Marketing changes

Marketing Changes

Edited by
Susan Hart

THOMSON

Australia • Canada • Mexico • Singapore • Spain • United Kingdom • United States

THOMSON

Marketing Changes

Copyright © Thomson Learning 2003

The Thomson logo is a registered trademark and used herein under licence.

For more information, contact Thomson Learning, High Holborn House, 50/51 Bedford Row, London, WC1R 4 LR or visit us on the World Wide Web at: http://www.thomsonlearning.co.uk

British Library Cataloguing-in-Publication Data
A catalogue record for this book is available from the British Library

ISBN 1–86152–673–3

First edition 2003

Typeset by Photoprint, Torquay, Devon
Printed in Croatia by Zrinski d.d.

Contents

Contributors

Tim Ambler
London Business School

Stephen Brown
School of Marketing, Entrepreneurship and Strategy
University of Ulster, UK

John Cadogan
Aston Business School
Aston University, UK

Sally Dibb
Warwick Business School
University of Warwick, UK

Pavlos Dimitratos
Department of Marketing
University of Strathclyde, UK

Christine Ennew
University of Nottingham Business School, UK

Martin Evans
Cardiff University Business School, UK

John Fernie
Heriot-Watt School of Management
Heriot-Watt University, UK

Jim Hamill
Department of Marketing
University of Strathclyde, UK

Susan Hart
Department of Marketing
University of Strathclyde, UK

Gillian Hogg
Glasgow Caledonian Business School
Glasgow Caledonian University, UK

Frank McDonald
Manchester Metropolitan University, UK

Robert Morgan
School of Management and Business
University of Wales Aberystwyth, UK

Lisa O'Malley
Department of Management and Marketing
College of Business
University of Limerick, Ireland

Stefano Puntoni
London Business School

Michael Saren
Department of Marketing
University of Strathclyde, UK

Eleanor Shaw
Department of Marketing
University of Strathclyde, UK

Alan Stevenson
Consultant
Parallel 56

Heinz Tüselmann
Manchester Metropolitan University, UK

Nikolaos Tzokas
University of East Anglia, UK

The changing context of marketing

CHAPTER 1

Introduction and overview of 'Marketing Changes'

Susan Hart

In recent years, research in marketing has broadened in scope, from being concerned with describing, analyzing and predicting 'rational' buying behaviour in both mass and business markets to embracing trends and issues from cognate social sciences and the humanities. Perusal of the top journals in marketing in Europe and the US reveals deepening concern with a broad range of issues such as the construction and nature of marketing knowledge, marketing in post-industrial and transitional economies, organizational learning, the development of customer relationships and the influence of technology on marketing. Yet this trend is still largely in contrast to essential and recommended texts, which still tend to emphasize a 'marketing management' approach to the discipline. At the other end of the spectrum are texts which explore the ideological and philosophical domains of marketing, but which remain largely specialist and in many cases beyond the scope of what is deemed essential material for marketing students. The risk of this type of polarization, however, is that research becomes increasingly removed from marketing syllabi and that academic research becomes removed from the interests and concerns of a whole group of students that could be not only informed but also inspired by interesting, novel, original approaches to an area of business which thrives on creativity. The purpose of this book is to bridge this gap between changing research agendas and the slowly evolving marketing syllabi.

Essentially a collection of essays written by leading, authoritative marketing academics in Europe, the book aims to explore and synthesize major developments in marketing thought outside the marketing management rubrique of the 4 – or even the 7 – Ps. The book is intended for students of marketing who have already studied the key elements of marketing management and who wish to develop an advanced appreciation of how the subject is changing.

Structure of the Book

There are three parts to the book. The first part contains chapters that explore and discuss changes in various aspects of the business environment which affect marketing. The chapters in Part 2 deal with the various approaches to marketing and its role within the organization, including marketing-relevant concepts from organizational learning, market orientation literature, relational and network marketing. The part ends with a postmodern take on postmodern marketing. Part 3 takes as its focus elements of marketing operations from market research and segmentation, product development, marketing communications, e-marketing and, finally, measuring marketing performance.

Part 1: The Changing Context of Marketing

Chapter 2, written by Dimitratos, McDonald and Tüselman focuses on four elements of the changing environment for marketing: globalization, changes to the international monetary system, changes to trading and investment, and changes in the competitive, social and environmental considerations that impinge on firms' culture and operations. These are themes which are picked up in several other chapters also, from other perspectives, as they are of direct relevance. E-marketing (Chapter 14), for example, acknowledges the changed global competitive environment in its argument for a customer-led approach to business growth. Logistics and the supply chain (Chapter 4) are equally affected by international economic changes while consumers' preoccupations, motivations and behaviours (Chapter 3) are increasingly affected by social and environmental conditions. In this wide-ranging discussion, the authors cover aspects of international business from the introduction of the Euro and frequent financial crises to the doggedness – despite the Uruguay agreement – of trade barriers. Into this melee, the growth of the anti-capitalist movement and business ethics are also considered for their effect (if any) on the activities of the multi-national enterprise.

Chapter 3, written by Gillian Hogg, begins with the arresting observation that the twentieth century began on horseback and ended with the Internet. Given that leap in technological sophistication, perhaps there is little wonder that understanding consumers and consumption has also had to change radically. In examining these changes, the chapter traces early consumer booms in the sixteenth and eighteenth centuries, bringing a necessary historical perspective to the search for understanding consumers. Equally, the chapter links the economic perspective of the 'consumer society' with its cultural and communicative, integrating ideas of individual and social identity on the journey. Changes to consumers that are discussed and theoretically developed include: the level of choice consumers have in the developed world; their level of education, knowledge and demands; the rise of women consumers; the growing influences of (the lack of) time and (the pervasiveness of) technology.

Chapter 4, the last in Part 1, shows how these sophisticated, demanding consumers have pulled and been satisfied by changes in supply chain technology, from information handling to sophisticated logistics planning and execution.

The chapter, written by John Fernie, begins by outlining key theoretical perspectives on supply chain management, emphasizing the synthetic nature of the subject, and its shifting base from one drawing on geography, economics, operational research and mathematics, to one encompassing strategic management and relationship marketing (see links with Chapter 7). The chapter explains specific concepts such as efficient consumer response, warts and all, the retail supply chain and the major challenges for the future.

These three chapters in Part 1 present, explain and analyze principal elements of the marketing environment which shape the development of marketing as a management practice and an area of academic study. They set the scene for parts 2 and 3 of the book which are described below.

Part 2: Changing Approaches to Marketing's Role in Organizations

The first chapter in this part is Chapter 5 by Robert Morgan, who examines the concept of organizational learning, drawing together its multidisciplinary roots and integrating concepts from the development of marketing theory. In so doing, the chapter examines the origins of market-based organizational learning and addresses issues further explored by Chapter 6 on market orientation. The discussion notes that the role of the marketing function within firms has undergone much practical and reflective change, from a departmental function in large, bureaucratic organization designs prevalent in the 1950s and 60s, to the contemporary conceptualization of marketing as an overarching culture within new forms of organization which take account of relational approaches to customers and markets. The role of information in the post market-orientation view of marketing is examined, introducing themes that are later examined by Chapter 12 on new product development, notably those concerned with capabilities.

Chapter 6, by John Cadogan, examines in detail the origins and manifestations of research into market orientation, providing not only an overview of the variety of the 'original' overall conceptualizations of market orientation but also how its subdimensions have been treated subsequently by researchers. In the analysis, the link between the marketing concept, customer focus, coordinated marketing and a cultural perspective are covered as a platform from which a unifying framework is developed. The influences of firms' industry sectors and contexts are also examined, as is the level of analysis employed by different research studies into market orientation.

Chapter 7, by Lisa O'Malley reviews the development of relationship marketing (RM). Noting that relationships have been implicit to marketing discourse since its beginnings, the chapter examines the origins of more formal treatments of RM through the 1970s and 80s. Twin routes to the development of the so-called 'new paradigm' are cited as business-to-business marketing, encapsulated by much of the work of the Industrial Marketing and Purchasing Group (IMP) and the development of services marketing. In exploring these avenues of research, the chapter focuses on the changing emphasis from transaction to relationships, buyer–seller interaction, and the development of primary relational constructs including commitment, trust, cooperation and bonds. The chapter then goes on to review the more recent considerations of relationships in consumer markets, the related concept of loyalty and the benefits of relational approaches to marketing to buyers and sellers alike. The practical difficulties of deploying RM and the areas for improvement are also presented in detail.

Chapter 8, by Eleanor Shaw, tackles marketing through alliances and networks, an approach related in development and conceptualization to RM. Again, citing as origins the work of the IMP group of European researchers, the chapter begins by examining the forces which have forged the development of cooperative arrangements among organizations. Here the chapter echoes ideas introduced in the first part of the book, notably globalization and the supply chain. The discussion emphasizes the concept of 'business networks' but shows how RM and services marketing have contributed to the development of thinking on these networks. Since the markets-as-networks view has been described as a synthesis of economics and sociology, the chapter considers the concept of social networks to tease out the relevant concepts for interorganizational networks. The chapter finishes with a discussion of emerging research directions and their implications.

The part on changing approaches to marketing – as an area for academic study and a business function – draws to a close on platform 9¾ with an infotainment chapter by Stephen Brown to set you up for Part 3. All aboard!

Part 3: Marketing Operations

The third part opens with a formal consideration, by Christine Ennew, of market research. Chapter 10 begins with the observation that market research has a long history, often quite distinct in academic treatments from other aspects of marketing. Echoing previous chapters (notably 5 and 6) with the observation that market knowledge had emerged as a renewed conceptualization of market research, the chapter explores the nature, provenance and importance of market knowledge. This is followed by a discussion of the evolution of the market research process, and a discussion of the somewhat patchy use of market research by managers. The chapter concludes by considering the future prospects for market research.

Chapter 11, by Sally Dibb, reviews the state of knowledge and evolution of market segmentation, one of the key areas of use of market research. Building on sections covering the need for segmentation and the process, the chapter contrasts consumer and business markets approaches to market segmentation and reviews research which reports on actual practice of segmentation in industry. Related traditional concepts of targeting and positioning are discussed in preparation for a discussion of the applications of information technology and the emergence of one-to-one marketing as a concept which might replace that of market segments. This discussion relates to numerous issues covered elsewhere in the book, but particularly chapters 3, 7 and 14.

Chapter 12 by Tzokas, Hart and Saren re-examines the success and failure literature in new product development and teases out the importance of market information – often characterized as the voice of the customer. In the chapter, the central role of all types of information is reconsidered as a major change emanating from new product development (NPD) research, and attention is drawn to the idea that in order to develop further, researchers must widen the scope of their studies to embrace what information is needed, where, when and by whom. This then leads into a discussion of 'market information capability' and its influences throughout an organization's processes developing new products. The changed focus is on integrating the different levels at which market information for NPD is gathered, processed and used.

Chapter 13, by Martin Evans, reviews the changes in marketing communications, focusing on the key driver of data. Picking up on the idea mentioned in Chapter 11, namely one-to-one marketing, the rise in personalized communications is discussed, with the observation that this is, in theory anyway, more measurable in its effects than mass communications. (See Chapter 15 for a link across here.) Links are equally drawn between knowledge management, customer relationship management and integration of all the ways in which organizations communicate with customers (known as touchpoints). The social aspect of all these one-to-one communications are explored in the chapter, as is the inward-looking tendency of the systems being installed to manage one-to-one communications.

Chapter 14 by Jim Hamill treats a related field – focusing on Internet marketing through the lens of customer relevance. Again the one-to-one concept is raised, along with others focused on the idea of 'quality customers': customer lifetime value, performance metrics, and cross-functional integration in an organization. The chapter reviews the business benefits of being customer led in developing Internet or e-marketing and situates the development of e-marketing within a customer-centric and strategic view. From a change perspective, what is interesting about this chapter is that the very recent changes in technology leading to e-marketing are having less impact than predicted due to the accompanying abandonment of fundamentals.

The last chapter, by Tim Ambler and Stefano Puntoni, opens with the observation that marketers have long striven to show how marketing contributes to the financial health of their organizations. Indeed, much of the preoccupation in the market orientation literature is precisely in this area, a factor also discussed in this chapter. Beginning with a review of the theoretical underpinnings of performance assessment, encompassing control, agency and institutional theories, the chapter goes on to examine managerial practice in the task of assessing marketing performance. The evolution of metrics is discussed, focusing on concepts such as brand equity, benchmarks and customer-based measures. These ideas are built into a conceptual framework before reporting on a recent study which shows the extent to which there has been little change, and even less satisfaction, with the way managers measure their marketing efforts.

In summary, therefore, this book of readings traces the histories, presents and futures of primary areas of marketing and the differences in approaches, theoretical backgrounds and writing style all provide testimony to a varied and challenging area of study and business practice.

August 2002

CHAPTER 2

International economic and environmental changes

Pavlos Dimitratos, Frank McDonald
and Heinz Tüselmann

This chapter discusses the key economic changes that have taken place in the international environment during the recent years and the implications that they entail for firms and marketing strategies. Traditionally, these changes in the international economic environment have been considered to be part of the 'uncontrollables' that firms and marketing practitioners should cope with. Nonetheless, apart from major challenges that these economic 'uncontrollables' may cause for the firm, they can entail significant opportunities that successful firms may take advantage of. In order for firms to take advantage of these opportunities they have to implement suitable strategies at the corporate and the functional-marketing level. One should note that these two levels of analysis can be closely interrelated.

This chapter discusses four key economic changes that have taken place in the international marketplace recently, and is organized as follows. The first section deals with globalization and its related terms, i.e. internationalization and regionalization, in an attempt to clarify these notions and illuminate what they mean for the firm. This section also examines implications and strategies that firms may implement in order to deal with globalization challenges. The second section investigates the changes to the international monetary system and the consequences for firms. Specifically, this section investigates the European Monetary Union and the introduction of the Euro, the development of new exchange rate regimes, and the occurrence of the serious financial and currency crises that have seriously affected the macroeconomic environment in which firms operate. The third section discusses changes to the trading and investment system including multilateral trade and investment liberalization, and regional trading blocs as well as what these changes imply for firms. The fourth section examines the recent changes to the global competition, social and environmental regulatory system and what they entail for the firm. The chapter concludes with a section that stresses the need for more research into the theme of the association between the international economic changes and their impact on firms and marketing managers.

Globalization, Internationalization and Regionalization: Different Degree and Focus of International Business Operations

Perhaps the major economic change that has affected firms and their respective marketing strategies, especially since the 1980s, has been the increasing marketization of the marketplace worldwide. The growth of trade and investment flows, and the perception that large multinational enterprises have become very powerful have led to concern that the economic, social and environmental implications of the so-called globalization process are unprecedented in human history (Giddens, 1999; Ohmae, 1990). However, others have sought to place the globalization process into context by pointing out that the level of marketization of the world economy was at least as large as it is today in the period 1870 to 1914 (Eichengreen, 1998).

The terms most commonly used to describe this escalating economic integration internationally have been 'globalization' and 'internationalization'. While these notions may have positive or negative connotations for some people, it appears that globalization and internationalization are processes that firms should seriously take into consideration and examine when formulating their strategies. At a macro-level, globalization is associated with 'the increasing integration of economies around the world, particularly through trade and financial flows' (IMF, 2000: 36). Globalization can be viewed as a process by which the economy worldwide is changed from a set of national markets to a set of markets that operate without paying attention to national boundaries (Hood and Young, 2000a). Foreign direct investment (FDI) by large multinationals is the engine that largely drives this process, inasmuch as the 500 largest multinationals account for 90 per cent of the world's FDI and over half of its trade (Rugman, 2000). Much of the world's trade takes place between subsidiaries of these large multinationals, yet international trade is also generated by alliances whereby often smaller firms participate (OECD, 1992).

In general, it seems that there have been few efforts to differentiate globalization from internationalization (Young, Slow and Hood, 2000) despite the fact that both of them constitute the other side of the coin for marketization (Rodrik, 1997). Some researchers (e.g. Dicken, 1992; Prasad, 1999) appear to use the term globalization and internationalization as synonyms. There seem to be increased international business operations worldwide in industries which are often called globalized, such as microelectronics, consumer electronics, office machinery, household appliances and financial services. Nonetheless, the globalization process is far from complete as many researchers suggest (Dunning, 2000; Micklethwait and Wooldridge, 2000; Rondinelli and Behrman, 2000). In fact, Hood and Peters (2000) estimate that around 50 per cent of the world's gross domestic product (GDP) is considered to be at the early stage of globalization, and essentially local in its focus. Hence, it is better to view globalization and global firms as industry-specific phenomena rather than as holistic trends that extend to all industries and countries uniformly (cf. Berry, Dimitratos and McDermott, 2002). The world is far from being globalized, a statement which seems to apply to both industries and firms (Hood and Young, 2000b).

Levitt in 1983 argued that because of the emergence of global markets, global or 'universal' products will dominate the international marketplace. Ever since that time, other authors have also argued in favour of the homogenization of world products and services (e.g. Ohmae, 1990). Nevertheless a truly global strategy, which involves a standardized product and a homogenous marketing mix worldwide (Yip, 1989) only appears to be implemented to a limited extent by multinationals. For instance, even McDonald's, which is often cited as a global company with operations worldwide, has to accompany its menu with beer in Germany and wine in France in order to adapt to local customer needs. The marketing literature is replete with blunders of firms which failed to take into consideration local differences and idiosyncratic demands of foreign countries. Such were the cases of General Motors, which tried to sell its Chevrolet Nova in Latin America without changing the car's name (No Va means 'does not go' in Spanish) or Disneyland Paris, which had to modify its strategic profile to look more French and European rather than American in order to become profitable.

Rugman (2000) also posits that globalization is essentially a misleading term since global operations for a firm really mean regional operations, i.e. operations in the triad markets of North America, the European Union (EU) and Japan. He suggests that most trade and investment by multinationals nowadays are intra-firm and take place within triad-based business networks. Many researchers also support the implementation of a regional strategy (e.g. Baden-Fuller and Stopford, 1991; Mirza, 2000; Morrison, Ricks and Roth, 1991; Roth, 1992), although there does not appear to exist an agreement on whether this implies operations in the triad markets or in regionally trading groups of countries which may not necessarily belong to the triad (such as the EU, North America/North American Free Trade Agreement (NAFTA), south-east Europe etc.).

The third section of this chapter will elaborate on the regional trading groups and what consequences these may entail for firms and marketing managers. At this point, it should be stressed that for the firm, regionalization can be viewed as an intermediate stage of the process towards increased marketization. Internationalization, regionalization and globalization should not be considered as static and completely different alternatives but rather as intermediary stages towards increasing international business operations (cf. Berry, Dimitratos and McDermott, 2002). This statement is in accord with the views which perceive globalization as a continuum (Makhija, Kim and Williamson, 1997; OECD, 1997; Young, Slow and Hood, 2000). Compared to globalization and internationalization, regionalization appears to have a particular geographic focus of countries. Compared to internationalization, globalization is linked to a comparatively higher extent of international operations with customers which are well beyond the national borders. Internationalization is mainly a phenomenon of the 1950s, 1960s and much of the 1970s, while globalization is mainly a phenomenon of the 1980s and 1990s (OECD, 1999). Nevertheless, globalization should not be viewed as an ideal state, an end in itself that the firm must reach in order to succeed internationally.

What exactly does the difference between globalization and internationalization mean for the firm? Dimitratos (2001) supports the view that there are two aspects that are important to this difference. First, firms which follow the globalization route perform international business operations to a comparatively higher extent, faster speed and greater number of foreign markets. These firms also do not appear to pay much attention to a foreign country's 'psychic distance'. As suggested by Johanson and Vahlne (1977), psychic distance refers to dissimilarities in language, culture, political system, business practices, etc. that interfere adversely in the flow of information between the firm and that foreign market. Second, firms which follow the globalization route go abroad instantly, often with advanced forms of market servicing modes, such as licensing, joint ventures and subsidiaries. In other words, these firms tend to disregard the initial exporting modes that incremental models of international business would support (Johanson and Vahlne, 1977; 1990; Johanson and Wiedersheim-Paul, 1975). These firms also frequently employ international networks and alliances when expanding through the advanced modes for their operations abroad.

Implications for Firms and Marketing Managers

Many governments of triad market regions have raised significant barriers for firms which are not members of these specific regions (Brewer and Young, 2000b). In order to overcome these problems many 'outsider' firms resorted to mergers and acquisitions of 'insider' firms.These moves are particularly noticeable across the triad blocs of Europe and North America (Rugman, 2000). Such noticeable moves that took place recently involve the mergers of Chrysler and Daimler, Bankers Trust and Deutsche Bank, and Nissan and Renault. As the data in Table 2.1 reveals, the merger and acquisition activity in the key markets worldwide has increased significantly lately. It is worth noting that mergers and acquisitions have become more important than greenfield developments for FDI, accounting for around 70 per cent of the total value of inward investment in developed countries between 1986 and 1990 (United Nations, 1995).

In spite of the popularity of the merger and acquisition activity, business practitioners have to be extremely cautious in these endeavours. Evidence suggests that fewer than one quarter of mergers and acquisitions achieve their financial objectives, as measured in terms of share value, return on investment, and postcombination profitability (e.g. Marks and Mirvis, 2001; Porter, 1987).

Networks formed between firms from different countries seem to be an effective and viable alternative to tackle the globalization challenges nowadays. They have been employed by firms to gain access to all foreign markets regardless of the geographic regions of countries involved. Such networks can take the form of

TABLE 2.1 Value of mergers and acquisitions during 1994–1999 (US$ billion)

Year	USA	Europe	Asia
1994	227	150	30
1995	356	300	80
1996	495	350	60
1997	657	500	80
1998	1,192	600	70
1999	1,426	1,250	240

Source: Thomson Financial Securities Data.

strategic alliances, joint ventures, licensing or loose interorganizational arrangements. Generally alliances are especially common in industries such as information technology, biotechnology, autos, and new materials (Brewer and Young, 2000a). They are used by firms in order to acquire clout in the foreign market or alleviate resource constraint problems that they may have. Whereas traditionally the acquisition of knowledge concerning foreign markets has come through the establishment of subsidiaries abroad, nowadays this can also be achieved through the development of market networks (Berry, Dimitratos and McDermott, 2002). Through such networks, firms often internationalize from the inception of their business operations, something which appears as the 'born-global firm' phenomenon in the literature (e.g. Knight and Cavusgil, 1996; Madsen and Servais, 1997; Rennie, 1993). In the age of 'alliance capitalism' (Dunning, 1995), implementation of effective strategies appears to move from the individual-firm to the dyad-network level.

Another successful strategy that many firms, and especially the smaller ones, have effectively followed is targeting similar market niches worldwide (Simon, 1996; Voudouris *et al.*, 2000). The business operations of many large firms, which target big and homogenous customer segments worldwide, appear to leave market space for smaller firms. Clearly big firms are not the only winners in the global economy (*cf.* Naisbitt, 1994). Hence, many smaller firms pursuing this 'deep niche strategy' seek to satisfy the needs of well-defined and specific segments or niches of foreign markets. In terms of customer demands, these niches have very similar characteristics across countries. In effect, the underlying idea in this strategy is that firms employ global market segmentation, whereby they identify specific segments of individual consumer groups with homogenous attributes across countries, which are likely to show similar buying behaviour (Kumar and Nagpal, 2001). Subsequently they are in a position to service these segments or niches with a very similar product offering and marketing mix worldwide.

Another strategy that successful firms often implement in the era of globalization is introducing new products fast. Because of the increasing competition in consumer markets, product lifecycle stages seem to become shorter. Hence, a response by firms to preempt competition may be to come up with completely new products that rapidly appear in the market (e.g. Julien, 1996). Such was the case by Gillette, which launched its Mach 3 razor in 100 countries within 18 months of its release in 1998. Unlike its competitors, which only experience a shortened portion of time in the market, the firm, which is among the first-to-market, enjoys full utilization of the product's lifecycle and increased sales. Nowadays globalization pressures seem to intensify and technological improvements render products obsolete very quickly. Hence, product life cycles are shrinking and being among the first-to-market appears to gain key importance (Ali, Krapfel and LaBahn, 1995). This is corroborated by evidence which suggests that speed to market pays: first-to-market firms and their fast followers score better than their competitors on many dimensions of new product performance (e.g. Dyer, Gupta and Wilemon, 1999).

Changes to the International Monetary System

In the 1990s three major changes to the international monetary system led to important implications for firms and marketing managers. The first major change has been the introduction of a new major world currency, namely the Euro. The second change is the development of a variety of exchange rate regimes that seek to establish stability within the floating exchange system which governs the main currencies of the world. The third change is connected to the occurrence of frequent financial and currency crises, for example, the Asian crisis of 1997, the Russian crisis of 1998, and the crisis in Brazil and Argentina in 1999 and 2001 (Brealey, 2001; Krugman, 1999a; 1999b).

European Monetary Union and the Euro

The introduction of European Monetary Union (EMU) has profound implications for the economies of the members of the union and for the rest of the world (De Grauwe, 1998; Emerson *et al.*, 1992; Gros and Thygesen, 1998). EMU is based on a single currency (the Euro) with a central bank (the European Central Bank) responsible for monetary and exchange rate policy. The members of EMU (Euroland, i.e. Austria, Belgium, Finland, France, Germany, Greece, Ireland, Italy, Luxembourg, Portugal, Spain and the Netherlands) completed the process of converting to a single currency in February 2002. The members of the European Union (EU) that are not currently part of Euroland, i.e. Denmark, Sweden and the UK are facing strong pressure to join Euroland. All future members of the EU must join EMU after they satisfy a set of conditions contained in the Maastricht Treaty and the treaties of membership. The emergence of Euroland has created a large economic area with a single currency which is likely to become bigger. If the UK joins, Euroland will include the four largest economies in Europe and will rival the USA in terms of output, and size of capital and money markets.

The introduction of the Euro removes exchange rate risk and currency conversion costs by replacing different currencies with a single currency. The adoption of a common monetary policy by the European Central Bank (ECB) ensures that inflation rates in the members of Euroland will not diverge significantly other than in the short-run. EMU therefore provides a solution to exchange rate risk for intra-Union trade and to distortions to the price mechanism that arise from floating exchange rate regimes, but only within Euroland. If the monetary policy of the ECB delivers low and stable inflation, the value of the Euro within

Euroland will be stable. However, the Euro floats against the other major currencies of the world and thus its value on a global scale will not necessarily be stable. The rapid decline of the Euro against the US dollar in the aftermath of its introduction in 1999 indicates that monetary unions do not necessarily deliver a currency with a stable international value. EMU has removed the problems of floating exchange rates for its members but has not eliminated these problems for international business activities conducted outside Euroland.

Monetary unions do not remove the need to make adjustments between their members if economic imbalances exist. Unexpected economic changes that lead to different impacts across countries (asymmetric shocks) may lead to imbalances between the economies of a monetary union. In order to restore balance it is necessary to adopt respective policies. The common monetary policy and a single currency mean that countries with imbalances cannot use changes in monetary conditions or exchange rates to restore balance. In Euroland, a 'stability pack' constrains the use of fiscal policy thereby further constraining the tools available to curb imbalances. This means that the main adjustment processes to asymmetric shocks are 'supply side' policies that encourage changes to labour costs and thereby adjustments to prices to restore balance (De Grauwe, 1998).

If the EU develops into some type of political union with the ability to directly levy taxes and with public expenditure powers, the adjustment problem will become mainly a challenge for regional development. The example of the USA illustrates how adjustment takes place in an economic and political union. In the USA, if some states suffer a decline in economic activity relative to other states, federal tax revenues fall in those states that suffer decline and federal expenditures rise. This reduces the adjustment problem because federal taxes/expenditure systems redistribute income to those states that are suffering from reduced economic activity. Labour will also move from the states with problems to the more economically active states. In the USA differences in the income levels of the states exist to a considerable extent, indicating that it is not always possible to adjust to changes in competitive positions even within an economic and political union.

Euroland does not currently have such a political underpinning, although monetary union is likely to lead to increased pressures to develop some kind of political union. The ability of Euroland to adjust to imbalances is not as large as that of the USA because not only does it not have an effective redistributive tax/expenditure system, but also it lacks the level of labour mobility that exists in the USA. These factors suggest that the regional adjustment problem in Euroland will be considerably more difficult than is the case in the USA. The lack of political underpinning for Euroland further strengthens the need to use 'supply side' policies by the governments of the members of Euroland and for firms to adjust unit labour costs to maintain competitiveness.

The creation of the Euro introduces a major currency that could rival the US dollar as a world currency. The Euro may become a major reserve currency used by central banks for the international financial transactions of governments. Large bond and equity markets denominated in Euros are emerging leading to large-scale use of the Euro in international capital flows. The Euro could also displace the dollar as the major vehicle currency, and as the main currency for invoicing and means of payment in international business transactions. These developments would lead to the emergence of a bipolar international monetary system dominated by the USA and the EU, with Japan playing a minor role. It is not clear if this would lead to a more stable international monetary system.

New institutional systems are likely to be required to deal with the emergence of the Euro as a major world currency (Henning, 1997). The introduction of the Euro backed by the large economy of Euroland means that for the first time since the early part of the twentieth century there exists a potential rival to the US dollar as a world currency. However, it will take time for Euro money and capital markets to develop to be feasible rivals to dollar markets. Moreover, Euroland currently lacks the type of political union that would allow it to rival the US as a political force in international monetary matters. Nevertheless, EMU has the potential to radically change the international monetary system. Whether this will increase the stability of the system or lead to crises and instability is not known at this stage. It has been argued that history suggests that stable international monetary systems depend on the existence of a hegemonic power – Britain in the gold standard and the USA in the Bretton Woods system (Eichengreen, 1998). If this is true, the growth of the use of the Euro as an international currency will have serious implications for the stability of the international monetary system, unless new institutional systems can be developed to secure effective cooperation between the USA and the EU.

Firms face choices to move from the use of the dollar to the Euro for international business purposes. Given the large fixed costs in moving from the use of the dollar due to the need to alter accounting, payment and treasury management systems, it is unlikely that this will happen quickly. However, as Euro markets develop, it may become attractive to use the Euro instead of the dollar, or as a complement to the dollar. The possibility of the development of a new international monetary system based on the twin pillars of the dollar and the Euro holds the prospects for the emergence of a different system with unknown characteristics.

New Exchange Rate Regimes

In the wake of the collapse of the Bretton Woods system, the major economies of the West introduced a series of different types of regimes to counter the harmful effects of floating exchange rates. None of them was successful and they were either abandoned or collapsed (Eichengreen, 1998). However, the risks and costs to international business activities associated with floating exchange rates, and the emergence of high inflation in the 1970s and 1980s stimulated attempts to find partial solutions in order to inject some stability into exchange rates. The liberalization of capital markets in the 1980s and the subsequent growth of international capital flows contributed to the volatility of exchange rates because of the large growth in short-term capital flows. These factors increased concern about the effects of floating exchange rates for international business activities. Solutions were sought for three major problems:

1. Exchange rate risk for firms engaged in international business.

2. Differential inflation rates among major trading partners leading to uncertainty about the level of future revenues and costs from international business transactions.
3. Volatile exchange rates leading to rapid and unpredictable changes to the prices of traded products.

The private sector provided solutions to the first problem by developing hedging instruments to reduce exchange rate risk. Firms also developed techniques to reduce exchange rate risk, such as transfer pricing, international cash flow management techniques as well as internal hedging instruments (Moffett and Yeung, 1999). These solutions involve costs in terms of management time and the purchases of hedging instruments. Nevertheless, there is little evidence that the costs of hedging and managing international cash flows significantly reduce international business transactions including FDI (Aggarwal and Soenen, 1989). Yet it is a problem for small and medium-sized businesses that lack the resources to acquire the means to reduce exchange rate risk (Storey, 1994).

The other two problems are more serious for the stability and growth of international business activities and affect even large multinationals. Unanticipated differential inflation rates and exchange rate volatility lead to uncertainty about future cash flows because of the distorting effects of such inflation and exchange rate changes on prices, and therefore on the real value of transactions. These distortions to the price mechanism increase uncertainty about the financial outcomes of engaging in international business transactions, and act as a deterrent to the expansion of such activities (Baldwin, 1990). Fluctuating currencies can also lead to problems for exporters that are difficult to hedge fully against because a currency can suddenly become strong and remain so for a long time. The rise of the UK pound against the Euro in the 1999–2001 period illustrates this problem. Moreover, the distorting effects of international monetary instability contribute to uncertainty in domestic business transactions and consequently lower economic activity.

The failure of policies to establish fixed exchange rate regimes led to an emphasis on other methods to reduce international monetary instability. Two major systems have emerged to overcome the problems posed by floating exchange rate regimes: crawling peg systems and currency boards. These approaches seek to reduce the problems of fixing exchange rates that arise from speculative pressures. The need for such arrangements stems from the power of speculators to organize very large capital flows to attack fixed exchange rate systems. This has forced defenders of fixed exchange rate regimes to devise systems that are less vulnerable to speculative attacks. In the case of crawling peg systems there is also an attempt to lessen the problems of adjustment to fundamental imbalances (Williamson, 1999).

Crawling peg systems

Crawling peg systems link a currency to an anchor currency that is strong and will enforce monetary discipline on the home country. Normally, the anchor currency is the US dollar. The economic conditions in the USA are likely to be different from those of the home country. Therefore, the trend is for the weaker home currency to depreciate against the dollar. The crawling peg system accommodates this by establishing a value around which the exchange rate can vary to a given per cent. The crawling peg system alters the exchange rate according to assessments of the divergence between conditions in the economy of the anchor and those of the home currency. An alternative to the use of an anchor currency, such as the dollar, is to use a basket of currencies as the anchor. The advantage of this is that the home currency is fixed to a group of countries and is therefore less likely to be caught up in changing economic conditions that mainly affect the country of a single anchor currency.

Crawling peg systems seek to achieve stable parities that adjust slowly and in a predictable manner, and therefore reduce the costs associated with floating exchange rate regimes. They also impose a degree of domestic monetary stability by linking the home country to an economy with a good anti-inflationary stance. The crawling peg permits slow adjustment to the divergent conditions between the anchor (or basket currency group of countries) and the home country. It is conceivable that discipline of the crawling peg system will lead to convergence between the home and anchor countries and thereby to a fixed exchange rate system. The attraction of the crawling peg system is that it may prevent speculative attacks because divergence between the two economies is adjusted for by the crawling peg. Crawling peg systems do not eliminate exchange rate risk but they make exchange rate changes more predictable, and therefore lessen the need for hedging instruments and other means of managing the risks.

However, if significant differences emerge between the economic conditions of the anchor and home countries, speculators will spot the opportunity to profit from the devaluation necessary to restore balance. This happened to the crawling peg system that Mexico established in 1991 using the dollar as the anchor currency. Speculative pressures on the peso emerged due to a financial crisis that highlighted economic differences between Mexico and the US, and this led to the abandonment of the system in 1994.

Currency boards

Establishment of a currency board leads to a rigid fixed exchange rate system. The currency board is required by law to link the growth of domestic money supply to its holdings of a given currency, usually the US dollar. The attraction of currency boards is that they provide strong curbs to the growth of domestic money supply and thereby deliver a very creditable anti-inflationary policy. However, if the dollar rises against most currencies because of economic conditions in the USA, the countries that fixed their currency to the dollar will also rise in value. Unfortunately, this may lead to a serious loss of competitiveness for countries that fixed their currencies against the dollar.

The most well-known case of this problem is the recession that afflicted Argentina when its main trading partner, Brazil, devalued its currency against the US dollar. In 1991 Argentina established a currency board to provide a creditable anti-inflationary policy to escape a long history of hyperinflation. The currency board was very successful in providing stable domestic monetary conditions in Argentina. However, the devaluation in 1999 of the Brazilian currency against the US dollar significantly reduced the competitiveness of Argentina. The sudden loss of competitiveness following from the devaluation led to reduced exports and disinvestments by multinational companies that had used Argentina as a base to supply the Brazilian market. These problems led to the onset of a severe recession in Argentina. In contrast, Brazil experienced increased growth because of its improved competitiveness. Moreover, Brazil did not suffer from high inflation because of the devaluation, and its financial markets did not enter into a period of chaos. Indeed, financial markets in Argentina have been more volatile than those in Brazil. The conflicting experiences of Argentina and Brazil illustrate the problems of using currency boards to reduce monetary instability (Krugman, 1999b). It appears that currency boards are susceptible to severe adjustment problems like all other types of fixed exchange rate systems.

Financial and Currency Crises

Traditional theories identify the causes of crises as fundamental structural changes in economies or policy inconsistency by governments. However, the inability of orthodox models to explain financial and currency crises other than by reference to special circumstances that prevail at the time of crises calls into question the validity of these models. Three main theories of currency crises have been put forward: the first two are compatible with the orthodox model of exchange rate determination, but the third casts doubt on the validity of this model (Krugman, 1999a).

1. *Canonical or classical models.* In fixed exchange rate regimes currencies are supported by buying and selling of currencies in excess demand and supply. However, reserves to defend parities are finite, and therefore continuing attempts to defend exchange rates will eventually deplete reserves unless adjustment policies to solve imbalances can be successfully made. The expectation that imbalances are due to fundamental structural differences between economies reinforces the view that a change in the exchange rate is inevitably stimulating capital flight, and thus ensuring the depletion of reserves.
2. *Second generation models.* Canonical models assume that governments cannot, or will not, adopt domestic policies to cure fundamental economic imbalances. However, governments normally respond to divergent economic conditions by using macroeconomic policies that seek to tackle the sources of imbalances. For example, they can raise the interest rates to support a beleaguered currency and in the longer-term to solve the differential inflation rates that cause difficulties in maintaining exchange rate parities. However, the markets may expect that the required macroeconomic changes are not feasible for political reasons or that they will further worsen the underlying economic imbalances. In that case, the markets will expect that the trade-off between conflicting economic policies (fixed exchange rate and required macroeconomic policies) will break down and the currency will have to devalue.
3. *Contagion and herding models.* If investors suspect that major economic imbalances exist due to, for example, financial crises from asset price bubbles, some investors will withdraw short-term capital to reduce exposure to debt default. This will lead to capital flight if other investors join the herd and withdraw short-term capital. Concern may spread to other similar countries. This contagion effect strengthens the herd instinct and spreads capital flight to other

countries. This may happen even if the direct economic and financial links between these countries are small because the herd instinct leads investors to fear for the safety of their investments in what they regard as similar countries. The dramatic growth in short-term capital flows to emerging economies is thought to encourage herding and contagion because investors often have poor information about conditions in these economies. This leads to large-scale and rapid capital flight when information becomes available which indicates that economic and financial conditions in emerging economies are deteriorating.

The herding and contagion theses on the origins and development of financial and currency crises suggest that financial markets do not operate in the rational and efficient manner assumed in orthodox economics. The crises caused by herding and contagion behaviour suggest that modifications to the international institutional system are necessary to help prevent crises, and to reduce the likelihood of these crises spreading from financial markets to the real economy and causing high economic, political and social costs (Dornbusch, 2001; Eichengreen, 1999; Radelet and Sachs, 1998; Stiglitz, 2000). In this view, the international monetary system has become very unstable and a threat to the wellbeing of the world economy.

Implications for Firms and Marketing Managers

The changes in the international monetary system have a number of important implications for marketing managers.

Pricing decisions need to take account of the complexity of the various exchange rate regimes that have developed. Whereas floating exchange rates prevail between the major currencies of the world, fixed and quasi-fixed exchange rate regimes exist but are often not stable. Therefore, assuming that prices will not be affected by exchange rate changes due to the existence of a fixed or quasi-fixed regime will prove to be a costly mistake if the regime is abandoned or collapses.

The international monetary system appears to be subject to periodic financial and currency crises, especially in emerging economies. This has implications for pricing decisions and for the stability of economic conditions in emerging economies. In these circumstances, the outcome of marketing strategies that have significant involvement with such economies will be subject to high levels of uncertainty. Systems to monitor developments in emerging economies and to deal with crises are therefore necessary for such marketing strategies.

The introduction of the Euro effectively eliminates exchange rate and un-anticipated differential inflation risk for intra-Euroland transactions. However, these uncertainties remain and may well increase for extra-Euroland transactions. Marketing strategies must be adapted to take into consideration these changes in uncertainty for both intra and extra-Euroland operations.

The introduction of the Euro also means that marketing and pricing decisions within Euroland could have many characteristics of domestic marketing operations, because exchange rate risk is eliminated and the risk from unanticipated differential inflation across the members of the monetary union is small. However, marketing in European countries that are not members of Euroland will continue to face exchange and unanticipated inflation risks. In these circumstances it might be worth considering treating Euroland as a type of a domestic market, and the rest of Europe as an area requiring international marketing and pricing policies.

The use of the US dollar as the major world currency is likely to decline as more use is made of the Euro for international financial purposes. Marketing managers need to assess their use of the dollar relative to the Euro as a means to finance international transactions, and as a vehicle to reduce the uncertainties that arise from currency fluctuations.

The institutional framework that underpins the international monetary system is undergoing significant modification in response to these new conditions, and it is not clear whether the emerging system will be more or less stable than the old system. Therefore, marketing managers need to be aware of the fluidity in the system and factor into their strategic plans effective monitoring systems and crisis management schemes to cope with upheavals in the system.

Changes to the Trading and Investment System

Since the Uruguay agreement on trade liberalization it seems that little progress has been made to further the objective of removing barriers to trade and investment. The process of multilateral trade and investment liberalization appears to be bogged down in disputes about agricultural products and textiles, and failures to make progress in the liberalization of services and investments. The admission of China as a full member of the World Trade Organization (WTO) holds the prospects of new developments in trade and investment liberalization. This is because China may bring a new perspective to negotiations as it may represent many of the views of the emerging economies. In the past, emerging economies have not had a powerful voice in WTO negotiations, and consequently, discussions have reached stalemate when the powerful players from the developed economies have been unable to persuade the emerging economies to accept their views. Nevertheless, there are also many unresolved issues between the developed economies in areas such as liberalization of services and in the development of new rules for trade involving new technologies, for example, e-commerce and genetically modified organisms. There has also been little progress towards finding solutions to disputes about the trade and investments distorting effects of health and safety regulations.

The growth of anti globalization movements, as witnessed by demonstrations at many summits of government leaders, and international trade and financial organizations, have also led to the development of a defensive attitude by many governments which has further limited the development of multilateral liberalization of trade and investments. Notwithstanding the slow progress in multilateral liberalization, regional integration blocs, such as the EU, NAFTA and Mercosur have made significant progress in liberalizing markets. In addition, political pressures and activities by non-government organizations are reinforcing business operations in the triad region (Brewer and Young, 2000b; Rugman, 2000). The validity of these statements is strengthened by the fact that there exist significant problems in multilateral negotiations which promote the acceptance of regional agreements (Brewer and Young, 2000a).

Bilateral deals between the regional integration blocs and third countries (especially between third countries and the EU) have led to the creation of a web of agreements that extend trade liberalization across a large number of countries (El Agraa, 1997). NAFTA has also developed significant links with third countries and a free trade area for all of the Americas is beginning to emerge (Schott, 2001). Some progress has also been made to develop institutional systems to enhance free trade among the countries of the Pacific Rim (Scollay and Gilbert, 2001). Thus, although multilateral trade and investment liberalization is not making significant progress, the same is not true of regional trade liberalization. Moreover, due to the evolution of the network of agreements that the main regional blocs have developed this regionalization process embraces a large number of countries.

Multilateral Trade and Investment Liberalization

The General Agreement on Tariffs and Trade (GATT), negotiated in 1947, remains the basis for world trading rules and dispute settlements. In 1994 the WTO replaced the secretariat of the GATT and it provides the forum for developing trading rules and settling trade disputes. The work of the WTO extends to services because of the General Agreement on Trade in Services (GATS). The agreement on Trade-Related Investment Measures (TRIMs) covers the development of a regime of rules and codes of practice for international investments. The Trade-Related Intellectual Property System (TRIPS) seeks to develop rules for disputes about intellectual property that arise from international trade and investment.

The Organization for Economic Cooperation and Development (OECD) also influences international trade and investments because of the development of codes of practice, such as the 1976 *Guidelines for Multinational Enterprises*. Moreover, in 1995 the OECD attempted to negotiate a Multinational Agreement on Investment (MAI), but discussions on the agreement broke down in 1998 and negotiations on this agreement were referred to the WTO. The WTO and the OECD also affect international trade and investments by providing a forum for developing the dialogue on proposals to agree rules for liberalization of the barriers that restrict the free movement of goods, services, capital and labour. These and other organizations also seek to develop dispute resolution procedures in order to facilitate the removal of obstacles to the evolution of a more liberal trade and investment system (Brewer and Young, 2000a; Trebilcock and Howse, 1999). Although there have been no large scale developments in multilateral trade and investment liberalization since the Uruguay Agreement, the WTO continues to develop rules and dispute procedures over an ever-widening range of goods, services and trade-related investments.

Regional Integration Blocs

Regional integration blocs pose a threat to the attempts to promote multilateral trade liberalization by the WTO because regional integration blocs only remove trade barriers among a subset of WTO members. Consequently, regional integration breaks the spirit of the multilateral approach to trade liberalization adopted by the GATT agreement in 1947. The main problem is that regional integration blocs do not grant all members of WTO most-favoured-nation (MFN) treatment. That is, they do not grant to countries that are not members of the regional integration bloc the same treatment in the application of tariffs, quotas and non-tariff barriers (NTBs) as they do to members of the bloc. GATT rules permit regional integration blocs to grant preferential treatment to its members providing that tariffs, quotas and non-tariff barriers applied to non-members do not increase because of the formation of the bloc.

Some argue that regional trade blocs create significant trade diversion and thereby lead to welfare losses because of the failure to apply MFN treatment (Bhagwati, 1993). This harmful outcome is counterbalanced if regional blocs use trade liberalization among their members as a route to extend the same trading privileges to non-members by the preferential trade agreements which they have with countries linked to the bloc and eventually to all WTO members (Bhagwati, 1991). The EU has a large number of such preferential trade agreements, and NAFTA is moving towards such agreements with Latin American and Asian countries. Cooperation between the EU and NAFTA to extend their preferential trade arrangement to all countries linked to these blocs would encompass many of the members of the WTO. If the Asia Pacific Economic Cooperation (APEC) free trade area makes progress and the EU develops links with this area, most of the WTO members would become involved in multilateral trade negotiations via a number of regional integration bloc agreements. This would be a very complex way to make progress towards multilateral trade liberalization. Such a route is likely to lead to complex negotiations and therefore may prove to be a difficult but realistic way to promote multilateral trade liberalization (Frankel, 1997).

Negotiations between the EU and the USA on trade liberalization already exercise a strong influence on negotiations on trade liberalization in areas where the WTO struggles to reach multilateral agreements, such as agricultural products, health and safety rules, and regulation of international e-commerce. The large economic size of the EU and NAFTA gives them considerable power in trade liberalization programmes and agreement between these blocs appears to be prerequisite for progress at WTO negotiations. Given the power of these regional integration blocs, complex negotiations between these blocs may be the only feasible way to make progress in multilateral trade liberalization.

Regional economic integration encourages the development of large concentrations of economic activity to serve the growth in trade resulting from multilateral and regional integration bloc trade liberalization. This gives these large blocs market power and first mover advantages in industries that are subject to growth in trade resulting from trade liberalization. The blocs therefore become reluctant to threaten these advantages by extending MFN treatment. The initial effect of regional integration helps multilateral trade liberalization because removing trade barriers permits concentration of firms that leads to economies of scale. The process of concentration will be most pronounced in areas close to large markets to take advantage of low transport cost and to gain advantages of being close to a large number of customers. This will lead to the creation of clusters of firms in large economic integration blocs that can also supply the rest of the world from operations within the bloc. However, as the process of regional integration develops the advantages bestowed to these clusters may be threatened if trade liberalization is granted to third countries. Granting trade concessions in these circumstances may lead to the transfer of operations from clusters within regional trade blocs to lower cost locations in third countries (Bagwell and Staiger, 1998; Either, 1998).

Often the protection offered to clusters within regional integration blocs is lodged in non-tariff barriers. Hence, regional integration blocs are often willing to remove tariff and quota barriers on a multilateral basis, but removal of non-tariff barriers normally proves to be a more difficult objective to achieve. In these circumstances, regional integration blocs are helpful in the early stage of trade liberalization which mainly involves reducing tariffs and quotas. However, the advantages gained to clusters by multilateral trade liberalization create the conditions in which further trade liberalization becomes difficult.

Implications for Firms and Marketing Managers

The continuing progress towards dismantling barriers to trade and investment, and to develop effective dispute resolution procedures has a number of implications for marketing managers.

The WTO and other international organizations are likely to extend liberalization measures, especially in the areas of services and trade-related investment. This will require strategic plans to develop appropriate responses to the removal of the existing barriers to trade in services and trade-related investment. These developments will make it easier to develop integrated supply chains across frontiers and to focus on new strategies to market services across frontiers. This will require firms to undertake market entry strategies involving exporting, licensing, franchising and FDI to supply liberalized markets in the services sector, and to develop transnational supply chains.

Agreements on health and safety regulations, and new technologies are likely to emerge from the WTO. This will require strategic planning to ensure conformity to the new regulations and to take advantage of new marketing opportunities that arise from these regulations, or to defend existing markets from new entrants.

The resolution systems for disputes developed by the WTO must be monitored and effective procedures put in place to lodge and prosecute claims for unfair treatment in foreign markets, and to defend or alter the practices of firms that are accused of unfair procedures or practices.

The liberalization programmes of regional integration blocs and the development of agreements with third countries create new and complex liberalization environments. Marketing managers need to monitor and assess these developments to gather information on changing regulatory and competitive environments.

Decisions need to be made on marketing variables, such as the level of product standardization, appropriate networks for distribution and sales, and the development of promotion systems in the light of the complex regulatory frameworks that emerge from regional integration blocs. The extension to third countries from the network of agreements that exist between regional blocs and third countries further complicates the process of ensuring compliance with regulatory frameworks. Decisions on these issues must also include assessments of the opportunities and challenges of dealing with the competitive position that results from the complex regulatory frameworks which are developing from regional integration blocs.

Effective monitoring of developments at organizations, such as the WTO and the major regional integration blocs, is necessary to ensure that the changes at these organizations are identified, and that responses to the complex and perhaps conflicting regulatory and dispute resolution procedures are incorporated into the strategic marketing planning process.

Exerting influence on the development of the complex liberalization processes by lobbying national governments and international organizations involved with trade and investments may be worthwhile if changes in proposals in these areas can be achieved. Given the complex nature of the liberalization process this requires effective monitoring and lobbying of the decision-making systems in national governments, international agencies and the major regional integration blocs. For most firms, apart from very large multinational enterprises, the resource costs of such monitoring and lobbying may be prohibitive. In these circumstances, the development of networks of cooperation within industries or sectors may provide an alternative means of influencing the liberalization process. The complexity and cross-frontier nature of many of the proposals for liberalization makes the development of transnational networks to monitor and lobby the various agencies a worthwhile objective.

An effective alternative to global strategy and 'universal' products appears to be pursuing a regional strategy which emphasizes regional requirements of customers. Ohmae (1985) has foreseen the significance of regional operations, and suggested that firms should establish manufacturing and marketing operations in each of the triad areas. As this strategy calls for economies of scale to be achieved, it may be often implemented by large firms whose size advantages render them capable of producing and marketing their products at a large scale. In fact, Rugman (2000) found that all twenty large multinationals that he examined have succeeded internationally through the implementation of regional strategies.

Changes to the Global Competition, Social and Environmental Regulatory System

The social and environmental implications of globalization are increasingly affecting the strategic and operational activities of firms. The growth of the anti-capitalist and environmental movements, and the fears of many emerging and developing countries about the costs (to these countries) of globalization have led to calls for constraints on the activities of multinational enterprises. Governments in developed economies have expressed concerns about the need to develop systems to ensure that cross-frontier mergers and acquisitions do not undermine the competitive structure of markets. The ability of multinational enterprises to take advantage of different approaches to competition policy in their host countries in order to distort international competition has also led to calls to develop rules on competition policies to prevent the creation and maintenance of unfair advantages in trade and investment flows. The growth of business ethics as an important strategic factor in response to these concerns indicates that firms cannot divorce themselves from the social and environmental implications of their activities (Stajkovic and Luthans, 2001).

Organizations such as the WTO and the OECD are developing dialogue about the need for rules to settle disputes that arise in international trade and investment because of national differences in areas, such as environmental and labour regulations as well as competition policies (Brewer and Young, 2000a). The OECD has developed a number of guidelines and conventions to encourage good practices by multinational enterprises (OECD, 2000). The regional integration blocs such as the EU, NAFTA and Mercosur are also developing rules on these issues (Frankel, 1997). The various agencies of the United Nations (UN) have also developed agreements and programmes on the social and environmental impact of globalization (ILO, 2000a; 2000b; 2000c; UN Division for Sustainable Development, 1999).

The OECD guidelines for multinational enterprises include guidance on dealing with combating bribery of public officials, principals of corporate governance, and guidelines for consumer protection for e-commerce, transfer pricing and corporate taxation (OECD, 2000). The OECD's guidelines for multinational enterprises also encourage the fulfilling of UN declarations in the area of social and environmental policies. The guidelines are voluntary and are not legally enforceable. However, the governments that are members of the OECD have approved in principal these guidelines and are committed to upholding them in their own countries, and to exerting pressure on multinational enterprises that are located in their countries in order to adopt policies and programmes that fulfil the conditions outlined in the guidelines.

The various agencies of the UN have been very active in generating declarations and programmes to encourage greater social and environmental responsibility by multinational enterprises. For example, the UN agency, namely the International Labour Office (ILO), has recently developed three major declarations on labour issues. These are the *Declaration on Fundamental Principals and Rights at Work*, the *Tripartite Declaration concerning Multinational Enterprises and Social Policy*, and the *International Programme on the Elimination of Child Labour* (ILO, 2000a; 2000b; 2000c). These declarations and programmes call on multinational enterprises to develop good practice in employment and social matters. These include recognizing trade unions, promoting equal opportunities (especially for women), seeking to contribute to the general improvement of social conditions in developing countries and combating the use of child labour.

The declaration at the Rio summit on sustainable environmental development led to the Agenda 21 programme to promote the objectives agreed at the Rio summit (UN Division for Sustainable Development, 1999). This declaration includes a chapter on the role of firms in achieving the objectives of Agenda 21, which involves development of recycling processes, investment in cleaner production and distribution systems, and development of environmental auditing systems for all aspects of the operations of firms. Agenda 21 also calls for governments to work with firms to monitor environmentally-damaging activities and to engage in cooperation to reduce or limit these activities.

As is the case with the OECD declarations, the UN declarations and programmes are not legally enforceable but have been agreed by the member states of the UN. Therefore, they can be used by pressure and interest groups that are opposed to the harmful aspects of globalization to exert pressure on governments and firms. Moreover, in some countries the law courts may take note of these guidelines and declarations in consideration of cases brought before them against governments and/or firms. In the public relations war between multinational enterprises and anti-capitalist/environmentalist groups the attempts to seek to abide by the conditions outlined in guidelines and declarations may become an important battleground which can be significant for marketing strategies.

The development of rules by the WTO and the regional integration blocs on social and environmental issues involve more than public relations battles. WTO rules and regulations from regional integration blocs may involve legally enforceable conditions on matters connected to trade and investment that are associated with social and environmental issues. Rules on competition policy will also directly impinge on firms. The WTO has reached no agreements on these issues but they are an important part of their agenda.

However, the regulatory framework of NAFTA and the EU in these areas does impinge on firms that operate within these blocs, even if their headquarters are located outside of these blocs. For example, multinational enterprises that operate in the EU must abide by the employment law of the EU and they must establish a European Works Council to provide an institutional framework for consulting their European workers. Moreover, firms that operate in the EU are subject to the competition policy of the Union even if they are not European companies. The decision by the European Commission to prohibit the merger between General Electric and Honeywell (although it had been approved by the US authorities) effectively prevented these companies from merging. Similarly, the decisions of the US authorities can prevent European companies from merging or from engaging in anti-competitive practices, even in their European operations. NAFTA has also developed rules on labour regulations and environmental conditions for goods and services traded across the frontiers of NAFTA. Clearly, some of the international rules and conventions on social, environmental and competition policies are already legally enforceable.

Implications for Firms and Marketing Managers

In the public relations war that is emerging between multinational enterprises and anti-capitalist and environmental groups, adherence to the principles outlined in the various international guidelines and declarations will be important elements in the battle. Marketing managers need to take into account the implications of these guidelines and declarations to be able to counter adverse publicity that could undermine the goals of their strategies.

Corporate governance systems that focus on social and environmental responsibilities require firms to be sensitive to principles outlined in these guidelines and declarations because marketing strategies that clearly break them may lead to serious implications for the companies. Monitoring of the development of these guidelines and declarations, and attempts to influence their development can be valuable.

Compliance with regulatory frameworks governing social, environmental and competition policy issues by national governments and regional integration blocs is required for any marketing strategy. Monitoring and lobbying national governments and international agencies to influence the development of new regulatory systems in these areas are essential for those firms engaged in extensive international marketing activities.

Conclusions

This chapter has examined four major economic changes that have taken place in the international marketplace during the recent years. These are: (a) globalization and internationalization of firms' business operations; (b) changes to the international monetary system; (c) changes to the trading and investment system; and (d) changes to the global competition, social and environmental regulatory system. These international economic developments cannot be predicted by firms, yet effective strategies and responses exist to some extent and have been discussed in this chapter. Generally, successful strategies for large firms include international marketing operations in the triad region, continuous monitoring of the changes to the international monetary, trading/investment and regulatory system, and lobbying national governments and international organizations. Successful strategies for smaller firms include international networking and targeting similar market niches worldwide.

Prima facie, the theme of international economic changes and its impact on firms and marketing managers should have been investigated to a large extent and knowledge on it should have been significant. However, surprisingly there has been little research concerning the impact of international economic changes on firms' strategies (Young, 2001). Clearly researchers have to delve into these issues which are of primary importance to business and marketing operations of large and small firms alike. Although these economic 'uncontrollables' largely cannot be influenced by firms, this chapter identified that there are often 'best practices' which firms can implement in order to succeed in an increasingly competitive international marketplace. More investigation is essential in order to come up with other viable strategies on the theme of international economic changes and their impact on firms' strategies.

CHAPTER 3

Consumer changes

Gillian Hogg

The 100 years after the death of Queen Victoria saw massive social, technological and scientific development which, with the exponential growth characteristic of such change, saw society alter more radically in the final 15 years of the twentieth century than it had for the preceding 500. A century that began on horseback ended with the Internet. The implications of this change for consumers have been enormous. Even looking back over the last 15 or 20 years the availability of technology, advances in medical science, market forces and their subsequent effect on the lifestyle of consumers clearly indicates that our understanding of consumers must have changed. At the same time, the rise in the education level of consumers, both generally and with regard to their specific rights and responsibilities, has led to a growth in consumerism and an increasingly demanding consumer presenting a managerial challenge for marketers. It is impossible in one chapter to give a comprehensive description of all consumer change over the last few decades; rather this chapter provides an overview of some of the main developments in consumption and attempts to identify the drivers of change that will illuminate our understanding of the twenty-first century consumer.

In tracking the development of theory marketing academics have traditionally turned to metaphor to enlighten the process (Hunt and Menon, 1993). Woodruffe (1997a) uses a theological image, tracing our understanding of consumption and changing understanding of the consumer from orthodoxy, through fundamentalism to liberalism. This metaphor implies a development, a moving through stages and a distinction between perspectives. Clearly there is a risk that close adherence to a metaphor will mislead rather than enlighten, however metaphor does help illuminate understanding. In discussing the way that we understand consumers the metaphor of religion is helpful as we can trace developments in theoretical perspective, the faith, alongside clear changes in the nature of the consumer (the congregation) and in managerial responses to consumers (the church). The purpose of this chapter is to examine these developments, both within society and in marketing theory and to consider the impact this has had on management – or is likely to have in the next decade. First the foundations of consumer behaviour theory are introduced, the orthodoxy of Woodruffe's metaphor; second, this understanding is traced through fundamentalism to liberalism linked to the development of our understanding of the modern, and postmodern, consumer and to changes in the environment in which consumers live their lives. Finally, the chapter examines the emerging issues in consumer behaviour and, based on forecasts of consumer changes, considers the challenges likely to be faced by marketers in meeting the demand of the next generation of consumers.

Now Let Us Praise Famous Men (and Women) . . .

Behaviour and beliefs are historically and culturally conditioned: to understand the present it is necessary to consider how we got here. The roots of consumer behaviour lie in economics and therefore the traditional view of the consumer has its central focus on exchange and the need to understand the behaviour of markets. This perspective was fundamentally sales orientated, considering what and how consumers buy. The view of the consumer as a rational, economic, problem solver dominated early consumer behaviour theory and is important when considering current consumers because it explains so much that the view of the postmodern consumer rejects. As Fuat Firat (1995) states, 'consumer behaviour theories believe in consistency and orderliness of consumer behaviour' (p. 3) and most of the considerable attempts to build models of consumer behaviour throughout the twentieth century are predicated in some way upon this fundamental rationalism that can be modelled. From the early models of Nicosia (1966) and Howard and Sheth (1969) through to more complex models of Schiffman and Kanuk (2000), or Baker (2000) academic researchers have sought to provide a framework for understanding the decision process and consumer buying behaviour. Many of these models attempt to include the behavioural, socio-economic or psychological drivers of consumer behaviour, yet remain intrinsically unsatisfactory as they are fundamentally rooted in consumption as an economically driven, decision-making process. As Loewenstein (2001) points out, whilst this may have intuitive appeal and managerial and practical resonance, it raises a number of problems, not least the overwhelming demands made on human cognitive capabilities (Gabaix and Laibson, 2000). Individuals are inconsistent, particularly in their attitude towards risk, and as Ross and Nisbett (1991) argue, interpersonal decision-making is much more a function of how people construe situations than of how they evaluate and weigh up attributes. Consumers are variety seekers; part of consumption can be explained in what Holbrook and Hirschman (1982) sum up as 'feelings, fantasy and fun', whilst at the same time they are identity seekers, constructing their social identities through consumption (Campbell, 1989; Elliot, 1999). In a society when a person's identity is no longer based on what he or she makes, but what is consumed (Keaney, 1999; Lee, 2000) and the role of women as consumers is inadequately explained by theory (Catterall, Maclaren and Stevens, 2000), the challenge for marketers is to find a means of coming to terms with a non-rational, identity-seeking consumer, focused on the symbolism of consumption as much as the commodity itself. As Holbrook (1999) points out, how we frame a problem greatly affects the conclusions that we reach. If, therefore, consumer behaviour theorists continue to frame the understanding of the consumer in terms of decision making, models will predominate. If, however, we look to reveal the consumer to be a 'creature more wondrous than we have heretofore imagined' (p. 146) as Holbrook suggests, then modelling behaviour has less attraction. Rather than rehearse these arguments in detail or attempt to put forward an alternative perspective, this chapter attempts to discuss contemporary consumption by examining the consumption context of the later twentieth to early twenty-first century and the implications of this for understanding consumers.

Theoretical Perspective

Whilst the economic prosperity of late twentieth century Western economies has been regarded as the defining moment of the consumer society, consumer booms are not a modern phenomenon. McCracken (1988), tracing the expansion of consumerism in Europe, notes two particularly interesting times; the consumer boom in late sixteenth century England and the 'explosion' in the fashionable use of consumer objects in the eighteenth century. On both occasions the rise in 'fashionable' consumption – and the consumption of fashion – had clear political and class overtones. Conspicuous consumption was the mark of a nobleman, essential in Elizabethan England to be noticed at court, and therefore receive favours from the Crown. Whilst at home he was indisputably at the top of the hierarchy, at court the noble was one of the crowd and had to wear more magnificent clothes, give better feasts or more gifts in order to stand out. The consequences of this consumption was that less money was available for family and hereditary possessions than the new, the fashionable and different (see also Mukerji, 1983). As a result the court became increasingly divorced from the country as they lived in different consumption universes (Corrigan, 1997). By the eighteenth century, consumption conveyed wealth, status-competition based on the ability to pay rather than inherited status – put simply, if you could afford it, you could have it. With the explosion of imitative behaviour on the part of low-standing consumers (McCracken, 1988, p. 40) the upper classes were driven to differentiate themselves once more, only once more to be imitated, resulting in a cycle of fashionable consumption. As eighteenth century Europe was relatively prosperous, the world of fashion and consumption was opened to more social classes and the consumer society flourished. McKendrick, Brewer and Plumb (1982) describe the demand side of the industrial revolution, notably the commercialization of fashion, which turned the bourgeoisie into avid spenders (p. 361). This separation of needs and wants is a defining feature of consumer society. As Campbell (1989) states, 'The crucial role of the modern consumer is to want to want under all circumstances and at all times, irrespective of what goods and services are actually being acquired or consumed' (p. 282). Thus want satisfaction becomes an end in itself in a way that could not have happened when production was linked to consumption. By the time Veblen wrote his *Theory of the Leisure Classes* in 1899 the idea of wealth as social currency was established. If one possesses wealth and desires social honour, it follows that one must demonstrate that one is wealthy and Veblen identifies two main ways that this can be accomplished; conspicuous leisure and conspicuous consumption. Whilst the head of the house could not pretend to leisure, as he was engaged in providing for his household, he could engage in vicarious leisure via his wife: from which comes the idea of a wife displaying the affluence of her husband by not working. This is important when we come to examine the changing role of women as consumers and the way in which female consumers have been traditionally viewed in marketing theory below. Campbell (1989), discussing what he terms the 'puzzle' of modern consumerism, considers in depth the cultural significance of the status aspects of consumption and concludes that they are, in general, not tenable in a modern society. Not only is the status of the upper – and therefore leisure – classes as fashion leaders debatable, but he questions the reasoning that suggests consumption that gives the 'correct' social signals is defensive. Whilst Veblen's theories may provide some answers to the apparent insatiability of consumption, they do not offer an explanation of the dynamic of modern consumption (see Campbell, 1989 for a full discussion).

A consequence of the need to establish status though consumption is, inevitably, a change in the nature of goods, or commodities. Marx in 1867 outlined two dimensions of value in objects, use value and exchange value. Use value refers to the actual concrete uses an object may be put to; exchange value is what makes a commodity exchangeable in the market. Whilst Marx's concern was with goods no longer produced for their use value but for exchange value and the relationship between production and consumption, this did not include the understanding of objects from the point of view of the consumer. Clearly consumption not only marks social difference, but also represents how we relate to each other or 'weave the web of culture' (Belk, 1995, p. 69). Understanding the changing consumer, therefore, requires a consideration of commodity and consumption in contemporary culture. Slater (1997) suggests that there is a temptation for every generation to see their variant on consumer culture as new and unique. However, as Gabriel and Lang (1995) point out, what sets modern consumption apart from earlier patterns is not only the growth in spending power across the social classes, but choice as a social phenomenon. At no previous time have consumers had so much choice of what to spend surplus funds on, and importantly, so much surplus to spend. Whilst the gap between the 'haves' and 'have nots' may be widening (Mintel, 2000), it is still smaller than at any other time in our history. At the beginning of the twentieth century consumers spent approximately two thirds of their available income on food; by the end of the century this had dropped to less than 10 per cent. As a result of this increased affluence the distinction between 'need' and 'want' becomes confused. Lee (2000) argues that it is not simply availability of material needs that distinguish us from our grandparents, but our hopes, aspirations and dreams are 'fulfilled under a very different expectancy'. For him the question that then arises is how consumers negotiate a material world largely constructed through, and by, commodities and importantly, the extent to which the necessary consumption of the commodities either empowers – or disempowers – us as individuals or groups.

Clearly consumption and consumer activities do not merely have economic effects, but cultural and communicative aspects. Increasingly, contemporary social theory recognizes that consumption is a vital part of the construction of social reality (Campbell, 1989; Douglas and Isherwood, 1978; Elliot, 1999), central to which is the idea that consumers do not only consume products for their material benefits, but for the images they communicate. Consumption of the social meaning of goods therefore regulates and expresses the way that individuals participate in social relationships. As Fiske (1989) states:

> In a consumer society, all commodities have cultural as well as functional values. To model this we need to extend the idea of an economy to include a cultural economy where the circulation is not one of money, but of meanings and pleasures.
>
> (Fiske, 1989, p. 27)

It is this search for an understanding of the meaning that consumers attribute to goods and the association between objects – and the role of marketing in determining these meanings that has dominated the understanding of consumers in the last 20 years. Postmodern consumer theory is predicated upon this belief that consumption is as much about the symbolic meaning of products or their images as it is about the product itself. According to Baudrillard (1981) therefore, products become commodity signs, the fragility of which makes their interpretation problematic. As Elliot (1999) points out, to complicate matters further, much of consumers' symbolic interpretation of these signs and symbols is essentially non-rational and does not obey the conventional codes of language. It is not the purpose of this chapter to explore the methodological implications of such claims, indeed Holbrook (1999) has already done so. The important point for considering consumer changes is that the symbolic meaning of products defies rational or logical model building. However, even if much of modern consumption takes place within the realm of illusion (Debord, 1977) or virtual reality (Baudrillard, 1988), the challenge for marketing is to understand how, as Gabriel and Lang (1995) put it, consumers learn to ignore the 'noise' of commodities, signs and images and use them in their everyday lives.

Possessions are an integral part of self identity (see for example, Celsi, Rose and Leigh, 1993; Hogg and Michell, 1996; Schouten and Alexander, 1995). As Dittmar (1992) states, consumption is located at the individual-society interface and represents one way in which the relationship between individual and society is realized. This interdependence of self and society is summed up by Berger (1966, p. 109): 'One identifies oneself, as one is identified by others, by being located in a common world'. As Hogg and Michell (1996) state, consumption is an activity which creates, confirms, maintains or transforms situated identities. Gabriel and Lang (1995) describe identity as the 'story which an individual writes and rewrites about him or herself, never reaching the end . . .' (p. 86). As this story is incomplete consumers are constantly constructing their identities. Whilst identities have previously been drawn from personal and family groups, work and achievement, Bauman (1992) argues that, in Western societies at least, the work ethic has now been displaced by the consumption ethic, with consumers able to buy an 'off the peg' identity through brands (see also Keaney, 1999). Thus Davidson (1992) states, 'Ours is a world in which products tell our stories for us' (p. 15), and the twenty-first century consumer is a consumer primarily of brands and the symbols they convey. Brands then take on a life of their own and as Sampson (1993) states, choice of brands, like choice of friends becomes personality-dictated and choice becomes choice between brands.

It has become axiomatic to state that consumers have more choice then ever before. Gabriel and Lang (1995) point out, however, choice is not as simple as the number of items available; if these are undifferentiated and the consumer does not have the information on which to base choice, then it becomes meaningless and a source of confusion – or overload (Gabriel and Lang, 1995; Jacoby, Speller and Kohn, 1974). Ridderstrale and Nordstrom (2000) refer to this as the 'surplus society' and give examples of such excess choice as the 200 newspapers available to Norway's 4.5 million citizens, 5,000 separate watch models produced by Seiko, and the claim by the Disney corporation to develop a new product – film, book, CD, etc. – every five minutes. However, Howard (2001) argues that many consumers today question the messages and images associated with the brands and products they have purchased and are looking for information and advice they think they can trust. This need to find trustworthy sources of information leads to increased reliance on word of mouth and social networks to validate the marketing messages and interpret information (Gabriel and Lang, 1995).

The Changing Consumer

There are a number of demographic and lifestyle factors that have been documented that suggest that the twenty-first century consumer has changed. Firstly, simple demographics reveals that in the UK, as in most of the Western economies, we have an ageing population. This is due to a combination of falling birth rates as women choose to start families later, have fewer children (or none at all), and have increased life expectancy: the twenty-first century consumer enjoys an average life expectancy of 80 for women and 75 for men. At the same time, life expectancy for men has improved to nearer that of women to the extent that there is predicted to be a growth of five per cent in the numbers of men over the age of 60 in the next five years (Mintel, 2000). The consequence of these demographic changes is that increasing numbers of children are born into families whose parents are further into their careers and have greater disposable income to spend on their families. There has also been a large increase in the number of people choosing to live alone, indeed Mintel (2000) predicts that by 2010 single person households will account for 40 per cent of all UK households. This rise can be accounted for by both declining marriage rates and increasing divorce rates. The Office of National Statistics predicts a 46 per cent growth in the numbers who will never marry by 2021 and a 51 per cent rise in divorce. These changes in household composition are mirrored by changes in consumer lifestyle. The traditional age distinctions are becoming increasingly blurred; in fashion, lifestyle and attitude people are staying younger longer, and are increasingly aware of the need to take responsibility for their own health. Sport and keep-fit facilities were the growth areas of the 1990s and there has been a corresponding growth in over-the-counter medicines and health supplements, 'healthy eating' food ranges, and a plethora of diet and exercise books and videos. Body image has become an obsession with the 'ideal' (thin) shape promoted as an ideal and beauty being associated with goodness (see Dion, 1972; Grogan, 1999). Achieving this ideal requires constant scrutiny and suffering (Docscha and Ozanne, 2000). Attitudes towards leisure time have also changed, consumers want to use their leisure time more effectively and to treat themselves – as Hart (1998) points out, there is a debit and credit mentality amongst many consumers that means that they are willing to reward themselves for good behaviour – if they use the stairs rather than the lift they can eat a chocolate bar. Mintel (2001) found that 75 per cent of their respondents would spend money on something for themselves as a treat. The numbers eating out regularly has grown to 87 per cent of the population and as the cost of international air travel has become cheaper consumers are taking more holidays, indeed taking holidays is regarded as a necessity by over half of the population (Mintel, 2000). These trends are not restricted to the younger generation: leisure activities once confined to teenagers are now visited by older adults searching for a more exciting experience, with consequent implications for the more 'traditional' venues; visitors to zoos and historic houses have fallen as themed attractions such as Alton Towers become more popular (Mintel, 2000). (For a fuller discussion of the contemporary search for authenticity in heritage attractions see Goulding, 2000.) As a consequence of these lifestyle changes there are an increasing number of consumers who fall into debt. In January 2002 the official Bank of England figures for personal borrowing showed consumer debt to be at its highest since they began collecting this type of data and that consumers were generally rate insensitive. Credit is widely and easily available and consumers are not willing to 'save up' before making a purchase but are demanding immediate gratification (Hogg and Moore, 2001).

These changes in household and lifestyle have important consequences for the way that consumers consume. Howard (2001) suggests that consumers are increasingly searching for 'fulfilment and sources of identity' (p. 95), what Mintel (2000) refers to as a 'centre of gravity'; as trust in both government and established religion declines they need some other unifying force (see also Palmer, 2002). The decline of the 'nuclear' family, with increasing divorce rates and greater teenage independence, suggests a greater reliance of social networks and friendship groups as a source of reference (Mintel, 2000). The importance of the social group in understanding consumer behaviour has been widely recognized (see, for example, Solomon, Bamossy and Askegaard, 2000), it is in the importance of these groups that the changes have occurred. As noted above, in defining identity there is interdependence between the individual and society (Dittmar, 1992; Goffman, 1959), manifested in a sense of community. Community, as a number of authors point out, has been largely over looked in studies of consumption behaviour (see Cova, 1997; McGrath, Sherry and Heisley, 1993; Muniz and O'Guinn, 2001). Community assumes that there are a set of common values to which members of the group subscribe that determine consumption patterns and are a direct reflection of the commitment of individuals to the ethos. These groups may be based on a number of different criteria such as ethnicity or national identity (Bouchet, 1995; Fuat Firat, 1995), interest (Schouten and Alexander, 1995) or increasingly, consumption (Muniz and O'Guinn, 2001). In postmodern community non-territorial mutual interest groups, based on an assortment of factors such as shared activities or tastes, have replaced geographical medieval notions of community and subculture (Muniz and O'Guinn, 2001). A subculture of consumption emerges as people identify with certain objects or activities and, through them, with other people. Unifying these activities is a set of common values, which determine consumption patterns and are a direct reflection of the commitment of individuals to the ethos. Brands take on specific meaning within the subculture; by understanding the process of self-transformation and the meaning associated with certain products, marketers can 'take an active role in socializing new members and cultivating the commitment of [t]he current one' (Schouten and Alexander, 1995, p. 62).

A related issue to this community emphasis is the desire to find ways of creating a fairer society. Howard (2001) points out that as the division between selfishness and altruism is becoming blurred, it is possible for today's consumers to satisfy themselves and 'do good' at the same time – a principle that lies beneath initiatives such as *The Big Issue*. The aim of *The Big Issue* is that consumers should see the exchange as a commercial one, where they are paying money for a quality magazine. However, at the same time they are helping the homeless; indeed in this case, uniquely, the donor comes face-to-face with the beneficiary as the vendors are themselves homeless (Hibbert, Hogg and Quinn, 2002). The responsibility of society to care for 'excluded' members is not new, it is the emphasis placed on 'inclusion' that is a feature of the late twentieth to early twenty-first century. Byrne (1999) argues exclusion is not a property of individuals or even of social spaces, rather it is a necessary and inherent characteristic of an unequal post-industrial capitalism (p. 128). Social exclusion is defined as 'the inability of our society to keep all groups and individuals within reach of what we expect as a society and the tendency to push vulnerable and difficult individuals into the least popular places' (Watt, 2001, p. 175). Differences in life expectancy between socio-economic groups have widened, mainly as a result of faster rates of improvement in affluent groups rather than a decrease in poorer communities (Watt and Ecob, 2000). As a result areas have become 'deserts' to certain types of retailer, notably food retailers (Cummins and McIntyre, 1999). This is important when considering consumer change as not all consumers are equal; change for many consumers who, because of age, income or handicap, are excluded from mainstream consumption can result in the withdrawal of opportunities.

The Rise and Rise of Women Consumers

One of the most important changes in consumers in the last 20 years is the increased economic and social power of women. Although marketing and consumer behaviour theorists were always aware of the commercial power of women this was a patriarchal and stereotypical view of 'Mrs Consumer'. Indeed the consumer has traditionally been viewed as female. The verb 'to consume' means to use up and is associated with extravagance whilst production, being the domain of the male was socially useful and positive. In marketing research gender has long been the most common segmentation variable yet; as Catterall, Maclaren and Stevens (2000) point out, this was generally at the level of acknowledging that differences exist (or do not exist) between male and female consumption behaviour, rather than any attempt to investigate how and why these differences were found. Woodruffe (1997a) suggests that our understanding of consumers is fundamentally flawed as it is built on 'false truths – illusions arising out of gendered assumptions about women as consumers' (p. 668). Similarly, Hirshman (1993) demonstrated the dominant masculinity in marketing research and Knights and Odih (1999) show that the male 'breadwinner' characterizes marketing's view of the household.

In 1979, when Margaret Thatcher became the first woman to become Prime Minister of Britain, over 60 per cent of the women in the UK had finished full-time education by the age of 15 and fewer than 10 per cent had benefited from higher education. Although only a quarter of women worked full time this was an increase on previous decades and the ensuing affluence of these households was used to explain the rise in ownership of white and brown goods (Gray, 2000) yet only 2.5 per cent of households had a dishwasher and fewer than 50 per cent a refrigerator. By the end of the century female participation in the workforce almost equalled male; indeed, the Department of Education and Employment estimate that by 2006 80 per cent of women aged 25–34 will be working. This has been aided by a shift in employment patterns away from traditional heavy industry to white collar jobs more open to women (Mintel, 2000). With this rise in working women comes an increasing acknowledgement of the economic power shift this implies. As more women become financially independent their economic power increases and their importance as consumers rises.

This has not, however, led to any better understanding of the gender issues in marketing (Catterall, Maclaren and Stevens, 2000), indeed despite social and economic prosperity marketers have awakened to the 'women's market' relatively late. As Ridderstrale and Nordstrom (2000) point out, it took car manufacturers almost 100 years to understand that women are not small men, they do not look for the same features in a car and do not use the same decision-making criteria. Popcorn (2001) goes further and suggests that a major failing in marketing strategy has been to assume that women are like men. She argues that women and men differ in crucial ways in which they receive and evaluate information and therefore respond to different marketing stimuli. She attributes these differences to key neurotransmitters in the brain, as a result of which women have 'peripheral vision' a dislike of 'in your face' marketing techniques and a preference for more subtle messages that directly relate to the lives they lead. Women still do 80 per cent of housework and yet hold down demanding jobs and are the primary carers of children (Mintel, 2000). They are, therefore, looking for products and services that make their lives easier and help them to juggle their myriad responsibilities. The amount of free time available to women is declining as increasing numbers are employed in senior positions. As a result there has been a rise in consumption of labour saving devices, leisure items and in services such as cleaning. Indeed Mintel (2000) predicts the return of the household servant as more and more women look for help in running a home.

A second trend associated with the rise of the female consumer is the growth of more fluid attitudes towards gender and gender divides. It is estimated that 10 per cent of the population are gay and the traditional hostility to 'alternative' sexual orientation is decreasing with a move towards the legitimizing, in legal terms, of homosexual unions, property rights and inheritance. At the same time the traditional gender-based consumption patterns are altering. This is evidenced by the growth in the market for male cosmetics, magazines and fashion items traditionally thought to be the preserve of women (Sturrock and Pioch, 1998); the rise in alcohol consumption by women and 'gender free' clothes (Mintel, 2000). In 1972 it was considered 'inappropriate' for a woman to wear trousers to work and a female teacher was suspended for not conforming to such a dress code. Today such restrictions would be considered a breach of human rights. This re-

and de-gendering is important in consumption terms as it is indicative of a wider trend in society towards individualism and the drive by consumers to assume their identities not through social class, age or sex, but from a smaller reference group of people with common interests.

One setting in which concern for women and their requirements has tradition-ally dominated is the shop. Shopping has long been regarded as a women's activity, indeed the department store developed as women's public space, an 'Adamless Eden' (Corrigan, 1997, p. 50). Nava (1996) describes the importance of shopping as part of women's everyday life at the end of the nineteenth century. Department stores provided a safe and socially acceptable context for the wives of the new middle classes to interact socially without chaperones, indeed Laermans (1993) describes the early department stores as 'female leisure centres'. Shopping fitted the traditional role of the woman, as the primary homemakers shopping for the family and household was a female responsibility and at the same time, in keeping with Veblen's theories, allowed the leisured wives of the affluent to demonstrate their non-working status in public. Yet the place of shopping as a leisure activity is itself a gender issue. Traditionally, shopping has been viewed as a low-skill, repetitive, tedious and economically insignificant act. Invariably classified as a 'female-type' task, and a female responsibility (South and Spitze, 1994), aside from the various political implications of such categorizations, shopping participation studies consistently identify that women shop more frequently and for longer periods of time than men (Boedeker, 1995; Underhill, 1999). For many women shopping, at least for necessities, is as much work as pleasure. Eccles and Woodruffe-Burton (2000) provide evidence that women take their role as shoppers seriously. A study of Christmas gift-buying noted that women appeared to regard this as important work whilst men saw it as 'play'. Clearly not all shopping is equal. Retail therapy, or compensatory consumption, has been extensively studied (see for example, Eccles and Woodruffe-Burton, 2000; Elliot, Eccles and Gournay, 1996; Woodruffe, 1997) particularly in relation to 'normal' consumption activity, as a response to psychological problems and as a form of self-expression. Underhill (1999) suggests that women take pride in their ability to shop prudently and well and, despite the social and economic changes discussed here, they still do 80 per cent of non-household shopping, although household shopping is now more of a shared activity (Nava, 1996). Men may become more involved in their own shopping (Underhill, 1999), but a study by Moore, Doyle and Thomson (2001) on the fashion purchasing of divorced men demonstrated that in a stable partnership women buy most of their men's clothes. Unfortunately, as a female-dominated activity shopping is frequently viewed as a frivolous and mundane occupation. Even the terminology used implies that shopping is a lesser activity when undertaken by women than men; for example, purchasing a car or a computer is a male-dominated consumption decision and is rarely referred to as 'shopping'. Men see themselves as specialist consumers, becoming more heavily involved in the acquisition of high involve-ment purchases (Laroche *et al.*, 2000), fulfilling an instrumental need as opposed to shopping for the sake of shopping (Otnes and McGrath, 2001).

Whilst this image may be changing with the increased number of men venturing into shops, the dominant image of a man shopping is of one under duress. As Miller *et al.* (1998) point out, however, shopping is a prerequisite of consumption. Theorizing consumption as a social process rather than as a single isolated exchange requires that we take account not only of what we buy, but the context in which we do so. Shopping psychology has developed in sophistication and experts can now predict and manipulate the way that the consumer navigates the shop, what falls in their line of gaze and which colours and brands they are most likely to respond to (for a full discussion of shopping behaviour see Underhill, 1999). Increasingly however, retail has become 'retailment', a form of entertainment within a retail experience.

Time and Technology

One of the most urgent pressures on twenty-first century consumers is time. Time, according to Ridderstrale and Nordstrom (2000), is the religion of our age and we are addicted to speed. Time has long been considered a factor in understanding consumer behaviour (see for example, Solomon, Bamossy and Askegaard, 1999). Time is an economic variable and consumers develop their own time style to allocate this resource (Bergadaa, 1990). The Henley Centre classes time into 'good' time and 'bad' time. Although working hours are falling the UK average working week is still the highest in Europe and unlikely to fall further (Mintel, 2000). There is, therefore, increasing pressure on consumers to use their leisure time effectively, and not to 'waste' time. Time, as Howard (2001) notes, is a currency that we feel we should invest in and save, rather than squander. Keeping busy has traditionally been considered a good thing whilst doing nothing signals waste; consumers are therefore likely to plan their time more carefully than in the past and to indulge in leisure time activities that make use of time. For example, the recent growth in DIY home and garden activities have created a group of products that would not have been considered consumer products 30 years ago (Mintel, 2000). Compared to their counterparts 20 years ago consumers are relatively cash rich but time poor, as the pressure to control time and account for quality time increases. As noted above, consumers, especially female consumers, are more willing to pay for labour-saving products and services that will provide them with more free time; Mazur (2002) singles out 'convenience' as the most significant consumer trend of 2001. At the same time consumers search for leisure time experiences that intensify their free time, even the simplest cup of coffee becomes an experience in Starbucks or Coffee Republic. This group, referred to by the Henley Centre as 'time converters' are focused on making the best use of their time, at all times.

Technology has assisted this search for time by providing not only the labour-saving devices, but the means and opportunity to use time more efficiently by 'polychronic' activity (see Kaufman, Lane and Linquist, 1991). Telephone banking, for example, means that bills can be paid at any time of the day or night – banking in pyjamas. The rise of the mobile phone has ensured that time traditionally seem as wasted, for example in a taxi to a meeting, can now be used to make telephone calls, and to send and receive e-mail. Mobile phones are no longer a luxury item for the rich; 66 per cent of UK adults and 77 per cent of 14–16 year olds own a mobile (Mintel, 2000). Technology allows shopping over the Internet with Tesco alone delivering £125 million of groceries a year. Whereas the previous generation of consumers had been amazed at what technology can do, the current generation are surprised when technology can not do something. This 'technolust' is driven by a desire to have more control over their environment and decision making (Brosnan, 1998). Technology in general, and the Internet in particular, is breaking down the traditional geographical boundaries to information search as product and service information is available from all over the world (Ward and Lee, 2000). Whereas previously search costs would have rendered the acquisition of such information too expensive, it is now available at the click of a mouse.

It has been estimated that by 2003 the UK market for e-commerce will be worth at least £2.5 billion by 2003 (Retail e-commerce Task Force) with development reliant on the access to the Internet until new platforms such as digital television (DTV) become more widespread. It is predicted that services offered through the television have greater potential as they are able to attract the levels of advertising revenue to make web-based services commercially viable (Stevenson, 1998). The advantages for the consumer of e-commerce that emerged from this research are: the 24 hour, 7 day access, quality and topicality of product information; ease of comparison; immediate access to certain products (for example, electronic documents, financial transaction); customer involvement in product and service innovation; and convenience (Retail e-commerce Task Force). One of the main inhibitors of online purchase is the perceived security of Internet payments. Research by Karakaya and Charlton (2001) suggests that lack of confidence in the security of transactions was one of the main reasons why consumers did not purchase over the Internet, whilst a report by *Which? Online* (1998) reported that almost half of respondents believe that the Internet encourages fraudulent practices (see also Cook and Coupey, 1998).

Arguably the most dramatic effect of the information-empowered consumer will be felt in those services where access to information has been traditionally regarded as the preserve of the professional such as medicine, law and financial services. The Internet has the power to change fundamentally the informational asymmetries which have characterized the delivery of professional services (Jadad, 1998). Professional dominance and power in the service encounter has conventionally been based on the existence of an imbalance in knowledge and expertise between the professional and service user (Wilson, 1994). The Internet, with its breadth of information and, more significantly, its scope for interaction among consumer communities through providing virtual discussion forums, has the potential to redress these informational asymmetries and empower consumers to challenge the established dominance of service professionals. This image of an Internet-empowered consumer has been noted in health, for example, by anecdotal accounts in the letters pages of journals such as the *British Medical Journal* and *New England Journal of Medicine* from health care professionals describing consumers arriving for a consultation armed with reams of Internet printouts (see Coiera, 1996; Eysenbach and Diepgen, 1998). Problems have been identified, however, in the veracity of the information patients gather. For example, an article in *The Sunday Times* (12 March 2000) suggested that of 41 pages giving advice on treating a child only four gave advice that an independent doctor considered appropriate. Indeed, as consumers make increasing use of

Internet sites for obtaining information, the nature and reliability of the informa-tion becomes increasingly important.

The anarchic nature of the Internet and the lack of control over material accessible over the web causes problems for consumers and suppliers alike. Increasingly they are expecting suppliers to not only have a web presence but for this to include the possibility of an Internet transaction. Channel proliferation, however, does not help suppliers unless it is accompanied by increased revenue. At the same time the opportunity for the development of consumer communities to develop online to share information, discuss matters of mutual interest and compare product performance vastly increases the potential for word of mouth, both positive and negative (Muniz and O'Guinn, 2001). Whilst received wisdom in consumer behaviour was that a dissatisfied customer told 10 or 12 others, the Internet can increase that to thousands or even millions. The problem for suppliers is that this type of information is almost impossible to control and yet for consumers has the credibility of other forms of word-of-mouth information. The need to find trustworthy sources of information, discussed above, drives this reliance on word of mouth and at the same time raises concerns over the validity of the source.

[handwritten margin note: amazon + eBay rate reliability of seller]

The Knowledgeable Consumer

Over the last three decades the numbers of adults entering further and higher education has doubled to almost 50 per cent (Mintel, 2000). Kress, Ozawa and Schmid (2000) suggest that education is a good benchmark for measuring consumers' sophistication and that those with at least one year of college tend to be more analytical and questioning in their behaviour. As a result, we can conclude that as levels of education rise consumers become more demanding of the goods and services they receive. Alongside this overall rise in education there has been a rise in consumers' knowledge of their rights and consequently a move towards enshrining consumer rights in law. Legal remedies for production failures are not new; King Hammurabi in the Babylonian Empire (*circa* 1800 BC) intro-duced a law which stated that a builder whose house fell down and killed its owner was liable. The growth in consumer activist groups throughout the twentieth century is documented in detail by Gabriel and Lang (1995) (see also Quazi, 2002). The key point is that there has been an increasing trend towards consumer protection legislation, a move from *caveat emptor*, let the consumer beware, to *credat emptor*, let the consumer trust. At the same time consumers have become more aware of the rights that they have, and importantly their entitle-ments. The range of interests covered by consumer policies is normally defined in the context of the range of consumer 'rights' agreed and ratified by the United Nations in 1985; i.e., the right to safety, choice, information, redress, education to be an informed consumer, basic needs, a healthy environment and, importantly, the right to be heard. These general consumer rights are linked by the IOCU (1987) to the overall rights of the citizen, although as Gabriel and Lang (1995) point out, their realization across national boundaries is a Promethean task. Of more interest in discussing consumer change is the impact of television and consumer rights programmes.

Broadcasting in Britain has evolved as a 'quasi-public' institution which has traditionally adopted a role of both educating and entertaining. For example, 'The Archers' was originally designed to provide the Ministry of Agriculture with a method of disseminating information about farming developments. Whilst there has been a change in this conception of broadcasting following the enterprise culture of the 1980s, reflected in the BBC's increasing emphasis on ratings, and more recently the need to meet the challenge of new technologies, the prevailing culture is still one of paternalism. A BBC policy document in 1995 recognized this change, suggesting that audiences are 'more discerning, more aware of their power . . . less willing to be patronized or talked down to . . .'. The media consumer is, therefore, an increasingly powerful force in determining programming, both content and policy, and at the same time programmes which inform them of their rights and allow them to express their dissatisfaction with the goods and services they receive are perennially popular. From pioneering consumer programmes such as 'That's Life' in the 1970s to 'Watchdog' the emphasis has been on championing consumer rights against amorphous organizations. The link between consumerism and citizenship is emphasized by the Consumer Association who, as part of their mission to educate consumers, are increasing school-based education of consumer issues, and citizenship is now becoming part of the national curriculum in England. The result of this growth in consumerism has been an increase in complaining, a willingness by consumers to stand up for their rights and to express their dissatisfaction. This may be beneficial to marketers as there are positive effects on satisfaction from well-handled complaints and Bennett (1997) has demonstrated the cathartic effect of complaining leading to the psychologically gratifying relief of frustration, and hence to higher post-complaint repurchase behaviour. The implication is therefore that consumers who are aware of their rights and complain will be more satisfied than those who do not complain. The crucial managerial issue is that these complaints must be dealt with and appropriate action taken. Zeithaml, Parasuraman and Berry (1990) identify the 'zone of tolerance' of what consumers regard as acceptable. This zone moves in a recovery situation; i.e., in order to satisfy a customer it is necessary to do more than if the service had been right first time.

The Demanding Consumer

Satisfaction was the mantra of the late 1980s and 1990s. As Fuat Firat, Dholakia and Venkatesh (1995) point out the sovereign consumer was both idealized and idolized. The need to understand and deliver customer satisfaction – and its link to the other goal of the time, quality – dominated the business literature. However, businesses are not in business to create satisfied customers, they are in business to make money; it just so happens that satisfied customers are profitable. Marketing in particular awoke to the economic reality of customer satisfaction, in part based on an increasing recognition that by focusing on attracting new customers marketing practitioners were devoting little effort on retaining existing customers, a potentially more profitable group (Anderson and Mittal, 2000; Heskett *et al.*, 1994; Rust, Zahorik and Keiningham, 1995). Axioms abounded that it was two, four, 10 or 12 times more profitable to retain existing customers than recruit new ones, according to the industry sector or research methodology, and that the way to retain customers was to satisfy them (Fornell and Wernerfelt, 1988; Yu and Dean, 2001). Conceptualizing satisfaction proved more difficult and the customer satisfaction literature was dominated by the (dis)confirmation of expectations paradigm. Satisfaction (and, confusingly, perceived quality) is assumed to be a function of expectations minus perceptions (see, for example, Anderson, Fornell and Lehmann, 1994; Churchhill and Suprenant, 1982; Zeithaml, Parasuraman and Berry, 1990). According to this 'gap' model, when an experience is better than expected there is positive disconfirmation of the expectation and quality/satisfaction is predicted: when the experience is worse than expected dissatisfaction or poor perceived quality results. Whilst this model has the attraction of parsimony, there has been increasing acknowledgment that it is necessary to look beyond this simple equation to arrive at an understanding about how consumers assess either satisfaction or quality (see Anderson, Fornell and Lehmann, 1994; Buttle, 1996; Churchill and Surprenant, 1982; Oliver, 1993; Zeithaml, Berry and Parasuraman, 1990 for a full discussion of these issues). These operationalization issues did not prevent a continuing exhortation to concentrate on delivering customer satisfaction, and over the course of the 1980s simple customer-driven axioms, like 'the customer is always right' and 'stay close to the customer', were widely proclaimed in business publications (e.g., Albrecht and Zemke, 1985; Peters and Waterman, 1982). An American-based retailer, Stew Leonard, famously displayed his customer policy, 'Rule 1: The customer is always right. Rule 2: If the customer is ever wrong, re-read Rule 1'. Berry (1995) provided case studies of successful companies who had responded to customers as role models for the rest and the cult of the customer ruled.

The reality is less simple. Not every customer can be satisfied and, inevitably, not all satisfied customers can be retained. Economically it is not profitable to retain every customer as the cost escalates sharply in response to offering better service/products (Anderson and Mittal, 2000; Reichheld and Teal, 1996). Slowly, both academics and business executives started to acknowledge that customers are not always right and businesses would be better advised to stay away from certain groups of customers (Bitner, Booms and Mohr, 1994; Lovelock, 1994). Gummesson (1998) characterizes this as a 'tug of war', arguing that the strain of keeping every customer was simply a shift from 'marketing myopia' (Levitt, 1960) to 'marketing myopia 2'. Whereas once the issue was organizations being inward-looking (i.e., production-oriented) and following established rules and traditions of the industry, they then had an equally short-sighted outward aspect (i.e., customer-oriented), still not based on reflection. Such a shift of mindset only signified moving from one extreme to another of the same myopic continuum. Iacobucci, Grayson and Ostrom (1994) suggest that 'the claim "the customer is always right" is utter nonsense' (p. 94), and Lovelock (1994) points out that 'nobody really believes that the customer is always right. In truth, the customer is sometimes horribly wrong, and it's silly to pretend otherwise' (p. 223). So where does this leave customers? Having been deified in the early 1990s were they then to be villainized? The emphasis by the late 1990s was for organizations to identify the 'right' customers for them, their target group, whom the company should be able to serve well and profitably compared to the 'wrong customers, whose needs it cannot profitably serve' (Jones and Sasser, 1995, p. 90). At the same time was the development of the relationship marketing paradigm, with its recognition that transactions are rarely 'one off' but fit into a pattern of transactions, and that the benefit to the organization was in developing long-term, mutually beneficial relationships with key customers. A recent Institute of Bankers study suggested that the 80:20 rule still predominates and companies make 80 per cent of their profit from 20 per cent of their customers, whilst only 20 per cent of their marketing effort goes into retaining that profitable section. Relationship marketing is discussed in Chapter 7; the key point for this chapter is the emphasis that is being placed on loyalty and customers as assets that required to be managed to ensure maximum benefit. This management was assisted by the technology trigger of mass data mining and an industry grew up around customer relationship management (CRM). From a consumer perspective, however, organizations have the technology and information to truly know their customer and to produce goods and services based on customer-defined needs and wants. These databases allow for a better analysis of the 'cause and effect' relationships at work in consumer behaviour and the variables with predictive power. But even the strongest causal relationships do not lead to 100 per cent prediction. Ridderstrale and Nordstrom (2000) argue that this is because getting to know customers is not very difficult: 'Any customer, in any industry, in any market wants stuff that is both cheaper and better, and they want it yesterday . . . . The simple truth is that the typical customer will always ask for improvements within the present frame' (p. 157). The reality, as they point out, is that listening to customers or studying their past behaviour is not enough, customers have neither the imagination or technical knowledge to know what is possible. Prediction comes not from knowing customers, but from *understanding* them, a challenge most organizations find harder to meet.

The Thinking Consumer

Concern for the environment was one of the major global issues of the 1990s (Chuckman, 1990; Kirkpatrick, 1990; McDaniel and Rylander, 1993; Roberts, 1996) and the indications are that this concern continues (de Simone and Popoff, 1997; Kilbourne and Beckmann, 1998). Recent research certainly suggests it is not a 'consumer' fad (see UK Business and the Environment Trends Survey 1997) and as a result there has been increased media attention paid to environmental issues and the need to be 'greener' in our individual behaviour. The problem, as Beckman, Christensen and Christensen (2001) point out, is that consumers tend to act contrary to their beliefs about the environment, and are willing to express their concern about environmental issues but not to change their consumption behaviours, indicating a 'words/deeds inconsistency' and a weak relationship between what consumers say and what they do. Whilst some authors (see, for example, Ottman, 1998) have identified a change in societal values away from consumerism to stewardship and conservation, there is no evidence for a consumer-led force for change. Many consumers are willing to pay a price premium for green products, referred to by the Roper Organisation (1990) as 'green back greens' after the slang for dollar bills. The implication is that these consumers would rather pay extra than change their behaviour in any radical way (Bloemers, Magnomi and Peters, 2001). There has, however, been a growth in the highly principled group of 'ethical' consumers (Shaw and Clarke, 1999). As well as being concerned about general environmental issues, ethical consumers are distinguished by their concern for deep-seated problems, such as those of the Third World and armament manufacture (see, for example, Gabriel and Lang, 1995). This distinction between 'green' and 'ethical' consumerism is important, since more wide-ranging ethical issues can add significantly to the complexity of consumer decisions (Shaw and Clarke, 1999). Ethical consumerism may only account for a small proportion of the market, however they are indicative of a growing trend in consumer behaviour to question the supremacy of organizations and to attempt to redress the power balance between consumer and supplier. The rise in Fair Trade products, for example, is indicative of the fact that consumers are willing to consider the social impact of their own consumption (Shaw and Clarke, 1999).

Conclusion: Consumer Changes and the Changing Consumer

To detail all of the changes that have effected consumption in the last 20 years would require a volume of its own and would comprise the social history of the late twentieth century. Consumption dominates our lives so that the decision of what (and what not) is consumed permeates social relationships, perceptions and images, and consumption has become the 'unchallenged ideology of our time' (Gabriel and Lang, 1995, p. 1). The picture of the twenty-first century consumer is unclear. Traditionally the marketing concept viewed consumers as rational, sovereign and seeking to maximize the benefits of personal acts of choice. More recently attention has turned to ways in which consumers interpret the signs and symbols of consumption and relate to each – consumption not only marks social difference but represents the means through which we relate to each other. Keaney (1999) suggests that consumption has been 'elevated to a status equivalent to the pinnacle of human achievement. More cynically, it is promoted as the likely pinnacle of most humans' achievement' (p. 696). At the same time as marketers celebrate individualism, and governments in the EU promote economic and fiscal convergence, nationalism remains a dominant force with issues of cultural identity and religious intolerance causing widespread unrest. Values of national and ethnic cultures impact upon buying motives: as incomes converge, cultural values remain stable, resulting in increased emphasis on cultural values as an influence on consumption in increasingly affluent Western societies – the more we strive to be different the more we want to be seen as part of something. The need to belong is a consistent theme of social research and increasingly we demonstrate our belonging though our consumption activities (Gabriel and Lang, 1995).

What has not changed is the vital requirement of all organizations to understand their customers and to develop goods and services based on this understanding. In their review *2020 Vision: Tomorrow's Consumer* Mintel (2000) predicts that society will follow the principle of entropy; i.e., the tendency of all natural systems to move towards a disordered state. This will be evidenced by the decline in importance of established social and economic institutions, the increased focus on the individual consequent from the increase of single person households, greater social isolation, greater cultural diversity and the information society. These tends are already apparent. The challenge for marketing is to connect with these customers and to produce what they want to consume, when they want to consume it. Ridderstrale and Nordstrom (2000, p. 183) state: 'People do not get their kicks from celibacy and savings. . . . Leisure and pleasure are the new reality. Instant gratification is expected.' Technology allows production to be individualized in a way that was common before the industrial revolution, but on the scale and in the time frame that industrialization delivered. Instant gratification helps the consumer cope with the postmodern 'empty self' and consumption is equated with happiness (Keaney, 1999). A number of commentators have observed a shift towards individualism in Western societies (see, for example, Palmer, 2002), increasingly consumers are asking 'what's in it for me?' and a failure to demonstrate the benefits to consumers is a key reason why marketing efforts fail. Relationship marketing, aimed at developing long-term mutually beneficial relationships between consumers and suppliers, addresses this in theory, but in practice frequently fails to add value for the customer in any meaningful way. As transaction cost economics demonstrates that relationships are more likely to be sustained when there is benefit to both parties, basing marketing efforts on an understanding of customers is vital (Palmer, 2002).

CHAPTER 4

Changes in the supply chain

John Fernie

The concept of supply chain management (SCM) is relatively new in the management literature. This is due to the major changes which have occurred in both industrial and consumer markets in the last 30 years. The IMP group was in the forefront of research into buyer–seller relationships as companies embraced 'lean' thinking to eliminate waste in supplying industrial products. The reduction in the supply base and long-term partnerships with fewer supplies ensure a lean, cost-efficient supply chain incorporating Japanese-derived concepts such as Just-in-Time (JIT) production. The notion of time as a driver to gain competitive advantage is also evident in consumer markets. The acronyms QR and ECR (quick response and efficient consumer response) illustrate how responding quickly to market changes became an important element of supply chain strategy for companies involved in the logistics of fast-moving consumer goods. The shift from a mass production/mass consumption environment to one of mass customization, where more variety and customization is required without a corresponding increase in costs, posed a new set of challenges for supply chain managers. The 'lean' model is not so relevant here because of its focus on cost and its inflexibility. In the 1990s the notion of 'agile' supply chains was deemed more relevant to companies/industries involved in turbulent markets. An 'agile' chain attempts to minimize lead times across the supply chain in its pursuit of end customer demand. This necessitates internal flexibility within and across firms in the supply chain.

This chapter will explore these concepts within the evolution of SCM. The role of SCM in the management literature and its relevance to marketing will provide the backcloth to the key concepts and the ones which underpin SCM. Specific focus will be on the role of SCM in competitive advantage. The notion of time-based competition will be discussed, evaluating concepts such as quick response and efficient consumer response. Finally, the impact of e-commerce on traditional supply chains will be assessed.

Supply Chain Management: Theoretical Perspectives

The roots of SCM as a discipline is often attributed to the management guru, Peter Drucker and his seminal article in *Fortune Magazine* in 1962. At this time he was discussing distribution as one of the key areas of business where major efficiency gains could be achieved and costs saved. Then, and through the next two decades, the supply chain was still viewed as a series of disparate functions. Thus logistics management was depicted as two separate schools of thought; one dealing with materials management (industrial markets), the other with physical distribution management (consumer goods markets), see Figure 4.1. In terms of the marketing function, the IMP group has focused upon buyer–seller relationships and the shift away from adversarial relationships to those built upon trust. At the same time a body of literature was developing, mainly in the UK, on the transformation of retail logistics from a manufacturer-driven to a retail-controlled system (Fernie, 1990; Fernie and Sparks, 1998; McKinnon, 1989).

In both industrial and consumer markets, several key themes began to emerge:

- The shift from a push to a pull, i.e., a demand, driven-supply chain.
- The customer is gaining more power in the marketing channel.
- The role of information systems to gain better control of the supply chain.
- The elimination of unnecessary inventory in the supply chain.
- The focus upon core capabilities and increasing the likelihood of out-sourcing non-core activities to specialists.

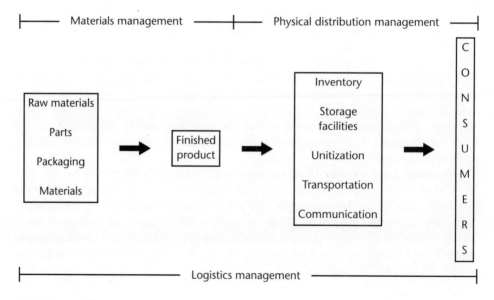

FIGURE 4.1 Logistics management

To achieve maximum effectiveness of supply chains, it is imperative that integration takes place by 'the linking together of previously separated activities within a single system' (Slack *et al.*, 1998, p. 303). This means that companies have had to review their internal organization to eliminate duplication and ensure that total costs can be reduced, rather than allow separate functions (including marketing) to control their costs in a sub-optimal manner. Similarly, supply chain integration can be achieved by establishing ongoing relationships with trading partners along the supply chain.

Throughout the 1970s and 1980s attention in industrial marketing focused upon the changes promulgated by the processes involved in improving efficiencies in manufacturing. Total quality management, business process re-engineering and continuous improvement brought Japanese business thinking to Western manufacturing operations. The implementation of these practices was popularised by Womack, Jones and Roos' (1990) book *The Machine that Changed the World*. Not surprisingly much of the literature on buyer–seller relationships focused upon the car manufacturing sector.

During the 1990s this focus on lean production was challenged in the US and UK because of an over reliance on efficiency measures rather than innovative responses. Harrison, Christopher and Van Hoek (1999) show in Table 4.1 how lean and agile supply chains differ. Agility as a concept was developed in the US in response to the Japanese success in lean production. Agility plays to US strengths of entrepreneurship and information systems technology. Harrison, Christopher and Van Hoek (1999) have therefore developed an agile supply chain model (Figure 4.2) which is highly responsive to market demand. They argue that the improvements in the use of information technology to capture 'real-time' data means less reliance on forecasts and creates a virtual supply chain between trading partners. By sharing information, process integration will take place between partners who focus upon their core competencies. The final link in the agile supply chain is the network where a confederation of partners structure, coordinate and manage relationships to meet customer needs.

TABLE 4.1 Alternative supply chain processes

	Efficient/function (lean)	Innovative/responsive (agile)
Primary purpose	Supply predictable demand efficiently at lowest cost	Respond quickly to unpredictable demand in order to minimize stockouts, forced mark-downs, and obsolete inventory
Manufacturing focus	Maintain high average utilization rate	Deploy excess buffer capacity
Inventory strategy	Generate high turns and minimize inventory	Deploy significant buffer stock of parts
Lead time focus	Shorten lead time as long as it doesn't increase cost	Invest aggressively in ways to reduce lead time
Approach to supplier selection	Select primarily for cost and quality	Select primarily for speed, flexibility and quality

Source: Harrison *et al.* (1999).

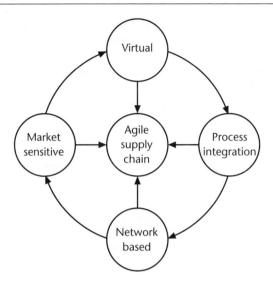

FIGURE 4.2 The agile supply chain

From this background to the evolution of SCM, it is clear that SCM draws upon a range of disciplines with regard to theoretical development. Initially, much of the research was geared towards the development of algorithms and spatial allocation models for the determination of the least cost locations for warehouses and optimal delivery routes to distribute to final customers. The disciplines of geography, economics, operational research and mathematics provided solutions to management problems.

As SCM has developed into an integrated concept seeking functional integration within and between organizations, the theories to explain empirical research have been increasingly drawn from the strategic management or economics literature, although much of what is discussed below has relevance to relationship marketing which is the subject of another chapter in this book.

The key concepts and theories in SCM are:

- the value chain concept
- resource-based theory (RBT) of the firm
- transaction cost economics
- network theory

The thrust of all these theories is how to gain competitive advantage by managing the supply chain more effectively. The concept of the value chain was originally mooted by Michael Porter (1985) and his ideas have been further developed by logisticians, especially Martin Christopher (1997). In Figure 4.3, a supply chain model is illustrated which shows how value is added to the product through manufacturing, branding, packaging, display at the store and so on. At the same time, at each stage cost is added in terms of production costs, branding costs and overall logistics costs. The trick for companies is to manage this chain to create value for the customer at an acceptable cost. The managing of this so-called

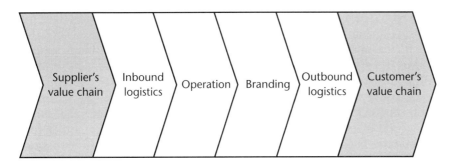

| Supplier's value chain | Inbound logistics | Operation | Branding | Outbound logistics | Customer's value chain |

FIGURE 4.3 The extended value chain

'pipeline' has been a key challenge for logistics professionals, especially with the realization that the reduction of time not only reduced costs but also gave competitive advantage.

According to Christopher there are three dimensions to time-based competition which must be managed effectively if an organization is going to be responsive to market changes. These are:

time to market: the speed at bringing a business opportunity to market
time to serve: the speed at meeting a customer's order
time to react: the speed at adjusting output to volatile responses in demand

He uses these principles to develop strategies for strategic lead-time management. By understanding the lead times of the integrated web of suppliers necessary to manufacture a product he argues that a 'pipeline map' can be drawn to represent each stage in the supply chain process, from raw materials to customer. In these maps it is useful to differentiate between 'horizontal' and 'vertical' time: Horizontal time is time spent on processes such as manufacture, assembly, in-transit or order processing; vertical time is the time when nothing is happening, no value is added but only cost and products/materials are standing as inventory.

It was in fashion markets that the notion of 'time-based competition' had most significance in view of the short time window for changing styles. In addition, the prominent trend in the last 20 years has been to source products offshore, usually in low cost Pacific Rim nations, which lengthened the physical supply chain pipeline. These factors combined to illustrate the trade-offs which have to be made in SCM and on how to develop closer working relationships with supply chain partners. Christopher has used the example of The Limited in the US to illustrate his accelerating 'time to market'. The company revolutionized the apparel supply chain philosophy in the US by designing, ordering and receiving products from South East Asia to stores in a matter of weeks rather than the months of its competitors. New lines were test marketed in trial stores, orders communicated by electronic data interchange (EDI) to suppliers which also benefited from CAD/CAM technology in modifying designs. The products, already labelled and priced, were consolidated in Hong Kong where chartered 747s airfreighted the goods to Columbus, Ohio, for onward despatch to stores. The higher freight costs were easily compensated for by lower markdowns and higher inventory turns per annum.

Along with The Limited, another catalyst for much of the initiatives in lead-time reduction came from work undertaken by Kurt Salmon Associates (KSA) in the US in the mid 1980s. KSA were commissioned by US garment suppliers to investigate how they could compete with Far East suppliers. The results were revealing in that the supply chains were long (one and a quarter years from loom to store), badly coordinated and inefficient (Christopher and Peck, 1998). The concept of quick response was therefore initiated to reduce lead times and improve coordination across the apparel supply chain. In Europe, quick response principles have been applied across the clothing retail sector. Supply base rationalization has been a feature of the last decade as companies have dramatically reduced the number of suppliers and have worked much closer with the remaining suppliers to ensure more responsiveness to the market place.

The resource-based perspective builds upon Porter's models by focusing upon the various resources within the firm which will allow it to compete effectively. Resources, capabilities and core competences are key concepts in this theory. As a supply chain perspective to competitive advantage increases the resource base within which decisions are taken, this theory links to transaction cost analysis and network theory. Thus, firms have to make choices on the degree of vertical integration in their business, to 'make or buy' in production and the extent of outsourcing required in logistical support services. Building upon Williamson's (1979) seminal work, Cox (1996) has developed a contractual theory of the firm by revising his ideas on high asset specificity and 'sunk costs; to the notion of core competences' within the firm. Therefore a company with core skills in either logistics or production would have internal contracts within the firm. Complementary skills of medium asset specificity would be outsourced in a partnership basis and low asset specificity skills would be outsourced on an 'arms-length' contract basis.

The nature of the multiplicity of relationships has created the so-called network organization. In order to be responsive to market changes and to have an agile supply chain, flexibility is essential. Extending the resource-based theory, the network perspective assumes that firms depend on resources controlled by other firms and can only gain access to these resources by interacting with these firms, forming value-chain partnerships and subsequently networks. Network theory focuses on creating partnerships based on trust, cross-functional teamwork and interorganizational cooperation.

In industrial markets, especially the automobile and high technology sectors, a complex web of relationships has been formed. This has led Christopher (1997) to claim 'that there is a strong case for arguing that individual companies no longer compete with other stand alone companies, but rather, that supply chain now competes against supply chain' (p. 22). Tiers of suppliers have been created to manufacture specific component parts and other supplier associations have been formed to coordinate supply chain activities. In these businesses the trend has been to buy rather than make and to outsource non-core activities.

Benetton, which has been hailed as the archetypal example of a network organization, is bucking the trend by increasing vertical integration and ownership of assets in the supply chain (Camuffo, Romano and Vinelli, 2001). While it is retaining its network structure, it is refining the network from product design through to distribution to its stores. While Benetton customized around 20 per cent of its ranges to satisfy national markets, it has reduced this to around five to 10 per cent in order to communicate one image of Benetton in global markets. The streamlining of its brands and in-store testing has allowed it to respond quicker to changing market trends.   *Zara, H+M → same products globally.*

Benetton is renowned for its relationship with small and medium-sized enterprises (SMEs) in north-eastern Italy. These SMEs supplied the labour intensive phases of production (tailoring, finishing, ironing) while the company kept 'in house' the capital intensive parts of the operation (weaving, cutting and dyeing). In the last five to 10 years it has established a high-tech production pole at Castrette, near its headquarters, to cope with increased volumes. The Castrette model has been recreated in foreign production poles in Croatia, Egypt, Hungary, India, Portugal, South Korea, Spain and Tunisia with an SME network which focuses on specific products and skills in the area. For example, t-shirts are made in Spain and jackets in eastern Europe.

Control also has been increased both upstream and downstream of production. The company now controls 85 per cent of its textile and thread suppliers to ensure speedy quality control and reduce lead times to workshops. In retail distribution, Benetton operates most of its store network through agents who set up a contract relationship with owners. However, Benetton had tended to trade from small outlets which often cannot display the full range of casual wear. They are opening 100 megastores worldwide in prime locations to promote Benetton brands. It will own and manage these outlets to glean first-hand experience of customer's responses to new lines.

Efficient Consumer Response (ECR)

The notion of time-based competition through JIT and QR principles was given further credence in the fast moving consumer goods (FMCG) sector with the advent of efficient consumer response (ECR).

ECR arrived on the scene in the early 1990s when Kurt Salmon Associates produced another supply chain report, *Efficient Consumer Response*, in 1993 in response to another appeal by an US industry sector to evaluate its efficiency in the face of growing competition to its traditional sector. Similar trends were discerned from their earlier work in the apparel sector; excessive inventories, long uncoordinated supply chains (104 days from picking line to store purchase) and an estimated potential saving of US$30 billion, 10.8 per cent of sales turnover.

During the last nine years the ECR initiative has stalled in the US; indeed, inventory levels remain over 100 days in the dry grocery sector. Nevertheless, ECR has taken off in Europe from the creation of an European Executive Board in 1994 with the support of European-wide associations representing different elements of the supply chain: AIM, the European Brands Association; CIES, the Food Business Forum; EAN International, the International Article Numbering Association; and Eurocommerce, the European organisation for the retail and wholesale trade.

It was in 1994 that initial European studies were carried out to establish the extent of supply chain inefficiencies and to formulate initiatives to improve supply chain performance (Table 4.2). ECR Europe defines ECR as 'a global movement in the grocery industry focusing on the total supply chain – suppliers,

TABLE 4.2 Comparisons of scope and savings from supply chain studies

Supply chain study	Scope of study	Estimated savings
Kurt Salmon Associates (1993)	US dry grocery sector	10.8 per cent of sales turnover (2.3 per cent financial, 8.5 per cent cost)
		Total supply chain US$30bn, warehouse supplier dry sector US$10bn
		Supply chain cut by 41 per cent from 104 days to 61 days
Coca-Cola Supply Chain Collaboration (1994)	127 European companies. Focused on cost reduction from end of manufacturers' line. Small proportion of category management	2.3 per cent – 3.4 per cent percentage points of sales turnover (60 per cent to retailers, 40 per cent to manufacturer)
ECR Europe (1996 on going)	15 value chain analysis studies (10 European manufacturers, 5 retailers)	5.7 per cent percentage points of sales turnover (4.8 per cent operating costs, 0.9 per cent inventory cost)
	15 product categories	Total supply chain saving of US$21bn
	7 distribution channels	UK savings £2bn

Source: Fiddis, 1997.

manufacturers, wholesalers and retailers, working close together to fulfil the changing demand of the grocery consumer better, faster and at less cost'.

One of the early studies carried out by Coopers & Lybrand (1996) identified 14 improvement areas whereby ECR principles could be implemented. These were categorized into three broad areas of product replenishment, category management and enabling technologies (Figure 4.4). Most of these improvement areas had received management action in the past, the problem was how to view the concepts as an integrated set rather than individual action areas.

As the ECR Europe movement began to gather momentum, the emphasis on much of the work conducted by the organization tended to shift from the supply side technologies (product replenishment) to demand-driven initiatives (category management). This is reflected in the early ECR project reports which dealt with efficient replenishment and efficient unit loads. While the supply side is still important as reflected in projects on transport optimization and unit loads identification and tracking, the majority of recent projects have focused upon consumer value, efficient promotion tactics, efficient product introductions and collaboration in customer-specific marketing.

Commensurate with this change in emphasis has been the topics under discussion at the annual ECR Europe conference. At its inception in Geneva in 1996, the concept was being developed and efficient replenishment initiatives were prominent on the agenda. Subsequent conferences at Amsterdam 1997, Hamburg 1998, Paris 1999, Turin 2000, Glasgow 2001 and Barcelona have tended to emphasize demand-driven initiatives and emerging issues such as e-commerce.

It can be argued that the early work focused upon improving *efficiencies* within the supply chain and later collaborations have stressed the *effectiveness* of the supply chain. Thus, the focus now is on how to achieve profitable growth as there is little point in delivering products efficiently if they are the wrong assortment, displayed in the wrong part of the store!

The ECR Europe prime objective is to develop best practices and to disseminate these benefits to all members of the food supply chain in Europe. To date it has been highly successful in moving towards this objective. The early conferences were well attended (over 1000 delegates) but events in the twenty-first century have attracted over 3000 people. ECR initiatives are now formally organized in 14 European countries and the work in these countries is formally recognized through representation on the Executive Board. The Board itself is comprised of 30 senior executives from leading retailers and branded manufacturers in Europe who established the policy agenda to initiate new pilot projects and develop demand and supply strategies.

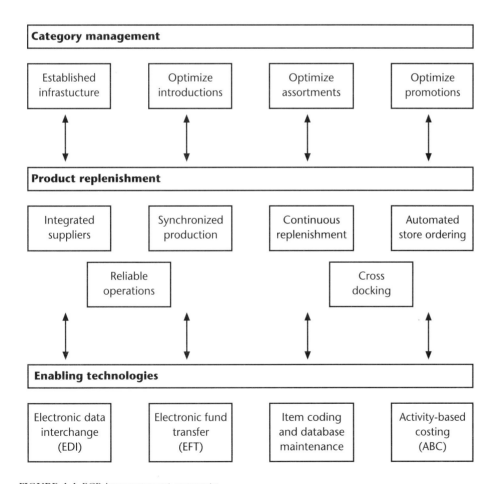

FIGURE 4.4 ECR improvement concepts

It is clear, however, that ECR will not be a panacea for all companies. The improvement areas suggested in Figure 4.4 provide a tariff of initiatives from which companies will choose according to their own particular objectives. Each company will have a different starting point and a different agenda depending upon the current nature of supplier–retailer relationships. Nevertheless, a common theme applicable to all retailers is the limited number of relationships which are established with suppliers. The large grocery retailers deal with thousands of suppliers and have only formal partnerships or initiated pilot projects with a small number of suppliers; for example J Sainsbury has supply chain forums which bring together senior supply chain staff with 19 of their counterparts (suppliers) which account for a large part of Sainsbury's volume business. A criticism of ECR Europe conferences and of those held in the UK, is that these venues are packed with representatives from the largest retailers and their multinational FMCG suppliers. Such concentration, the argument goes, can only lead to restricting consumer choice, high profit margins and higher prices. So much for the consumer in ECR! With Wal-Mart's entry into the European market, this is hardly true in view of the intense price competition in Germany and the UK, the initial target markets. ECR can in fact enable companies to compete better in such competitive markets. It is true, however, that smaller companies have been slower to hop on the ECR bandwagon because of the time and resource commitments required to carry out ECR initiatives. Nevertheless, smaller companies such as those operating convenience stores have achieved significant increases in sales through working with key suppliers which have acted as 'category captains' in developing assortments within stores.

The Retail Supply Chain

The implementation of ECR initiatives has been identified as the fourth and final stage of the evolution of grocery logistics in the UK. Fernie, Pfab and Marchant (2000) classify this as the relationship stage which relates to a more collaborative approach to supply chain management after decades of confrontation. The UK is often mooted to have the most efficient grocery supply chain in the world and a key contributor to the healthy profit margins of its grocery retailers.

This logistical transformation of UK retailing has occurred in a short period of time. In the first stage of evolution (pre-1980) the dominant method of distribution to stores was by manufacturers who stored products at their factories or field warehouses for multiple drops to numerous small shops. As the retail multiple gained in prominence (especially on the abolition of resale price maintenance in 1964), retailers invested in regional distribution centres to consolidate deliveries from suppliers for onward delivery to stores. This was the first step change in the supply of FMCGs in that buying and distribution became a headquarter function in retailing and the logistical infrastructure created a market for third-party logistics service providers.

To all intents and purposes, this marked the abdication of suppliers from controlling the supply chain. This period of centralization throughout the 1980s enabled retailers to reduce lead times, minimize inventory and give greater product availability to customers in their stores. The 1990s witnessed a consolidation of this process. In many cases inventory had only been moved from store to RDC. By implementing JIT principles, retailers began to focus on their primary distribution networks (from supplier to RDC) demanding more frequent deliveries of smaller quantities. Clearly this created a problem for many suppliers in that they could not deliver full vehicle loads of product. To ensure that vehicle utilization could be maximized, consolidation centres have been created upstream of the RDC and retailers have established supplier collection programmes to pick up products from suppliers' factories on return trips from stores.

In the early years of the millennium, retail networks continue to be upgraded as ECR initiatives are enacted and grocery retailers accommodate the increase in non-food products through their distribution centres. Furthermore, the greater sharing of information, especially through Internet exchanges, has fostered collaborative planning, forecasting and replenishment (CPFR) initiatives to reduce supply chain response times.

It should be stressed that UK retail logistics is relatively unique and this has implications for marketing practitioners. UK retailing is dominated by food retailers who have become the dominant force in the UK supply chain. These retailers not only control the supply chain but have taken over marketing responsibilities which were once the sole domain of the manufacturer, for example, product development, branding, advertising and distribution. The high level of own label penetration by these companies has enabled them to build up store loyalty and diversify into other businesses such as banking.

For around 20–30 years the British grocery consumer has tended to do the 'one-stop' shop as superstores became the predominant retail format with convenience stores providing a 'top-up' service. This pattern of shopping has shaped the logistics support infrastructure of large RDCs, often composites, to superstores. In other countries a more fragmented store offering is apparent and different store choice attributes are evident. For example, price and promotions are key drivers of consumer choice in the US, Germany and France compared with the UK. This means the consumer buys in bulk and the retailer 'forward buys' promotional stock which needs to be housed in distribution centres. Of course, in these markets land and property costs are relatively low compared with the UK so that the savings in buying costs can outweigh the additional logistics costs. It is interesting to note that Safeway in the UK has adopted a high/low promotional strategy in order to compete with Asda (Wal-Mart) and this has led to significant changes in the operation of its RDC network.

Even in Western European markets with strong retail consolidation, the manufacturer's brand continues to be important to consumers compared with the UK. Ironically this has led to more conflict between manufacturer and retailer than is currently the situation in the UK. ECR initiatives were embraced by UK companies because it was the only way ahead to maximize benefits for supply chain partners. In these price-orientated markets, it has been difficult for companies to change their attitudes after inherent rivalries which have built up over decades. Yet for any significant supply chain benefits to happen, the breaking down of cultural barriers within organizations will be necessary. To achieve such change as advocated by the IMP group, organisations will need to change from a functional

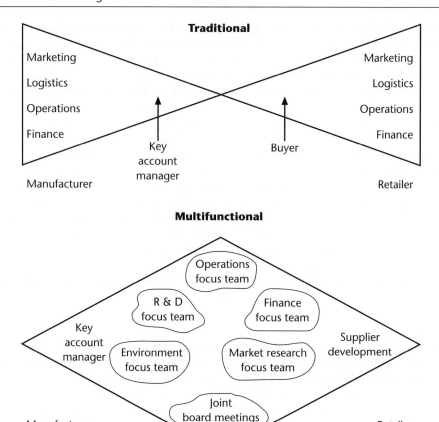

Source: Fiddis (1997)

FIGURE 4.5 Transformation of the interface between manufacturer and retailer

'silo' internal structure to that of a multi-functional external structure. The role of the account manager and the retail buyer will therefore have to change from the 'bow tie' organizational form to that of the cross-functional team approach depicted in Figure 4.5.

Future Challenges

Whilst members of the supply chain sought ways to foster collaboration, the rise of e-commerce posed another set of challenges for companies. The rise and subsequent fall of many dot.com companies led to a high degree of speculation as to the reconfiguration of the business to consumer (B2C) channel. Ultimately, e-fulfilment, especially the 'last mile' problem of delivering goods to the final customer, holds the key to success in this channel. The business to business (B2B) channel, however, has more to offer members of the supply chain because of the number and complexity of transactions and the greater adoption of Internet technology by businesses compared with consumers. There have been numerous B2B exchange marketplaces created since the late 1990s with most of these exchanges being created in highly concentrated global markets sectors with a 'streamlined' number of buyers and sellers; for example, in the automobile, chemical and steel industries.

The FMCG sector has been a laggard in new developments. The more proactive retailers developed B2B Internet exchanges as an extension of the EDI platforms created a decade earlier. This has enabled companies such as Tesco, Sainsbury and Wal-Mart to establish their own private exchanges with suppliers to share data on sales, product forecasting, promotion tracking and production planning. There are major benefits to be derived from pooling EDI efforts into a smaller number of B2B platforms. For example, it is easier to standardize processes for communication, reduce development costs and give members access to a larger customer base.

In 2000, several Internet trading exchanges were created promising a revolution in product procurement. The two major exchanges, Global Net Exchange (GNX) and World Wide Retail Exchange (WWRE), have made some progress but the performance of e-market places have not met initial expectations (see Table 4.3 for details). Although the Global Commerce Initiative established draft standards for global Internet trading, many issues need to be resolved to ensure the seamless flow of data across the supply chain. The complexity of dealing with thousands of SKUs has meant that retailers have had to be selective in the projects which can be routed through their private exchanges compared with these global exchanges. To date the focus of the GNX exchange has been on special promotions, perishables and own label products, for example, 600 out a potential 2000 suppliers of Sainsbury's own label products are on GNX.

In the business to consumer (B2C) market, the rise and fall of Internet retailers has brought a touch a realism to the evolving market potential of online

TABLE 4.3 Profiles of GNX and WWRE

GlobalNetXchange – www.gnx.com	*WorldWide Retail Exchange – www.wwre.org*
• Founding equity partners include Carrefour, Metro AG, Sainsbury's, Karstadt Quelle, Sears Roebuck, Pinault-Printempts-Redoute, Kroger, Coles Myer, Oracle and Pricewaterhouse Coopers	• WWRE has 60 retail members with combined sales of more than US$845bn (£579bn)
• There are 30 retail members	• Members include Ahold, Delhaize, Dixons, Gap, Kingfishers, John Lewis, Kmart, Casino, Boots Company, Toys R Us, Tesco, Safeway Inc. Safeway plc (UK), C&A Europe, Target and Marks & Spencer
• In 2001 GNX customers conducted more than 2600 online auctions, with a total value of approximately US$2.1bn (£1.4bn)	
• GNX's main areas of business are online auctions, collaborative supply chain management programmes, collaborative product development (own-brand) and a perishables exchange	• WWRE claims to have saved its members more than US$270mn (£185mn) through online negotiations
	• WWRE aims to reduce costs and improve efficiencies throughout the supply chain, employing product and service solutions

Source: Retail Week, May 10, 2002.

TABLE 4.4 Online shopping forecasts by product category 1999–2005

	1999		2004		2005	
	Online shopping £mn	Online as % of all retail sales	Online shopping £mn	Online as % of all retail sales	Online shopping £mn	Online as % of all retail sales
Grocery	165	0.20	3 665	3.7	4 960	4.9
Clothing and footwear	5	0.01	1 210	2.7	1 843	4.0
Computer software	122	9.97	934	35.6	1 502	1.9
Electricals	18	0.17	668	5.3	993	7.6
Music and video	85	2.87	592	16.0	782	20.4
Books	106	5.15	430	17.2	473	18.3
Health and beauty	1	0.01	213	1.6	355	2.5
Other	79	0.17	1 125	1.8	1 625	2.4
Total	**581**	**0.29**	**8 837**	**3.6**	**12 533**	**5.0**

Source: Verdict Research Ltd (2000) *Electronic shopping*, UK, p. 126.

shopping; however, forecasts are still being made of up to 12.5 per cent of retail sales in both the US and UK by 2005. This seems unduly optimistic in view of fulfilment and other problems which still have to be overcome and will be discussed later in the chapter. Table 4.4 provides a forecast by Verdict Research of UK online sales by category in 2004/05. This confirms that sectors such as computer software, music, videos and books will continue to increase their penetration of these retail markets. In these product categories, many consumers know what they want and online retailers are more competitive than their high street counterparts. It is interesting to note the forecast for electrical goods from £85 million to £782 million. Price is a key store choice variable in this sector and the Internet may bring savings to consumers.

In Europe, grocery retailers are powerful 'bricks and mortar' companies and the approach to Internet retailing has been reactive rather than proactive. Most Internet operations have been small and few pure players have entered the market to challenge the conventional supermarket chains. Tesco is one of the few success stories in e-grocery.

The situation is different in the US where a more fragmented, regionally-orientated grocery retail structure has encouraged new entrants into the market. In the late 1980s this came in the form of Warehouse Clubs and Wal-Mart Supercenters; by the 1990s dot.com players began to challenge the traditional supermarket operators (Table 4.5 identifies the key players, along with Tesco for comparison). Unfortunately these pure players have either gone into liquidation, scaled down their operations or they have been taken over by conventional grocery businesses.

Why have pure players failed? Laseter *et al.* (2000) identify four key challenges:

1. Limited online potential
2. High cost of delivery
3. Selection-variety trade-offs
4. Existing entrenched competition

TABLE 4.5 The major existing and former e-grocers

	Tesco UK	Webvan USA	Streamline USA	Peapod USA
Background	The biggest supermarket chain in the UK	Started as a pure e-grocer in 1999	Started as a pure e-grocer in 1992	Started home delivery service before the Internet in 1989
Investments in e-grocer development	US$58mn	Approx. US$1200mn	Approx. US$80mn	Approx. US$150mn
Main operational mode	Industrialized picking from the supermarket	Highly automated picking in the distribution centre	Picking from the distribution centre, reception boxes, value adding services	Picking from both the distribution centre and from stores
Current status	The biggest e-grocer in the world. Expanding its operations outside the UK. Partnering with Safeway and Groceryworks.	Operations ceased July 2001.	Part of operations were sold to Peapod in September 2000. The rest of operations ceased in November 2000.	Bought by global grocery retailer Royal Ahold. Second biggest e-grocer in the world.

Source: Yryola, Tanskanen and Holmstrom, 2002.

Ring and Tigert (2001) came to similar conclusions when comparing the Internet offering with the conventional 'bricks and mortar' experience. They looked at what consumers would trade away from a store in terms of the place, product, service and value for money by shopping online. They also detailed the 'killer costs' of the pure play Internet grocers, notably the picking and delivery costs.

The gist of the argument presented by these critics is that the basic Internet model is flawed. Laseter *et al.* (2000) suggest that the US Internet sales forecasts for 2004 are highly optimistic. Nevertheless, the researchers took Forrester Research's sales forecasts, assessed Internet penetration in the key US cities identified by pure players for their expansion plans and built a forecast model on the drivers of local delivery economics – sales concentration and population density. They conclude that only New York City offers an attractive market for online sales potential.

Regardless of the nature of the 'accepted' e-grocery model of the future, the 'last mile' problem continues to pose difficulties for e-grocers. In many ways, the initial pure players in the US have pioneered the various fulfilment models (see Table 4.5). Webvan raised US$360 million of share capital in October 1999 partly to fund the construction of 26 giant warehouses, each greater than 300,000 square feet in 26 cities. The model is a hub and spoke logistics system in each of these regions. The highly automated warehouses stocked around 50,000 SKUs and orders were picked and moved by conveyor belt to loading trucks which transported products to 10 to 12 sub-stations in the region. Here, loads were broken down into customers' orders for onward delivery by company trucks. Webvan could not generate sufficient volume to cover the fixed costs of the investment in its warehouse infrastructure and ceased operations in July 2001. Streamline, the other innovative US pure player, did offer value-added services. It was the pioneer of unattended reception whereby the Stream Box was accessed by keypad entry systems in the garage. The company also offered to automatically replenish inventories of key value items for customers in addition to other services such as dry cleaning, video rental and shoe repairs. This fragmentation of offering did not build up a customer base quickly enough before the company ran out of cash in 2000.

In the UK much of the early experimentation with online grocery focused upon the London region because of the high density of drops which could be achieved. Tesco opted for the store fulfilment model while its main competitors, Sainsbury and Asda, developed picking centres. Waitrose, a major South East of England chain, developed its Waitrose @ work, delivery to the workplace of key businesses along the M4 corridor.

The two main fulfilment models are illustrated in Figures 4.6 and 4.7. The store-based model makes use of existing distribution assets as products pass through regional distribution centres (RDCs) to stores where orders are assembled for delivery to online customers (Figure 4.6).

The advantages of the store model are the low initial investment required and the speed of rolling out the service to a wide geographical market. Customers also receive the same products online as available in stores. The problem here, however, is that 'out of stocks' and substitutions of products are prevalent as online shoppers compete with in-store counterparts for products.

The dedicated order picking model (Figure 4.7) uses e-fulfilment centres to pick and deliver orders to customers. The advantages of this system is that it is dedicated purely to e-commerce customers so 'out of stocks' should be low and delivery frequencies should be higher. These picking centres, however, have less

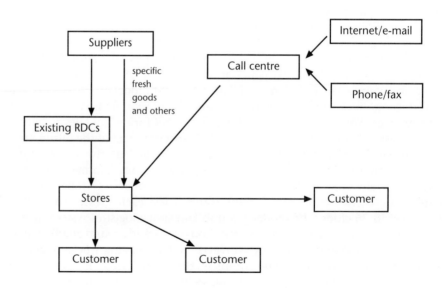

FIGURE 4.6 Logistics model for store-based picking of e-commerce orders

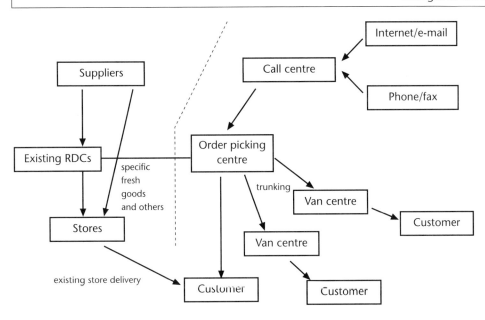

FIGURE 4.7 The dedicated order picking model

of a product range and they need to be working at capacity to justify investment costs.

Ultimately the picking centre model will be the long-term solution to online grocery fulfilment. The problem is that the economics of order fulfilment and delivery is so poor in the short run that companies are abandoning this approach or going bankrupt (Webvan). In the UK Asda has closed two picking centres in London and Sainsbury is developing a hybrid model. Only Tesco appears to have solved the online problem. It has stuck with its store picking model and continues to increase its market share at the expense of its picking centre competitors. By early 2002 it was supplying 95 per cent of the British population from 273 stores and attracting 80,000 orders a week.

So why has the so-called least efficient fulfilment model proven successful? The answer is simple. You need to create market demand before you invest in costly infrastructure. Indeed, there are parallels here with the evolution of centralized distribution to stores in the 1970s and 1980s. Asda, centralizing in the late 1980s, had national geographical coverage compared with Sainsbury which only had one store in Scotland at that time and only built an RDC in 2001! Market penetration into new markets is restricted by centralization as evidenced by regional chains such as Waitrose, Morrisons and Wm. Low (prior to its take-over by Tesco). Tesco is currently delivering 'direct' from stores rather than centralizing its e-commerce operation. When demand reaches sufficient levels (and Tesco does not foresee this occurring in the near future), a gradual switch to picking centres will occur. Tesco now claims that their e-grocery business is profitable. This can only be achieved with a store-based model where all investments and general running costs are allocated to the traditional business.

The US critics mentioned earlier in the chapter claimed that it was the order fulfilment and delivery costs which were the 'killer costs' undermining e-grocery businesses. In the UK, it has been estimated that the cost of order processing, picking and delivery for groceries is between £8–£20 per order depending on system operated and utilization of vehicle fleet (DTI, 2001). As the delivery cost to the customer is around £5 per order, it is clear that unless the order value is high, retailers will make a loss on every delivery they make.

Some of the solutions to this 'last mile' problem are to:

- install unattended reception boxes based on the Streamline model
- deliver to agreed local collection points
- persuade customers to accept more flexible 'time windows' as a trade-off for lower delivery charges

Research by Helsinki University of Technology has shown that unattended reception, using a reception box installed into the customer's house or garage can lead to significant savings by optimizing vehicle utilization (Punakivi and Saranen, 2001; Punakivi, Yrjola and Holmstrom, 2001). Savings of 40–60 per cent in home delivery costs are quoted in these surveys. More recently Punakivi and Tanskanen (2002) have explored another possible solution to unattended deliveries, the shared reception box. These researchers used a sample of point of sales data from one of the largest grocery retail companies in Finland. The results from the modelling exercise show that transport costs using shared reception are 55–66 per cent lower in comparison with the Tesco concept of attended reception and two hour delivery time windows. It is interesting to note, however, that Tesco is testing a new delivery structure whereby lower charges (£3.99) are levied at off-peak times with higher charges at peak periods (£6.99).

Conclusion

The challenges outlined in the last section highlight the major changes which have occurred in the supply chain in a relatively recent period of time. The direct channel of distribution, often neglected in the channel literature, becomes the panacea for new marketing opportunities. Alas, building market awareness needs time and resources to create demand in addition to an efficient logistical support system to deliver the goods.

Despite several false dawns, e-commerce is here to stay and B2B and B2C channels will increase in importance once established standards for data transfer across the supply chain are realized. Already, the information revolution has been the catalyst for improving supply chain efficiency and for fostering stronger relationships between supply chain partners. Private Internet exchanges developed by leading retailers, such as Wal-Mart with their Retail Link network, have enabled them to respond quickly to consumer choice at store level. Indeed, much of the focus of this chapter has centred upon how competitive advantage can be achieved through companies responding flexibly and quickly to changing market needs, hence the acronyms of JIT for lean supply chains and QR and ECR for agile supply chains.

Regardless of sector or industry, however, supply chain integration can only be achieved through greater collaboration and coordination of functions across supply chains. This means partnerships, alliances and networks are created within and between organizations. Traditional functions such as marketing can no longer be viewed in isolation or 'silos' independent from the workings of other parts of their own and other businesses. Cross-functional teamwork and inter-organizational cooperations will therefore hold the key to future developments in supply chain management.

Changing approaches to marketing's role in the organization

CHAPTER 5

Market-based organizational learning

Robert E. Morgan

Management readings and academic business journals demonstrate that executives and academicians alike devote much attention respectively to organizational learning (hereafter, OL) as a social technology (Probst, Raub and Romhardt, 2000) and a theoretical prolegomena (Crossan, Lane and White, 1999). The reason for this business executive interest is attributed to OL providing a means for combating the sophisticated level of competitive behaviours observable in most consumer goods and industrial marketplaces. Further, there is now a realization among executives that knowledge assets and intellectual capital can best serve to act as sources of potential incremental advantage over competitors, in comparison with the processing of traditional inputs such as the economic factors of production (land, labour, capital and equipment).

It was established more than a decade ago by Handy (1990) that the value of a firm's OL capabilities and knowledge assets is frequently several times that of its material assets. Even in the wake of market shakeout in worldwide technology stocks, and the various market corrections that have taken place in other knowledge-intensive industries, the value of OL to all firms is as vital today as ever (Dickson, Farris and Verbeke, 2001). For instance, taking market capitalization as an indicant of firm value,[1] General Electric and IBM currently find that only 14 per cent and 23 per cent of their respective capitalization is attributed to tangible assets, while this proportion reduces to 1 per cent when considering Microsoft (Kluge, Stein and Licht, 2001). Consequently, knowledge and learning developed from customers, competitors, suppliers and strategic partners of products, technologies and ways of working provide a considerable input to the intangible assets that are valued so highly by investors. In the face of such overwhelming knowledge considerations, there is a somewhat evangelical tone common in the prescriptive OL literature that has resulted in sceptical executives posing the question: Why should organizations aspire to 'learn' and improve knowledge? Such a question has frequently been challenged by a rhetorical question: Why should organizations not 'learn' and create knowledge? Despite the higher-order debate surrounding the empirical evidence concerning OL benefits, which will be developed later, the original question warrants some attention. Prior to preparing *The Fifth Discipline Fieldbook*,[2] Art Kleiner, who coordinated the drafting for this project, suggested a lengthy section in one of the chapters devoted to specifically address the question of why organizations should learn. However, the nomenclature used in this case was more accurately, *'Why Bother?'* with OL and the contents of such a section are summarised in Table 5.1.

As can be seen from this table, there are many implicit and explicit advantages of OL. Nonetheless, such a battery of legitimate reasons masks the reality. Often times, executives concern themselves with the ways in which OL can be levered to create some form of benefit to their firms, which commit vast resources to such an activity, in the faint hope that, at a minimum, the mere action of OL will reduce corporate anxiety about the future. Such scepticism has been echoed in the literature concerned with strategic planning where the rationale for planning has been questioned little due to its intuitive benefits but the empirical evidence justifying such a practice has generated mixed results (*cf.* Brews and Hunt, 1999). The perspective adopted in this chapter is one which considers OL as a 'black box' – the extent to which direct and measurable OL capabilities influence hypothesized performance outcomes may be empirically uncertain, but there is a compelling logic which drives this relationship and draws inductively from the strategic planning-performance thesis (*cf.* Priem, Rasheed and Kotulic, 1995).

As an area of academic inquiry, OL has matured to such an extent that it can now be described as an institutionalization of a body of knowledge (Gherardi, 1999). In this sense, OL has developed significantly since the pioneering work of Cangelosi and Dill (1965) to be positioned as an important theme to arguably reframe many topics in the organizational, social and administrative sciences (Cohen and Sproull, 1991). Nonetheless, underlying the apparent maturity of the

TABLE 5.1 'Why bother' with organizational learning: a prescriptive viewpoint

Some suggested reasons

- In order to create sources of competitive advantage that will allow us to realize superior performance.
- For customer relations purposes.
- To avoid decline in our business.
- To improve quality of our processes and overall activities.
- To understand risk and diversity to a greater extent.
- For innovation benefits.
- To increase our ability to manage change proactively.
- For greater understanding and insight into our organizational routines, systems, procedures, methods and everything else that makes us tick.
- For an energized and committed workforce.
- To expand boundaries.
- Because times demand it.

Source: Constructed from Kleiner, A (2001) *'Why a Learning Organisation?'*. www.world.std.com/~WhyLO.html

OL literature lies the proliferation of disciplines that claim aspects of this theoretical territory, each with their own ontological premises and schools of thought resulting in frequently conflicting theories, which often reflect a diverse pattern of phenomenological domains, interpretative issues, methodological predilections and conflicting operationalizations.

The marketing literature is characteristic in detecting elements in cognate disciplines and introducing them within the guise of mainstream marketing thought (Zinkhan, 1999). Consequently, it was a matter of time before marketing academicians became interested in exploiting seams of OL research that were relevant to areas of marketing management, marketing strategy and marketing information. While much of this work on OL in marketing reinvigorated the interest in the closely related subjects of market information use (Deshpandé and Zaltman, 1982; Menon and Varadarajan, 1992; Moorman, 1995; Sinkula, 1994) and market orientation (Baker and Sinkula, 1999a; Baker and Sinkula, 1999b; Hurley and Hult, 1998; Morgan, Katsikeas and Appiah-Adu, 1998), it has now become a topic in its own right with the term market-based organizational learning (hereafter, MBOL) being coined to represent its developing manifestation in conceptual, theoretical and empirical respects (Boussoura and Deakins, 1999; Moorman, Kyriakopoulos and Wallman, 2000; Morgan and Chimhanzi 2001; Morgan and Turnell, 2001; Sinkula, Baker and Noordewier, 1997). Furthermore, this burgeoning interest coincided with the Marketing Science Institute establishing learning about markets as a research priority for US firms toward the end of the last decade (Marketing Science Institute, 1998).

In this chapter, an attempt will be made to address the following: to delineate the OL concept by reviewing the multidisciplinary contributions and considering OL levels, processes, types and capabilities; to evaluate the intellectual roots to MBOL by considering its theoretical heritage; to propose a model of the theoretical properties of MBOL; to consider the extent to which market-based organizational theory satisfies criteria for theory construction in marketing and organization science; to identify critical gaps in our knowledge of MBOL; to indicate the contextual issues surrounding the development of MBOL programs in firms.

Delineating the Organizational Learning Concept

Multidisciplinary Contributions to Organizational Learning

Ackoff (1999) suggests that a hierarchical view can be adopted in characterizing OL and in doing so he distinguishes among data, information, knowledge, understanding and wisdom. Data are considered to be discrete and are limited to 'objective' facts. Data act as carriers of both information and knowledge and can be stored, transferred and processed. Information is derived from this but is subject to the manner in which such data are perceived which, in turn, provides the basis for knowledge which is regarded as the, '. . . fluid mix of framed experience, values, contextual information and expert insights that provides a framework for evaluating and incorporating new experiences and information. It originates and is applied in the minds of knowers. In organisational routines,

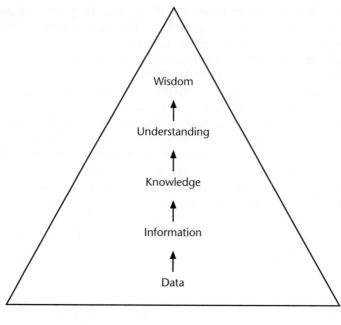

Source: Ackoff (1999)

FIGURE 5.1 Hierarchy of organizational learning

processes, practices and norms' (Davenport and Prusak, 2000, p. 5). While information is descriptive in nature, related only to past and present events and situations, knowledge is specifically predictive in that it allows future insights to be gained from past and current circumstances (Kock, McQueen and Corner, 1997). With ingrained knowledge, coherence in understanding develops from higher-order cognitions, which leads to a holistic understanding described as wisdom. Information and knowledge management are central pillars in OL, but they have also developed as specific streams of interest, simultaneously developed as a practice pioneered by management consulting firms and as an intellectual remit using information technology within management science (Hansen, Norhia and Tierney, 1999). Nonetheless, the focus here is on the collective whole of OL and in order to gain an understanding of this term, a broad evaluation of its ascribed meaning is necessary.

As a term, 'learning' has been considered synonymous with other organizational concepts such as 'coping', 'adapting', 'planning', 'developing' and 'changing'. However, as with most definitions of theoretical issues, following a growth in the literature distinct connotations are signalled, some of which are correct and some incorrect, while others fall into a midrange founded upon varying degrees of (mis)interpretation. As is inevitable in such a literature, identifying an appropriate definition from among the Babel of languages that develops is subject to the discipline to which one subscribes. While OL is particularly distinct in the literatures of strategy, sociology and organization theory, and management science, Table 5.2 identifies the main disciplines related to studies of management and business organizations where OL has been recognized as a notable area of interest. For an extensive treatment of OL from many of these disciplines see: Crossan, Lane and White (1999); DiBella (1995); Dodgson (1993); Easterby-Smith (1997); Fiol and Lyles (1985); and, Huber (1991). Table 5.2 describes the main relevant disciplines and develops the ontological basis of each with a brief description of the main theoretical coverage within the discipline, along with various difficulties identified in developing learning activities and an indication of a set of writers, intended only to illustrate some of the work performed within these areas.

At the expense of a marginal digression, readers should be aware of the overlap between 'organizational learning' and 'the learning organization'. It is suggested that the learning organization is the manifestation of distinctive OL capabilities, procedures, systems, behaviours and cognitions; therefore, a tautology exists therein.[3] The same parallel can be drawn with interpretations of market orientation and the market-oriented firm. The latter is a description of an organization that maintains a high degree of market orientation. Although there is an implied dichotomy within these views (i.e., market oriented versus non-market oriented; learning organization versus non-learning organization), such terms have become popularized but the distinction is not technically correct on the basis that the properties of both OL and market orientation are gauged by 'degree' (e.g., ordinal measurement) and not by 'either/or' classification (e.g., nominal measurement) (Morgan and Strong, 1998).

Efforts to provide a coherent conceptual framework for understanding OL are absent from the literature. Indeed a damning indictment was recently levelled at researchers in this field by Lähteenmäki, Toivonen and Mattila (2001) who argued that 'No successful attempts to create a holistic model of organisational learning have been accomplished, although the elements for its construction should be inexistence. . . . Instead it has only lead to the oversimplification of complex phenomena' (p. 115). Nonetheless, the following sections are concerned with a general overview of individual and organizational levels of learning and their interplay, the OL process and types or modes of learning, and OL capabilities.

Organizational Learning Levels and Processes

Some of the more conventional approaches define learning organizations as, 'Organization[s] skilled at creating, acquiring and transferring knowledge, and at modifying . . . [their] . . . behaviour to reflect new knowledge and insights' (Garvin, 1993, p. 80); 'Organizations where people continually expand their capacity to create the results they truly desire, where new and expansive patterns of thinking are nurtured, where collective aspiration is set free, and where people are continually learning how to learn together' (Senge, 1990, p. 1). However, the distinction is not clear as to the interplay between individual-level and organizational-level learning. Learning occurs at many levels within the organization – individual, group, department or function, business unit, and so on. Although these levels interact, it is generally contended that learning follows a sequential path between individuals, organizations and environments (Argyris and Schön, 1978; Popper and Lipshitz, 2000).

TABLE 5.2 Organizational learning – disciplines, ontological bases and theoretical interests

Discipline	Ontological basis	Theoretical domain	Problem areas
Cultural anthropology	Meaning systems	Culture as cause and effect of organizational learning; role of belief systems and potential cultural 'superiority'	The inherent 'instability' of culture and the relative properties of culture acting as an inhibitor to the transfer of ideas; whose culture dominates?
Economics	Internal efficiency	Founded upon both game-theory and agency perspectives where the productivity problem is explained as error handling	Identifying the individual's motivation to admit, detect and correct error within productivity
Entrepreneurship	Firm growth and development	The interactions effects that learning capabilities can play in the entrepreneurship process	Entrepreneurs should attempt to develop an appropriate learning style; the perceived conflict between aspiring to learn and commercial realities of operational decision making
Management science	Information systems	Knowledge systems and codification; 'informating'	Non-rational behaviour; imperfect information; varying degrees of time horizon; information overload; unlearning
Marketing	Information processing and market-based performance	Synergistic effects of learning and market orientation on business performance; learning commitment; information stocks and flows; behavioural elements in information processing; adaptation	Structural and organizational constraints; business unit culture; path dependency
Production management	Efficiency mechanisms	Productivity; learning curves; endogenous and exogenous learning sources; inputs to production design	Unidimensional measurement limitations; risk and uncertainty of outcomes
Psychology and organization development	Human development	Organizations as hierarchies; relevance of context-specific issues; perception and cognition; values and learning styles; dialogue	Defensive routines; cultural manifestations; unlearning; individual viz. collective learning
Sociology and organization theory	Social structures	Power structures and their configuration; hierarchy effects; ideology and rhetoric; conflicting multiple actors' interests	Organizational politics and power struggles; sources of conflict
Strategy	Competitiveness	Organization-environment interface; alliance learning; network and interaction effects; industry-level learning and market evolution; levels of learning and learning competencies	Dynamic fit between organization and environment; competitive pressures; technical versus general learning; learning transfer; speed of innovation practices

Source: Adapted from Easterby-Smith (1997, p. 1087) and developed further from Dodgson (1993) and Polito (1995).

While individual learning is fundamental to this process, continuity is established by developing,

> . . . operating procedures, mental models and implicit assumptions [which] operate as a kind of supra-individual memory (Walsh, 1995) that preserves learning. True, the individual that has engaged in and interpreted organisational actions and outcomes might possess richer knowledge than the organisation. However, organisational learning enables individuals other than the progenitor to engage in similar actions (Sinkula, 1994) and thus increase the likelihood of reliability and continuity (Hannan and Freeman, 1984). Learning at the organisational level, thus, transcends the individual (Moorman and Miner, 1997).
>
> (Kyriakopoulos, 2000, p. 64)

While these insights provide a conceptual platform for consideration, understanding needs to be gained of how OL can be articulated by the firm. Referred to as, '. . . organisational learning via learning processes' (Kilmann, 1996, p. 207), the role of organizational processes and mechanisms is critical to appreciating the manner in which OL may be manifest. Accordingly, OL represents: 'The process of improving actions through better knowledge and understanding (p. 83) . . . the development of insights, knowledge and associations between past actions, the effectiveness of those actions and future actions' (Fiol and Lyles, 1985, p. 811). This view is akin to the work of Levitt and March (1988) among others, who adopt a learning process perspective in their assessment of OL. Moreover, the process of OL can both incorporate and encourage experimentation in practice, the unlearning of previous methods and conventions, and the development of an environment where multiple viewpoints are the norm with debate being encouraged (including the types of OL identified above).

Aligned with this more liberal view of the OL process are Cummings and Worley (1997) who suggest that, '. . . organisational learning is a process aimed at helping organisations to develop and use knowledge to change and improve themselves continuously' (p. 492). This is a cyclical view of OL which is consistent with Nonaka's (1994; 1996) tenet whereby the cycle of knowledge creation commences with tacit knowledge becoming explicit knowledge at first by individuals, then by groups and finally by the organization. Echoes of Kolb's (1984) theory of experiential learning arise here and Dixon (1994) has developed this specifically for cycles of OL to suggest that in generating meaning from information, experiential learning, collective sharing and experience interpretation are all crucial determinants in the process of developing OL. In an effort to generate a more holistic model of OL, Lähteenmäki, Toivonen and Mattila (2001) claim that attempts should be made to draw more readily upon other closely-related concepts with the literature associated with management and business organizations. In doing so, they draw heavily upon change management and argue that OL can be considered a gradual, stepwise process which emphasizes frequent shifts in activity. Such behaviour-based change is also frequently the consequence of strategic market planning activities within the firm (Morgan, McGuinness and Thorpe, 2000).

Research has long since recognized that strategic market planning is a process founded upon a pattern or stream of decisions reflecting an identification phase, development phase and selection phase of strategy (Schwenk, 1995). Most strategy process typologies such as this (for instance, Gerbing, Hamilton and Freeman's (1994) study assessing management participation in strategy formation) adopt the assumption of decisional rationality where a systematic process is followed in establishing a logical and sequential pattern of decisions from goal formulation through to strategic choice and strategy implementation – such a concept has been referred to as 'procedural rationality' (Dean and Sharfman, 1993, p. 587). Often therefore, strategic market planning refers to the information processing and learning activities that underlie the setting of goals, the analyses that underlie the generation, evaluation and selection of strategies necessary to achieve these organizational goals, and the implementation efforts that result in the behaviour-based modification discussed above (Morgan, McGuinness and Thorpe, 2000). Therefore, it can be argued that OL concerns both the '. . . allocation of resources and the development of organisational processes necessary to achieve the long-term goals of the organisation' (Vorhies, 1998, pp. 5–6).

A strategic process such as OL can, therefore, be reflected in an organizational capability (Morgan, Katsikeas and Appiah-Adu, 1998; Ulrich and Lake, 1990). Grant (1996a) considers this issue within the boundaries of the knowledge-based view of the firm. He suggests that analysis of the organization as an integrator of knowledge is an appropriate frame of reference for researchers to diagnose organizational capability. Moreover, Grant (1996b) specifies that organizational (learning) capability is a consequence of sophisticated assimilation of knowledge, where productive activity is a function of the firm's capacity to harness and integrate knowledge attributed to multiple individuals and groups. However, caution should be exercised here in noting that OL capability depends upon the firm's mechanisms and processes of knowledge integration, rather than the extent of knowledge that individuals and groups possess *per se*. In this respect, it has been advanced that strategic capabilities such as OL may be augmented as strategic market planning processes that facilitate new organizational methods and procedures for OL (*cf.* Anderson, 1982; Ramanujam and Venkatraman, 1987).

Organizational Learning Capabilities

Arguably, one of the responsibilities of management is to develop and exploit organizational capabilities (Barney, 1991). It is this harnessing of resources which is central to the resource-based view of the firm and its satellite, the knowledge-based view, that focuses attention upon the intangible resources which are seen to play a key role in the determination of competitive advantage (Spender and Grant, 1996). This theoretical lens provides a viewpoint upon the creation, transfer and application of learning (Nonaka, 1994) and, as DeCarolis and Deeds (1999) have reported:

> The knowledge-based view argues that the heterogeneous knowledge bases and capabilities among firms are the main determinants of performance differences . . . The underlying knowledge of firms may be conceptualised by both stocks and flows (Dierickx and Cool, 1989) of knowledge which contribute to superior firm performance. Stocks of knowledge are accumulated knowledge assets which are internal to the firm

and flows of knowledge are represented by knowledge streams into the firm or various parts of the firm which may be assimilated and developed into stocks of knowledge.

(p. 954)

As Hamel and Prahalad (1994) have indicated, merely aspiring to being a learning organization is not sufficient; in contrast, the organization must attempt to translate these learning processes into capabilities. This view of OL processes being reflected in organizational capability has only recently been explicitly developed (Chaston, Badger and Sadler-Smith, 2000; Li, Nicholls and Roslow, 1999). Various researchers have demonstrated that firm capabilities result from an adaptive and evolutionary process, and learning develops to favourably influence organizational effectiveness (Hart, 1992; Winter, 1987). The potential competencies that might be gained by a firm from engaging in mechanisms and processes for planned learning can be characterized as OL capabilities (*cf*. Slater and Narver, 1994). Two particular forms of OL capability have been identified: utilitarian and psychological (Morgan, Katsikeas and Appiah-Adu, 1998).

Typically, utilitarian capabilities can be conceived as the knowledge-based skills and organizational mechanisms that are derived from OL. Specific capabilities likely to be included here involve a clearer strategic perspective, improved managerial skills and development, better internal communication and greater coordination of strategic activities (*cf*. Ramanujam and Venkatraman, 1987). On the other hand, psychological capabilities are the cognitive benefits that arise from OL processes and mechanisms. They embrace the extent to which managers are committed to the organization, its goals and development resulting from OL practices (Lyles and Lenz, 1982).

Much of the literature reviewed here has been drawn from strategy, organization development and management science. However, the basis of marketing's interest in OL needs to be specifically addressed. In the following section, consideration is given to the background of MBOL and commentary is devoted to establishing the antecedents underlying the current interest in developing a new concept for marketing.

Origins of Market-based Organizational Learning

Market-based Organization

Marketing has witnessed a significant change in its applied practice and theoretical coverage over the last 40 years (Varadarajan, 1999). The marketing concept was idealized as the saviour of companies in the 1960s, while this was challenged in the 1970s due to marketing being unresponsive to societal issues leading to the dawn of macromarketing. During the 1980s marketing induced strategic failures for many companies by over-segmenting markets and overstating the value of consumers' expressed needs, while during the last decade marketing was considered as 'everything' (McKenna, 1991, p. 65). It is too early to consider what this decade will be remembered for in marketing terms but indications abound (for a discussion of various postulates see *Journal of Marketing* (1999), special issue).

One avenue of inquiry that does appear to be particularly fertile, which is also not new, is the role of the marketing function which has altered considerably from its departmental position in the large, bureaucratic hierarchy of traditional design in the 1950s and 1960s to the contemporary overarching and culture-binding function of new forms of structural configuration evident today (Moorman and Rust, 1999). Many reasons account for the role of marketing within the firm having changed: relationships with customers are commonly founded upon collaborative partnership through cohesive means; relationships with channel intermediaries are proliferating through different and innovative methods of distribution, and channel parties are mobilising greater influence and exercising more power in the value stream; and, relationships with competitors have changed from direct, open offensive behaviour to selective collaboration and competition. The importance and value in studying the contribution and influence of marketing within the organization is therefore fundamental (Homburg, Workman and Jensen, 2000). Day (1997) states:

> As organisations evolve toward hybrid structures, using self-directed process teams . . . the importance of all functional departments will inevitably be diminished. Nonetheless, some functions will be relatively more powerful than others – that is, they will control more resources and have more influence in the strategy dialogue. Will marketing be the lead function, rather than operations, sales, finance, engineering or technology?
>
> (p. 89)

Given that there is a lack of empirical research in this area (Homburg, Workman and Krohmer (1999), academicians are at a loss to explain the extent to which marketing exercises its relative influence in key areas of management and business. Consequently, because of these characteristics and fundamental shifts in organizational practice, potentially relevant inferences can be made from market orientation studies as suggested by Hunt and Lambe (2000): 'If there were any contribution that marketing could make to business strategy that might be considered universally to be uniquely marketing, it would be that of market orientation' (p. 25).

Market Orientation

Market orientation can be considered a cornerstone of marketing thought. For five decades, this construct has been ubiquitous within pedagogic readings and, not without criticism, provided a focus for business executive interests. Advances in this area were made during the late 1980s where efforts were directed toward determining the conceptual domain, scope, interpretation and measurement of market orientation (Deshpandé and Webster, 1989; Houston, 1986). From this period, two conceptual frameworks in particular have enjoyed longevity, stimulated debate and established well-received operational approaches for market orientation measurement: Kohli and Jaworski (1990) incorporating measures in Kohli, Jaworski and Kumar (1993); and, Narver and Slater (1990).

Kohli and Jaworski (1990) define market orientation as: the organization-wide generation of market intelligence which concerns both existing and potential customer needs, and exogenous factors likely to influence these needs; disseminating such intelligence throughout the organization; and, responding accordingly on an organization-wide basis. Narver and Slater (1990) posit that market orientation is a unidimensional construct with three components being customer orientation, competitor orientation and inter-functional coordination. These components respectively concern: understanding customer needs in a manner that allows superior value to be provided; being aware of both existing and potential competitor activities such that appropriate actions may be taken to respond to identified opportunities and threats; and, the integrated effort of organization-wide constituencies and resources towards creating superior value for customers.

These conceptualizations of market orientation share certain similarities (Jaworski and Kohli, 1996). First, the customer is central to market orientation. Second, both balance an internal and external business view of the specific environmental situation. Third, there is an explicit sentiment that the whole firm should respond to identified customer needs. Fourth, the scope of market orientation goes beyond customers and incorporates competitors (Narver and Slater, 1990) or the forces shaping customer needs such as technology, regulation and such like (Kohli and Jaworski, 1990). Beyond the parallels that can be drawn between these two schemata, notable differences emerge from closer examination. Kohli and Jaworski (1990) focus on the activities and behaviours that underlie the generation and dissemination of market intelligence and the associated response by all parties within the firm. In contrast, although Narver and Slater (1990) consider behavioural elements within their conceptualization of market orientation, they also include a cultural perspective (*cf.* Deshpandé, Farley and Webster, 1993) suggesting that specific activities involving information processing (Kohli and Jaworski, 1990) are a natural product of market orientation rather than the orientation *per se*. To this end, they have defined market orientation as: 'The organisational culture (i.e., culture and climate – Deshpandé and Webster, 1989) that most effectively and efficiently creates the necessary behaviours for the creation of superior value for buyers and, thus, continuous superior performance for the business' (Narver and Slater, 1990, p. 21).

Since these contributions to the literature, market orientation research has developed to consider the capabilities of market-oriented firms (Day, 1994a), levers underlying market orientation (Jaworski and Kohli, 1993) and the effects of market orientation upon firms' business performance (Greenley, 1995), product innovation (Atuahene-Gima, 1996), comparative advantage (Hunt and Morgan, 1995) and OL (Baker and Sinkula, 1999b; Slater and Narver, 1995), along with contingency issues such as the context of cross-cultural comparisons (Desphande, Farley and Webster, 1993) and the setting of small business (Pelham and Wilson, 1996), to list a few settings reflecting the historical interest in this subject.

Notwithstanding the developments surrounding market orientation, it has been argued that, for a firm to maximize its capacity to learn about markets, creating a market orientation is only the beginning (Day, 1994b). Moreover, contemporary thinking suggests that:

> A market oriented culture can achieve maximum effectiveness only if it is complemented by a spirit of entrepreneurship and an appropriate organisational climate, namely, structures, processes and incentives for operationalising cultural values. Thus, the critical challenge for any business is to create the combination of culture and climate that maximises organisational learning to create superior customer value in dynamic

and turbulent markets, because the ability to learn faster than competitors may be the only source of sustainable competitive advantage (deGeus, 1988; Dickson, 1992).

(Slater and Narver, 1995, p. 63)

Thus, the firm capacity for OL and the inherent capabilities exhibited are a fundamental issue in the contribution of market orientation to business competitiveness. Nonetheless, the incorporation of OL in the marketing context has, until recently, remained at the formative stages of theory development (Sinkula, Baker and Noordewier, 1997).

Beyond Market Orientation

Despite the vast literature devoted to market orientation and the development of information processing, the manner in which organizations manage knowledge and develop higher-order cognitions is now of greater interest to executives and academicians than merely assessing the impact of market orientation on various firm consequences (McNaughton *et al.*, 2001). Indeed a central question driving much of marketing theory is OL in marketing (Varadarajan and Jayachandran, 1999) or more specifically, 'Understanding the learning dynamics of firms and markets is key to understanding the evolution of firms and markets and long-term competitive and comparative advantage' (Dickson, Farris and Verbeke, 2001, p. 227).

Slater and Narver (1995) have explored the potential capabilities arising from the strategic processes of planned learning and consider that:

> In the learning organisation, planning is guided by a stable vision and operationalised through a flexible, responsive overlay of task oriented planning teams. The motivating vision is grounded in a sound understanding of the market, guides the business' competitive advantage efforts, and is communicated continuously throughout the organisation. The shared vision sets the broad outlines for strategy development and leaves the specific details to emerge later. A robust vision enables the organisation to learn and adapt.
>
> (p. 70)

Beyond this, Ruekert (1992) observed an association between market orientation and elements of organization structure, systems and processes created to sustain the firm's interest on the market. He develops the argument to suggest that a high level of market orientation may be difficult to achieve for firms because of organizational factors impeding such a strategic focus (Kelley and Amburgey, 1991) and conversely implies that such influences, if appropriately managed, can act as a cataylst in enhancing market orientation.

Bentley (1990) similarly extols the virtues of market-oriented firms with their organizational style, structure and climate that ensure a setting for learning about customers' needs is paramount. Also, Kohli and Jaworski (1990) propose various change efforts that can be made to lever market orientation such as attempts to minimize functional conflict and increasing flexibility of organization-wide systems that can be exhibited in processes of OL. It is interesting, however, to contrast this with Schein's (1996) notion of 'organisational disabilities' (p. 235), which are phenomena likely to impede organizational mechanisms and processes of learning that might consequently constrain market orientation. Nonetheless, the challenge of environmental diversity dictates that:

> The . . . information-based organisation leverages time and efficiency and its reaction capabilities to market opportunity. It will need to (1) be directly wired to the pulse of its markets and (2) have the flexibility to react to market signals with a customised and immediate response.
>
> (Achrol, 1991, p. 79)

On the basis that organizations being highly market oriented must adhere to these prescriptions, firms able to benefit from the mechanisms and processes derived from OL capabilities will be in a strong position to achieve their posture toward a market focus (*cf.* Baker and Sinkula, 1999b; Dickson, 1996; Hurley and Hult, 1998; Menon and Varadarajan, 1992; Sujan, Weitz and Kumar, 1994). Furthermore, it could be claimed that the extent to which firms use market information is a function of what they have already learned (Sinkula, 1994). However, it remains that relatively limited conceptual and empirical attention has been devoted to the theme of OL in marketing contexts. Indeed this embryonic stage of theory development with its formulation and basic level of theoretical questioning was reflected recently in a statement providing the basis to a study by Baker and Sinkula (1999b): 'We refer merely to illustrate that . . . these scholars believe that (1) learning is an important facilitator of competitive advantage, and (2) market orientation and learning are not one and the same' (p. 411).

A Model of Market-based Organizational Learning

Toward a Conceptualization of Market-based Organizational Learning

At the outset of this chapter, it was indicated that there are a number of intuitive benefits from engaging in the practices of OL (Table 5.1). Beyond these prescriptive outcomes, Pfeffer and Salancik (1978) have argued that high-performing firms tend to be loosely coupled because of the buffer effect between organization and environment. First, firms able to benefit from OL capabilities will be in a strong position to achieve their posture toward an effective product–market position, with a responsive organizational mindset ready to detect signals and adapt to conditions; successful decision makers are those that:

> . . . use more information, consider more alternatives and seek a greater amount of advice. Instead of departing from the analytical requirements of comprehensive decision-making, they accelerate their cognitive processes. The quick decisions resulting from comprehensive decision processes lead to better performance.
>
> (Goll and Rasheed, 1997, p. 584)

Second, OL tends to be focused upon envisioning any future considerations that limit the effect of potential shocks and enable an anticipatory element to be built into decision making where organizational preparedness enables the organizational members to better understand changes in the internal, competitive, industry, market and allied environments (Courtney, Kirkland and Viguerie, 1997).

Third, learning organizations reportedly enjoy sound working relationships with stakeholders, and symbiotic interactions based upon an attitude of mutual accommodation can be realized when unanticipated problems arise (Lukas, Hult and Ferrell, 1996). Fourth, it has been suggested that learning organizations often exhibit flexibility which means that rapid organizational actions can be implemented in order to exploit and extinguish emerging opportunities or threats, respectively (Slater and Narver, 1995). Fifth, given that information typically flows efficiently within the organization, transaction (information processing) costs can be minimized and economies of information may be achieved (Bharadwaj, Varadarajan and Fahy, 1993) – referred to as the Williamson Principle (Williamson, 1975). Sixth, learning activities promote innovation skills and result in business performance gains (Baker and Sinkula, 1999a; Hurley and Hult, 1998). Consequently, learning activities provide the basis for considerable benefits. If a firm's market orientation and capacity for OL can be characterized as phenomena exhibiting:

> . . . (1) inimitableness, because processes of generating market knowledge are embedded in organisational cognitive activities and are not observed readily from outside; (2) immobility, because these processes are created within the firm and cannot be purchased in the market; and, (3) undiminishableness, because unlike machines, whose value depreciates over time, the utility of these processes does not diminish with usage
>
> (Li and Calantone, 1998, p. 14)

how can we better understand these issues and what frameworks are available within which to consider a concept known as MBOL?

For some time, theorists have commented upon the evolving symbiosis between issues traditionally considered strategic and those commonly concerned with marketing (Day and Wensley, 1983). The opinion of many writers is that marketing activities must be synchronized with other organization-wide structures and processes if an ambition to be market oriented is to be realized. Doing otherwise handicaps the potential for marketing programs and actions to contribute to organizational wellbeing. MBOL is similarly an organization-wide concept that is the responsibility of more than merely the marketing department. In order to respond to the reality of market-based change, organizations must create a coherent and focused agenda on MBOL which is defined here as *the learning values, capabilities, processes and behaviours that facilitate the dynamic fit between organizations and their marketplace environments*. Within the following conceptual framework of MBOL, many facets of OL *per se* are incorporated in order to reflect the overlap between market-based learning and general learning. As is the case for delineating among corporate, business and functional (e.g., marketing) strategy, the argument for mutual exclusivity among strategy levels is tenuous and as Varadarajan and Clark (1994) observe, '. . . a cursory analysis of strategic practice reveals that while some issues do indeed fall unambiguously into the corporate, business or functional area strategic domains, there is also considerable overlap' (p. 93). Consequently, the development of MBOL cannot be far removed from that of OL. Figure 5.2 displays a working conceptualization of MBOL, which is characterized by six main elements. These are not antecedents or consequences of MBOL, nor are they inherently the properties of MBOL, but they serve to

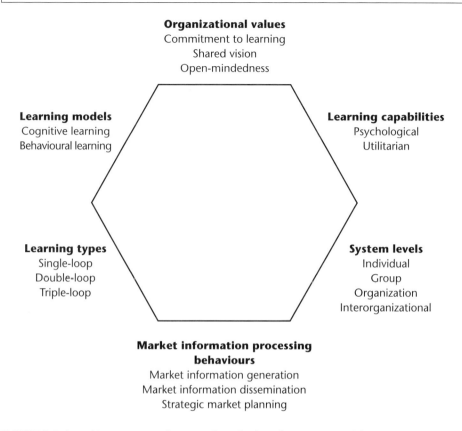

Organizational values
Commitment to learning
Shared vision
Open-mindedness

Learning models
Cognitive learning
Behavioural learning

Learning capabilities
Psychological
Utilitarian

Learning types
Single-loop
Double-loop
Triple-loop

System levels
Individual
Group
Organization
Interorganizational

**Market information processing
behaviours**
Market information generation
Market information dissemination
Strategic market planning

FIGURE 5.2 A working conceptualization of market-based organizational learning

demonstrate the perspectives through which MBOL can be considered within organizations.

In order to explain these characteristics, Table 5.3 describes each perspective in turn. Organizational values, '. . . influence the propensity of the firm to create and use knowledge . . . [This] . . . influences the degree to which an organisation is satisfied with its theory in use and, hence, the degree to which proactive learning occurs' (Sinkula, Baker and Noordewier, 1997, p. 309). The elements that compose these values have been proposed as a commitment to learning, shared vision and openmindedness. For an extensive discussion of organizational values in relation to MBOL see Sinkula, Baker and Noordewier (1997).

Learning capabilities have become central to assessing the extent to which organizations are positioned to take advantage of future opportunities. Research ranges from the purely theoretical (Lei, Hitt and Bettis, 1996; Van den Bosch, Volberda and Boer, 1999) to the applied setting (Goh and Richards, 1997) but consistently the argument is levelled that firms need to become more 'learningful'. Commonly considered synonymous with the concept of absorptive capacity, learning capabilities describe the psychological and utilitarian phenomena that arise from '. . . the firms ability to identify, assimilate and exploit knowledge from the environment' (Cohen and Levinthal, 1990, p. 569).

TABLE 5.3 Market-based organizational learning

Perspectives and sub-themes	Theoretical properties
Organizational values	
Commitment to learning	The value the organization holds towards market-based learning and the propensity for a learning culture to exist. Related to Senge's (1990) consideration of 'learning principles' and the fact the culture must be amenable to market-based learning in order for an improvement in understanding of products and markets to occur over time (Dickson, Farris and Verbeke, 2001).
Shared vision	Captures the direction of market-based learning (Sinkula, Baker and Noordewier, 1997). Limits 'tribal mentality' and 'silo-thinking' within the organization and encourages a coherent focus for responsiveness and learning values (Day, 1994b; Slater and Narver, 1995).
Open-mindedness	Mental models represent the way the world is viewed (Day and Nedungadi, 1994) and dynamic thinking requires flexibility in these perspectives (Dickson, Farris and Verbeke, 2001).
Learning capabilities	
Psychological	The consequences of values supportive of market-based learning mean that capabilities are developed in cognitive terms (Li and Calantone, 1998; Moran, Katsikeas and Appiah-Adu, 1998).
Utilitarian	Knowledge-based skills and effective mechanisms that allow market-based learning processes to be explicated – ranging from improved strategic perspective to effective internal communication and greater coordination (Day, 1994a; Hunt and Morgan, 1997).
System levels	
Individual	The extent and capacity that individuals have to learn (Damanpour, 1991).
Group	The development of collective market-based learning established by individuals working together to synchronize learning and stimulate intellectual synergy from symbiosis (Homburg, Workman and Jensen, 2000).
Organizational	The higher-order functioning that derives from market-based learning activities, mechanisms and processes at an organizational (usually strategic business unit) level (Workman, Homburg and Gruner, 1998).
Interorganizational	The network advantages gained from sharing knowledge between organizations – most notably within strategic alliances and similar collaborative arrangements where market-based learning can be shared for mutual gain (Lukas, Hult and Ferrell, 1996).

TABLE 5.3 Market-based organizational learning *continued*

Perspectives and sub-themes	*Theoretical properties*
Market information processing behaviours	
Market information generation	As cognitive entities, organizations process information. Following from market orientation, the complexion of information generated provides the rootedness to decision-making and actions that follow from market-based learning (Hurley and Hult, 1998; Sinkula, 1994).
Market information dissemination	Merely gathering information and making intelligence from information is a first principle, information must be shared in order to encourage debate and test the meaning underlying interpretations (Baker and Sinkula, 1999b).
Strategic market planning system characteristics	The nature and form of strategic market planning systems play a role in determining the form, extent and timing of information generation and dissemination (Day, 1994b; Dickson, Farris and Verbeke, 2001; Slater and Narver, 1995).
Learning types	
Single-loop	'Detections of error' in product markets. Recognizing issues via feedback and control and adapting accordingly (Slater and Narver, 1995).
Double-loop	Testing assumptions underlying learning (values, capabilities, etc.) and recognizing that creativity and flexibility stimulate frame-breaking developments (Slater and Narver, 1995).
Triple-loop	Encouraging 'discovery' and contingent responsiveness – new circumstances call for new, unlearned responses (Baker and Sinkula, 1999a).
Learning models	
Cognitive learning	Learning for the sake of broadening the knowledge base of the organization and to store in the organizational memory, as for conceptual information use (Menon and Varadarajan, 1992).
Behavioural learning	Market-based learning with a specific form of response behaviour in mind. As for instrumental information use, with a stimulus (information, interpretation and meaning) comes a response in the form of innovation (Menon and Varadarajan, 1992).

Learning occurs at many levels and thus requires management of this intra- and extra-organizational knowledge. Specifically, individuals' actions lead to organizational responses, which interact with the environment, leading to outcomes that are then interpreted by individuals' belief systems and correspondingly responded to by the organization (Morgan and Hunt, 2002). The properties of this sequence are codified and preserved in the organizational memory, beliefs, routines, scripts and physical artifacts (Hansen, Nohria and Tierney, 1999). In marketing terms, for instance, field sales employees (individual level) may inform their department (group level) of issues, which in turn, result in organizational responses (organization level) and potentially interorganizational responses to joint marketing programs (interorganizational level).

Market information processing behaviours essentially describe the manner in which information is transformed into knowledge (Huber, 1991) through the generation and dissemination of information, which forms the prime inputs to strategic market planning behaviours. Likened to aspects of market orientation, these behaviours are closely entwined in organization-wide OL (Baker and Sinkula, 1999a/b).

In determining the nature of learning types or modes, the concept of feedback is a facilitator of improvement. MBOL types can be considered in three related respects. First, 'single-loop', 'adaptive', 'adjustment', 'first-order' or 'Model I' learning is about coping; utilizing knowledge gained to improve quality and efficiency of existing operations. Second, 'double-loop', 'generative', 'second-order', 'higher-level', 'turnover' or 'Model II' learning, goes further and involves creating; forming new practices, perspectives and frameworks, questioning assumptions and stimulating frame-braking views, so as to continuously expand capability. Third, 'triple-loop', 'deutero', 'turnaround' or 'Model III' learning reflects an even greater form of creating; the rules governing assumptions are questioned and learning recognizes that organizational habits and routines are formed which frequently require adjustment to particular situations and according to specific market dynamics. A common explanation of this form of learning is where firms learn how to learn.[4] Each of these learning types operates independently of one another but they each still offer a potent input to MBOL.

Beyond the types of learning, MBOL models also exist in terms of cognition or behaviour. Mainstream studies have tended to argue either for a cognitive perspective (specifically discounting the learning–behaviour modification link) or a behavioural perspective (incorporating the association between learning and resultant changes in behaviour). This distinction can be recognized in conceptual and instrumental forms of information use respectively (Caplan, Morrison and Stambaugh, 1975). Conceptual use describes the situation where the indirect application of information serves to broaden the knowledge base of decision makers without specifically providing an input to a decision or future strategy. Instrumental use, however, is characterized by the information being used directly to guide a specific decision scenario or identified management problem. Thus, where conceptual use of information is made there is an expectation that no immediate behaviour modification will take place (cognitive perspective), while the corresponding form of instrumental use suggests that managers will consciously decide to modify behaviour by developing a tactical response or considering a contingency strategy, for instance. By considering both of these perspectives, the combined approach can provide a rich platform upon which to articulate MBOL. From the cognitive perspective comes the broad base of understanding and the means of interpreting prior behaviours and actions (Daft and Weick, 1984; Fiol and Lyles, 1985) while the behavioural perspective introduces 'stimulus–response chains' (Hedberg, 1981), 'cycles of action and outcome' (Cyert and March, 1963), and 'theories in action' (Argyris and Schön, 1978). By building both approaches into attempts to understand these issues it has been suggested that studies may be more substantive and OL practices may be better captured by researchers (Huber, 1991).

Criteria for Theory Construction and Theory Verification

The Development of Theory in Marketing

Early writings on marketing were mainly descriptive and it was not until the 1940s that the discipline received recognized theoretical attention by researchers. The most significant contributions in this area at that time were provided by Alderson and Cox (1948) and Bartels (1951), who debated the position of marketing as a scientific discipline. The development of marketing thought was not at all rapid and, in 1964, Halbert (1964) provided a damning indictment of the status of marketing. He concluded that marketing had no defensible theory on the basis of logical consistency, experimental rigour or adequate philosophical grounding. Indeed, theoretical developments were so limited that somewhat later, Bartels (1974) suggested that there was an 'identity crisis' (p. 73) in marketing. Thereafter, a trend toward the examination of marketing theory emerged which provided a resurgence of interest in developing the foundations of the academic discipline.

The last two decades have witnessed numerous contributions to the field, which now form the basis of contemporary marketing theory. Writers have approached this field of examination from several perspectives. For example, some see marketing theory in terms of its scientific content, managerial perspective and meta-theoretical foundations. Despite this significant research attention, numerous opportunities still exist within the marketing discipline for generating new theories and providing a substantial contribution to knowledge (Sheth, Gardner and Garrett, 1988). This has been further emphasized by Howard *et al.* (1991) who suggested that, in order to gain greater recognition, the marketing discipline must now generate an exemplary body of theory which, '. . . provides not only a continued interest in . . . fundamental theory questions, but a raison d'être for the current increase in scholarly attention being given to marketing' (p. 15).

In order to understand what constitutes theory and what is currently acceptable as such, some discussion needs to be given to the nature of scientific inquiry. Historically, it was considered that the role of science was to convert 'doxa' (what is believed to be true) into 'episteme' (what is known to be true) (Zinkhan and Hirschheim, 1992). However, this suggests that contentions can somehow be proven. The contemporary philosophical view tends to suggest that knowledge is not infallible but, moreover, tends to be conditional upon particular circumstances. Arguably, one of the foremost commentators on the philosophy of science, in present times, is Robert Dubin. His opinion of a sound theory building approach is described, in two parts, as follows:

> A theoretical model starts with variables or (1) units whose interactions constitute the subject matter of attention. The model then specifies the manner in which these units interact with each other as (2) the laws of interaction. . . . Since theoretical models are generally of limited portions of the world, the limits as (3) boundaries must be set forth within which the theory is expected to hold. Most theoretical models are presumed to represent a complex portion of the real world, part of whose complexity is revealed by the fact that there are various (4) system states each of which the units interact differently with each other. . . . The theorist is [then] in a position to derive conclusions that represent logical and true deductions about the model in operation or the (5) propositions of the model.
>
> (Dubin, 1978, pp. 7–8)

However, the early stages of theory building represent conceptual aspects, whereas the final two reflect empirical considerations. Therefore, it follows that:

> Should there be any desire to determine whether the model does, in fact, represent the real world, then each term in each proposition whose test is sought needs to be converted into (6) an empirical indicator. . . . The next operation is to substitute the appropriate empirical indicators in the propositional statement to generate a testable (7) hypothesis. The research operation consists of measuring the values on the empirical indicators of the hypotheses to determine whether the theoretically predicted values are achieved or approximated in the research test.
>
> (Dubin, 1978, p. 8)

Therefore, theory building can be considered to be a disciplined, systematic and rigorous approach to formulating and testing models of knowledge. Furthermore, Dubin's (1978) seven-stage sequence, outlined above, is believed to be a generic framework for theory building and one that is not solely applicable to social science disciplines.

In considering the specific role of theory building in marketing, Hunt (1983) has extensively reviewed definitions of theory and recognised some broad underlying common themes in various writings. He subsequently defined the scope of marketing theory as follows: 'A theory is a systematically related set of statements, including some lawlike generalisations, that are empirically testable. The purpose of theory is to increase scientific understanding through a systematised structure capable of both explaining and predicting phenomenon' (Hunt, 1983, p. 228). Accordingly, marketing theory has three components; systematically-related themes, lawlike generalizations and empirical testability. The first two of these components are fundamental criteria for any scientific explanation. That is, phenomena cannot be viewed in isolation and must be considered within the framework of broader and interconnected variables. The justification for the final component of empirical testability is explained by Hunt (1983) in that '. . . any systematised structure which is not empirically testable will suffer from explanatory and predictive impotence' (p. 243). Therefore, in order to claim some form of inference from a model, the theory must possess an empirical grounding.

Market-based Organizational Learning Theory(?)

The literature of OL documents several principles, disciplines and vignettes of successful learning (Kilmann, 1996). However, beyond these conceptual and anecdotal insights it remains that little is still understood of the dimensions underlying the processes and mechanisms of MBOL. Moreover, the nature of association between features of MBOL and other related concepts (e.g., market orientation and information use) remains at the formative stages of theory development.

Although the OL field is diverse, such an eclectic blend of contributions to this literature means that we now have a sufficient theoretical foundation to conduct evaluation and assessment of the state-of-the-art. However, the method for performing this evaluation of theory construction is itself problematic with methods in marketing ranging from Bagozzi's (1984) *Prospectus for Theory Construction* to Hunt's (1990) suggestion of evaluation according to scientific relativism, across to those in other areas of social and administrative science who espouse generic sets of rules for assessment (Cohen, 1980). However, Bacharach (1989) suggests a framework for evaluating theories in organizations. Figure 5.3 presents an outline of the main premises underlying this evaluation.

As can be seen from Figure 5.3, the matrix is composed of the properties of any theory, which reflect the conceptual development and empirical issues identified above – variables, constructs and their proposed or hypothesized relationships. These are contrasted against the two premises of theory evaluation – falsifiability (the extent to which theories are empirically refutable) and utility (the usefulness of theoretical systems considered as explanation and prediction). Comments can be observed within each of these cells indicating the extent to which existing theories and underlying theory development is robust. These observations indicate that MBOL theory suffers from mixed conceptual foundations, confusion surrounding the domain and boundary of MBOL, empirical problems ranging from measurement inadequacy, through to research design constraints reflecting limitations of explanatory potential and questionable bases for hypothesis development.

Considering the origins of these difficulties it may be useful to consider the theoretical roots in the broader field of published work on OL. Here most accounts are conceptual in nature rather than empirical (Harvey and Denton, 1999). Prescriptive writings are also ubiquitous, proclaiming the virtues of learning from customers and the marketplace (McKean, 1999; Rubinstein and Firstenberg 1999) but there are rare examples of coarse-grained empirical research in mainstream OL; examples include the work of Adler and Cole (1993) and Edmondson (1996). Consequently, it has been posited that: '. . . the ratio of systematic, empirical learning research to learning theories is far too low. . . . The current popularity of learning as a practical vision for managers increases the need for rigorous systematic research' (Miner and Mezias, 1996, p. 95).

When considering the development of OL within the marketing literature however, the traditional dominance of the neo-positivist approach (Gummesson, 2001) has meant that empirical studies concerned with aspects of MBOL have developed at a far greater pace than either qualitative or conceptual developments. It can be argued, therefore, that empirical research has lacked robust

	Falsifiability	Utility
Variables	**Measurement issues** Variable definition unclear both in constitutive and operational terms; conflicting forms of operationalization; limited coherence within measurement–validity and reliability; constraints in MBOL measurement over time.	**Variable scope** Ensuring parsimony while being mindful of sufficient scope in measurement; tendency to overemphasize 'focus' at the expense of capturing the true and full extent of MBOL; leading to MBOL theories that are 'compilations of isolated variables and constructs'.*
Constructs	**Construct validity** Ill-conceived notions of MBOL in conceptual terms; discriminant validity limitations with similar constructs; problems of convergent validity – the responses from different measures of MBOL must share variance.	**Construct scope** As studies indicate, MBOL should be capable of quantitative and qualitative asessment; although there has been a tendency to favour the former.
Relationships	**Logical adequacy** Logic embedded in the hypotheses proposed; arguably many antecedents to MBOL may be tautological. **Empirical adequacy** MBOL studies are empirically adequate on the basis that analyses are rarely spatially bound – a single case study at one point in time.	**Explanatory potential** Explanatory potential is modest; most studies claim an exploratory basis; causal linkages are often dictated by methodological convenience and are assumed to be linear. **Predictive accuracy** Probabilistic preditions have no basis in MBOL; theory-based predictions do exist following development of specific hypotheses.

* Bacharach, 1989, p. 507.

FIGURE 5.3 Market-based organizational learning: criticism of extant theory

theoretical underpinnings in MBOL. The tendency has been too heavily skewed towards a traditional approach in marketing of logical empiricism whereby, '. . . we use research methods more geared towards confirmation than discovery, and more towards verification than generation' (Deshpandé, 1983, p. 106).[5] Rather, appreciation needs to be given to the view that, 'Theory construction is *as* important as theory verification' (Deshpandé, 1983, p. 107; author's emphasis). Essentially, the predilection of marketing researchers for quantitative methods has meant that our understanding of MBOL is in need of evaluation so as to create improved future insights. While the quantitative biases in extant research have a significant contribution to make, caution should be exercised in making conclusions from this work because of the inherent limitations in this paradigm which is fundamentally a '. . . positivistic, hypothetico-deductive, particularistic, objective, outcome-oriented, and natural science world view' (Reichardt and Cook, 1979, pp. 9–10). Consequently, investigators should be aware of this imbalance and its implications for theory development.

Beyond these considerations, several other specific limitations of extant knowledge exist. For instance, there has been an overemphasis upon the economic (DeCarolis and Deeds, 1999), developmental (Quinn, 1980) and normative (Garvin, 1993) schools at the expense of the capability school of thought (Grant, 1996a). Also, most research is limited to discrete methods or modes of learning 'without careful consideration as to how these ideas fit together into a more comprehensive view of learning that offers richer insights for theory and practice' (Moorman, Kyriakopoulos and Wallman, 2000, p. 1). In addition, much of the extant research assumes that organizations have access to 'full relevant knowledge' (Deligönül and Çavuşgil, 1997, p. 67) whereas, in practice, such perfect information is erroneous and the behaviour of firms dictates that competitive situations mean they learn at different paces with the marketplace being a source of knowledge discovery (Hunt and Morgan, 1997).

Beyond these issues, it is important that researchers and other investigators in the MBOL area guard against what has become commonplace in certain domains of marketing interest – populist 'theory'. As has been exclaimed elsewhere:

> If theorists don't take the rules of theory seriously, individually they may well continue to cling to theories in almost cultist fashion. Getting beyond this clinging behaviour, which tends to drive theorists from fad to foible, demands a precise discourse, one which allows theorists to focus on the specific strengths and weaknesses of particular theories.
>
> (Bacharach, 1989, p. 512)

Critical Gaps in Knowledge

Several avenues of future investigation exist which warrant attention by investigators of MBOL. First, an interesting notion advanced by Winter (2000) recently is the extent to which learning capability reaches a threshold level. Based upon the satisficing principle applied to the learning of capabilities *per se* and not solely learning capabilities, Winter (2000) purports that there may be a level at which firms generally suspend overt learning behaviours and declares that, '. . . there is generally no clear-cut or automatic answer to the question of when an organisation should be expected to cut back its learning efforts and affirm that the desired capability has been achieved' (p. 981). Although seemingly counterintuitive, this notion addresses a valuable point regarding the worth or utility of market-based learning insights. This echoes a point made by Miner and Mezias (1996) who proposed the question: to what extent is all learning valuable. That is, an organization may well be advanced in terms of MBOL activities, processes and behaviours but this needs to be articulated in such a way as to realize positioning advantage in the marketplace. Otherwise, the situation of 'learning without doing' is likely to arise. Therefore, questions could be raised concerning what the extent and nature of MBOL such as: what should we learn?; how much do we wish to learn?; why do we learn?; and, what do we do with what we learn?

Second, interorganizational learning is now of significant interest to firms. The strategic alliance literature has devoted much attention in recent years to learning between organizations (Khanna, Gulati and Nohria, 1998) and many network theories have been developed to explain the learning synergies that can arise from sharing insights within a network (Beeby and Booth, 2000). Indeed many small and medium-sized businesses that lack the processes and utilitarian capabilities that underlie effective MBOL, find this form of learning most effective. However, attempts must be made to better understand how these networks function optimally. This is also of great interest to public policy makers and regional development authorities specifically within the interests of small firm growth and development. Furthermore, these issues readily apply to large firms such as BT plc, the UK-based telecommunications and high-technology services corporation. This organization does not exist solely as a provider of traditional telephony services for domestic and business customers, but rather the vast proportion of its revenue streams are generated from a myriad of other activities in which alliances and partnerships play a key role in providing value-based propositions, primarily to the business market. These individual relationships number nearly 600 and the potential for interorganizational learning from these arrangements are significant. Moreover, it is often the case that in such strategic alliances, especially non-equity agreements, that one party learns about proprietary processes and technologies to such an extent that the acquisition of these new capabilities undermine the rationale for engaging with the other party(ies) in the first place.

Third, there is limited knowledge concerning MBOL in international respects – ranging from export market learning for small firms to multinational enterprise learning and knowledge transfer within global operations. For the latter, the structural, process and communication challenges are vast, and given the inertia toward encouraging greater autonomy within work groups and business units on a global scale, global players are finding it more difficult to codify, share and disseminate knowledge. One of the best known proponents of shared learning and knowledge transfer on a global scale is Jack Welch at General Electric and this organization has proven that the management of MBOL, as well as organization-wide learning, can be achieved whatever the scale of commercial activity and geographic scope.

Fourth, the value of replication and extension in business management literatures has recently been rejuvenated (Easley, Madden and Dunn, 2000) – this is especially important in the light of the exploratory research in MBOL literature to date and the limited descriptive and causal studies that exist. Replicability plays a fundamental role in scrutinizing research conclusions and such a recommendation is made here. Thus, future extension studies may serve to determine the scope and parameters of richer MBOL conceptualizations by testing whether they can be generalized to other reference comparisons (e.g., '. . . other populations, time periods, organisations, geographical areas, measurement instruments, contexts and so on', Hubbard, Vetter and Little, 1998, p. 244).

Fifth, the emerging view of organizations as collections of 'processes' instead of 'functions' provides an alternative view of business that has particular relevance to MBOL (Workman, Homburg and Gruner, 1998). The distinction is a valuable one in that processes tend to transcend functional boundaries and more accurately represent the workflows in organizations, thus representing more accurately the channels of MBOL. Also, operationalization and measurement issues are central considerations to both MBOL researchers and managers alike, and improved batteries need to be developed with robust testing of their reliability and validity (Lähteenmäki, Toivonen and Mattila, 2001). Tracking studies using techniques such as data envelopment analysis may also prove to be potentially useful in attempts to profile learning dimensions on a longitudinal basis.

Sixth, insights have been developed into the way in which 'adaptive sense-making' practices (Bogner and Barr, 2000) can be employed in high velocity contexts. These practices have evolved from the conventional sensemaking literature in which methods have been established for dealing with temporary turbulence – with the advance being that these methods are practiced indefinitely under hypercompetitive circumstances. Furthermore, given that an understanding of changes both internal and external to the organization are vital for business performance gains, adaptive sensemaking may offer opportunities for standard operating learning procedures to be developed by firms in order to create institutional learning norms (see Bogner and Barr (2000) for an elaboration here).

Seventh, future investigations should consider the role of contingency issues such as environmental turbulence, product-market characteristics and industry setting that might affect the emphasis, direction, nature and form of MBOL. Also, given that market-based learning is cumulative and organizations build upon what is already generally known (Cohen and Levinthal, 1990), studies should consider the role of MBOL in firms pursuing pioneering, innovative and prospector-type strategies seeking first-mover advantage in new markets. These insights might help understanding of whether certain MBOL approaches are best suited to particular business strategies.

Market-based Organizational Learning Programs in Firms

In the late 1980s it was suggested in the services marketing literature that in order for the contribution of marketing to be fully realized within the organization, all internal constituencies needed to recognize their implicit role in the marketing function. In the same way that these non-marketing specialists were called upon to be to become 'part-time marketers', all organizational personnel must now engage in MBOL. While firms need to move beyond the syndrome that the Chief Marketing Officer is responsible for all marketing, the same applies to the role of the Chief Knowledge Officer – often perceived as of semi-divine influence, shrouded in mystique whose activities involve actually conducting learning and knowledge management on behalf of those in the organization, thus abdicating learning responsibility for others. In a successful marketing firm, the Chief Marketing Officer's role becomes superfluous, and the aim of the Chief Knowledge Officer should be the same – to become occupationally redundant. Indeed, in a recent survey conducted by McKinsey and Company (Kluge, Stein and Licht, 2001), it is concluded that, for corporate success to be achieved, MBOL needs to be an organization-wide phenomenon:

> The best companies have seen the fallacy of a narrow definition and have not one but all of their employees with being self-standing chief knowledge officers. Starting with the chief executive, then going on to the middle managers, and finally the frontline employees, everyone in a company must recognise the value of knowledge, and everyone must participate in the knowledge management program.
>
> (p. 201)

Managers should also consider the means by which they can initiate or augment their MBOL practices. The argument that most organizations nowadays 'learn' is a truism, but it is the learning bar that is important to market performance gains. Consequently, firms should conduct learning audits in order to evaluate their dormant potential. Moreover, a balance should be struck in that, for certain organizations, the development of a 'learning climate' may be crucial (e.g., a service firm) or emphasis on 'boundary spanners as environmental scanners' (e.g., a company offering a standardized product where the sales force is a large dependent function) may be key to understanding the business. Therefore, it should be appreciated that MBOL is a multidimensional, multiattribute concept that is particularly contingent upon the firm circumstance.

In an analysis of current advances in learning strategy, Slocum, McGill and Lei (1994) present a series of case scenarios and propose a way forward in implementing MBOL. By developing such an approach they emphasize that:

> Firms cultivate their capabilities to give customers what they want, when they want it and where they want it. . . . To develop the flexibility, responsiveness and rapid learning they will need, organisations will have to implement practices that facilitate both customer intimacy and experimentation with new products and processes. This pursuit of continuous learning is the route to achieving renewable competitive advantage.
>
> (Slocum, McGill and Lei, 1994, p. 35)

In practice, this means that managers must gauge their learning practices. Jackson and Schuler (2001) present an acronym to assist mangers in doing this – LEARN: *L*everage knowledge and learning to satisfy key stakeholders; *E*mbed knowledge and learning in all activities; encourage and allow *A*ccessible and accessed knowledge; *R*enew and regenerate continually; and, *N*on-financial measurement should be used to supplement financial indicators (p. 13).

Business managers must measure their 'information literacy' (Mutch, 1999, p. 323) as an input to MBOL. Organizations and their actors must assess the utility they make of data and information, and to what extent they are 'literate' in this process. The management and organization literature has emphasized processes and methods that support the construction of meaning without paying sufficient attention to the constraints upon this form of construction. Although there are substantial efforts that managers can make in their attempts to understand and use information appropriately, there are also formidable barriers and obstacles to overcome in constructing a complete, uniform, consensual and accurate understanding of markets and the competitive dynamics that underlie their explication. Moreover, questions need to be asked of the frame of analysis ('know-what'), understanding the underlying dynamics ('know-why'), and the properties of competitive and industry influences (know-how). Moreover, given the nature of complex dynamic systems, such 'chaos' does mean that the pursuit of order and understanding from this randomness is not straightforward. Consequently, it might be more pragmatic to resign ourselves to the fact that, '. . . a complete understanding of some of the things we plan may be beyond all possibility' (Cartwright, 1991, p. 54). Thus MBOL has limits. However, the question is not whether to learn or not, but whether to learn well or learn badly. Some, if not most, MBOL outcomes at time tx^1 restrict the range, as well as the desirability and feasibility, of both strategic and tactical options at tx^2 where 'x' may be only days or even weeks in high velocity environments. To never learn about markets, customers, suppliers and competitors is an unfortunate reflection upon the individual, the work team and the organization – such complacency will eventually be rewarded by loss of market share, customer switching behaviours, ill-conceived innovations, employee turnover, commercial losses and other natural consequences of competitive deterioration. The MBOL bar is increasing for all firms with no sanctuary from the fact that intellectual capital, knowledge management and the application of market learning is the prerequisite to merely existing in competitive marketspace – doing market-based organizational learning well is what distinguishes successful firms from their unsuccessful counterparts.

Acknowledgements

I should like to acknowledge Barrie Oxtoby, formerly Director of Organizational Learning at the United Nations and now Senior Executive Consultant with Industry Forum, Society of Motor Manufacturers and Traders, whose insight and experience has assisted in the market-based organizational learning conceptualization outlined within this chapter.

Notes

1 Market capitalization generally reflects investors' expectations of a firm's ability to generate future earnings. Although volatile and subject to significant shocks, this indicant of firm value provides an objective, non-partisan and comparable reference for future success based against current position.
2 This is the executive and consulting workbook that outlines various principles of organizational learning implementation (Senge *et al.*, 1995). It is based upon the best selling book by Peter Senge (1990) entitled, *The Fifth Discipline: The Art and Practice of the Learning Organisation*, Doubleday/Currency, New York, NY.
3 However, for a more extensive treatment of the distinctions between organizational learning and the learning organization, see Addelson (2001), Jones and Hendry (1994), Malhotra (1996) and Sugarman (2001).
4 For an elaboration upon these types of learning see Argyris and Schön (1978). In addition, for an interesting discussion of a hierarchy of market knowledge broadly reflecting types of OL, see Sinkula (1994, Figure 1) where he characterizes modes of OL according to the following questions: *'What is?'*; *'What has been?'*; *'What is the espoused way of doing things?'*; *'How things are actually done?'*; *'Why things are done the way they are?'*;

'How should things be done?'; *'How does the organization create knowledge and learn?'* (p. 39).

5 The author of this chapter includes some of his own previous work in this criticism.

Selected Websites for Resource Materials

Useful websites for elaboration on (market-based) organizational learning include:

- www.solonline.org
  The Society for Organizational Learning (SoL) is the brainchild of Peter Senge (Sloan School of Management, Massachusetts Institute of Technology), author of the seminal book, *The Fifth Discipline: The Art and Practice of the Learning Organisation.* This is an international membership network of like-minded researchers, company executives and consultants interested in organizational learning. With regular members' meetings and a structured set of activities, this is an active society to become familiar with. Visit their valuable website for access to excellent source material.

- www.stanford.edu/group/SLOW
  This is the website of the Stanford Learning Organisation Web (SLOW); a network of business executives, researchers, staff and students, associated with Stanford University, interested in the development of learning organizations and their functioning.

- www.members.aol.com/iqduru/knowledge.htm
  This is an extremely comprehensive review of several hundred organizational learning resources on the web including sub-classifications of: 'Institutions and Organisations'; 'Articles, Journals and Similar Resources'; 'Conferences'; and, 'Consultancies and Related Product/Service Companies'.

- www.gpsi.com/lo.html
  This site provides details of web-based resources concerning organizational learning and if you follow the specific mailing list subscription information links, you can subscribe to Group Performance Systems, Inc.'s latest information on organizational learning.

- www.jiscmail.ac.uk/lists/know-org.html
  Here you will find a mailing service (with archives) provided specifically for researchers and students interested in the field of organizational learning.

- www.world.std.com/~WhyLO.html
  Visit this site for a collage of comments as responses to the questions: 'Why do we want learning organizations?'; 'Why do you want to build learning organizations?'; and, 'Why do you want your own organization to be more of a learning organization?'.

Multiple perspectives on market orientation's domain specification:
Implications for theory development and knowledge accumulation

John W. Cadogan

The development of a market orientation is central to the marketing discipline. For nearly five decades, it has been a broadly accepted tenet of marketing thought that a market orientation is required as a platform from which to compete in the marketplace. The case is clearly presented, in introductory and advanced marketing text books alike, that a market orientation is a prerequisite for business success. Over the decades, marketing scholars have continuously argued the case that more market-oriented firms outperform their less market-oriented counterparts. Despite this history of anecdotal support, until relatively recently, empirical evidence concerning the impact of market orientation on business performance was scarce. Fortunately, the publication of several important theoretical and empirical contributions in the early 1990s signalled a change in this respect, since they provided both the impetus for researchers to start developing conceptual models concerning market orientation's system of relationships with other key variables, and the means by which researchers could empirically assess their models. Numerous scholars have found their interests drawn in this direction, and as a consequence, market orientation has emerged as a field of research in its own right.

Critically, this growth in interest in market orientation has gone hand in hand with a proliferation in competing definitions of the concept. Uncertainties arise from this situation. Most importantly, a lack of agreement on the conceptual content of the market orientation construct is worrying simply because of market orientation's prominence at the centre of marketing 'thought'. Currently, superficially similar studies into market orientation run into severe comparability problems, because the central construct, market orientation, has been defined differently across the studies.

In turn, this lack of comparability across studies has contributed to a situation whereby marketing scholars – those charged with the task of education and with the responsibility of providing guidance to managers – are faced with two problems. First, numerous research studies have attempted to provide empirical evidence on the pivotal role that market orientation has in determining business performance. Unfortunately, different studies, many adopting different definitions of market orientation, have come to very different conclusions. For example, although much of the empirical research undertaken has provided evidence that firms with higher levels of market orientation outperform their less market-oriented counterparts, a substantial and growing body of evidence has provided evidence to suggest that (a) some firms can 'get away' with low levels of market orientation, and (b) some firms with high levels of market orientation are actually outperformed by their less market-oriented counterparts! A tempting conclusion to draw from findings such as these is that a market orientation might not be such a good thing after all. Another possibility is that the results researchers obtain when studying the performance outcomes of market orientation are partly a function of the conceptualizations and measures they have adopted. It seems clear: if researchers adopt competing and different definitions of market orientation, and measure market orientation differently from each other, then it should come as no surprise if the results of their efforts do not tally. Consequently, the development of a more coherent picture of the potential benefits and performance outcomes of market orientation would be aided if researchers were to use similar conceptualizations (and hence measures) of the core concept (market orientation).

Assuming that the development of a market orientation is a good thing for at least some businesses, marketing scholars face a second problem. That is, what recommendations should be made to managers who wish to improve their business's performance via increased levels of market orientation? What is problematic here is that, since there are differences in opinion regarding what market orientation is, there are also differences in recommendations about how firms should go about modifying their market orientation levels. Given this situation, it is hardly surprising to find that most managers simply do not understand what it means to be market-oriented (Day, 1999), and that many experience enormous difficulties implementing and maintaining a market orientation (Harris, 1999).

It can be seen, therefore, that definitional issues pertaining to the market orientation concept are instrumental in blocking the development of a more complete understanding of market orientation's performance outcomes, and are hindering efforts to learn how to leverage market orientation to the benefit of the firm. In this chapter, I attempt to provide a way forward for those interested in the market orientation phenomenon. Specifically, I examine the evolution of market orientation's multiple definitions and, building on recent theoretical developments, present a holistic picture of how market orientation can be conceptualized. In doing so, I point out where current theoretical perspectives and approaches are impeding theory development and knowledge accumulation.

In the following section, I provide an overview of the various ways market orientation has been conceptualized in the literature, highlight the key contributions within the field, and describe the competing cultural definitions of the concept proposed by various scholars. Based on an assessment of this literature, I then provide an integrated multi-level conceptualization of market orientation which, I argue, should provide a basic framework from which to direct future discourse and research in this area.

I then go on to discuss in more detail the numerous subdimensions that have been used in different definitions of market orientation. Here, I explain how these different focuses have evolved, comment on their relevance, and describe how their proliferation threatens the development of a clear understanding of market orientation's domain, and its consequences and antecedents. I then provide recommendations concerning the explicit inclusion or exclusion of such focuses in market orientation's definition.

Following this, I address the issue of the appropriate level of analysis of the market orientation concept. Here, scholars' differing viewpoints are contrasted, implications for market orientation theory development and knowledge accumulation are presented and conclusions are drawn.

The chapter concludes with a summary of the issues raised.

What is Market Orientation? Multiple Cultural Perspectives

Basic Definitional Issues – The Pivotal Role of the Marketing Concept

Market orientation finds its roots in the marketing concept. First developed and articulated in the 1950s and 1960s, the marketing concept holds that (a) all areas of the firm should maintain a customer focus, (b) all marketing activities should be coordinated, and (c) that long-term profits, not just sales, should be the organizational goal. At the very heart of the marketing concept is the notion of customer focus, of which customer sensing (i.e., the identification of customer needs) and customer satisfaction (i.e., providing goods and services which will satiate the needs and wants of customers) are fundamental elements.

Market orientation's relationship with the marketing concept is fairly straightforward. Specifically, over the decades, and as the marketing concept became a central tenet of marketing thought, the term market orientation came to refer to the implementation of the marketing concept (Lafferty and Hult, 2001). Thus, a market-oriented firm is one which has adopted the marketing concept (see Kohli and Jaworski, 1990; Shapiro, 1988). Although this simple platform for defining market orientation is not without its critics, the fact is that the majority of definitions of market orientation are deeply embedded in the marketing concept.

At this stage, providing a more detailed definition of market orientation starts to become a little more problematic. This is because market orientation research is still a developing field of study, with multiple perspectives on the construct's domain being touted. When looking at the definitions available in the literature, it makes sense to first examine the key theoretical contributions to the divergent development of market orientation's conceptual content. Foremost of these are the works of Deshpandé, Farley and Webster (1993), Kohli and Jaworski (1990) and Narver and Slater (1990).

Key Contributions

First came the seminal article by Kohli and Jaworski published in the April 1990 issue of the *Journal of Marketing*. Here, Kohli and Jaworski (1990) initially defined market orientation as being the implementation of the marketing concept. Following empirical analysis in the form of a large scale qualitative study, however, a more refined perspective of market orientation was proposed: 'the meaning of the market orientation construct that surfaced in the field is essentially a more precise and operational view of the first two pillars of the marketing concept – customer focus and coordinated marketing' (Kohli and Jaworski, 1990, p. 3). They went on to formally define market orientation as being a one dimensional construct consisting of three organization-wide activities: market intelligence generation, the dissemination of this intelligence across departments in the firm, and the responsiveness to intelligence. Perhaps because of the intuitive logic of Jaworski and Kohli's approach, and the relative ease with which their basic concepts can be measured (see Jaworski and Kohli, 1993; Kohli, Jaworski and Kumar, 1993), many scholars have adopted this definition when conducting research into market orientation (e.g., Bhuian, 1998; Cadogan *et al.*, 2002b; Diamantopoulos and Hart, 1993; Homburg and Pflesser, 2000; Kwon and Hu, 2000; Pitt, Carvana and Berthon, 1996; Pulendran, Speed and Widing II, 2000; Raju, Lonial and Gupta, 1995; Vorhies and Harker, 2000).

The second approach which has also held a dominant position in the marketing literature is that of Narver and Slater whose initial research appeared in the October 1990 issue of the *Journal of Marketing*. Specifically, Narver and Slater (1990, p. 21) first defined market orientation as 'the *culture* that most effectively and efficiently *creates* the necessary behaviours for the creation of superior value for buyers and, thus, continuous superior performance for the business'. They then elaborated on this conceptualization by arguing that market orientation consists of five components: customer orientation, competitor orientation, inter-functional coordination, a long-term focus, and a profit focus. Narver and Slater (1990) also provided a description of their measuring instrument for market orientation. Over the years, numerous researchers, keen to test a wide variety of theoretical issues, have adopted Narver and Slater's (1990) conceptualization and measurement approach (see, e.g., Farrell, 2000; Gatignon and Xuereb, 1997; Greenley, 1995a; Han, Kim and Srivastava, 1998; Kumar, Subramanian and Yauger, 1998; Lukas and Ferrell, 2000; Siguaw, Brown and Widing II, 1994; Slater and Narver, 2000; Van Egeren and O'Connor, 1998).

Less widely used for empirical research purposes, but still highly influential, are the works of Deshpandé and colleagues. These authors have argued that market orientation and customer orientation are synonymous concepts (Deshpandé, Farley and Webster, 1993). From a definitional perspective, customer orientation is a type of organizational culture (Deshpandé and Webster, 1989): it is 'the set of beliefs that puts the customers' interest first, while not excluding those of all other stakeholders, such as owners, managers and employees, in order to develop a long-term profitable enterprise' (Deshpandé, Farley and Webster, 1993, p. 27). Although relatively few studies have used Deshpandé, Farley and Webster's (1993) measuring instrument – exceptions include Baker, Simpson and Siguaw (1999) and Steinman, Deshpandé and Farley (2000) – their notion that market orientation is a cultural phenomenon has found favour with many recent authors (e.g., Harris, 1998; Harris and Ogbonna, 2000; Homburg and Pflesser, 2000; Hooley *et al.*, 1999; Webster, 1995).

Market Orientation – Philosophy and Behaviour

Looking at these three key contributions, an important conclusion can be drawn. Specifically, influential marketing scholars have disagreed in terms of the extent of market orientation's cultural content. Thus, some researchers believe that market orientation is a philosophical concept, deeply rooted within the firm's culture. Dreher (1994, p. 155) summed this 'philosophical' perspective up in the following way: market orientation 'can best be described as [being] . . . embedded in the cognitive sphere and influenced by personal factors, leading to a certain view of reality and forming organizational characteristics such as goals, strategies, structures, systems and activities'. Thus, from the 'philosophical' perspective, market orientation is an organizational cognition – an intangible organizational state-of-mind – which emphasizes philosophical notions such as customer-oriented values, norms and beliefs, market and customer focus, and customer commitment. From this perspective, market orientation is more of an 'intangible' concept – only the *consequences* of a market orientation are behavioural. That is, the outcome of a market-oriented philosophy is organizational behaviour which should be consistent with the cultural values held by the firm, and which then feeds into the firm's performance. (*cf.* Deshpandé, Farley and Webster, 1993; Narver and Slater, 1990).

Kohli and Jaworski (1990), on the other hand, placed less emphasis on organizational states-of-mind when defining market orientation, concentrating instead on the behavioural manifestations of market orientation. Specifically, the behavioural perspective focuses on the set of the information processing activities which underpin market orientation. Numerous researchers agree with this perspective and, although terminology may differ, the consensus among the behavioural camp appears to be in agreement with Kohli and Jaworski's (1990) proposition that a business is market-oriented to the degree that it gathers market intelligence, disseminates that intelligence, and analyzes and responds to that intelligence (e.g., Deng and Dart, 1994; Hunt and Morgan, 1995; Kohli and Jaworski, 1990; Ruekert, 1992; Shapiro, 1988). Jaworski and Kohli (1996, p. 121) have provided something of a justification for adopting a behavioural perspective:

> an organization may believe something is important, but fail to act on its beliefs for a variety of reasons (e.g., resource constraints). Thus, from a manager's perspective, it may be more important to focus on what an organization actually does than what it feels is important. The choice between focusing on values/beliefs or activities/behaviors is an important one, with direct implications for . . . implementing organizational change interventions.
>
> Jaworski and Kohli (1996)

Thus, from the behavioural perspective, the adoption of the marketing concept as a philosophy does not necessarily mean that the firm will be market-oriented in its behaviour. Rather, it is the manifestation of market orientation that those adopting the behavioural approach are interested in: asking managers whether they are customer focused is not good enough; asking them what they do about it is preferable. In essence, while attitudes and cognitive structures consistent with the marketing concept *may* be important antecedents to a market orientation, they are not considered to reflect the construct itself. Indeed, coming from a behavioural perspective, Pulendran and Speed (1996, p. 2034) have suggested that the 'distinction between the business philosophy (marketing concept) and the specific activities required for implementation of that philosophy (market orientation) has now been widely accepted within the research community'.

Interestingly, while Narver and Slater (1990) initially defined market orientation as more of a philosophical phenomenon, grounded in the beliefs and values held by organizational members, three of the dimensions that they used when refining their definition (customer orientation, competitor orientation, and interfunctional coordination) were behavioural in nature. Specifically, Narver and Slater (1990) argued that customer and competitor orientations involve developing a sufficient understanding of one's target buyers and competitors, while interfunctional coordination involves using company resources to create superior value for customers. Narver and Slater then provided a measuring instrument to capture a firm's degree of market orientation. The questions asked of managers when assessing a firm's market orientation, while including items capturing organizational states-of-mind, were also concerned with organizational behaviours. Consequently, Narver and Slater's view of market orientation is mostly philosophical – they have clearly and repeatedly defined market orientation as a philosophical state-of-mind, 'an overall organizational value system' (Slater and Narver, 1995, p. 67) – but has behavioural overtones, since aspects of market orientation are considered to have behavioural manifestations. Thus, it seems that Narver and Slater do not really differentiate, on conceptual or operational grounds, between (a) the philosophical beliefs, values and norms which underpin a market-oriented culture, and (b) the activities which underpin market-oriented behaviour.

Not surprisingly, the fact that dominant market orientation definitions are, apparently, somewhat contradictory has been noticed by numerous researchers. However, for most, the differences in the underlying definitions of market orientation have merely been a matter of differing terminology. Consequently, researchers have adopted either Narver and Slater's (1990) or Deshpandé, Farley and Webster's (1993) more philosophical definitions, or Kohli and Jaworski's (1990) behavioural definition with little by way of justification. Yet the choice of adopting a philosophical or a behavioural perspective also has implications for theory construction and testing, since market-oriented values/beliefs are fundamentally different concepts from activities/behaviours. One needs to be aware of where, within a theoretical model, one should place the key concepts, and how these concepts should relate to other concepts: this is likely to differ depending on how the concepts are defined. If care is not taken in this respect, incorrect conclusions are likely to be drawn.

For example, potential problems have arisen from the presence of alternative definitions of market orientation. Deshpandé, Farley and Webster's (1993) findings indicated that firms' self-evaluated levels of market orientation (conceptualized as a deeply cultural concept, at the level of values and beliefs) do not correlate with firm performance. Other studies (e.g., Jaworski and Kohli 1993; Narver and Slater, 1990; Ruekert, 1992; Slater and Narver, 1994), however, measuring market orientation as behaviour, have suggested that firms' self-evaluated levels of market orientation are significantly and positively correlated with aspects of firm performance. These findings need to be interpreted very carefully: does Deshpandé, Farley and Webster's (1993) study indicate that a market orientation is not a useful business approach? Not really. Rather, one needs to be aware that market-oriented behaviours and market-oriented values and beliefs are not the same things. As a result, market-oriented values and beliefs are likely to operate on performance in a different way to market-oriented behaviours. Specifically, the relationship between values/beliefs and performance is likely to be mainly indirect (i.e., by influencing other variables), whereas the relationship between behaviour and performance can be relatively direct. One outcome of this is that the relationship between business success and a firm's market-oriented values and beliefs is likely to be weaker, and thus more difficult to observe, than the association between market-oriented behaviours and firm performance. In fact, Deshpandé, Farley and Webster's (1993) lack of a significant relationship between market-oriented values/beliefs and organizational success can be put down to a lack of sensitivity in the methods used to capture the relationship, rather than a lack of a relationship in the first place.

However, methodology issues aside, these competing results do illustrate a critical issue which arises as a result of having different definitions of market orientation. Specifically, as Churchill (1979, p. 67) has pointed out, the potential problem with a situation like this is that 'the use of different definitions makes it difficult to compare and accumulate findings and thereby develop syntheses of what is known'. Clearly, there is a danger that the multiple definitions of market orientation being used may be impairing researchers' ability to understand fully market orientation and its place and significance within a wide variety of theoretical frameworks. Ideally, then, it seems that it would be beneficial if there was consensus about what is meant by the term 'market orientation'. Some sort of consolidation of the theory of the composition of market orientation would appear to be in order.

A Unifying Framework

Perhaps what has been impeding researchers' work has been a lack of an explicit appreciation of market orientation's complexity. It seems that market orientation is not a single phenomena: it has many facets. Yet, for the most part, researchers have been lured into trying to treat market orientation as though it were a 'one-dimensional concept'. Consequently, leading scholars such as Narver and Slater (1990) have argued that market orientation is a business philosophy which has behavioural manifestations. This, in itself, makes sense. However, Narver and Slater (1990) have also implicitly assumed that the business philosophy and the behavioural manifestations of which they talk of are one and the same thing. This is not a perspective I subscribe to.

In this section, I argue that for market orientation research to make further strides forward, there needs to be an explicit recognition on the part of marketing scholars that market orientation is multifaceted. Only then can the competing definitions of market orientation, and the broad body of empirical research they engender, be synthesized into a meaningful body of knowledge.

The work of Homburg and Pflesser (2000) may be key in this respect. Specifically, they have developed, in their own words, 'a multiple-layer model of market-oriented culture'. Their approach was straightforward. If market orientation is an organizational culture – as some have argued in detail (e.g., Deshpandé, Farley and Webster, 1993; Slater and Narver, 1995) – then in order to truly appreciate market orientation's domain, a detailed understanding of what is meant by the term 'organizational culture' is required. Based on the meanings of culture derived from anthropology, sociology and organizational science, Homburg and Pflesser (2000) argued that market orientation consists of a hierarchy of components which are inter-related, but are conceptually distinct.

Drawing on Homburg and Pflesser's (2000) notion of a multifaceted market orientation concept, and integrating it with the works of other scholars within the market orientation field (e.g., Harris, 1998; Kohli and Jaworski, 1990), I now attempt to delineate the basics of a theoretical framework from which to view market orientation.

At the most abstract level of culture – and the most deeply rooted from a cultural perspective – are market-oriented values and beliefs. Perhaps most obvious of these would be valuing the marketing concept as a guiding business philosophy. This basic value provides a focus for the firm in terms of what its goals are and how it will achieve them. For instance, by valuing the marketing concept as a business philosophy, a firm has a set of beliefs – a view of reality – which centre around the notion that superior performance is achieved through the delivery of goods and services that most closely match customers' needs and wants. This perspective of market orientation aligns most closely with the conceptualization promoted by Deshpandé, Farley and Webster (1993) (see also Harris (1998)). Somewhat controversially, Homburg and Pflesser (2000) viewed organizational values as external to a market orientation. For them, organizational values can only provide supportive conditions under which a market orientation can thrive: values can support a market orientation but are not part of the concept itself. However, most scholars, including myself, would place market-oriented values at the heart of the market orientation concept (e.g., see Harris, 1998).

A second level of market orientation consists of 'norms for market orientation'. Norms are different from values in that 'norms guide behaviours in a specific context, whereas values represent general guidelines' (Homburg and Pflesser, 2000, p. 451). Furthermore, norms provide a kind of behavioural pressure, such that a norm for market orientation would describe a market-oriented behaviour that organizational members pressure each other to follow. Thus, a norm for interfunctional coordination would describe a set of expectations that employees have regarding appropriate levels of, and ways of, approaching the coordination of marketing activities within the firm. A norm is market-oriented when the focus of the norm is towards the visible manifestations of market orientation – specifically, those artifacts and behaviours which are market-focused. Importantly, it is also likely that in firms with strong market-oriented values, stronger norms for market orientation will also be present.

Market-oriented artifacts comprise a third level of a market-oriented culture. In short, market-oriented artifacts provide a kind of symbolic representation of market orientation in the form of stories, arrangements, rituals, and the language used within the firm. Homburg and Pflesser (2000) identify several such artifacts, including stories about heroes of market orientation (e.g., company founder, CEO, etc.), arrangements for market orientation (buildings and exterior styling, styling and organization of reception area, etc.) rituals of market orientation (reward systems, special events, etc.), and market-oriented/non-market-oriented language. Reinforced by market-oriented values and norms, artifacts are themselves likely to influence the activities of organizational members. Thus, because of their symbolic power, market-oriented artifacts are thought to influence the degree to which firm members behave in a market-oriented way.

Finally, the fourth level of market-oriented culture is market-oriented behaviour. As noted earlier, most scholars agree that the latter is defined as the generation of market information, the dissemination of the information to appropriate decision makers, and responses to the information. Thus, strategy making and implementation are covered under the umbrella of market-oriented behaviours. Interestingly, Homburg and Pflesser (2000, p. 452) are of the opinion that only market-oriented behaviour influences organizational performance: '[v]alues, norms, and artifacts are not assumed to have a direct impact on market performance. Rather … they indirectly affect performance through market-oriented behaviours'. While this statement makes sense, it should also be recognized that values, norms and artifacts might also influence performance in other ways (i.e., through a route other than via market-oriented behaviours). For example, some market-oriented values and norms may enhance organizational cohesion, leading to increased staff morale, lower levels of staff turnover and heightened efficiency and productivity levels, while market-oriented artifacts, such as store frontage and layout, may have a direct impact on trade (and hence on sales and profits) in their own right.

The above conceptual picture of market orientation's domain is both convenient, since the hierarchy of values, norms, artifacts and behaviours is reasonably well-established in organizational research, and comprehensive, since most aspects of market orientation are captured within the hierarchy. The conceptualization also recognizes that market orientation's domain is multifaceted: market orientation is a broad concept – too broad to have a single meaning. The implication is that a firm cannot be described simply as having a certain level of market orientation, because a firm may have differing degrees of market orientation depending on the facet of market orientation one is describing. For instance, while a firm may have strong customer-focused values and beliefs, it may not be able to transfer effectively its market-oriented philosophy into market-oriented actions. Alternatively, a firm may behave in a market-oriented way, but not have strong market-oriented values and beliefs. Here, perhaps, activities have become somewhat ritualized, but their meaning has been lost.

However, although such differences can occur, it does make sense to view the multiple components of market orientation as being linked in some way. That is, although individual components of market-orientation are not linked in a deterministic fashion, one can argue that they are linked in the sense that the presence of one element within the firm increases the likelihood that other elements will also be present. For example, market-oriented values and norms are likely to facilitate market-oriented behaviours, since they provide the direction, goals, and guidelines against which to judge behaviours.

From a theory construction and testing perspective, of course, it is important to be explicit about the precise level about which one is theorizing. For example, a researcher studying the antecedents to market orientation will need to explicitly detail whether s/he is interested in identifying factors which directly shape market-oriented *values* within the firm, or whether s/he is interested in identifying those factors which facilitate or impede the emission of market-oriented *behaviours*. This is because (a) the forces which directly shape values are likely to be very different from the forces which directly shape behaviours, (b) values may be important determinants of behaviours, or even (c) behaviours, especially when repeated over time, may influence the value system within the firm. Thus, the conceptual models for the antecedents to market-oriented values versus market-oriented behaviours are likely to differ significantly.

Has the problem of market orientation's competing definitions been solved as a result of the above recommendations? Unfortunately not. The debate on market orientation's conceptual domain goes beyond researchers failing to recognize the distinctions between the multiple facets of a market-oriented culture.

The Devil's in the Detail: Multiple Evolutionary Paths

In reality, in addition to the works of Kohli and Jaworski (1990), Narver and Slater (1990) and Deshpandé, Farley and Webster (1993), a multitude of alternative conceptualizations of market orientation have been put forward (e.g., Balakrishnan, 1996; Cadogan, Diamantopoulas and Pahud de Mortanges, 1999; Dawes, 2000; Deng and Dart, 1994; Dobni and Luffman, 2000; Gray et al., 1998; Hooley, Lynch and Shepherd, 1990; Lado, Maydeu-Olivares and Rivera, 1998; Langerak, 2001; Ruekert, 1992; Thirkell and Dau, 1998). Some have adopted more of a 'market orientation as philosophy' perspective, others have adopted more of a 'market orientation as behaviour' perspective. All, however, differ in some way in terms of how they define the underlying components of a market orientation. These 'differences in the detail' have come about as a result of two main issues.

First, even though most scholars agree that market orientation is the implementation of the marketing concept, there is much disagreement as to what the concept of implementation really means. That is, the core pillars of the marketing concept have not always been treated in the same way when implementation of the marketing concept has been undertaken. Second, the conceptual domain of market orientation has also been evolving over time in a seemingly *ad hoc* fashion. As a result, multiple focuses have been proposed as components of the market orientation concept. However, different researchers have adopted or rejected specific focuses depending on their personal preferences.

In itself, there is nothing inherently wrong with changes occurring in a construct's meaning. It is only natural that, as a field of study matures, understanding and perceptions of the central constructs will change and become more refined. As Edwards and Bagozzi (2000, p. 157) have noted,

> [c]onstructs themselves are not real in an objective sense ... they are elements of scientific discourse that serve as verbal surrogates for phenomena of interest. ... Some constructs may demonstrate ongoing usefulness, whereas others initially considered useful may be modified or abandoned as knowledge accumulates. These advances may occur even when the phenomenon of interest remains unchanged.

However, what is interesting about the changes to market orientation's meaning is that multiple evolutionary paths have been followed in parallel. There is no single line of evolutionary development. Thus, while modification to market orientation's domain might be seen as signifying advancement in our understanding of the concept, the fact that these changes have occurred more or less concurrently actually compromises the accumulation of knowledge about market orientation and its system of relationships with other variables. Confusion is bound to occur when attempting to extract meaning and compare research findings from studies which have market orientation constructs comprising of different dimensions.

In this section, I try to unravel the confusion caused by these competing definitions, and point a way forward for theory development and knowledge accumulation. In doing so, I describe the various directions in which market orientation's construct domain has been extended, and in places I discuss the relevance and correctness of the definitions proposed. I conclude by providing a recommendation concerning the appropriateness of both context-rich and context-free definitions of market orientation for theory development and practice.

Implementing the Pillars of the Marketing Concept

When defining market orientation as the implementation of the marketing concept, different researchers have interpreted the term 'implementation' in different ways. That is, not all definitions of market orientation place an equal weighting on the marketing concept's core elements of customer focus, long-term profitability, and coordinated marketing.

Starting on a point of agreement, however, an examination of the many definitions of market orientation proposed in the literature shows that the concept of customer focus plays a major role in all approaches. Thus, the importance of understanding customers' needs and wants and responding to these is universally recognized across conceptualizations. Therefore, a market-oriented firm is generally recognized as having adopted and/or implemented a customer focus, either in its value system or at a behavioural level (depending on how the researcher in question views market orientation's cultural status). This is perhaps the only definitional aspect of market orientation about which all marketers broadly agree.

The second component of the marketing concept is long-term profitability. Thus, if one is trying to determine what it might mean to implement the marketing concept, then one could argue that it makes good sense to operation-alize the implementation of the idea that 'long-term profits should be an organizational goal', as specified by the marketing concept. However, only a few researchers have explicitly incorporated a profit-focus notion within their defini-tions of market orientation. For example, Deng and Dart (1994), Dobni and Luffman (2000), Gray *et al.* (1998) and Thirkell and Dau's (1998) conceptualiza-tions of market orientation all included a profit-focus component. Thus, for these scholars, if a firm does not have a strong profit emphasis (either in its value system and beliefs, or in its behaviours), its level of market orientation is reduced.

On the other hand, a strong case has been made to exclude profit focus as an explicit element of market orientation. Specifically, Kohli and Jaworski (1990) suggested that defining the marketing concept strictly in terms of the literature perspective or the 'received view' (i.e., in terms of the three pillars of customer focus, profitability, and coordinated marketing) severely limits the concept's practical value. Rather, Kohli and Jaworski (1990, p. 3) argued that their field interviews with managers provided a more realistic and practical perspective of marketing orientation's domain:

> In sharp contrast to the received view . . . the idea that profitability is a component of market orientation is conspicuously absent in the field findings. Without exception, interviewees viewed profitability as a *consequence* of a market orientation rather than part of it.

Kohli and Jaworski (1990) reinforced their argument by quoting Levitt (1969, p. 236) who objected so strongly to viewing profitability as a component of market orientation, he asserted that it would be 'like saying that the goal of human life is eating'. From Kohli and Jaworski's (1990) perspective, profitability is viewed as a desirable outcome for a business, while a market orientation is a way of achieving a business's desired outcomes: thus, profitability is external to market orientation.

Interestingly, Narver and Slater (1990) originally included both a 'long-term horizon' component and a 'profit-emphasis' component as 'decision criteria' (i.e., values and norms) within their definition of market orientation. Conceptually speaking, these facets were meant to capture the marketing concept's long-term profitability notion. However, Narver and Slater (1990, p. 33) were unable to develop reliable measures of these two elements, and had to drop them from their study, arguing that:

> [o]ur attempt to develop a valid measure of profit orientation and long-range focus as part of a one-dimensional concept of market orientation was unsuccessful. Future studies might address this issue by including additional items that represent these constructs and testing their relationship with [other dimensions of market orientation] and with a business's performance.

However, in their following empirical studies (e.g., Slater and Narver, 1994), no attempt was made to rectify this situation, and the concepts of profit orientation and of long-term focus were dropped permanently from market orientation's conceptual domain. Indeed, in a subsequent article, Slater and Narver (1996, p. 161) went on to argue that:

[t]he market-oriented business will realize its performance potential by either: 1) maximizing profit at the expense of expanded sales, 2) maximizing sales at the expense of profit margin, or 3) balancing the trade-off between profitability and sales growth for superior overall performance.

Here, at least implicitly, Slater and Narver (1996) appear to be acknowledging the difficulty of operationalizing the idea of profit orientation into a definition of market orientation, since the relative emphasis on profits in the short- and the long-term is likely to differ across companies and industries.

Kohli and Jaworski's (1990) and Narver and Slater's (1990) treatments of the profit focus concept appears to have followed Edwards and Bagozzi's (2000) scenario of a concept being abandoned as knowledge accumulates. In this respect, I suggest that there are two main reasons why a profit focus should be excluded from market orientation's conceptual domain. First, its inclusion would imply that a firm that seeks to balance profitability with sales growth would be less market-oriented than a firm seeking profits at the expense of sales. This does not make good sense, and would surely reduce market orientation's predictive capability in terms of business success (the latter is, itself, a multifaceted concept). Second, including a profit focus within market orientation's domain greatly reduces the utility of the market orientation concept for organizations which do not seek profits, such as charities and certain public sector organizations.

Clearly, the exclusion of profitability from market orientation's conceptual domain has serious implications for the interpretation of market orientation studies. Specifically, an exclusion of this sort raises doubts about the validity of theoretical and empirical research studies which are based on conceptual definitions of market orientation that include a profit component. Thus, if a study has based its assessment of market orientation in part on firms' levels of profit focus, the results of the study should be ignored, since market orientation has been assessed on the basis of something other than the concept itself.

The final pillar of the marketing concept is coordinated marketing, and there is confusion about how (or, indeed, whether) 'coordination' should be included in market orientation's conceptual domain. Narver and Slater (1990) were explicit in this respect, since they defined interfunctional coordination as a behavioural component of market orientation. For them, coordinated marketing represented the 'coordinated integration of the business's resources in creating superior value for buyers' (Narver and Slater, 1990, p. 22). This concept clearly has some overlap with the general notion of market-oriented activities (see Cadogan and Diamantopoulos, 1995). However, for Narver and Slater (1990), regardless of the activities in question, the focus of their concept was 'integrated effort': a sort of 'pulling together' orientation grounded in an organization's value system. Several other researchers followed Narver and Slater in this respect, specifying coordination as a component of market orientation (e.g., Deng and Dart, 1994; Gray *et al.*, 1998; Thirkell and Dau, 1998).

In my own research, I was also influenced by Narver and Slater's (1990) inclusion of a coordination concept, and included it as a formal dimension of market orientation. Drawing on a variety of literature sources, together with my own field research (see Cadogan and Diamantopoulos, 1995; Diamantopoulos and Cadogan, 1996), I proposed that the coordination component of market orientation (what I termed a coordinating mechanism) is endowed with several key characteristics. These were (a) communication leading to common understanding within the firm, (b) common work-oriented goals, (c) a lack of dysfunctional conflict, and (d) an organizational culture emphasizing the values of responsibility, cooperation and assistance. However, unlike Narver and Slater, I did not consider coordination to be part of a single market orientation entity. Rather, from my perspective, market orientation is made up of interlinking components, of which coordination is one and behaviour is another. In this respect, I made a distinction between the behavioural manifestations of market orientation (i.e., market intelligence generation, dissemination and responsiveness) and the more philosophically grounded coordinating aspect of market orientation. Thus, from this perspective, coordination is a guiding system of values, norms and artifacts which act to facilitate the implementation of market-oriented behaviours (see Cadogan *et al.*, 2001; Cadogan, Diamantopoulos and Siguaw, 2002a).

Kohli and Jaworski (1990) were less explicit in their discussion of coordination's place within market orientation's domain. They did describe a concept which is similar to coordination – what they termed an organization-wide responsibility for market-oriented activities – and even included it in their formal definition of market orientation. However, they did not elaborate on this concept in any real detail. Indeed, in their theoretical model of the antecedents to market orientation, elements of coordination (i.e., interdepartmental conflict and interdepartmental connectedness) were modelled as an antecedent factors, implicitly excluding these coordination concepts from the domain of market-oriented behaviour. This treatment is consistent with Kohli and Jaworski's (1990) view that market orientation is purely behavioural in context. That is, if market orientation is behaviour only, and if coordination comprises of values, norms and artifacts, then for Kohli and Jaworski, coordination would be external to market orientation.

Taking the issue even further, prominent researchers have explicitly argued that coordination should *not* form part of a definition of market orientation. Specifically, Hunt and Morgan (1995, p. 11) stated that they 'do not include interfunctional coordination [in market orientation's definition] . . . because, though it is a factor that can contribute to implementing successfully a market orientation, such implementation factors should not appear in a concept's definition'. Again, this assertion makes sense given Hunt and Morgan's mainly behavioural view of market orientation's domain. Hunt and Morgan (1995) were merely adopting the stance that (a) market orientation is behaviour, (b) coordination is an antecedent to market orientation, thus (c) coordination cannot be market orientation and antecedent to market orientation at the same time. However, if market orientation is viewed as comprising market-oriented values, norms, artifacts and behaviours there is no such conflict, since coordination can be considered as a component of a market-oriented culture which can act as an antecedent to market-oriented behaviours.

Consequently, drawing once more on Edwards and Bagozzi's (2000) argument that concepts' definitions are dependent on their utility and common usage, and synthesizing the above ideas, I suggest that coordination *is* an important component of market orientation. However, I limit the concept to the perspective of a ~ in terms of firms' values, norms and artifacts. Values for coordination provide goals and guidelines for thinking about the integration of organizational activities. Norms for coordination provide expectations about how specific activities should be undertaken and integrated. Artifacts for coordination provide the more overt manifestations of the concept in the form of rituals for coordinated actions, and stories and myths about such activities. Market-oriented behaviours themselves, on the other hand, are best conceptualized at the level of specific information processing activities. As Hunt and Morgan (1995) argue, it is probably best to think of these activities as being completely separate from the coordination concept. Thus, coordination can facilitate the manifestation and effectiveness of market-oriented behaviours, but does not constitute market-oriented behaviour in itself. Furthermore, as discussed later in this chapter, the domain of coordination is itself very much dependent on the level at which market orientation is conceptualized within the firm.

The Evolution of Additional Focuses

The above discussion has described three levels of 'focus' which, grounded in the marketing concept, have been attributed to the market orientation concept (customers, profits, coordination). However, a great many other focuses have been proposed (or can be implied) as components of market orientation.

The most widely recognized of these is likely to be the competitor orientation dimension. In itself, a competitor focus is not an explicit component of the marketing concept; however, the latter does have an implied competitor focus. That is, the marketing concept is considered to be a method by which a firm can achieve sustainable competitive advantage (SCA), and as such, the rationale of the marketing concept is partly based on the notion that a firm's customer value-creating activities must be considered relative to the value-creating activities of competitors. 'The logic of SCA is that for a buyer to purchase offering X, the buyer must perceive that the expected value to him of that offering . . . exceeds the expected value to him of any alternative solution' (Narver and Slater, 1990, p. 21).

In this respect, Narver and Slater's (1990) inclusion of a competitor orientation dimension in market orientation's domain was a formalization of this idea (since competitors provide alternative solutions), and was a natural extension to the ongoing debate in the marketing literature concerning the dangers of focusing on customers to the exclusion of competitors (e.g., Day and Wensley, 1988). This competitor focus concept was rooted in the firm's cultural values and norms – but was endowed with behavioural manifestations. Concerning the latter, Narver and Slater (1990, pp. 21–22) stated that '[c]ompetitor orientation means that a seller understands the short-term strengths and weaknesses and long-term capabilities and strategies of both the key current and the key potential competitors'.

Most other scholars have also included some reference to competition in their definitions of market orientation (e.g., Deng and Dart, 1994; Kohli and Jaworski,

1990; Ruekert, 1992). For example, Kohli and Jaworski (1990) included competition in their behavioural definition by arguing that a market-oriented firm generates, disseminates and responds to competitor information (in addition to other types of information). However, Deshpandé, Farley and Webster (1993, p. 27) were not convinced, arguing that 'a competitor orientation can be almost antithetical to a customer orientation when the focus is exclusively on the strengths of a competitor rather than on the unmet needs of the customer'. Not surprisingly, their definition of market orientation did not formally incorporate competitor issues. Similarly, Dawes (2000) excluded a competitor orientation from his implied definition of market orientation. Dawes rationalized this approach by stating that the key priority for the company managers he interviewed was the analysis and response to customer needs and preferences – not competitors' strategies and activities. In other words, Dawes' view was that a competitor focus was superfluous to market orientation's definition because the managers interviewed did not believe that competitive issues were relevant to their businesses. Possibly, Dawes' (2000) sample of managers worked in industries characterized by very low levels of competitive intensity.

This does raise the question: is a competitor focus relevant for all businesses? If it is not, then should all firms' levels of market orientation be judged (partly) on their levels of competitor orientation? According to Narver and Slater's (1990) model, a competitor focus (at least partly) defines a firm's level of market orientation. Therefore, Dawes' (2000) finding that his sample of managers focused on customers' needs and wants to the exclusion of competitor issues indicates (from Narver and Slater's perspective) that these firms were not very market-oriented. This is not a conclusion that Dawes appears to subscribe to (see also Deshpandé, Farley and Webster, 1993). Who is right?

The problem is made even more complicated by the fact that there are other focuses which might also be useful. Kohli and Jaworski's (1990) treatment of market orientation went beyond the inclusion of a focus on customers and competitors. They argued that a market-oriented firm should generate, disseminate, and respond to all information about markets in which the firm operates or may potentially operate in, and that the information should cover the whole range of exogenous factors which may influence customers' needs and wants, now and in the future. Consequently, the implied focus is broadened from customers and competitors to businesses in different industries, suppliers, regulatory forces, technological changes, and a host of other environmental factors (see also Slater and Narver, 1995). Should market orientation contain dimensions which address all these issues as well?

Some researchers have taken steps in this direction. For instance, Langerak (2001) proposed a new conceptualization of market orientation which included a formal 'supplier orientation' component. Similarly, Lado, Maydeu-Olivares and Rivera (1998) proposed a 'distributor orientation' element to market orientation's domain. Greenley and Foxall (1998) examined multiple stakeholder orientations, which some may argue should form an important focus for some market-oriented firms (*cf.* Slater and Narver, 1995). Finally, Gatignon and Xuereb (1997) examined various strategic orientations (e.g., technological orientation) which would not look out of place in an expanded or comprehensive market orientation concept, especially for firms operating in technologically turbulent business environments.

The Role of Focuses in Defining Market Orientation

In order to clarify the issue of the appropriate inclusion or exclusion of different focuses from market orientation's definition, it is worthwhile looking at the role of focuses in defining the market orientation construct. The conceptual approach underpinning most researchers' definitions of market orientation can be represented using the following general equation:

$$MO = [F_1 \times I_1] + [F_2 \times I_2] + ... + [F_n \times I_n] \qquad (1)$$

where, MO represents the strength of the market orientation of the firm; each of the F_i ($i = 1, 2, ... n$) represent the different potential focuses available, and; each of the I_i represent the importance attached by the researcher to the associated F_i, and can take on a value of 0 (i.e., the specific level of focus does not contribute to market orientation's domain) or of 1 (i.e., the specific level of focus contributes to market orientation's domain).

Thus, the equation to model Deshpandé, Farley and Webster's (1993) approach to the role of focuses in market orientation's definition is pre-specified in nature since we know that it will be:

$$MO = [F_1 \times 1] + [F_2 \times 0] + [F_3 \times 0] + [F_4 \times 0] + ... + [F_n \times 0] \qquad (2)$$

where F_1 = customer focus and, say, F_2 = competitor focus, F_3 = coordination, F_4 = supplier focus, and so on. Here, it can be seen that Deshpandé, Farley and Webster's approach defines a firm's level of market orientation by that firm's level of customer focus only. Thus, for Deshpandé, Farley and Webster, when $i > 1$, $I_i = 0$. Narver and Slater's (1990) equation, although pre-specified, is different:

$$MO = [F_1 \times 1] + [F_2 \times 1] + [F_3 \times 1] + [F_4 \times 0] + ... + [F_n \times 0] \qquad (3)$$

where F_1 = customer focus, F_2 = competitor focus, F_3 = co-ordination and, say, F_4 = supplier focus, and so on. Here, when $i > 3$, $I_i = 0$.

It can be seen that equations (2) and (3) are not equal. That is, since researchers have also tended to make the assumption that the various F_is can vary independently, such that the correlation between any two F_i can take on any value between −1 and +1, the degree of market orientation implied in equation (2) for firm A is different from the degree of market orientation implied in equation (3) for firm A. Viewed from this fairly simplistic algebraic perspective, it becomes obvious that market orientation studies adopting different focuses are highly likely to come to different conclusions about firm A's level of market orientation.

Kohli and Jaworski's (1990) conceptualization is interesting to look at from this perspective. Kohli and Jaworski did not put any parameters on market orientation's focuses. That is, their definition of market orientation is pre-specified to the extent that it implies that $I_i = 1$ for all i up to $i = n$: a market-oriented firm will be interested in all exogenous market factors – not just one or two (Matsuno,

Mentzer and Rentz, 2000). The way they were able to do this is by *not* including specific focuses in market orientation's definition. To do so would have been impractical from a definitional perspective, since the absolute number of focuses that would need to be specified in market orientation's definition would be very great indeed (i.e., although no-one has attempted to put a specific value to n, it is probably safe to say that it is very large). As a result, it is difficult to write an equation that provides a comprehensive representation of Kohli and Jaworski's (1990) all-inclusive view of market orientation's domain, because there are so many facets that should be included. A part of the equation, however, might look something like this:

$$MO = F_1 + F_2 + F_3 + F_4 + F_5 + F_6 + F_7 + F_8 + F_9 + F_{10} + F_{11} + F_{12} + \ldots + F_n \qquad (4)$$

where, F_1 = a customer focus; F_2 = a competitor focus; F_3 = a supplier focus; F_4 = a technology focus; F_5 = a distributor focus; F_6 = a focus on businesses in other industry sectors; F_7 = a focus on societal changes; F_8 = a governmental focus; F_9 = a regulatory focus; F_{10} = a focus on consumer groups; F_{11} = a focus on unions; F_{12} = a focus on economic changes; and so on. Here, there was no need to include the I_is since they all have an implied value of 1. In this respect, the instrument Jaworski and Kohli (1993) developed to measure market-oriented behaviours was intended to reflect their definitional approach, since it contained questions aimed at capturing the *essence* of firms' market-oriented behaviours by sampling across a broad range of exogenous markets factors, rather than specifically focusing on individual potential focuses (see Matsuno, Mentzer and Rentz, 2000).

An alternative to these pre-specified approaches, one that has not been discussed in the marketing literature in any depth before, is to let the I_i vary depending on the relevance of the F_i for the firm in question. Under this 'conditional' approach, since all organizations operate in environments that vary from firm to firm, the importance of the various potential focuses are likely to vary from firm to firm.

Thus, under this approach, if F_1 = customer orientation, and customers are an important variable in a firm's environment, then I_1 = 1; on the other hand, if F_4 = supplier orientation, but suppliers are an unimportant factor in a firm's business operations, then I_4 = 0.

The conditional perspective to market orientation's definition differs conceptually from the pre-specified approaches. Under the latter, a firm cannot be market-oriented if it fails to have a strong competitor focus, for example (*cf.* Narver and Slater, 1990). However, under the conditional approach, it is theoretically possible for a firm to be market-oriented and not to have a strong competitor focus – provided that competitive forces do not play an important role in that firm's business environment (*cf.* Dawes, 2000). Viewed from this conditional perspective, the domain of market orientation can be thought of as being broad in its entirety, but narrower for specific businesses/industries. Thus, a market-oriented firm will be one that has an appropriate balance of various exogenous orientations. At any particular industry level of analysis, however, only specific exogenous orientations will be necessary. Unlike the pre-specified approaches, the qualitative focuses that define a market orientation in one industry or context may not equally define a market orientation in another industry or context; for example, some firms are less likely to require a competitor or supplier orientation than others (for empirical support of this basic idea see, e.g., Greenley, 1995b; Mavondo and Conduit 2000; Oczkowski and Farrell, 1998).

Which perspective is the most appropriate, the pre-specified or the conditional? Certainly, the pre-specified approaches have shortcomings and, from a practical perspective, are somewhat limiting. First, researchers fail to agree on which focuses should be pre-specified – that is, which focuses should or should not define market orientation. Second, even adopting Kohli and Jaworski's (1990) all-inclusive perspective, the pre-specified approach fails to acknowledge that certain aspects of firms' market environments may differ in relevance for firms in different industries. Consequently, Kohli and Jaworski's (1990) approach implies that, notwithstanding the environment in which a firm operates, if that firm wishes to be market-oriented, it should channel its resources into the development of a multitude of focuses, regardless of their relevance. The conditional approach is more flexible and accommodating for businesses operating in differing settings. Here, a firm wishing to increase its market orientation level need only concern itself with improvements which are relevant to its business context.

Furthermore, the use of different pre-specified definitions also impacts on theory testing and knowledge accumulation. For example, the inclusion of different focuses in market orientation's definitions means that the measures based on these definitions are not capturing exactly the same thing. Comparisons of such studies are therefore problematic. In addition, these different definitions cannot all be correct. Thus, it is likely that Narver and Slater's (1990) three levels of focus (customer focus, competitor focus, and interfunctional coordination) may not accurately represent the focuses which are necessary to capture the levels of market orientation of all firms. The situation is the same for studies that have included some focuses in and excluded other focuses from market orientation's definition (e.g., Dawes, 2000; Deng and Dart, 1994; Deshpandé, Farley and Webster, 1993; Gray *et al.*, 1998; Kumar, Subramanian and Yauger, 1998; Langerak, 2001). Empirical studies based on these definitional approaches may not provide the most accurate of representations of market orientation's system of relationships with other variables.

Context-specific Versus Context-free Approaches

If the conditional perspective holds promise, as seems to be the case, how can researchers and practitioners progress and make use of it? Two approaches to concept specification need to be considered in this respect.

Firstly, an implication of the conditional approach is that the qualitative focuses comprising market orientation are likely to differ across industries and business settings. Consequently, in order for the definition of market orientation to be generalizable across these settings, the concept needs to be defined in a fairly context-free manner. Definitions which contain context-specific focuses (e.g., reference to competitor, technology, or supplier orientations) will not be meaningfully transferable across industries and settings. Taking market-oriented behaviours as the example, a context-free definition could be: a firm which behaves in a market-oriented way is one which (a) generates market information relevant to the business's market operations and, hence, the provision of superior value to customers, (b) disseminates that information to relevant decision makers, and (c) designs and implements appropriate responses to that market information. This definition recognizes that the purpose of the market-oriented activities is the creation of superior customer value. Furthermore, the definition clearly identifies the focus of a firm's behaviours as being those elements of the exogenous market environment which are important in terms of the firm's ability to succeed in its customer value-creating activities. However, no mention is made of the specific types of exogenous factors which are important, since they may differ across business settings.

In this regard, the definition provided is something of an abstraction of market-oriented behaviour. Since measures of the latter based on this definition would also be context-free, these measures could be applied, and would allow theory testing, in any business setting. Furthermore (and unlike differing pre-specified approaches), these studies should be comparable, since the underlying conceptual meaning of the market orientation concept being applied to firms is the same regardless of the setting in which it is applied. That is, it is possible for a firm with a monopoly to be just as (or even more) market-oriented as a firm with many competitors since the specific concept of *competitor* orientation would not be incorporated as a dimension when measuring these firms' market orientation levels. Rather, the measures would simply capture whether the firms in question generate, disseminate and respond to that information which is relevant to the creation of superior customer value in their markets.

Secondly, as it stands, the abstract nature of the definition of market-oriented behaviour described above means that its practical utility on a firm-by-firm basis is more limited. Consequently, when using the definition to diagnose elements of market orientation in need of improvement within an individual organization, contextual focuses would need to be explicitly recognized. For example, consider firm A, which operates in a industry with changing customer dynamics, and where competitors' and suppliers' activities play the critical role in determining that firm's ability to provide superior value to customers. If firm A's management wish to leverage market orientation to their advantage, they must first identify the critical environmental forces impacting on their customer value-creating capabilities. If they do a good job of this, then they should end up with a conceptualization of market orientation couched in terms of firm A's customer, competitor and supplier-oriented values, norms, artifacts and/or behaviours. This would provide firm A's management with a platform for benchmarking and for the development of organizational change programmes.

In summary, I am not suggesting that an abstracted or context-free definition of market orientation should supercede context-specific definitions in all situations. Rather, I advocate the use of a context-free definition of market orientation for theory testing purposes. To do otherwise is to invite trouble in the form of inappropriate applications of the market orientation concept, inaccurate measurement of market orientation, and the drawing of incorrect conclusions concerning market orientation's system of relationships with other important variables. Furthermore, if an all-inclusive conceptualization of market orientation is adopted (i.e., similar to that of Kohli and Jaworski, 1990), the practical relevance of market orientation is reduced considerably for many organizations and businesses. On the other hand, when viewed from the perspective of manipulating and/or benchmarking market orientation within firms, managers need more information than is provided by a context-free definition. Here, for different firms, it is likely that different qualitative focuses will need to be included in market orientation's domain. It should be remembered, of course, that both the context-free and context-specific definitional approaches are, conceptually speaking, one and the same, since the context-free definition encapsulates *all* the multiple qualitatively distinct meanings of market orientation that arise when one starts to think about specific business environments.

Level of Analysis

A more subtle source of differentiation in market orientation's meaning has occurred over time as researchers have applied the construct at various different organizational levels. Thus, some studies have adopted more of a macro-level perspective, treating market orientation as a phenomenon that is applicable to the whole organization. Other studies have adopted various different micro-levels of analysis, treating market orientation as a phenomenon that occurs at various different sub-levels within the firm.

Macro-level Versus Micro-level Considerations

At the highest level of aggregation, market orientation has been described as a macro-level concept. Implicit to these descriptions is the assumption that it makes sense to describe the whole organization or corporation in terms of its level of market orientation. For example, Felton (1959) described the marketing concept (which may be considered to be a major driver of market orientation) as being a corporate state of mind. For Hooley, Lynch and Shepherd (1990, p. 14), market orientation is 'a unifying corporate culture', a guiding philosophy for the whole organization. Webster (1992) placed the responsibility for market orientation at the corporate level, while Wong and Saunders (1993) discussed market orientation's impact on corporate success. This macro-level perspective also seems implicit in Kohli and Jaworski's (1990, pp. 1 and 3; italics added) definition of the market orientation concept: 'a *market-oriented organization* is one whose actions are consistent with the marketing concept . . . a market orientation refers to the *organizationwide* generation, dissemination, and responsiveness to market intelligence'.

Underlying these descriptions seems to be the assumption that market orientation is pervasive or consistent across the unit of analysis being described – in this case, the whole corporation. Indeed, Kohli and Jaworski (1990) were insistent on this idea. Harris (1998, p. 361) also appears to provide support for this, arguing that 'a market-oriented culture should be conceptualised as a subculture which dominates over conflicting subcultures'. Thus, although various subcultures may exist within a market-oriented firm, they assume a minor role – market-oriented values, norms, artifacts, and behaviours are prominent across the firm.

Can these notions of market orientation as a pervasive corporate culture be reconciled with the possibility that in some organizations, different divisions or strategic business units (SBUs) may have different levels of market orientation? It appears so. For example, although Greenley (1995a, p. 5) measured an 'overall market orientation' concept at the corporate level (i.e., macro-level), his approach was not necessarily founded on the notion that market orientation is a pervasive culture that is invariant across the whole of the firm: no mention was made of an assumption of this kind. Rather, Greenley's approach can be interpreted as one that advocates consideration of a company's market-oriented values, beliefs and activities 'aggregated' across the corporation. From the latter perspective, it is meaningful to examine the organization as a whole in terms of, say, the broad degree to which its market information response activities are market-oriented, the degree to which the marketing concept acts as a guiding business philosophy across divisions and SBUs, or whether divisions and SBUs are coordinated in terms of strategic goals and activities. Thus, Greenley was interested in assessing the whole organization in terms of its degree of market orientation: whether market orientation levels varied across subdivisions within the firm or was pervasive across business units was not relevant.

However, Kohli and Jaworski's (1990) view that market orientation must be pervasive within an organization meant that their conceptualization of the concept was limited in its applicability. Seemingly in contradiction with their original stance, they argued that 'the appropriate unit of analysis appears to be the strategic business unit rather than the corporation because different SBUs of a corporation are likely to be market oriented to different degrees' (Kohli and Jaworski, 1990, p. 6). Thus, for Kohli and Jaworski, a whole organization could *not* be described in terms of its market orientation (because the latter may differ across the company's various SBUs or divisions): however, it was appropriate to discuss the market orientation of an individual SBU (presumably because market orientation was considered pervasive within the latter). Of course, the fault with Kohli and Jaworski's (1990) argument is that the consistency of market orientation levels within SBUs can also be called into question. Thus, applying Kohli and Jaworski's logic within an SBU, one could just as easily state that the appropriate unit of analysis is departmental rather than across the SBU, because different departments within an SBU are likely to be market-oriented to different degrees. The logic can then be applied again: the appropriate unit of analysis appears to be occupational rather than departmental, because people with different occupations within the same department are likely to be market-oriented to different degrees. The regress goes on, with the argument continually suggesting that alternative or more fine-grained perspectives of market-orientation are most appropriate.

How far can the situation be taken? Certainly, since market orientation is cultural in nature (i.e., values, norms, artifacts, and behaviours), there are many internally derived organizational subcultures to which it could be applied. For example, subcultures can be hierarchical (e.g., managers versus employees), they can be departmental (e.g., marketing versus R&D), they can be occupational (e.g., key account executives versus telesales employees – all of whom could reside within a sales department), they can be task-specific (domestic marketing employees versus export marketing employees), they can be geographic (from plant to plant), or even ethnic (ethnic grouping within the company). Some researchers have taken this to its logical conclusion, and have studied market orientation at an individual employee-level of analysis (see Kennedy, Lask and Goolsby, 2002; Strieter, Celuch and Kasouf, 1999) – since each employee within the firm is likely to have a different view of the organizational culture. Any of these cultural perspectives can serve as a level of analysis for market orientation, and all can be applied within a single SBU.

Furthermore, firms' levels of market orientation can vary, not just across subcultures within the firm, but also according to other criteria. Specifically, a single firm (or subculture within a firm) might vary across its markets in terms of its degree of market orientation depending on, for instance, the markets' relative growth or profit potentials, the markets' relative competitive conditions, or the markets' geographic locations. Similarly, a firm's market orientation levels may well differ across customers within a single market.

Very fine-grained levels of analysis now become possible: for instance, an individual within the firm might have different levels of market orientation in different product markets and may be more or less market-oriented towards different customers within each of those markets. Thus, for example, it becomes possible to combine an individual employee level of analysis with an individual customer level of analysis.

Clearly, we can see that no matter what level of analysis adopted when describing market orientation (e.g., corporate, SBU, departmental) some form of aggregation is required across units that may differ from each other in their levels of market orientation (e.g., aggregation across individual employees). This kind of aggregation was explicitly what Kohli and Jaworski (1990) were trying to avoid when they recommended the SBU as the appropriate focus for study. It seems, therefore, that we can safely reject Kohli and Jaworski's suggestion that *the* appropriate level of analysis is the SBU.

Theory Development and Knowledge Accumulation Issues

What, then, is the correct level of analysis? This is an inappropriate question. It makes as much sense to conceptualize market orientation at the corporate level as it does to conceptualize the concept at the SBU level or the export market level, or any other level that is of specific interest to a researcher. What should determine researchers' conceptualizations of market orientation is not some arbitrary notion that the concept exists only at some pre-specified level (e.g., the corporate or SBU level). Rather, researchers should choose their level of analysis depending on their research needs. As a result of this kind of reasoning, it can be seen that there are implications for theory building and knowledge accumulation.

First, in some cases, it is difficult to interpret study findings since the variables examined were conceptualized at different levels of analysis; as a consequence, the practical relevance and meaning one can attribute to empirically-derived relationships between these variables is questionable. For example, when examining the role of market orientation in driving export success, it is clear that the values, norms, artifacts and behaviours which are held and take place within the exporting function of the firm are most influential in determining export performance. Relative to a firm's export marketing activities, its domestic marketing activities are likely to play only a minor role in determining export business outcomes. Furthermore, many firms have very different levels of market orientation in their domestic markets relative to their export markets (Hooley and Newcomb, 1983; Rose and Shoham, 2002). Therefore, in light of the export-specific nature of the study objectives, it would make little sense to measure market orientation at a level which does not inform the researcher about businesses' market orientation levels in their export operations. Consequently, the most appropriate way of examining market orientation's relationship with export success would be to focus specifically on firms' exporting operations, and to exclude references to market orientation in firms' domestic markets.

Interestingly, several studies have not adhered to this principle. For example, Kwon and Hu (2000), Prasad, Ramamurthy and Naidu (2001), and Rose and Shoham (2002) have all attempted to identify market orientation's direct and/or indirect linkages with export success, and the possible environmental moderators of these relationships. However, in these studies, market orientation was measured at an organizational level (i.e., market orientation was assessed across firms' export *and* domestic markets). Consequently, the measures of market orientation used were unlikely to capture accurately firms' levels of market orientation in their export operations. As things stand, then, substantive insights of use to export practitioners are compromised by the fact that these studies' levels of analysis were not export-specific; their assessments of market orientation were contaminated by inclusion of reference to firms' domestic market orientations. Thus, Rose and Shoham's (2002) finding that the relationship between firms' levels of 'overall market orientation' (p. 218) and their levels of export success are positive and significant, regardless of environmental conditions facing those firms (e.g., competitive intensity, customer dynamism, and so on), does not actually furnish us with information which can be used with confidence to direct action and policy within firms' exporting operations. Only studies which explicitly examine market orientation at the 'exporting level' can provide this kind of information.

Second, the examination of market orientation at different levels of analysis (i.e., at levels other than at the SBU level) compromises researchers' ability to compare across studies (Uncles, 2000). However, it also opens up the possibility of new theoretical insights, since market orientation's system of relationships with other variables might not be consistent across levels of analysis. For example, Greenley's (1995a) study of UK firms and Slater and Narver's (1994) study of US-based SBUs were almost identical except for the fact that they measured market orientation at different levels of analysis within the firm (corporate and SBU levels respectively). However, the empirical findings resulting from these two studies were very different. For instance, Greenley (1995a, p. 10) concluded that his findings imply 'that market orientation may be uneconomic in some market environments'. In direct contradiction, Slater and Narver (1994, p. 53) concluded their empirical study by stating that 'businesses that are more market oriented are best positioned for success under *any* environmental conditions'.

Currently, one can only speculate as to why these differences in findings were observed. However, one possible explanation is that the relationship between market orientation and performance may differ depending on the level of analysis which one adopts. Perhaps aspects of market orientation at the corporate level (e.g., cooperation between SBUs) are a good thing, but only to a point (e.g., perhaps some degree of competition between SBUs is healthy), and this is what Greenley's findings were picking up. However, Slater and Narver's (1994) approach ignored such macro-level considerations since market orientation issues at the inter-SBU level were excluded from their study. Thus, for instance, coordination was conceptualized as a variable that pertained only to interdepartmental issues within a single SBU (unlike Greenley's (1995a) conceptualization, which pertained more generally to coordination at the corporate or inter-SBU level). Hence, Slater and Narver's (1994) finding that market orientation is always a good thing might be specific to the intra-SBU level of analysis, where, for example, competing business objectives and a lack of coordination in market-oriented activities may compromise performance.

Third, and following on from the above point, each level of analysis is likely to require the consideration of its own context-specific factors which may alter or reshape a theory which has been developed from the perspective of an alternative level of analysis. For instance, a model of the antecedents to firms' market-oriented behaviours was developed and tested by Jaworski and Kohli (1993). Since Jaworski and Kohli were not explicitly interested in studying firms' behaviours in their export markets, however, it is not surprising that their model had an implied domestic market bias. Consequently, from the perspective of exporting firms, Jaworski and Kohli's (1993) model was incomplete, since it excluded consideration of antecedent factors unique to firms with exporting operations (e.g., export coordination, export dependence, and export experience). Since the latter do not relate directly to equivalent variables within a purely domestic marketing context, it was only when the unique situation faced by exporters was explicitly recognized that these export-specific factors were identified and modelled (Cadogan et al., 2001).

Fourth, in some cases, the consideration of certain levels of analysis may require the development of a whole new theoretical framework. For instance, recent advances in marketing theory have demonstrated that market orientation can be conceptualized at an internal marketing level of analysis, as well as with a traditional external market focus (Lings, 2002). From this internal market orientation perspective, employees are viewed as internal customers of the firm, consuming wages and non-financial organizational offerings in return for physical and mental effort. The logic of the internal market orientation approach is based on the assumption that the more satisfied, committed and motivated staff are, the more effective a firm will be in its pursuit of an external market orientation, and the more successful it will be in its attempts to create superior value for external customers. Lings (2002) has argued that internal market-oriented behaviours are legitimate components of the market orientation concept. However, the antecedents and consequences of an internal market orientation are likely to be very different from those of an external market orientation. New theories will need to be developed as a result.

Conclusions

In this chapter, I have attempted to provide a broad-based picture of the ways in which market orientation has been defined. I have also attempted to impose some kind of structure on these definitions, dividing the latter into issues concerning market orientation's (a) cultural content, (b) multiple focuses, and (c) multiple levels of analysis. As a consequence, I hope that readers will come to a greater appreciation of market orientation's domain. I am also hopeful that I have provided a platform from which significant strides forward can be achieved both in terms of developing a greater understanding of market orientation's antecedents and consequences, and in terms of learning how market orientation can be leveraged to businesses' advantage. The conclusions to be drawn from my arguments are as follows.

First, I have suggested that market orientation is best conceptualized as a multifaceted cultural concept. That is, firms can vary in terms of their levels of market-oriented values, norms, artifacts and behaviours. Furthermore, since each of these cultural facets differs conceptually, and can vary independently from each other, it no longer makes sense to discuss market orientation as though it were a single concept. Rather, each type of market orientation merits attention in its own right. The benefit of this approach is that it provides a framework to guide knowledge accumulation, and ensures that inappropriate study comparisons and invalid generalizations do not occur. Consequently, a much richer and more complete appreciation of market orientation and its system of relationships with other variables can be developed.

I have also demonstrated that market orientation (whether defined at the level of values, norms, artifacts or behaviours) can be defined legitimately both in context-specific terms and in context-free terms. For theory testing purposes, I advocate the adoption of a context-free approach to market orientation's definition, since this should help ensure that the concept has the same meaning across business settings, and allows cross-study comparisons. From a practical perspective, however, the specific combination of focuses relevant to different business and industry settings will differ across those settings. Consequently, the qualitative dimensions that may characterize a market orientation for one business are unlikely to reflect accurately the market orientation of another business operating under differing environmental conditions. The implication is that businesses in different industries are likely to require their own industry-specific conceptualizations of market orientation; these conceptualisations are likely to comprise of very different focuses. One general outcome of my analysis in this respect has been to show that market orientation definitions that are based on a limited number of very specific focuses – such as Narver and Slater's (1990) customer orientation, competitor orientation and interfunctional coordination dimensions – are unlikely to provide valid representations of what it means to be market-oriented for all firms. Similarly, all-inclusive approaches, such as Kohli and Jaworski's (1990), are of limited practical value to many organizations.

Finally, I have argued that the level at which market orientation is conceptualized may have an important impact on our understanding of market orientation's system of relationships with other variables. Consequently, in terms of future studies, whether practical or theoretical in nature, level of analysis issues need to be considered carefully since validity can be compromised if an inappropriate level of analysis is chosen. In this respect, care must be taken when generalizing across studies which have adopted different levels of analysis, since the variables and/or relationships studied may lose much of their substantive meaning if inappropriately extended beyond their domain. This is especially important when making recommendations to management, since the practical implications arising from being market-oriented, or for leveraging market orientation, may differ substantively across different levels of analysis.

CHAPTER 7

Relationship marketing

Lisa O'Malley

Although relationships have been at the heart of marketing in an informal way since the first stirrings of commerce (Gummesson, 1994), as a formal approach to marketing relationship marketing is more recent. Specifically, in the late 1970s and early 1980s researchers in industrial, international and services contexts recognized the limitations of the dominant mix management (4P) view of marketing and began to articulate a radically different approach.

Marketing in the twenty-first century has been heavily influenced by the movement away from transactions and towards relationships, begun in the late 1970s and popularized in the early to mid 1990s. Although spanning different marketing contexts and incorporating diverse theories and concepts, this movement became known as relationship marketing (RM). By the mid 1990s, this new relationship-oriented approach was hailed as a paradigm shift both in the theory and the practice of marketing (Grönroos, 1994). RM offers a more holistic approach to understanding market dynamics and to developing and implementing marketing strategies. Its ideological emphasis is on the creation of greater value for consumers and organizations through fostering cooperative and collaborative partnerships (Tzokas and Saren, 1997).

There now exists a substantial literature on RM. Despite this, Sheaves and Barnes (1996) highlight that a fundamental flaw in the emerging literature is the lack of consideration given to what actually constitutes a relationship. As such, there exists a plethora of definitions and the choice between them is often a matter of convenience or researcher orientation. While these definitions are not necessarily mutually exclusive, they do capture different aspects and focus attention in quite diverse ways. For the purposes of this chapter, the definition employed is·

> [T]he identification, specification, initiation, maintenance and (where appropriate) dissolution of long-term relationships with key customers and other parties, through mutual exchange, fulfilment of promises and adherence to relationship norms in order to satisfy the objectives and enhance the experience of the parties concerned.
>
> (O'Malley, Patterson and Evans, 1997, p. 543)

Although initially developed as a means of combating the specific conditions prevalent in high-contact service and industrial marketing contexts, RM has recently seen its domain widened to include the arena of fast-moving consumer goods (FMCG) markets and relational approaches are becoming popular across the marketing spectrum. Such popularity does have attendant disadvantages. In particular, the early consistency in respect of subject matter has been lost to some degree, and understandings of RM vary widely.

This chapter provides an overview of the key themes in relationship marketing. The chapter is divided into several sections. First, a general overview of the origins and development of RM is provided. Here we highlight key research findings relating to the nature and management of relationships between organizations and their customers. Second, the chapter reviews RM in consumer markets paying particular attention to the motivation for relationship development by both consumers and organizations. Third, the chapter considers practical issues regarding the implementation of RM. Fourth, problems with RM in consumer markets are considered in some depth. Finally, the chapter offers some practical suggestions as to how the implementation of RM in consumer markets might be improved.

Origins of RM

RM emerged in the latter part of the 1970s and early 1980s as an alternative approach to understanding markets than that which had dominated in the previous 30 years (i.e., the mix management paradigm). In the early years RM enjoyed parallel development within services and industrial marketing.

The unique characteristics of services (inseparability, intangibility, heterogeneity and perishability), demanded that services marketers develop a different approach. Indeed, the dominant mix management paradigm was criticized for offering 'no guidance, no terminology, or practical rules for services' (Shostack, 1977, p. 73). Initially services marketers attempted to enhance the dominant paradigm through the incorporation of additional elements – people, processes and physical evidence (see Booms and Bitner, 1981) – but this approach proved less compelling than the development of strategies uniquely tuned to the important service characteristics outlined above. Service-based marketing strategies had to recognize and deal with the importance of people (customers and buyers) in the service delivery experience, and this led to a focus on understanding and managing the interaction between buyers and sellers (Grönroos, 1978). This new approach to services marketing became known as 'relationship marketing' (Berry, 1983) and represented an approach to developing formal, ongoing relationships between buyers and sellers in order to enhance customer retention (Lovelock, 1983). Today, the term RM is applied to any marketing situation where relationships are deemed important.

At the same time as services researchers were moving toward a relational approach, colleagues in interorganizational (business-to-business) marketing were independently coming to the same conclusions. Specifically, by the late 1970s European researchers working as part of the IMP Group recognized the centrality of relationships in business. Their understanding of the role and development of such relationships is captured in the interaction approach (Håkansson, 1982). Essentially, this conceptualizes relationships as the outcome of interaction between buyers and sellers. Within this view, both buyers and sellers are active, and both have similar roles in forming, developing and maintaining relationships (Ford, 1980; Håkansson, 1982). This is an important point because it had been previously assumed that buyers were generally passive, and, indeed, this remains an implicit assumption of the mix management paradigm (O'Malley and Patterson, 1998; Grönroos, 1994).

The focus on relationships in interorganizational exchange was not solely European-based. Although some work was conducted in the early 1980s in the USA (Anderson and Narus, 1984), it was really in the late 1980s and early 1990s that the relationship perspective came to dominate research and practice there. US interest was sparked by the success of the Japanese business format (with its emphasis on relationships) in America (Spekman, 1988; Webster, 1992). Furthermore, Dwyer, Schurr and Oh (1987) offered a compelling and insightful model of relationship development that presented clear guidelines for creating and managing customer relationships.

In contrast to the European researchers' focus on understanding relationships through qualitative research, American researchers were more concerned with articulating and testing the antecedents and consequences of business relationships. While their European counterparts intuitively relied upon an understanding of business relationships as a special case of interpersonal relationship, US researchers explicitly adopted social exchange theory (SET) as their conceptual underpinning. This resulted in a conceptualization of relationships as the outcome of increasing bilateral trust and commitment. Within this view, mutual goals are achieved through the creation and maintenance of relationships. Cooperation and communication are central to relationship development because they lead to trust which, in turn, leads to greater levels of commitment, cooperation and communication.

This brief historical review highlights that researchers operating in services and interorganizational marketing contexts independently came to believe that the fostering of long-term relationships underpinned successful exchange. Although these representations of RM did develop independently, a degree of commonality did emerge. This included:

- A focus on the interaction between buyer and seller.
- A distinction between transactions (one-off exchanges with no history and no future) and relationships.
- An understanding of those relationships in terms of deepening trust and commitment.
- A recognition that relationships develop and change over time (relationship life-cycle) and, that different strategies may be required at each stage.

Buyer–Seller Interaction and Relationships

Extant research on the mechanisms associated with relationship development suggest that relationships:

- Develop between people
- Develop as a result of extended or intimate interaction

Although buyer and seller interaction is distinguishable from other types of human interaction because it is purposive and highly task-oriented (Solomon *et al.*, 1985), interpersonal contact is still at the heart of a large proportion of relationships, particularly those relationships that are recognized and valued by all relational partners (see Sheaves and Barnes, 1996). As a result, researchers have paid close attention to the interaction between clients and providers (Grönroos, 1983) and on the service encounter generally (Solomon *et al.*, 1985). Indeed, the very nature of exchange in services forces buyers into intimate contact with sellers (Grönroos, 1978), thereby emphasizing the importance of people in service delivery and service quality (Czepiel, 1990). The emphasis on interpersonal interaction within RM can be further understood by distinguishing between the functional quality of the service encounter versus the technical quality experienced (Figure 7.1) (Grönroos, 1990; Gummesson, 1987).

Because more and more organizations achieve an acceptable level of technical quality, competition today is increasingly centred upon the delivery of higher functional (or interaction) quality. Interestingly, it appears that an organization is more likely to exceed customers' prior expectations (as a result of previous experience, word-of-mouth, etc.) through attempts to enhance functional rather than technical quality. Thus, many of today's organizations focus on improving customers' interaction experience through training, empowering and rewarding their staff appropriately.

Interestingly, interaction not only impacts upon a customer's perceptions of, and satisfaction with, the service (Grönroos, 1983; 1994), but also facilitates the development of social bonds (Berry and Parasuraman, 1991; Crosby and Stephens, 1987). Thus, deliberate attempts to foster customer relationships represent a viable and appropriate marketing strategy (Lovelock, 1983). However, even within a service context, it has been acknowledged that not all service encounters have the capacity to become relational. Indeed, some authors suggest that only

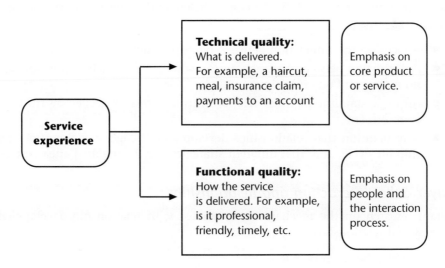

FIGURE 7.1 Technical and functional quality

those that are extended, emotive or intimate (Crosby, Evans and Cowles, 1990; Price, Arnould and Tierney, 1995) have such potential.

RM: Emphasis on Relationship Rather Than Transaction

Traditionally, marketing has focused on transactions rather than relationships. The archetype of a transaction is typical of the micro-economic worldview. It involves the exchange of money for some easily measured commodity. Thus, the identities of the actors are unimportant; indeed, they must be ignored or else relations creep in. This is embodied in Macneil's (1980, p. 60) definition of a transaction:

> Discreteness is the separating of a transaction from all else between the participants at the same time and before and after. Its pure form, never achieved in life, occurs when there is nothing else between the parties, never has been, and never will be.

The relational perspective goes beyond the one actor, given the goals perspective that has long dominated marketing. For example, the interaction approach popular among IMP researchers viewed a business purchase (transaction) as just 'a single *episode* among many in a *relationship* between the two companies' (Ford, 1997: p. xi). Thus, each purchase could only be understood within the context of that relationship.

In a relationship, the identity of the buyer and seller is of central importance, as is their history and the possibility of future exchange (see Dwyer, Schurr and Oh, 1987). However, despite recognizing the distinction between transactions and relationships 'most of the research and too many marketing strategies treat buyer-seller exchanges as discrete events, not as on-going relationships' (Dwyer, Schurr and Oh, 1987, p. 11). There has been some debate regarding the emphasis on relationships in all marketing contexts (particularly in mass consumer markets). This debate is best epitomized in the marketing-strategy continuum (Figure 7.2) (Grönroos, 1994).

Essentially, the marketing strategy continuum suggests that as one moves from left to right on the continuum, RM becomes more appropriate. Thus, the suggestion is that RM is most appropriate in services marketing, and to a lesser extent industrial marketing (where often extended interpersonal interaction occurs in order to facilitate exchange). The continuum further suggests that in consumer packaged goods the mix management paradigm remains the dominant

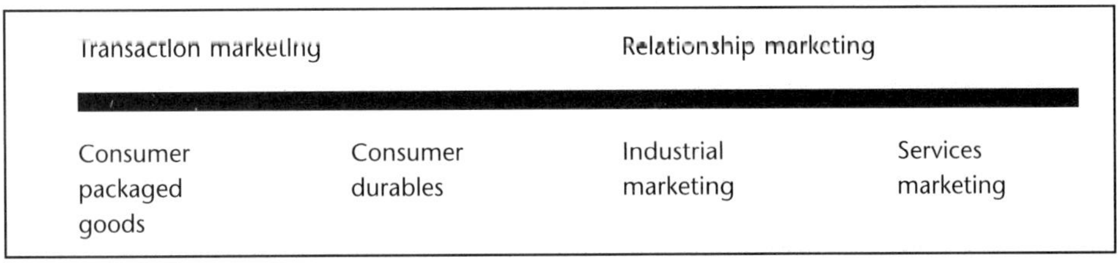

Transaction marketing		Relationship marketing	
Consumer packaged goods	Consumer durables	Industrial marketing	Services marketing

FIGURE 7.2 The marketing strategy continuum

perspective. This, Grönroos (1994) argues, is because the characteristics of consumer goods markets (particularly their size and anonymity) limit the applicability of a relational perspective. Grönroos' (1994) position is contested by numerous researchers and practitioners who suggest that RM has much to offer, even in consumer goods markets (Christy, Oliver and Penn, 1996; Copulsky and Wolf, 1990). Indeed, Grönroos (1996), contra to his earlier position now advocates the use of RM in consumer markets. This will be discussed in some detail later in this chapter. However, for now, it is sufficient to recognize that within the relational paradigm, relationships (and not transactions) become the appropriate unit of analysis.

Understanding Relationships

Relationships are often described in terms of increasing levels of trust and commitment, and in terms of the bonds that maintain the relationship. RM purports to be the marketing process that creates and manages successful relational exchanges. While marketing relationships are generally understood in terms of deepening trust and commitment, there are, in fact, a number of other important dimensions. For example, Wilson (1995) identifies 13 key relationship variables (Figure 7.3) that appear to underpin such success. Given the centrality of these issues in understanding and facilitating relational exchanges, some are discussed in more detail below.

Trust

Trust is the glue that holds a relationship together (Berry, 1995; Dwyer, Schurr and Oh, 1987; Moorman, Deshpandé and Zaltman, 1993). In the absence of trust, exchange becomes increasingly difficult because trust is central to all human interaction (Creed and Miles, 1996; Gundlach and Murphy, 1993; Morgan and Hunt, 1994; Tyler and Kramer, 1996). Indeed, given its significance to social and economic life, an entire academic school dedicated to the study of trust has

Trust	Social bonds
Commitment	Structural bonds
Cooperation	Summative constructs
Mutual goals	Shared technology
Interdependence/power imbalance	Non-retrievable investments
Performance satisfaction	Comparison level of alternatives
Adaptation	

FIGURE 7.3 Key relational constructs

emerged (see Gambetta, 1988). However, trust is a complex issue and, despite the extensive attention it has received, it remains elusive.

In marketing we generally understand trust as 'a willingness to rely on an exchange partner in whom one has confidence' (Moorman, Deshpandé and Zaltman, 1993, p. 82). This exchange partner may be an individual, for example, a sales representative (Schurr and Ozanne, 1985), an organization or something more abstract such as a quality symbol or brand. Put simply, we will engage in market exchanges when we trust (rely on or have confidence in) the word of an individual, organization or brand. According to Bowen and Shoemaker (1998) the fundamental building blocks of trust are:

- Achieving results
- Demonstrating concern
- Acting with integrity

Trust is variously viewed as a necessary antecedent to relational exchange (Morgan and Hunt, 1994), and as a psychological benefit of that exchange (Gwinner, Gremier and Bitner, 1998). A minimum level of trust is necessary for an individual to engage in exchange with a particular individual or organization, and, at the same time, trust in that individual or organization strengthens or weakens as a result of the exchange experience. Thus, the focus on trust appears to be relevant throughout the life of a relationship.

If one party to the relationship is seen to take advantage of a situation, or to act opportunistically, this undermines trust. This requires that organizations and their employees operate within the spirit of the law rather than simply adhering to its letter. Indeed, a trust-based relationship is a moral relationship rather than a contractual one, and ironically, trust is most necessary when contracts break down. Thus, service or product failure, or indeed any critical incident offers an outstanding opportunity to enhance trust.

Although trust is incredibly powerful in explaining exchange behaviour, it remains a troublesome concept. This is because trust is comprised of a global (attitudinal/affective) component and a specific situational one (Butler, 1991). That is, a person's ability or desire to trust the advice being given by, for example, a bank manager, will be influenced by their assessment of the integrity and expertise of that individual as well as their attitudes towards financial services providers in general. Individual organizations can attempt to foster trust through their communication, their behaviour, their staff training, and the extent to which employees are empowered and/or rewarded for behaving with integrity. However, as a result of the micro focus of many contemporary organizations, substantive general aspects of trust have been overlooked. For example, some professions (e.g., medical) appear to engender more trust than others (e.g., legal) and similarly, specific product markets have traditionally been viewed suspiciously (e.g., estate agents, second hand car salesmen).

Commitment

'The recognition that commitment is central to successful relationship marketing has triggered research on the factors that contribute to developing, maintaining and increasing commitment' (Geyskens *et al.*, 1996, p. 303). Commitment involves both behavioural and attitudinal dimensions and, in marketing, is typically associated with notions of solidarity and cohesion (Dwyer, Schurr and Oh, 1987). Moreover, without commitment, no relationship is believed to exist.

Relationship dissolution occurs when the levels of commitment to the relationship are questioned. In some cases the lack of commitment of one partner may be part of a deliberate strategy of withdrawal. In many others, however, the offending partner is not even aware of problems within the relationship. There may be a number of reasons for this. One possible explanation is that the expectations of one partner may have changed as a result of interaction or offers of interaction with other relational partners. An alternative explanation is that the relationship has become institutionalized. That is, routines exist and cease to be questioned, even though these routines are no longer relevant or appropriate. As Ford (1980, p. 51) explains, 'these institutional patterns of operation make it difficult for a company to assess its partner's real requirements and so it may appear less responsive or uncommitted to the relationship'.

Relationships are developed through interaction, cooperation and communication, with the latter referring to 'the formal as well as informal sharing of information or meaning between the distributor and the manufacturer firms' (Anderson and Narus, 1984, p. 66). The degree of communication and cooperation, in turn, signifies the level of commitment to the relationship (see Moorman, Deshpandé and Zaltman, 1993).

Bonds

Bonds are important elements in bringing buyers and sellers together in a relationship. Various different kinds of bonds exist and these can be more, or less, important, depending on the type of relationship. For example, Holmlund and Knock (1996) identify that both social and structural bonds can play an important role.

Social bonds relate to the degree of mutual personal friendship and liking shared by the buyer and seller (Wilson, 1995). These develop over time as a result of interaction (Gwinner, Gremier and Bitner, 1998; Turnbull, 1979) and are important in developing loyalty (Crosby and Stephens, 1987). Social bonds are believed to make individuals more tolerant of service failure (Crosby, Evans and Cowles, 1990) and to influence the amount of information shared and the motivation to resolve business conflicts. Ultimately, social bonds play an important role in the creation of the 'special status' that is so central to the recognition of a relationship (Barnes, 1997; Czepiel, 1990). Traditionally, social bonds have been effectively developed through corporate entertainment, playing golf, etc..

Structural bonds can be based on technical, knowledge, legal or economic elements, and can create a strong impediment to relationship termination (Wilson, 1995). For example, in a retail banking context, restricting the use of ATMs to a banks' own customers only is evidence of a structural bond (Holmlund and Knock, 1996). Equally, as information on customers builds up over time, and/ or, as the number of different services provided by an individual institution increases, the strength of the structural bond increases. This happens because the customer perceives it to be too difficult to switch suppliers. Legal and economic bonds 'emerge when contracts and other agreements are signed and when payments are made' (Holmlund and Knock, 1996, p. 290). For example, ensuring minimum tie-in periods for particular offers and charging fees if an account is closed within a specific period of time are examples of legal and economic bonds which ensure that customers are 'locked-in' (Barnes, 1994; 1995). In such situations, although customers appear to be loyal (i.e., remain with the organization), it is likely that they will switch suppliers at the earliest possible opportunity (Dick and Basu, 1994).

While both social and structural bonds are important elements in successful relationships, social bonds appear to represent a more sustainable strategy as they engender more positive emotions toward the service provider (Rowe and Barnes, 1998).

Relationship Lifecycle

In attempting to understand how relationships develop, a number of researchers have attempted to model the process (Table 7.1). These models are generally conceptualized as a series of sequential stages that characterize the move from transactional to relational exchange (Borys and Jemison, 1989; Dwyer, Schurr and Oh, 1987; Ford, 1980; Wilson, 1985). A key premise of these models is that participants assess the costs and benefits of increasing dependence and, due to increasing trust, move from transactional to relational exchange. It is also presumed that as the relationship develops, each party risks more but increases confidence that the other intends to respect promises. A broader conceptualization of the motivation for relationship development is captured in the concept of attraction (Dwyer, Schurr and Oh, 1987; Harris, O'Malley and Patterson, 2002). Essentially, attraction is defined as the extent to which relational partners perceive past, current, future or potential relational partners as appealing in terms of their ability to provide superior economic benefits, access to important resources and social compatibility.

In terms of the motivation for relationship development, it appears that the desire to reduce risk is highly significant. Thus, when the object of exchange is important and/or intangible the level of risk rises and the motivation for relationship development increases (see Sheth and Parvatiyar, 1995).

Personal contacts are frequently used as a mechanism or lubricant for relationship development (Turnbull, 1979) and the resulting relationship between buyer and seller is frequently long term, close and involves complex patterns of interactions. The match between supplier capability and customer need is further

TABLE 7.1 Process models of relationship development

Ford (1980)	Dwyer et al. (1987)	Borys and Jemison (1989)	Wilson (1995)
Pre-relationship stage	Awareness		Search and selection
Early stage	Exploration	Defining purpose	Defining purpose
Development stage	Expansion	Setting boundaries	Boundary setting
Long-term stage	Commitment	Value creation	Value creation
Final stage		Hybrid stability	Hybrid stability
	Dissolution		

accomplished by adaptation on the part of either or both of them (Håkansson, 1982). Indeed, both parties are likely to be involved in adaptations of their own processes or product technologies to accommodate the other, and neither party is likely to make unilateral changes to its activities without consultation or at least consideration of the reaction of their opposite number in the relationship.

Although the models of relationship development suggest a linear sequential development, with the implicit assumption that the relationship will progress so long as the appropriate strategy is successfully implemented, this is not always the case. As Ford (1980, p. 44) notes 'relationships can fail to develop or regress depending upon the actions of either party or of competing buyers and sellers'. As such, relationship maintenance is not inevitable (Dwyer, Schurr and Oh, 1987). Thus, the success of RM may depend not only on the particular strategy or implementation process, but also on the preferences of the individual customer (Christy, Oliver and Penn, 1996; Gwinner, Gremier and Bitner, 1998). That is, customers' orientations toward relationships are likely to differ (Jackson, 1985) and, therefore, relationship investment may only be worthwhile for certain customers (Bendapudi and Berry, 1997; Christy, Oliver and Penn, 1996; De Wulf, Odekerken-Schroder and Iacobucci, 2001). These are those customers who (a) represent a significant profit to the organization and (b) who are open and positive toward relational approaches by that organization. As such, factors influencing the maintenance and dissolution of relationships are deserving of greater research attention.

Recent Developments: RM in Consumer Markets

The consumer marketplace of the late 1980s and early 1990s was especially dynamic and competitive. According to McKenna (1991, p. 4) 'with so much choice for customers, companies face[d] the end of loyalty'. In such an environment, core product and service offerings were becoming increasingly similar (Rowe and Barnes, 1998) and customers were happy to switch suppliers at the slightest provocation (Holmlund and Knock, 1996; Sisodia and Wolfe, 2000). The economics of customer retention suggested that if customers could not be retained, marketing costs would soar while marketing successes would dwindle. Mass consumer marketers thus viewed RM, with its emphasis on customer retention through the development of mutually rewarding exchange relationships, very positively.

In its original conception the relationship developed between the customer and the organization (Dwyer, Schurr and Oh, 1987; Sheth and Parvatiyar, 1995). However, in recent years there have been increasing calls to consider relationships at the level of the brand (Aaker, 1997; Ambler, 1999; Blackston, 1992; Palmer, 1996). Furthermore, within a service context it may be more acceptable to consider relationship development at a more fundamental interpersonal level (as with customers and their personal bankers). Thus, it may be that the object of a relationship could be the organization, the brand, the product/service, or the individual service provider.

The roots of RM are metaphorical in nature (Hunt and Menon, 1995; O'Malley and Tynan, 1999; Sheaves and Barnes, 1996) and theory is heavily influenced by analogies with close personal relationships and, in particular, marriage (Levitt, 1983; Dwyer, Schurr and Oh, 1987). For example, according to Levitt (1983), 'the sale merely consummates the courtship. Then the marriage begins. How good the marriage is depends on how well the relationship is managed by the seller'. The marriage metaphor guided researchers toward the marriage literature (e.g, McCall, 1966) as a basis for conceptualizing and operationalizing their model of the process of relationship development. McCall's (1966, pp. 197–8) conceptualization of marriage in turn adopted a social exchange perspective: 'Marriage [is a] restrictive trade agreement. The two individuals agree to exchange only with one another, at least until such time as the balance of trade becomes unfavourable in terms of broader market considerations'. Thus, the very notion of a relationship has implications in terms of the values with which it is associated. Specifically, commercial relationships are compared with interpersonal relationships generally, and explicitly with close, personal and long-term relationships (i.e., marriage). Therefore, the values that we associate with marriage are immediately linked with commercial exchange (see Hunt and Menon, 1995; O'Malley and Tynan, 1999). Because relationships are viewed as central to the successful conduct of our daily lives, even in a commercial context, they become positively regarded. As a result, academic and professional literatures, and even customer communications, promote relationships that are argued to:

- Offer mutual benefit (to organizations and consumers).
- Involve mutual trust, commitment and loyalty.

This puts forth a view of relationships as embodying a shift in the practice of marketing 'from manipulation of the customer to genuine customer involvement; from telling and selling to communicating and sharing knowledge; from last-in-line function to corporate-credibility champion' (McKenna, 1991, p. 68). Thus, RM has come to symbolize helpful and fair approaches to marketing that offer win-win outcomes for both consumers and marketers.

Despite suggestions that RM was less applicable to consumer markets than to other contexts (Grönroos, 1994; Barnes, 1994; 1995) the possibilities of RM in this context (see Dwyer, Schurr and Oh, 1987) have resulted in its becoming the new orthodoxy in consumer marketing (Petrof, 1997). The acceptance of RM in consumer markets has progressed through a series of sequential phases (O'Malley and Tynan, 2000):

- Until the early to mid 1980s, the mix management paradigm was the dominant approach to facilitating exchange in mass markets and served its proponents well.
- The recognition of RM by mass marketers in the latter part of the 1980s came as a result of the perceived decline in the utility of mass marketing (and, in particular, advertising) within an increasingly competitive and dynamic marketplace. Furthermore, affordable computing now offered mass marketers the means by which they could identify previously anonymous customers and personalize interaction with them (Dwyer, Schurr and Oh, 1987).
- RM as an approach to consumer markets became increasingly popular in the early to mid 1990s as the possibilities afforded by direct and database

marketing increased exponentially (Evans, O'Malley and Patterson, 1996). Moreover, the rationale for relationship development was explicitly documented through the economics of customer retention (Reichheld and Sasser, 1990). Although in the early 1990s there was some suggestion that RM might not be appropriate in a consumer context (e.g., Barnes, 1994; 1995; Grönroos, 1994) marketing practitioners were already doing RM – often in the form of loyalty or retention programmes (see Sheth and Parvatiyar, 1995).

- RM became increasingly popular throughout the latter part of the 1990s, and is still hugely popular today. Because RM in mass consumer markets relies so heavily on technology developments, it has come to be synonymous with database marketing and more recently with customer relationship marketing (CRM).

RM now represents 'enlightened self-interest' (Sheth and Parvatiyar, 1995, p. 265) for contemporary marketers. Interestingly, the benefits to organizations are widely discussed but, unfortunately, the benefits that accrue to customers have received less attention.

Relational Benefits

There is much literature on the firm's perspective that highlights the benefits of RM in terms of:

- Increased customer satisfaction and loyalty, and, as a result, decreasing customer turnover (Czepiel, 1990; Reichheld and Sasser, 1990; Sheth and Parvatiyar, 1995).
- Decreased price sensitivity on the part of consumers (Dwyer, Schurr and Oh, 1987; Sheth and Parvatiyar, 1995).
- Greater opportunities for up-selling and cross-selling (Dwyer, Schurr and Oh, 1987).
- Increased spend per customer (Pine, Peppers and Rogers, 1995).
- Increasing incidences of positive word-of-mouth (Colgate and Stewart, 1998).

As a result of these many benefits, marketing strategies are more focused and, subsequently, more cost effective. Customers get what they want and marketers reap significant rewards through improved effectiveness and efficiency (Sheth and Parvatiyar, 1995). As a consequence, relationships have come to be regarded as an important source of competitive advantage in today's marketing environment.

The consumer's side of the equation has attracted less attention. Indeed, there has been an implicit assumption that consumers want relationships and that these relationships represent some value for them (see Barnes, 1994; 1995). However, it is unlikely that any organization can maintain relationships with all of its customers, nor indeed that all customers will want a very close relationship (Barnes, 1997). Thus, an organization must be selective regarding its choice of relational targets, and in terms of the resources deployed to establish that relationship. Moreover, when the benefits to customers have been discussed these have been largely anecdotal with few, if any, consumers consulted for their experiences or opinions (O'Malley and Tynan, 2000). Despite this, consumers are assumed to seek ongoing relationships when:

- they wish to reduce uncertainty, improve exchange efficiency and when switching costs are high (Dwyer, Schurr and Oh, 1987).
- they want to reduce risk (Sheth and Parvatiyar, 1995).
- they want to enhance value (Peterson, 1995).
- it facilitates their goal attainment (Bagozzi, 1995).
- they are highly involved in a product or service category (Dick and Basu, 1994; Gordon, McKeage and Fox, 1998; De Wulf, Odekerken-Schroder and Iacobucci, 2001).

Although tangible benefits (e.g., special prices, discounts, reward schemes) often appear to be a central component in a relationship, recent empirical evidence suggests that these benefits are not that highly valued by consumers (Gwinner, Gremier and Bitner, 1998). In contrast, confidence benefits appear to be most highly valued by consumers across all service types. These relate to 'the sense of reduced anxiety, faith in the trustworthiness of the service provider, reduced perceptions of anxiety and risk, and knowing what to expect' (Gwinner, Gremier and Bitner, 1998, p. 116). Fundamentally, 'confidence benefits are critical outcomes of long-term relationships' (Gwinner, Gremier and Bitner, 1998, p. 120). This notion of confidence benefit is very close to, if not the same as, trust.

As suggested earlier, social benefits are also important to consumers. These include being recognized by service providers and, in certain cases, developing friendships with them. Finally, there are special treatment benefits that include skipping queues, receiving special prices or promotional offers, etc.. Preferential treatment relates to 'a customer's perception of the extent to which a retailer treats and serves its regular customers better than its non-regular customers' (De Wulf, Odekerken-Schroder and Iacobucci, 2001, p. 35). Interestingly, these appear to be valued when they are truly individualized and when they are actually important (e.g., mechanic coming to collect the car when it won't start) as opposed to being invited to a promotional evening for special customers (Gwinner, Gremier and Bitner, 1998). In summary then, the following benefits are believed to accrue to consumers as a result of maintaining a relationship with a service firm:

- Tangible benefits (monetary and non-monetary)
- Confidence benefits (most valued)
- Social benefits
- Special treatment

However, while all benefits can result from relational engagement with any service firm, confidence benefits appear to be most valued (irrespective of type of service firm). Interestingly, both confidence and social benefits 'are received more often and rated as important in those services characterized by high employee–customer contact. They are received less and rated least important for moderate-contact, standardised-type services' (Gwinner, Gremier and Bitner, 1998, p. 110).

The preceding review might suggest that both organizations and consumers are motivated to develop and maintain relationships because the outcomes are highly valued by all relational partners (Tzokas and Saren, 1997). However, problems with implementation, particularly in consumer markets (see Fournier, Dobscha and Mick, 1998) have led to suggestions that RM is often perceived as little more than rhetoric (see Fitchett and McDonagh, 2000; O'Malley and Tynan, 2000; Smith and Higgins, 2000). It is, therefore, worth considering how the ideology of RM (mutuality, trust, commitment and cooperation) is operationalized by many organizations.

RM in Practice

Contemporary discussions of relationship-oriented strategies in the context of mass markets tends to employ the term CRM rather than the more traditional RM. CRM is variously understood as Customer Relationship Marketing and Customer Relationship Management. Although philosophically in line with RM, the focus within CRM is on technology. In particular, the interest lies in technology that attempts to manage all customer touch points and which facilitates the integration of database systems to provide a single picture of the customer (O'Malley and Mitussis, 2002; Peppers, Rogers and Dorf, 1999). This picture encompasses the customer's needs, preferences, buying behaviour and price sensitivity and allows the CRM business to focus on building customer retention and profitability. We will now discuss in more detail the type of relationships that are advocated in consumer markets and the role of technology in developing and maintaining relationships.

Levels of Relationship

Given that the very notion of an exchange relationship is not clearly understood, it is difficult to identify exactly what constitutes an RM strategy. At one level, understandings of RM are influenced by comparison with good marriages resulting in an emphasis on trust, commitment, etc.. This view is one that tends to dominate in communications with customers. An opposing view of relationships is that they are simply a 'managed context' (Stone, Woodcock and Wilson, 1996). That is, rather than the unit of management being a particular brand or transaction, the customer and their lifetime potential become the focus of management attention. As a result of these conflicting views, it is not surprising that there is an understanding of 'different levels of relationship' (Berry, 1995).

- *Level one relationships* are primarily based upon pricing incentives and other tangible rewards and are the weakest level at which a relationship exists.

Tangible rewards are believed to represent the basic level of a relationship (Berry, 1995) and these include discounts, gifts, frequent flyer miles, etc. to customers as a reward for their continued patronage (Peterson, 1995). Many loyalty schemes represent an RM strategy in this sense (Sheth and Parvatiyar, 1995). Loyalty programmes operate within a classical conditioning framework of reward and punishment. However, there is increasing recognition that loyalty schemes often achieve little more than spurious loyalty despite significantly raising costs (Barnes and Howlett, 1998; Dowling and Uncles, 1997; O'Brien and Jones, 1995; O'Malley, 1998). More recently, De Wulf, Odekerken-Schroder and Iacobucci (2001) found that the tangible rewards generated by such schemes do not boost customer retention. However, their absence was found to disappoint customers.

- *Level two relationships* relate to the social aspects of RM as exemplified by regular communication with customers, recognizing them, and referring to them by name during an interaction. Communication is central to relationship development and maintenance (Duncan and Moriarty, 1998). For the majority of relational programmes involving massive numbers of customers, direct mail is a hugely important element of the relational strategy (Dwyer, Schurr and Oh, 1987).

- *Level three relationships* offer structural solutions to customers' problems. Such solutions are 'designed into the service-delivery system rather than depending upon relationship-building skills' (Berry, 1995, p. 241). At this level, relationships are integral to an organization's strategy, rather than being the intended outcome of that strategy.

It appears that level one relationships with their emphasis on tangible benefits are less valued by consumers (De Wulf, Odekerken-Schroder and Iacobucci, 2001). Moreover, because this approach to RM tends to be most widespread it may not actually reduce marketing costs nor make marketing more efficient (*cf.* Sheth and Parvatiyar, 1995). Indeed, despite more than a decade of relationship rhetoric (O'Malley and Prothero, 2003), consumer complaints in the USA are at an all time high (Fournier, Dobscha and Mick, 1998), and a recent National Complaints Culture Survey in the UK demonstrates that customer loyalty is actually decreasing (*Management Services*, 2000).

Level two relationships seem to offer more possibilities. Because level two relationships concentrate on social issues, attention should be focused on facilitating interpersonal interaction to promote social benefits. However, in many situations the emphasis tends to be on communication. While direct mail clearly has an important role to play (Dwyer, Schurr and Oh, 1987), its effectiveness in building relationships appears to decrease as consumers' exposure to mailings increases (De Wulf, Odekerken-Schroder and Iacobucci, 2001). In other words, in cultures that have traditionally been exposed to low levels of direct mail it is likely to be more effective than in cultures where consumers receive quite a bit. Thus, as the average amount of direct mail per head increases in the UK, its effectiveness is likely to decrease concomitantly.

The Role of Technology

Information on customers is critical to developing and maintaining customer relationships. While small organizations with very few customers find it relatively easy to collect and use relevant information in building customer relationships, larger organizations find this practically impossible to do. Thus, information technology, initially in the form of the database was regarded as 'an agent of surrogacy to be enlisted to help marketers to re-create the operating styles of yesterday's merchants' (Sisodia and Wolf, 2000, p. 526).

The ability to develop successful customer relationships lies in an organization's propensity to understand its customers, their individual preferences, expectations and changing needs. While today's markets are so complex that such customer intimacy may be precluded the database is employed by contemporary marketers to try to overcome this problem. In the absence of intimate knowledge of individual customers and interpersonal contact, the database promises an opportunity to capture information on customers in a useful and accessible fashion (Shani and Chalasani, 1992), allowing marketers to identify individual customers, monitor their buying behaviour (Blattberg and Deighton, 1991), and to communicate with them on an individual basis, often with personalized offers. Although these are essentially the basic elements of database marketing, RM (in theory, at least) uses this data to build a long-term relationship between company and consumer.

The creation of a special status between company and customers (Czepiel, 1990; Rowe and Barnes, 1998) relies on fostering customer intimacy (Jackson, 1985). In order to achieve this, data on transactions is held in the customer database and this is overlaid with demographic, geodemographic and lifestyle data, and a range of other data sources including country court judgements (CCJs), electoral register, etc.. The data are fused and held in a data warehouse where biographic data (Evans, 1998) on individual customers can be viewed. Thus, within an RM strategy, the database becomes a key knowledge tool for the organization and is used to simulate indicia of intimacy and connectedness. In addition to databases, other technologies have been developed that allow companies to maximize opportunities for meaningful communication with their customer. These developments include the Internet, telecoms, and computer-telephony in call centres. These technological developments have served to make systems that are supposed to support RM more affordable and, perhaps, more effective for companies operating in mass markets (Sisodia and Wolfe, 2000; O'Malley and Mitussis, 2002).

Some of these technologies have opened up new channels of dialogue, which can be customer-initiated as well as organization-initiated. This being the case, efforts must be made to capture data at all interactions and make that information available for subsequent conversations. This is possible when technology is used at the customer interface to secure real-time or near real-time interaction (Gordon, 2000). This has resulted in a need to move beyond the customer database as the basis of RM and to link the central information centre with call-centre software and Internet systems that allow direct interaction, as well as into other functions that contain histories of customer interaction (such as accounts and product service departments).

Problems with RM in Consumer Markets

The notion that RM may be applicable in mass consumer markets, although widely accepted today (Coviello, Brodie and Munro, 1997; Petrof, 1997; Sheth and Parvatiyar, 1995), must be tempered by the recognition that attempts to implement RM do not always have the desired result either ideologically (in terms of mutual benefit) or practically (in terms of increased customer retention). This may be because in attempting to reap the numerous benefits of RM, problems relating to the size and anonymity of markets have been found. The 'quick fix' offered by technology is particularly problematic (O'Malley and Mitussis, 2002) as are approaches that fail to take account of consumer concerns and issues. Both of these problems will now be considered in more detail.

Technology-led RM

> Organisations continue to approach relationship marketing using the same structures that were appropriate for the marketing era, a time when product, price, promotion, and distribution channels were discrete, pre-established and one-way. In short, today's organisation is often designed for the technologies and processes appropriate for transactions, not relationships.
>
> (Gordon, 2000, p. 506)

Thus, (relationship) language structures consumers' expectations but (transaction) technology structures their experiences (O'Malley and Mitussis, 2002). Many companies have attempted to implement RM without being familiar with the processes required to manage customer relationships and with little knowledge of the underlying technological systems (database marketing, accounts, etc.) required (O'Malley and Mitussis, 2002). This creates a significant challenge – companies use technology that they don't understand very well in order to help them implement a process (relationship management) that they are also unfamiliar with. Thus, it is exceedingly difficult to facilitate 'credible and responsive dialogue' (Sisodia and Wolf, 2000, p. 551) with all customers during all interactions.

O'Malley and Mitussis (2002) problematize the use of IT to implement RM in mass markets as follows:

- RM is adopted by the organization but only at a superficial level. This is part of RM rhetoric (O'Malley and Tynan, 2001), which achieves little more than raising customer expectations.
- If the whole organization does not buy into the need to develop and maintain customer relationships, attempting to force the purchase and implementation of CRM systems is likely to result in political infighting between marketing and other functional units, and, as a result, ultimately fail.
- CRM systems that are developed and implemented by different product or brand units that undertake their own marketing, sales and support, are also likely to be problematic. In such cases, there might be competition over access to the system, that, if left unchecked, might lead to conflicts when

the same customer receives competing communications from different parts of the organization (i.e., an offer for a credit card and a personal loan at the same time).

If relationship management support systems develop *ad hoc* from product unit customer databases a number of different CRM programmes may be implemented within a single organization (O'Malley and Mitussis, 2002). These systems might reflect the various organizational silos (e.g., product or brand divisions, direct marketing) or different channels (particularly true when Internet channels are introduced). As a result, customers may obtain a very different experience, offer or outcome depending on when, why and with whom in the organization they interact.

[handwritten margin note: importance of corporate/company culture]

From a more pragmatic viewpoint, there is little reduction in marketing costs because several divisions are incurring direct communication costs and may continue to maintain their own databases. Finally, the inconsistencies (in communication style, offer content and, occasionally, salutation) demonstrate to customers that they are unimportant (whilst simultaneously advocating a 'meaningful' relationship). Thus, there are several problems that result when RM is overlaid onto the existing organizational structure and systems without any consideration for how relationships might be appropriately pursued and developed (i.e., the relationship development process).

Consumer Issues

Marketers appear to be promising more than they can deliver. They have focused on database building (O'Malley, Patterson and Evans, 1997) yet have stressed the importance of customer relationships. While technology offers opportunities in facilitating relationship development by overcoming the need for interaction, it has created its own problems through exacerbating customers' physical and information privacy concerns (O'Malley, Patterson and Evans, 1997; Patterson, O'Malley and Evans, 1997).

Physical privacy relates to the physical intrusion of marketing communications into consumers' daily lives. While direct mail is often viewed as annoying, outbound telemarketing and door-to-door salespeople are viewed as much more intrusive. Information privacy relates to how information on consumers is used and relates largely to the sale and sharing of information between companies. While consumers are concerned that they have no control over their data they are also aware that invasions to their physical privacy (i.e., more direct mail and telemarketing) result because of this practice.

Consumers who are the targets of relationship building efforts are concerned about the increases in direct marketing that occur under the guise of RM. Organizations must recognize that attempts to build relationships without consumers' consent demonstrate a lack of respect for their customers that is (or should be) fundamental to an RM strategy (see O'Malley, Patterson and Evans, 1997). Moreover, the switch from interpersonal interaction to technology-mediated interactions may also prove misguided because the latter limit the opportunities for the creation of social bonds. Rather, there is now a greater emphasis on locking-in customers (Barnes, 1995) as epitomized by the prevalence of level one relationship strategies. It has been further argued that McKenna's suggestions that RM will result in more helpful and fair approaches to marketing amounts to little more than rhetoric (Alvesson, 1994; Desmond, 1997; Smith and Higgins, 2000). Moreover, customer care and loyalty schemes, while being promoted as customer benefits are widely viewed as attempts to up-sell, cross-sell or lock consumers into specific exchange relationships. Indeed, O'Malley and Prothero (2003) demonstrate that organizations are making promises they cannot deliver on and, consequently, the experiences of customers seems, ironically, to have deteriorated since RM has been popularized. Consequently, the extent to which RM has resulted in redressing power inequalities and created win-win outcomes between consumers and marketers is highly questionable. Indeed, it has been argued that RM does not actually 'achieve greater representation of the individual' (Fitchett and McDonagh, 2000) and ultimately RM programmes are important only because they 'add profit to the bottom line' (Buchanan and Gilles, 1990).

Improving Customer Relationships

Although there appear to be a number of problems related to current attempts to implement RM in mass markets, we must recognize that it is a relatively new topic for marketing practitioners and there is still insufficient research into how marketing strategies impact upon customer satisfaction and the development of trust. What we must acknowledge, however, is that such problems simply magnify the importance of ensuring that there is an appropriate customer-centric culture and employee skill-set prior to the introduction of a relational strategy. Indeed, it seems that companies that have successfully implemented RM have done so by trial and error rather than on the basis of any theory.

Prior to implementing RM (or indeed, when evaluating current programmes) organizations should:

- Evaluate the nature of the existing relationship. Specifically, how do customers, suppliers, employees and others currently regard the organization?
- Consider what level of relationship (see Berry, 1995) might be possible given their specific product/service, business context and resources (financial as well as human).
- Formulate an outline strategy to achieve the desired level of relationship, paying particular attention to:
    1. The requirements in terms of recruitment, training, motivation and rewarding staff.
    2. The changes necessary to existing systems (customer service, billing, accounting, product development, staff training, pay-related systems, etc.).
    3. The impact on current marketing strategies. Is there a need to develop new advertising, direct marketing etc.? Will a customer reward programme be necessary?

    4. Will new technologies be required in terms of relational databases, telecoms, Internet and computer-telephony?

    5. Calculate the costs involved in implementing the desired strategy in terms of all of the above.

- Consider the degree to which marketing is capable of implementing these organization-wide changes, and the costs in terms of human time and effort.

- Critically evaluate whether the benefits likely to accrue at that level of relationship are worthwhile considering the costs involved.

If, after considering all of the costs and benefits outlined above, the organization wishes to implement an RM strategy, there are a number of organizational attributes that may help foster sustainable customer relationships. These include:

- An organizational culture that focuses on customer service (Colgate and Stewart, 1998; Grönroos, 1990; 1995). Organizations must go beyond the simple purchase of a database or other IT systems if their efforts at RM are to be viewed by their customers as authentic (see Sisodia and Wolf, 2000).

- Employees with good skills in interpersonal communication must be re-cruited and rewarded within the organization. Good interpersonal communication influences how service providers interact with customers and helps to foster the social bonds that appear to be so central to truly successful relationships (Berry, 1995; Crosby, Evans and Cowles, 1990).

- Internal marketing/empowered employees (Berry, 1995; Bitner, 1995; Grönroos, 1995). Employee motivation and training will be more important:
  1. in services that involve high employee/customer contact;
  2. where social benefits are particularly valued;
  3. where technology plays a significant role in building and maintaining relationships (O'Malley and Mitussis, 2002).

- In order to manage customer relationships successfully, there is a need to integrate with non-marketing information systems. This moves RM support systems from being customer databases in the hands of product unit marketing teams, to being complex systems that must integrate with other information systems within the product units and beyond (O'Malley and Mitussis, 2002).

- Develop an ability to calculate relationship performance (Berry, 1995; Pine, Peppers and Rogers, 1995) and to assess the impact of marketing strategies on customer satisfaction, trust, commitment and loyalty.

RM has clearly a lot of potential in consumer markets as well as in service and interorganizational contexts. Ideologically, RM focuses upon mutuality and the synergistic outcomes of long-term cooperation and collaboration. It relies heavily on the creation and maintenance of trust and commitment. This chapter has outlined the role and importance of these, and other, central concepts. However, the chapter has also demonstrated that current approaches to implementing RM, particularly in consumer markets, do not necessarily foster relationships, and, in some cases, may actually undermine relationship development. People and their interaction lie at the core of RM and the current emphasis on technology actually limits opportunities for interpersonal interaction. More fundamentally, however, because technology has been seen as a solution to overcoming the lack of interpersonal interaction, many of the RM strategies today emphasize technology over people. This has proven to be both costly and short-sighted as the successful implementation of RM is determined as much by people and systems as it is by technology.

CHAPTER 8

Marketing through alliances and networks

Eleanor Shaw

From the mid 1980s business and management research, including marketing, has become increasingly interested in understanding organizational alliances, partnerships and networks. As the boundaries between organizations have become less clear and organizations have recognized the benefits of collaborating, even with their competitors, researchers have become interested in understanding the dynamics of these relationships and exploring their impact on organizational behaviour, decision taking and competitiveness. Within the business and management literature, the term 'network' has been loosely used to describe the ways in which an organization can manage and coordinate their activities and has received attention from a range of subjects, including transactional economics (Bradach and Eccles, 1989; Powell, 1990; Williamson, 1985; 1991; 1996); organizational behaviour (Kanter, 1989); small business management (Aldrich and Zimmer, 1986; Johannisson, 1986; Shaw, 1997) and organizational learning and development (Beeby and Booth, 2000; Khanna, Ghulati and Nohria, 1998). The diversity of business and management subjects interested in networks is such that the definition of 'network' is often determined by individual subject areas (Blois, 1990; Grandori and Soda, 1995; Kanter and Eccles, 1992). What is agreed upon is that for many organizations, involvement in collaborative relationships with other organizations and individuals can enhance their competitiveness. For example, networks have been found to assist small firms' acquisition of information and advice (Birley, 1985; Carson *et al.*, 1995; Shaw, 1997); improve the innovation processes of entrepreneurial organizations and provide access to finance and other resources (DeBresson and Amesse, 1991; Freeman, 1991; Oakey, 1993; Rothwell and Dodgson, 1991; Saxenian, 1990; Shaw, 1999).

Particular to marketing, research interests in organizational partnerships, alliances and networks have been pioneered by work of the Industrial Marketing and Purchasing Group (IMP) (Axelsson and Easton, 1992; Ford *et al.*, 1998; Hakansson, 1987). Research in this area regards organizations as existing within 'portfolios' of overlapping relationships with customers, suppliers, distributers, etc., which adopt a network-like structure. Such overlapping relationships are described as 'business networks' which present organizations with opportunities, for example access to the resources of a collaborating partner, as well as liabilities, for example investment made in joint ventures and strategic alliances. The building blocks of such networks are the relationships shared between collaborating organizations and work in this area has sought to explore the dynamics of the interactions, actors and activities of which such relationships are comprised. As a consequence of this focus, research in the areas of service and relationship marketing have also contributed to current understanding about marketing, alliances and networks. While each of these subjects are discussed in detail elsewhere in this book, networks and relationships are inherently linked and, as will be made apparent by the review presented below, it can be difficult to delineate between the two, and research which has considered the collaborative arrangements of sets of dyadic relationships is often inaccurately described as 'network' research.

This chapter opens by identifying the driving forces which have encouraged organizations to engage in collaborative alliances and organize their marketing activities through networks of relationships rather than market mechanisms or internal hierarchies. It then reviews marketing research interests in the area of alliances and networks. This review concludes that while network research has emerged as an identifiable area of marketing research, work in this area shares many of the criticisms that have been made of relationship marketing (*cf.* Gummesson, 1997; Li and Nicholls, 2000; Moller and Halinen, 2000; O'Malley and Tynan, 1999; Smith and Higgins, 2000). It is argued that as a consequence, to advance theoretical and practical understanding of marketing alliances and networks, there is value in tracing the roots and development of network theory and considering the extent to which this theory together with the 'embeddedness' perspective conceived of by economic sociology (Granovetter, 1985; 1992) can be applied to understand the network arrangements by which many organizations seek to organize their marketing activities. The chapter goes on to introduce the concept of a social network and describe Granovetter's 'embeddedness perspective' before presenting a review of emerging research in this area. Research and managerial implications are then considered before drawing conclusions.

Organizational Alliances and Networks: The Driving Forces

Since the mid 1980s cooperative arrangements between organizations have emerged as an important strategic issue and research interest in partnerships, alliances, joint ventures and all types of collaborative arrangements have grown at a fast pace (*cf.* Cravens *et al.*, 1993; Hamel, Doz and Prahalad, 1989; Nohria and Eccles, 1992; Varadarajan and Cunningham, 1995). Interest in such arrangements has intensified over the past decade as a result of a number of more recent trends or driving forces which have convinced organizations that collaborative arrangements with their customers, suppliers, distributors, competitors, indeed all parties in their value system, is critical to their competitive success (Henderson, 1989; Kanter, 1994).

Internationalization, rapid advances in technology, a changing industrial base and increasingly active customers are amongst those trends which have encouraged organizations to enter alliances, partnerships, joint ventures, licensing agreements and networks. Hakansson and Johanson (2001) argue that such changes have created a complex business 'landscape' (p. 1) which has implications for the amount and type of knowledge required by organizations as well as the ways in which knowledge is acquired: 'Business market situations are continually being transformed by changing technologies, forcing firms to learn and adapt'. Specifically, they argue that a fast-changing and complex business environment demands that organizations require greater knowledge and that this knowledge is most readily and speedily acquired through networks of relationships shared with other organizations. Using the example of internationalization, Hakansson and Johanson (2001) argue that when firms are exposed to new market situations about which they must learn, business relationships, that is interdependent, collaborative relationships shared with other organizations, can offer the quickest and most effective access to such information and knowledge: '[R]elationships are part of the knowledge-generating process. Thus business relationships do not simply facilitate learning, they also increase the number of opportunities to learn through expanding the total knowledge base' (Hakansson and Johanson, 2001, p. 9). Fisk (1997) agrees that the 'globalization of business relationships suggests that international interdependency is increasing. Consequently, network theory, relationship marketing and strategic partnering forms of business co-operation are attracting increased attention from academics as well as the business community' (p. 6).

Internationalization and the growing learning requirements of organizations are not the only drivers encouraging organizations to engage in collaborative arrangements. Recent collaborative arrangements, for example, within hi-technology industries, together with the 'downsizing' of large organizations and introduction of 'networks' of organizations connected by collaborative arrangements often with small and medium-sized firms, have encouraged researchers to explore collaborative arrangements agreed between organizations and identify the conditions under which they arise (Jarillo, 1993; Johnson and Lawrence, 1988; Miles and Snow, 1986; Powell and Brantley, 1992). In particular, advances in information technology have created an 'information rich environment' within which consumers have become better informed, more educated about their purchase demands and, as a consequence, have become increasingly active. Doherty, Ellis-Chadwick and Hart (1999) argue that the 'information revolution' is radically changing the way organizations and consumers operate, especially in services where, for example, the Internet has become a significant new channel for financial and travel products. Information asymmetries have changed: consumers have access to more and a greater variety of information at a faster speed than ever before, one effect of which has been a shift in the balance or 'equalizing' of power between organizations and customers (Hogg, Laing and Winkelman, 2002). Within today's 'information and communication rich environment', organizations are increasingly aware of the need to recognize the multiple sources of information and other relationships in which their customers interact and assess the likely impact these will have upon their relationships with customers.

A number of developments within the marketing literature have also encouraged researchers to explore the collaborative networks arrangements by which organizations are seeking to organize their activities. At the time of writing, relationships, partnerships, alliances and all forms of collaborative arrangements between organizations is one of the most pervasive subjects within the research and practice of marketing (Palmer, 2001). In particular, work within relationship and services marketing has encouraged an interest in marketing alliances and networks. Recognizing that consumers have become increasingly active, the relationship marketing literature argues that in developing long-term relationships, organizations and consumers engage in the exchange of more than goods and services for monetary payment. Instead relationships shared between organizations and consumers, particularly in industrial and business markets, are recognized as being comprised of multiple exchanges: information about competitors, customers and technology; friendship and social exchanges and advice about new technologies, for example (Hamfelt and Lindberg, 1987; Johanson and Mattson, 1987). Relatedly, it is now recognized that the relationships, exchanges and transactions shared between organizations and customers do not occur within a vacuum but instead are situated or, to borrow from economic sociology, are 'embedded' within a wider social context or network of relationships which impact upon and influence these interactions (Granovetter, 1985; 1992). As a consequence, an emerging area of interest within relationship, services and industrial marketing is the management of an organization's 'portfolio' of relationships (Ford *et al.*, 1998; Gronroos, 1991; 1994; Hunt, 1997; Turnbull and Wilson, 1989; Webster, 1992). Work in this area argues that while relationship marketing recognizes the benefits of building relationships with various stakeholder groups, it does not advocate that organizations should engage in relationships with all stakeholder groups (Gummesson, 1994). Instead, it is argued that to be effective, organizations adopting a relational approach should consider creating a portfolio of profitable, usually, long-term relationships (Gronroos, 1994; Hunt, 1997). In particular, the management of customer portfolios has received much attention. Research in this area has identified a number of criteria which can be used to develop a portfolio of profitable customer relationships: lifetime value of a customer; contribution to profitability; contribution to turnover; likelihood of repeat business; complaints and technical and commercial requirements (Ford *et al.*, 1998; Saren and Tzokas, 1998; Turnbull and Wilson, 1989; Webster, 1992).

Particular to service marketing research, key areas of interest include service quality and the management of service 'encounters' (Carlzon, 1987; Czepiel, Solomon and Suprenant, 1985; Gabbott and Hogg, 1998; Harris, Barron and Ratcliffe, 1995; Shostack, 1985). While these areas have traditionally 'paid little attention to the context of relationships' (Moller and Halinen, 2000, p. 38), the drivers discussed above, especially the emergence of increasingly active, informed consumers have encouraged important conceptual developments. Traditionally, the service encounter has been conceived as a process between dyadic parties: an active supplier and less active customer. It has been recognized however that within an information-rich environment, such a *dyadic* presentation of the service encounter may no longer be accurate. Instead wider conceptualizations which recognize the 'embeddedness' of the service encounter and the impact which complex networks of relationships will have upon the service encounter are being developed (Gummesson, 1995; Hogg, Laing and Winkelman, 2002).

Marketing, Alliances and Networks: A Review of the Research

Recognizing the drivers detailed above, marketing research has sought to explore the ways in which organizations can develop relationships with customers, competitors, suppliers and distributers through alliances, networks and collaborative ways of working. In particular, work in the area of industrial marketing has contributed much to current understanding about the ways in which organizations develop and manage relationships.

From the 1970s industrial marketing researchers have been interested in understanding the dynamics of collaborative arrangements shared between industrial suppliers and buyers. Since this time, the European International Marketing and Purchasing project (IMP) has collected and analyzed extensive empirical data about business relationships (Ford, 1990; Hakansson, 1982; Turnbull and Valla, 1986). Based upon this empirical data, an IMP perspective on 'business relationships' and 'business networks' has developed and represents a significant perspective or school of thought about the relationships, interactions and collaborations which typify industrial and business markets. Like transaction costs research, work in this area is interested in exploring and explaining the ways in which organizations arrange their marketing activities, including transactions with customers, through collaborative rather than market or hierarchical mechanisms. In contrast to transaction costs, while IMP research is specifically interested in understanding the ways in which industrial buyers and suppliers organize these collaborations, it is motivated more by an interest in understanding and explaining these arrangements than by calculating the extent to which they are cost effective (Ford, 1980; 1990; Hakansson, 1987; 1989; Hakansson and Johnson, 1992; Hakansson and Snehota, 1989; 1995). A second important difference is that while transaction cost literature can be characterized by robust conceptual developments (Coase, 1937; Powell, 1990; Williamson, 1975; 1996), IMP research is characterized by significant empirical research.

The IMP Perspective on Business Networks

This perspective on networks borrows from resource dependency theory and conceives of *organizational* or *business networks* as comprising of actors which engage in activities for instrumental reasons (Pfeffer and Salanick, 1978). By conceiving of organizations as comprised of resources, competencies and tacit knowledge, this perspective argues that organisations will interact and collaborate for the purposes of gaining access to resources, exploiting one another's competencies, linking with third parties and transmitting expensive or difficult to code knowledge and information (Ford, 1990). Morgan and Hunt (1994) explain that 'in alliances and partnerships, there are neither "buyers" or "sellers", "customers" nor "key accounts" – only partners exchanging resources' (p. 22).

This perspective also conceives of organizations as 'actors' that engage in collaborative arrangements or 'activities' which develop a mutual orientation. In contrast to the transaction cost literature, this perspective conceives of organizational collaboration as occurring within the context of a relationship. It is argued that within industrial markets, buyers and suppliers do not behave atomistically to select those organizing mechanisms that most effectively handle transaction costs. Rather, based upon the analysis of much empirical data, this literature argues that within industrial markets it is common practice for buyers and suppliers to engage in collaborative arrangements which do *not* offer the most cost-effective means of acquiring resources (Axelsson and Easton, 1992; Hakansson, 1987). This literature argues that over time, as collaborating industrial buyers and suppliers engage in recurrent and active interactions, individuals involved in the negotiation of these increasingly engage in 'social' as well as 'business' exchanges. As a consequence, social bonds are created and, when evaluating the cost-effectiveness of such inter-firm collaboration, personnel involved may consider the benefits that accrue to themselves personally in terms of friendships made, support received and shared experiences as well as to their organization (Hakansson, 1982; Hamfelt and Lindberg, 1987). Johanson and Mattsson (1987) argue that as these 'social' and 'business' exchanges are 'not independent of one another', the cost-efficiency of collaborative arrangements between industrial buyer and suppliers can be challenged. Building upon this, Axelsson and Easton (1992) explain that often, in evaluating collaborative arrangements, the parties involved will weigh the social exchanges comprised within these arrangements more heavily than the instrumental exchanges. As a consequence, they argue, it is 'possible that social bonds will transcend and even replace economic bonds as the raison d'être for the relationship to continue' (p. 12). In contrast then to transaction costs research, IMP literature argues that the presence of social exchanges within collaborative arrangements between industrial buyers and suppliers serves to increase their switching costs and, consequently, engender such collaborative arrangements as not always cost-effective. In doing so, this literature aligns itself more closely to the suggestion that organizations are embedded within a social context that impacts upon and influences their behaviour (Granovetter, 1985; 1992; Salanick, 1995). Moreover, such an 'interaction' approach contrasts with the traditional view of marketing 'which analyses the reaction of an aggregate market to the seller's offering' (Ford, 1980, p. 339), instead concentrating on interactions between the mutually active parties to business relationships. Simply put, while traditional marketing conceives of the selling organization as an active partner in the exchange of goods and services with passive, individual consumers, within the IMP perspective, both industrial sellers *and* buyers are active parties in a process of interaction. Conceived of in this way, it may be that relationship and interactional concepts developed by industrial marketing research have less relevance for consumer markets where organizations typically offer standardized products to mass markets comprised of relatively inactive individual consumers (O'Malley and Tynan, 1999).

Relationships

As the above review illustrates, within the IMP perspective, the *relationships* shared between industrial and business organizations, are the building blocks of *business networks*. Empirical research suggests that within industrial markets, interactions between organizations are characterized by long-lasting business relationships with a limited number of collaborating partner organizations (Ford *et al.*, 1998; Hakansson, 1989). This perspective contrasts with the traditional 'marketing mix' view which dominates consumer marketing. Within the IMP perspective, market transactions do not occur as isolated events. Instead, organizations interact, collaborate, adapt to and shape each others' activities, become interdependent and develop long-term relationships. For example, Hakansson and Johanson (2001) state that analysis of European IMP Project data found that the average age of business relationships for investigated firms was 15 years. One reason offered for such longevity is transaction costs: after comparing the cost of acquiring similar resources and/or information through market transactions or organizational hierarchies, collaborative relationships such as strategic alliances and joint ventures will be selected when they are most cost-effective (Ebers, 1994; Grandori and Soda, 1995). In such a way collaboration between organizations can reduce costs and so create value and benefits for each party and result in continued collaboration (Palmer, 2001). Hakansson and Johanson (2001) explain that the IMP study found that 'close coordination of production activities provides firms engaged in long-lasting relationships with the possibility of lowering joint production costs' (p. 3). As time and resources are required to establish and develop relationships, relationships are regarded as investments; when a company commits resources in specific relationships, important market assets are formed for future use (Johanson and Mattsson, 1987). Put another way, 'to establish and develop a business relationship is a resource-intensive process . . . [t]herefore, established relationships form an important asset for any company' (Anderson, Havila and Salmi, 2001, p. 579). In this way, business relationships constitute part of an organization's resource base (Hakansson and Johanson, 2001).

Within the IMP perspective, business relationships are conceived of as having a 'substance' (Ford *et al.*, 1998). As shown in Figure 8.1, the substance of business relationships refers to the actors, resources ties and activity links involved in such relationships (Hakansson and Johanson, 1992). Within this context, *actors* are the organizations and individuals party to business relationships. *Resource ties* are the technological, human, marketing and other resources which interacting organizations share and decisions about which can become dependent upon one another. *Activities* refer to the goods and services developed, manufactured, marketed, bought and sold by organizations sharing business relationships.

In addition to substance, another finding of the IMP project is that *interaction* between organizations is vital to the establishment and development of relationships. Coupled with the longevity of such relationships, this finding suggests that over time, as organizations engage in the repeat interactions typical of a relationship, they will adapt and coordinate decisions and resources and by doing so will become interdependent on one another. Interactions include all the actions necessary to establish business relationships, such as setting up and attending meetings, making and taking phone calls, processing customer orders, attending trade shows and signing joint venture and licensing arrangements. In addition, as described above, interactions also include 'social' interactions and the types of activities typical of a friendship relationship. By engaging in such interactions, the personnel involved bind organizations together in multiple ways and over time, such interactions increase the strength of such bonds. In particular, the

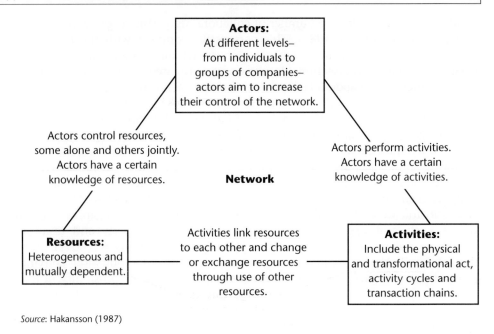

Source: Hakansson (1987)

FIGURE 8.1 Network model developed by Industrial Marketing and Purchasing (IMP)

personal investments made by staff can be identified as an important factor in maintaining the ongoing collaborations shared between industrial organizations (Axelsson and Easton, 1992).

A concentration on business relationships has encouraged work in this area to explore the value of applying the relationship metaphor to business interactions. Topics including trust, commitment, dependency and power of business relationships have, as is shown by the review below, received significant research attention (O'Malley and Tynan, 1997; Pels, 1997).

Business networks

Recognizing that the interactions between collaborating industrial firms do not exist in isolation, IMP researchers argue that the business relationships shared between sets of interacting, interdependent organizations will be affected by other relationships which they share with collaborating firms. Within the IMP perspective, sets of dyadic collaborating organizations are perceived to overlap to form a network-like structure which has been described as a 'business network' (Hakansson and Johanson, 2001; Hakansson and Snehota, 1995). As depicted in Figure 8.2 the A-R-A model, within business networks the relationship shared between focal organizations can be affected by an array of direct and indirect relational influences.

Building upon this conceptualization, Ford *et al.* (1998) explain that the frequency of interactions within business relationships is influenced by the other relationships in which parties are involved and assert that 'each relationship is

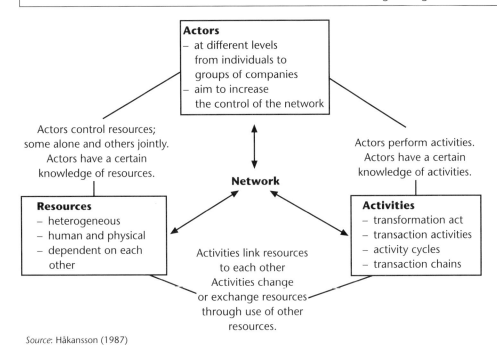

Source: Håkansson (1987)

FIGURE 8.2 The A-R-A model

In a business network

embedded in a set of connected relationships forming a network structure. It seems that business markets are networks of interconnected business relationships' (p. 4). Conceived of in this way, the network of business relationships within which industrial organizations exist represents opportunities in terms of transaction costs, learning and the 'ability to continue doing business with some degree of predictability and without cumbersome marketing and production costs associated with being forced to switch to new customers or suppliers frequently' (Hakansson and Johanson, 2001, p. 4). Business networks can help organize production more efficiently, provide the basis for the long-term development of products and processes, and give organizations access to resources including knowledge, technology and information held by organizations with whom they share direct and indirect relationships: 'Relationships are small pieces in a larger structure and the connections between them are important ways of creating efficiency and innovation' (Ford *et al.*, 1998, p. 44). Business networks also represent liabilities including investments made in establishing, developing and maintaining relationships with collaborating partners and loss of control which may result from interdependence, particularly when collaborating with larger organizations holding more of the bargaining power.

Within the IMP literature, the structure and position of an organization's business network has been an area of research interest. The structure of each organization's business network is unique to that organization, determined by the number and types of organizations with whom they share business relationships. Moreover, the structure of a business network is not fixed but can fluctuate. As a consequence, future network structure and the positioning of participating organizations will be dictated by the outcomes of past and current interactions between all organizations contributing to the business relationships of which the network is comprised. As Hakansson and Johanson (2001) explain:

> Since each firm is engaged in business relationships with a set of customer firms and supplier firms, which, in turn, are engaged in a number of business relationships, each firm is engaged in ever-extending business network structures. Thus, business networks are unbounded structures. When a firm interacts with its business relationship partners it modifies the network structure, which is also modified whenever other firms interact.

(p. 4)

An organization's network position has been described as consisting of 'its portfolio of relationships and the activity links, resource ties and actor bonds that arise from them' (Ford *et al.*, 1998, p. 49). The position which an organization holds within its business network can influence its reputation, widen or narrow the resources to which it has access and dictate obligations which it has to the network. Simply put, business networks can influence the ways in which a focal organization interacts with those organizations with whom it shares direct and indirect relationships.

Diads or Networks?: A Review of the Research Evidence

The section above reveals that conceptually, industrial marketing research perceives of organizations engaging in a range of overlapping relationships with different stakeholder groups including customers, suppliers and distributors, which overlap to form a network structure of business relationships. A review of empirical research on this subject reveals that industrial marketing researchers are conceptually aware of the networks of relationships within which industrial organizations are embedded, and recognize that the interactions by which individual business relationships are comprised are influenced by the other networks of relationships within which both parties are involved. Empirically however, research in this area has had a tendency to focus on understanding the dynamics of dyadic relationships held between industrial buyers and suppliers (*cf.* Dion, Easterling and Miller, 1995; Gardner, Joseph and Thech, 1993; Joseph *et al.*, 1995).

For example, within the innovation literature, while it has been recognized that organizations exist within networks comprised of overlapping informal and personal relationships which can help the innovation processes of industrial firms (Axelsson and Easton, 1992; Freeman, 1991; Hakansson, 1987; 1989), empirical research has tended to abstract sets of dyadic relationships from these networks. That is, while describing their work as network in focus, empirical studies of networks and innovation have concentrated at the lower level of abstraction of, for example, relationships between organizations involved in strategic alliances, licensing agreements, research associations and joint research and development activities (*cf.* Auster, 1990; Hagedoorn and Schakenraad, 1992; Littler and Wilson, 1991; Litvak, 1990; Rogers and Kincaid, 1981). Similarly, in exploring the trust, commitment, dependence, power and longevity of business relationships, interactions between industrial buyers and suppliers has been explored without considering the impact which the other relationships in which buyers and suppliers are involved are likely to have upon perceptions of trust and committment (Anderson and Weitz, 1992; Ganesan, 1993). For example, in Collins and Burt's (1999) study of business relationships in the internationalization of food retailers, the power and dependency of business relationships are explored by considering isolated sets of dyadic retailer–manufacturer relationships. Harland's (1995; 1996) review of the industrial marketing literature concurs that historically, empirical studies of business networks have concentrated on the lower level of abstraction of buyer–supplier relationships. She argues that existing work in this area, '... does not adequately recognize the significance of the network level of analysis' (1996, p. 78). Harland reasons that this may be because of the difficulties and time involved in collecting data from all relevant actors when studies are positioned at the level of a business network. Moreover, when the organization selected for study is large, as is common in industrial marketing research, the difficulties and time required to identify all actors contributing to business networks increase.

It has not been until more recently that empirical work in this area has positioned itself at the level of the network and sought to develop a more comprehensive understanding of network dynamics and the impact which a network of relational influences can have upon the behaviour of a focal organization. For example, recent case study research in the field of industrial supply chains has sought to explore the complexity of business networks. Ellis and Mayer (2001) borrowed from Gidden's (1984) notion of structuration to consider the effect which dyadic interactions can have on network structure. Their research established 'the reciprocal interplay between actions and structures' (p. 213). That is to say, their research of supply chains in the speciality chemicals industry found that not only can internal organizational activities, such as changes in marketing strategy, impact on the structure of such supply chains but also such structures can effect the behaviour of organizations interacting within the supply chain.

Advances to our understanding of marketing networks have also been made by recent work in the area of business network learning (Eriksson and Hohenthal, 2002; Hakansson and Johanson, 2001). Work in this area has explored the ways in which knowledge, especially tacit knowledge, can be acquired through interacting in individual sets of dyadic relationships as well as networks of 'learning business relationships'. Hakansson and Johanson (2001) reason that while business relationships may be 'unique', 'experience from one relationship may also be applicable in another' (p. 6), something they call the 'generalization of relationship learning'. Consequently, they argue, '[e]xperience from interaction in a business relationship can also lead to learning that develops links with other relationships' (p. 7). Specifically, they assert that as collaborating firms are usually involved in a set of interacting relationships and a business network, learning advantages can be acquired by coordinating activities across relationships. They also argue that the greater the variety of business relationships in which an organization is involved, the greater is the opportunity for that organization to learn from a range of interaction experiences and adopt a more flexible approach to their business structures and processes.

TABLE 8.1 Networks versus sets of dyadic relationships

	Networks	Partnerships
Focus	Individual relationships	Organizational relationships
Motivation	Voluntary	Voluntary or imposed
Boundary	Indistinct	Clear
Composition	Fluid	Stable
Membership	Determined by self/others	Determined by formal agreement
Formalization	Low	High

Source: Lowndes et al., 1997.

The review presented in this section suggests that while recent industrial marketing research, particularly on the subject of organizational learning, has sought to undertake empirical research which is positioned at the level of a 'business network', significant empirical work in this branch of marketing research has concentrated on exploring the collaborative arrangements between sets of *dyadic* business relationships. While conceptually industrial marketing recognizes that dyadic relationships are embedded within networks of business relationships, there is a scarcity of empirical research on the subject of business network dynamics, processes and influences. Borrowing from Lowndes et al.'s (1997) research on local government structures (Table 8.1), a useful discussion of the differences between dyadic and network perspectives together with the implications which this has for industrial marketing research on the topic of business relationships and networks can be presented.

The above table makes clear that by abstracting sets of dyadic relationships out of the social context in which they exist (Granovetter, 1985; 1992; Salancik, 1995), research positioned at the level of dyadic relationships is characterized by an interest in understanding the dynamics of relationships between organizations rather than the individuals by which they are established, developed and maintained. While such an interest is more common in transaction costs that industrial marketing literature, particular to both is the focus which they place on 'business' relationships; that is, relationships between organizations which are formally recognized rather than informally agreed. Where industrial or business networks have been selected as the level of analysis, Harland (1996) argues that rather than exploring the interactional dimensions of such networks, research has concentrated on their 'hard' or structural dimensions. As a consequence, research in the area of industrial marketing has yet to significantly contribute to current understanding about the impact which business networks can have on the behaviours and activities of those actors and collaborative relationships of which they are comprised.

The Embeddedness Perspective and Network Theory

In the same way that relationship marketing is currently in vogue but has been described as 'conceptually ambiguous' (Li and Nicholls, 2000) and 'characterised more by rhetoric than by rigorous examination' (Moller and Halinen, 2000,

p. 30), so too has organizational network research been criticized as popular but conceptually weak. Nohria (1992) for example has argued that while there is much to learn about organizational behaviour from a 'properly applied network perspective' (p. 3), a failure to do so is threatening to relegate the concept 'to the status of an evocative metaphor, so loosely applied that it ceases to mean anything' (p. 3).

In his editorial of the *Journal of Marketing Management*'s 'Special Issue' dedicated to the IMP's 15th Annual Conference in Dublin, Baker (1999) commented that, 'very little progress has been made since the Lyon Conference in 1992'. Borrowing from Powell's keynote address made at the conference, Baker suggested that if marketing is to make similar contributions to our understanding of organizational networks as those made by subjects including economic sociology, marketing researchers 'should take our own advice and look outwards rather than inwards in establishing "Interactions, Relationships and Networks"' (p. 583). Easton and Araujo (1994) have argued that the intellectual drivers of the industrial marketing perspective lie 'half-way between economics and sociology' (p. 82). Consequently, it is fitting that this chapter now turns to the sociological roots of network theory by introducing the concept of a social network and the 'embedded' perspective developed within economic sociology (Granovetter, 1985).

The Concept of a Social Network

Concept of a social network is not new to the social sciences. It has a strong heritage in the mature branches of sociology, anthropology and social psychology where it was developed in the 1950s and 1960s as a construct for analyzing the impact which the structure of society has on individuals, groups and the behaviour of society at large. Developed by social anthropologists as a construct for exploring and understanding social action and behaviour in terms of the social relationships shared between actors, the concept of a 'social' network offers a useful way of conceiving the environment in which organizations exist. As such, it is a useful construct from which to approach network studies of the organization and develop a comprehensive understanding of the relational influences impacting upon organizational behaviour, including marketing behaviour.

By viewing society as a 'network' structure of overlapping social relationships which bind individuals, groups and organizations together, social anthropologists believe that social action and behaviour can be understood in terms of both the positions which actors hold within these social networks and also as a consequence of the interactions which they share (Boissevain, 1974; Bott, 1957; Mitchell, 1969). For the purposes of analyzing the structural and interactional dimensions of social action and behaviour, networks are conceived to possess both *morphological* and *interactional* dimensions.

Morphological dimensions

Morphological dimensions consider the pattern and structure of social networks. The dimensions which Mitchell (1969) described as 'germane' to the structural analysis of social behaviour in network terms are anchorage, reachability, density and range.

Mitchell (1969) used the term *anchorage* to identify the focus of social network inquiries. While social network analysis is positioned at a lower level of abstraction than studies which seek to understand the behaviour of society at large, this does not imply that the anchorage of social network research must necessarily be positioned at the level of the individual. Rather, social network theory conceives of social relationships as lying along a continuum from personal relationships to interorganizational relationships between quasi-groups, corporate groups and institutions (Boissevain, 1974). Further, it regards any differences between the structures formed by social networks and those erected to organize the activities of organizations as being created by the level of abstraction at which the researcher operates rather than by any concrete differences (Mitchell, 1969). Consequently, the concept of a social network is a framework suited to analyzing the behaviour of individuals, groups and organizations.

Having identified the anchorage point or organization at the focus of a network enquiry, the *reachability* of the organization's network is useful in determining how many relationships should be involved in network research. It was mentioned above that the structure of business networks fluctuates and is shaped by the outcomes of interactions in business relationships. For this reason it can be difficult to identify how many relationships should be included in the network analysis of an organization's activities and behaviour. The reachability of an organization's network is helpful in making this decision. Reachability is a measure of how far and how easily an anchorage is able to contact other organizations and individuals, and can be used to identify all those relationships that should be involved in a network study. The reachability of anchorage is measured by the number of interactions, represented by the number of lines drawn on a network map, which they have to make in order to reach other parties (see Figure 8.3): the fewer the number of interactions, the greater their reachability. By giving an indication of the effort required to make contact via direct relationships with those to whom they are not directly connected, reachability assesses the extent to which relationships far removed from an organization have the potential to influence their behaviour.

While the image above simplifies the complex structure of overlapping relationships, it does capture the distinguishing feature of social network theory: a focus on both the direct and indirect relationships in which an anchorage, such as an organization, is involved. By providing an indication of the extent to which indirect relational influences can, via direct relationships, impact on organizational behaviour, measures of reachability draw attention to the importance which social network theory places on 'brokers'. Tichy, Tushmann and Forbrun (1979) define brokers as 'special nodes within the network' who link together social actors not sharing a direct relationship.

The third morphological dimension, *density*, also referred to as the 'connectedness', 'complexity' or 'social cohesiveness' of a social network, is a measure of the extent to which actors party to a network are connected to one another. Mitchell (1969) suggested that the density of a social network is calculated by the percentage of lines which actually exist in relation to the number which would potentially be created if every actor in the network were directly connected. He argued that measures of density could be used to distinguish between 'tight' and 'loose-knit' networks. By establishing the density of a network the ease, for

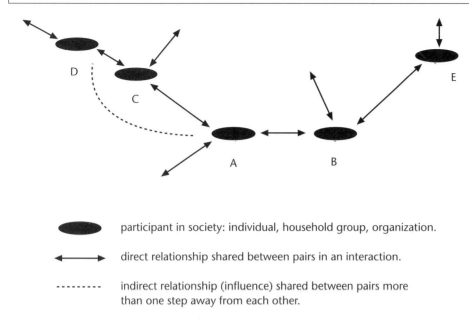

●●● participant in society: individual, household group, organization.

◄───► direct relationship shared between pairs in an interaction.

- - - - - - - - indirect relationship (influence) shared between pairs more
than one step away from each other.

FIGURE 8.3 A social network map

example, with which information spreads can be estimated. To illustrate this
latter point, Mitchell explained that in close-knit networks, the likelihood that
more participants will know one another increases and consequently, the more
likely it is that they will agree upon, communicate and reinforce behaviour that is
acceptable to the social norms created within their network. Applied to marketing
research, density is a measure of the extent to which organizations are connected
to other actors in their environment. Where a business network is loose-knit, few
of those organizations with which the anchor shares a business relationship are
known to one another. In contrast, in a tight-knit network, most organizations
sharing relationships with the anchor also share relationships. As a consequence,
within tight-knit networks, information is more quickly shared between the
anchor and other organizations and the potential for quickly learning about new
developments within the network is increased. It was mentioned that business
networks can present opportunities and liabilities, and in this respect the density
of an organization's network is an important structural dimension. Density can
impact on the variety of resources within a network to which an anchor
organization has access. For example, a tight-knit network can mean that the
variety of resources available to an organization are less than if its network was
loose-knit.

Related to this, the final morphological dimension, *range*, refers to the number
of actors in direct contact with anchorage and the social heterogeneity of these
actors. An organization's business network can be described as either 'narrow' or
'diverse' and Granovetter (1973; 1982) argues that the narrower the range of an
organization's network, the less opportunity the organization has of acquiring,
from its networks, a variety of information and advice. The range or variety of
types of organizations participating in a business network gives an indication of

the extent to which organizations sharing relationships have similar characteristics, and has implications for the variety of resources available within the network.

Interactional Characteristics

While it is revealing to examine the morphological dimensions of social networks, it has been argued that a concentration on analyzing these dimensions provides a restricted understanding of the relational influences on organizational behaviour (Mitchell, 1969). As the social à network concept was developed for the purposes of also understanding social behaviour as a consequence of the interactions shared between actors, it is conceived to possess a number of interactional or 'relational' dimensions. In contrast to morphological dimensions, the interactional aspects of social networks are particular to individual relationships. Consequently, they can only be understood by interpreting the perceptions which individuals have about the relationships in which they interact. Mitchell (1969) identified five interactional dimensions: content, intensity, frequency, durability and direction.

Mitchell (1969) defined *content* as a way of describing the meanings which people attach to relationships, and the understandings they have about the implications which their involvement in particular relationships have for their actions and behaviours in respect to these relationships. For example, if an actor defines a relationship as a 'friendship', they will engage in activities and behaviours that they perceive to be appropriate to those of a 'friend'. As the contents of relationships are not directly observable, Mitchell (1969) suggested that the meanings which social actors attach to relationships could be interpreted in terms of their information, communication or normative contents. Similarly, Tichy, Tushmann and Forbrun (1979) distinguish between four types of content: expressive, instrumental, cognitive and objective. Identification of these contents is however complicated by what Mitchell referred to as the 'multiplexity' of relationships. As social actors typically engage in a variety of interactions within the relationships which they share, a number of contents typically exist within each of these relationships. While recent discussion within business and management research has sparked debate over whether, for example, economic networks can be distinguished separately from those comprised of information and normative contents (e.g., Blackburn, Curran and Jarvis, 1990; Szarka, 1990) Mitchell (1969) emphasized that while social networks comprise of a variety of contents, this did not imply that each content represented a conceptually distinct network. Applied to marketing network research, the contents of relationships can help identify the opportunities and access to resources offered by business networks.

Drawing upon the work of Kapferer (1969), Mitchell (1969) explained that within multiplex relationships, the interactions between social actors are comprised of a variety of contents. For example, the same two people may share an employer–employee relationship comprised of an economic content and also a friend–friend relationship containing normative expressions. As a consequence, the behaviour of the social actors vis-à-vis multiplex relationships cannot be understood unless all of the contents of which they are comprised are identified. Mitchell defended this by explaining that where relationships contain more than one content, each content impacts upon the interactions by which the other contents are created. Using the same example, this uggests that when transacting parties also engage in friendship exchanges, their interactions in the former may condition those in the latter. Applied to business networks 'multiplexity' can help explain the longevity of business collaborations as increasing multiplexity might be indicative of increasing switching costs.

The second interactional dimension, *intensity* refers to the 'degree to which individuals are prepared to honour obligations, or feel free to exercise the rights implied in their link to some other person' (Mitchell, 1969). The intensity of a relationship provides an indication of the influence which relationships have on social action and behaviour. Considered alongside the dimension of multiplexity, intensity provides some indication of how complicated relationships within business networks can be. For example, where a relationship contains both economic and normative contents, the interactions involved in its economic content will be influenced by the obligations which actors feel towards one another as a consequence of the friendship which they share. As the intensity of a relationship cannot be observed, the frequency and durability of networks are suggested as suitable indicators.

Frequency refers to the amount of time social actors spend interacting in relationships. Social network theory asserts that a high frequency of interaction is indicative of intensity. Considered, however, alongside the content of relationships, Mitchell (1969) does caution that frequency is not always an appropriate indicator of the intensity of relationships comprised of normative contents. This, he explained, is because such relationships often have a low level of frequency yet share a very strong relationship. For example, while sisters living apart, one in Glasgow and the other in San Francisco, may not communicate on a regular basis this does not imply that the feelings of friendship and affection that they feel towards one another are diminished. Applied to marketing research, measures of frequency and intensity might usefully be employed to more fully understand the relationship between organizations and customer loyalty. Within industrial markets, intensity and frequency might be applied to better understand the collaborative arrangements which develop between, for example, suppliers and manufacturers as they engage in repeat interactions. Such measures might provide an explanation for the reasons why collaborating organizations adapt their processes and decisions and invest in relationship-specific investments to assist in their interactions with partners.

As participation in social networks fluctuates over time, the *durability* which they are conceived to possess is an indication of the length of time over which a relationship continues and is often used as a measure of the intensity of relationships. Affecting the durability of a relationship are not only the contents of which it is comprised, but also the extent to which both parties to the relationship perceive it to be mutually satisfying. The logic behind this assertion is that if parties to a relationship perceive that they are providing and receiving the type of behaviour which they expect from the relationship, they are more likely to continue to interact than if they perceive that their investment in the relationship is not reciprocated. Mutuality and reciprocity are, however, in turn dependent upon the final interactional dimension of *direction*. This refers to the actor from which a relationship is orientated and provides an indication of the direction of the power of a relationship. As with frequency, however, the extent to which relationships can be described as being orientated in one particular direction, is influenced by their content. For example, where relationships are comprised of normative expressions and are defined by their participants as 'friendship' relationships, their direction is less of an issue than where relationships are defined by their parties as 'economic'. This dimension is of particular relevance to firms that enter into the cooperative relationships typical of business networks. For example, where organizations share a partnering relationship, the orientation of the relationship may be such that the smaller of the firms holds a more vulnerable position.

The Embeddedness of Marketing Behaviour

Conceived of in this way, social network theory aligns itself with sociological explanations of economic activity which argue that like social action, business transactions and behaviours are socially situated and take place within or are embedded in ongoing structures and processes of interactions (Grabher, 1993; Granovetter, 1985; 1992). Granovetter (1992) asserts that as economic action is socially situated, social actors will simultaneously pursue economic and non-economic goals, such as sociability. He explains that:

> [O]ne (though) not the only reason why people conduct their economic action through networks of known personal acquaintances is that sociability, approval, status and power are central human motives and since economic activity is a large part of the lives of many actors, they could hardly be expected to play that large part in an arena utterly cut off from the chance to achieve these motives as would be the case in impersonal, atomised economic life.
>
> (p. 26)

As a consequence of what he describes as the 'embeddedness of social action' Granovetter (1985; 1992) proposes that if the actions and decisions taken by organizations are to be understood, the extent to which these are influenced by these concrete personal relationships and the obligations inherent within and between these have to be taken account of.

Considered alongside the industrial marketing literature presented above, it can be argued that, to date, industrial marketing research has borrowed from sociological and economic theories of personal and interorganizational theories of relationships and networks. However, it can also be argued that to advance our understanding of business network processes, dynamics, influences and outcomes on organizational behaviour work in this area would benefit from adoption of the more theoretically robust constructs proposed by work in more established branches of the social sciences. Applied to marketing studies of business relationships, partnerships and networks, social network theory and the related embedded perspective offer a number of advantages. As identified above, to date, marketing network research has primarily concentrated on understanding the arrangements negotiated between organizations party to resource-dependent, formally recognized, dyadic relationships. It was also mentioned that empirical studies have concentrated on the impact of network morphology, to the neglect of the contents and processes of interaction inherent in such networks (Mitchell,

1969). As a consequence, research to date has provided an incomplete understanding of the impact that relational influences have on the marketing behaviours and activities of organizations. Social network theory offers the potential to overcome some of these criticisms. By conceiving of social networks as possessing both morphological and interactional dimensions, social network theory affords the opportunity of acquiring a more comprehensive understanding of the relational influences impacting on organizational behaviour. Related to this, by recognizing the role of 'brokers', social network theory is a framework well suited to exploring the dynamics of today's 'negotiated' business environment. By considering the density of social networks, cross-sectional studies may reveal that depending upon the dynamics and structure of different industries, the density of the networks in which competitors are embedded, and hence information is circulated, may be less or more. For example, small firm research which has applied social network concepts to understand business development, has established that within the advertising and design industry the structure is such that the networks in which advertising and design agencies are embedded are 'tight' rather than 'loose' knit and as a consequence, competitor and other information is rapidly diffused (Shaw, 1997).

As mentioned above, applied to organizational research, the 'range' of an anchor's network is important in determining their access to available resources. Combined with other morphological dimensions, range can be usefully applied to ascertain the variety of information and other resources available within an organization's network and, once estimated, has potential to explain why some organizations have access to, for example, competitive market information while others do not. Simply put, by applying indicators of network range to studies of the organization, the adage, 'it's not what you know but who you know' is offered a legitimate framework of analysis and takes on a greater relevance. Finally, by conceiving of social networks as comprising of relationships which in turn are comprised of a variety of contents, social network theory offers the opportunity to acquire a clearer understanding of the reasons why and the ways in which relationships impact upon organizational behaviours and activities. Related to this, by recognizing the 'multiplicity' of relationships, social network theory may offer a useful construct for explaining why switching costs between collaborating organizations may increase, and organizations may be encouraged to continue in collaborative relationships even though they may not be cost effective.

Emerging Research

Relative to other business and management subjects, interest in business relationships and networks is at an early stage of development. As a consequence, a wide range of emerging research interests in the related areas of business and network interactions, structures and processes can be identified. Growing interest in this area of marketing, together with the overlapping theories and concepts which it shares with services and relationship marketing research, is such that a detailed review of emerging work in each of these related areas is not permissible here. However the brief review presented below provides an indication of the variety of emerging research interests in the area of business collaborations, interactions and networks.

It was mentioned above that more recent industrial marketing research interested in understanding the processes by which organizations learn has positioned itself empirically at the level of the network. Research in this area has explored the ways in which business networks can enhance organizational learning and argues that the diversity of business networks can enhance opportunities for organizational learning (Eriksson and Hohenthal, 2002; Hakansson and Johanson, 2001).

Also mentioned above, Ellis and Mayer's (2001) recent research in the field of industrial supply chains is an example of research which has explored, empirically, the impact that overlapping sets of interactions of which business networks are comprised have upon network structure. Specifically, their research established that interactions among sets of dyadic business relationships can affect the structure of industry supply chains, as well as be influenced by the structure of such supply chains.

Another area of emerging research is the impact which information technology, in particular the Internet can have on collaborative arrangements. For example, Abecassis, Caby and Jaeger (2000) have explored the extent to which electronic communication and networking impact on the social ties and trust inherent in business relationships. Particular to relationships with individual customers, recent research argues that while database technology has made it possible for organizations to identify and send communications to large numbers of individual customers, the extent to which such technology can be used to develop mutually interactive relationships between organizations and individual consumers is questionable (Patterson and O'Malley, 2000). Instead, these authors argue that, 'the decision to initiate a relationship is often one sided' (p. 96) where organizations use database technology to target communications and seek to develop relationships with their most profitable consumers who are uninterested in responding to such communications or developing 'relationships' with organizations. Such research suggests that the interactive, interdependent, mutually beneficial relationships of which business networks are comprised may be restricted to the business-to-business, industrial markets within which they were first identified and researched.

Related to this is emerging research which has raised questions about the benefits of collaborative relationships. Work in this area has challenged the extent to which partnerships, alliances and other collaborative arrangements pose a threat to competitive markets. Palmer (2001) argues that while organizational collaborations may add value for the partners involved, there is a need to distinguish between cooperative relationships that stimulate competitiveness and collusive arrangements which impact on economic welfare. Turnbull, Ford and Cunningham (1996) agree that: 'inter-company relationships are complex. It is simplistic to suggest that they can or should develop along a single continuum between 'distant' and 'close', 'good' and 'bad'. All inter-company relationships simultaneously exhibit conflict and co-operation with guile and self-seeking' (p. 46).

It was mentioned above that the relationships 'metaphor' has received wide-spread attention within the marketing research literature. Within the international marketing literature, emerging work has sought to explore the impact which culture can have on trust and cooperation (Harris and Dibben, 1999; Karunaratna, Johnson and Rao, 2001). Harris and Dibben, for example, have explored whether and to what extent national values may affect the development of business relationships between individuals in different countries. Their analysis of structured interviews with three founders and chief executives of medium-sized companies in the UK, France and Holland concludes that national values influence both the types of trust sought and the cooperation criteria used to assess whether to engage in inter-firm collaboration. They argued that as a consequence, the presence and impact of trust in developing international business relationships is complex and requires further study.

Also contributing to current understanding about business networks is emerging research in the related areas of small business and entrepreneurial marketing. One explanation for the growing body of network research in these fields may be the smaller size of small and medium-sized firms (SMEs). When applying network theory to organizations, the unit of analysis is the organization. As a consequence, network studies may be more readily undertaken in small business research. This is because small firms are characterized by the informality of relationships in which they engage and, as a consequence of their size, are embedded within networks which are smaller and more readily identified than those of their larger counterparts (Borch and Arthur, 1995; Donckels and Lambrecht, 1995; Perry, 1996). In contrast, as the size of the firm increases, so too does the size of the network in which it is embedded, and to identify and trace such business networks many months of data collection by a team of researchers may be required.

Within the small business and entrepreneurial marketing literature, networks have been identified as opportunity structures (Aldrich, 1987; Aldrich and Zimmer, 1986; Curran *et al.*, 1993; Johannisson, 1986; Szarka, 1990) and described as an important marketing tool which can be of strategic significance (Carson *et al.*, 1995; Shaw and Conway, 2000). For example, the networks of relationships within which smaller and entrepreneurial firms are embedded have been found to impact significantly on their innovation processes, improving new product development (Conway, 1997; Oakey, 1993; Shaw, 1998).

Particular to marketing, the networks within which entrepreneurs are embedded have been found to provide accurate information and advice that can be used to take marketing decisions and evaluate the validity of these decisions. Entrepreneurial organizations have been found to access information about customers from their networks and use this information to improve their pricing structures and tailor their communications (O'Donnell and Cummins, 1999; Shaw, 1998). One reason explaining why networks contribute to the marketing effectiveness of entrepreneurial organizations is that when lacking market information and knowledge, such organizations often make use of their personal contact networks to provide the market information and advice which they need if they are to develop their business. A second reason is the restricted time and resources which entrepreneurs and smaller, entrepreneurial organizations have available to them. As entrepreneurs rarely have the time, resources or inclination to purchase market research reports or seek the advice of business advisers, they often glean market information from their personal contact networks, typically when undertaking other activities such as liaising with suppliers. Simply put, for many entrepreneurs the conversations they have with people they interact with on a regular basis while running their business, constitute the market scanning which they undertake and use to keep up to date about conditions and changes in the market (Collinson and Shaw, 2001). Related to this, an important finding of such research is that the information and advice provided to entrepreneurs from their networks is trustworthy, reliable and can be acted upon (Hill and McGowan, 1997). This is because the individuals providing such information and advice have been found to share more than a transaction relationship with the entrepreneur and their organization. More commonly, they share multiplex relationships comprised of information, advice, friendship and trust.

Implications

While business networks are more likely to be theoretically constructed than they are to be identified by practitioners as physical structures, as a consequence of increasingly inter-firm collaboration, a number of managerial implications have been identified. As business networks can be regarded as opportunity structures comprised of important resources which organizations can access through a process of interacting in the direct and indirect relationships to which they are connected, 'network management' is an important managerial competency. Described within the industrial marketing literature as 'customer portfolio management', it is argued that the challenge for the managers of industrial organizations is, 'how to deal with an inter-connected portfolio of customers and suppliers' (Ford *et al.*, 1998, p. 12). Specific to relationships with customers, in particular key accounts, McDonald (2000) refers to this as 'relationship portfolio analysis' and argues:

> In the same way that the GE or directional policy matrix plots a company's portfolio or market segments against their strength in the market, key accounts can be analysed in order that appropriate strategies can be applied for each of them.

(p. 30)

Going further, Krapfel, Salmond and Spekman (1991) have suggested that in analyzing its network of relationships, organizations should consider the transaction costs, resource dependencies and the direction and power of individual business relationships, and use indicators of these to determine the management approach best suited to managing across the portfolio of business relationships in which they are embedded.

Remembering that business networks can represent liabilities as well as opportunities, effective network management requires analysis of auditing to identify the current impact of an organization's network in terms of the contents, and diversity of the network as well as the organization's position within the network. On the basis of such analysis, management are able to plan and implement any actions necessary to centrally embed their organization within a diverse network comprised of a variety of resources (Granovetter, 1982; 1995). As described above, research, particularly in the area of relationship marketing, has identified managerial implications inherent in managing a portfolio of relationships. However, if practitioners are to move beyond analyzing business networks from the perspective of individual sets of dyadic relationships and instead account for the impact which organizational behaviours and interactions vis-à-vis individual business relationships will have upon the structure and their position within business networks, they may benefit from seeking the advice of outside consultants and researchers. In this respect, parties external to an organization's business network can help. By working with management, outside consultants and researchers can help piece together the network structure within which an organization is embedded by identifying the overlapping sets of dyadic relationships with which management may be more familiar. Having identified all direct and indirect relationships of which their organization's business network is comprised, management are then in a position to undertake the portfolio analysis recommended above. On the basis of this they will have the necessary information about which to take decisions about how to make use of the opportunities presented within their network while also protecting their organization from any actual and potential liabilities.

When applying network theory to network studies of the organization, a number of research implications must be considered. As an understanding of the interactional dimensions of business networks is dependent upon the perceptions which participants have about the content, intensity, frequency, durability and direction of the relationships in which they are involved, qualitative methods are more appropriate than qualitative. Methods such as in-depth interviews and participant observation permit the researcher to get 'close' to participants to penetrate their realities and interpret the perceptions they have about the interactions in which they engage and the impact which they believe these to have had upon the behaviours and activities of their organization. Where a comprehensive understanding of the impact of network morphology and interaction is sought a questionnaire may usefully be employed to ascertain the reachability and range of an anchorage's social network, but it is unlikely that such a method will be successful in collecting data about network density or range. Consequently then, the application of network theory to studies of business networks implies that either qualitative or, at the least, mixed methods are appropriate.

Conclusions and Recommendations

This chapter opened by considering the environmental and theoretical drivers which have encouraged an increase in research and practice in the areas of interorganizational collaboration in the form of partnerships, alliances and networks. The chapter moved to provide a detailed description of the IMP perspective of business networks before presenting a review of research in this field. This review concluded that while industrial marketing conceives of business relationships as being embedded within network structures of overlapping relationships, it is only recently that empirical studies in this area have positioned themselves at the level of the business network and sought to understand the complex interplay between intra and interorganizational interactions and business networks structure, processes and outcomes. As a consequence, empirical industrial marketing research can be described as dyadic rather than network in focus. The argument was made that one reason for this dyadic-reductionism may be the lack of rigorously conceived network concepts within the marketing literature. Building upon this, it was further argued that marketing's understanding of business networks would benefit by borrowing from theories and concepts developed outside of the field in more established branches of the social sciences. The chapter went on to introduce social network theory together with the embeddedness perspective which were conceived of and have a strong history within sociology and economic sociology respectively. The ways in which these concepts could usefully be applied to marketing research were then considered before identifying emerging research in the areas including organizational learning and entrepreneurial marketing which are currently contributing to our understanding of business networks processes, dynamics and outcomes. The chapter drew to a close by identifying the managerial and research implications which have to be considered when managing and practicing marketing networks.

Postmodern marketing: Abutting for beginners

Stephen Brown

Curtain rises to reveal an anonymous office in an anonymous university. Piles of books and papers have accumulated on every available surface. A rickety desk occupies centre stage, though it too is strewn with unanswered letters, overdue library books, disposable coffee cups and yellowing memoranda marked 'urgent'. A middle-aged, pony-tailed professor enters stage right and saunters to the desk. He's wearing a dishevelled leather jacket, black T-shirt and torn designer jeans. Mutton dressed as lamb. He takes his place behind the desk, sighs heavily, glances at his watch and starts working his way through a mini-mountain of unopened mail. 'Rejection . . . rejection . . . rejection', he mutters to himself, as he flings the offending letters in the general direction of the waste paper basket. The telephone rings. He looks around, trying to work out where the sound's coming from and, after lifting several piles of paper, manages to locate the infernal contraption. 'Professor Susan Hart from Strathclyde University is on the line', says a disembodied secretarial voice, 'I'm putting her through'.

SUSAN: Get your ass in gear, Brown. I need a chapter on postmodern marketing and I need it now. Chop, chop.

STEPHEN: Hi Susan. Always nice to hear from you. You're winding me up, right?

SUSAN: Look, buster. Don't talk, just write. Ten K words, max. And none of your artsy-fartsy nonsense.

STEPHEN: Naturally I'm flattered by the invitation. Ah, but you really don't want a contribution from the likes of me.

SUSAN: What is your problem, Brown? Think yourself lucky. You're the bottom of my list, the scrapings of the scrapings of the barrel. Russ Belk's too busy. John Sherry's out of the country. Morris Holbrook wanted to do something about cats. I ask you. So, you're my last resort and you'd better make it good. Otherwise . . .

STEPHEN: Otherwise?

SUSAN: *Journal of Marketing Management.* Me editor, you contributor. Kappische? Or, do I have to spell out the consequences of your refusal?

STEPHEN: No, no, I catch your drift. And a very fine journal it is, too, Susan. However, I still think you'd be better off with someone else.

SUSAN: Why's that?

STEPHEN: Well, because postmodern contributions to edited books take all sorts of textual liberties. They stick out like a sore thumb. They lower the tone. People get upset. I've subverted several anthologies in my time and, if you're not careful, yours could be next.

SUSAN: All I want is a straightforward explanation of postmodern marketing.

STEPHEN: Ah, but then it wouldn't be postmodern.

SUSAN: What do you mean?

STEPHEN: The postmodern eschews straightforward explanations. So, if I explain it straightforwardly, it wouldn't reflect the non-straightforward character of postmodernism.

SUSAN: It doesn't eschew pretentious words like eschew, then? Or non-existent neologisms like non-straightforward?

STEPHEN: Oh, no. The more pretentious, the better. Neologisms a-go-go, don't you know.

SUSAN: Well, pretentiousness I can live with. Neologisms too. I'm the editor of a top-notch journal, remember. I've seen it all. But, tell me, why does an explanation of postmodern marketing have to be postmodern? Why must it reflect the character of the thing itself? Can't you just write *about* it?

STEPHEN: It doesn't. It mustn't. You can. There are quite a few published explanations of the postmodern that set it out in a fairly straightforward way. What it is. Where it comes from. Its basic premises, principal characteristics, practical examples and so forth.

SUSAN: Sounds good. I'll have one of those. You've got till Friday.

STEPHEN: Ah, but then it wouldn't be postmodern. That kind of thing is all very well, but it's basically a modernist explanation of postmodernism and, as such, it doesn't quite convey the iconoclastic postmodern spirit, which seeks to subvert even as it explains.

SUSAN: What do you mean?

STEPHEN: Well . . .

SUSAN: Oh, oh . . . wish I hadn't asked that.

STEPHEN: Well . . . um . . . you want a chapter on postmodern marketing. Right . . .?

SUSAN: Right! A.s.a.p. I've got a deadline, don't you know.

STEPHEN: . . . And I want to write one for you.

SUSAN: Glad we sorted that out. It took a while but we got there eventually. Get scribbling, sunshine.

STEPHEN: Ah, but it's not that simple.

Flings cowboy-booted leg over the arm of the chair.
A self-satisfied smirk crosses his face.

STEPHEN: If I'm going to contribute, it'll have to be a postmodern postmodern chapter, as opposed to a modern postmodern chapter, if you see what I mean. And a postmodern postmodern chapter has to be written in an unconventional manner. So . . .

SUSAN: What do you mean by unconventional?

STEPHEN: Dunno. A poem, perhaps. A short story, possibly. Is a phoney dialogue out of the question?

SUSAN: A phoney dialogue?

STEPHEN: Don't look so worried, Susan. The unconventional form disguises the conventional content. It'll still explain what postmodern marketing is; it just does it in an unconventional manner.

SUSAN: Hmmm. I'm not so sure about that. You must've heard about the *Kotler is Dead!* debacle in EJM, where someone wrote a phoney dialogue around Kolter's alleged demise. No-one knows who it was. Used a pseudonym. Pandemonium ensued. So, dialogues of any kind are out. You do understand, don't you?

STEPHEN: I do. I do. I understand completely. Disgraceful behaviour. But, do *you* understand *my* position?

SUSAN: No, not really. Why can't you just write it in a conventional manner?

STEPHEN: Ah, but . . .

SUSAN: . . . then it wouldn't be postmodern. I see. Couldn't you make an exception and at least try to write it properly. Just this once.

STEPHEN: Well, if I could do it *properly*, there's no-one I'd rather do it *properly* for. But it's the *properly* that's the problem. Who's to say what *properly* is? Why does every chapter have to be *proper*?

SUSAN: That's the way it is around here. We're supposed to be scholars, after all. At least some of us are. Scholars write in a scholarly fashion.

STEPHEN: Once again, it depends on what type of scholarship you're referring to. Marketers have traditionally aped the hard science model of explication, as have the social sciences generally. But there are other modes of scholarly enquiry. Take the humanities, for instance . . .

SUSAN: Do I have to?

STEPHEN: Yeah, I know what you mean. Much of it is impossible, impenetrable, infuriatingly obscurantist. And that's just the anthropologists. All I'm saying is that there are many ways to skin a scholar.

SUSAN: Maybe so. But not in my book, amigo. No dialogues will be entertained, thanks all the same.

STEPHEN: Not even entertaining dialogues?

SUSAN: Especially not entertaining dialogues.

STEPHEN: Then we have a problem, because I believe that postmodern marketing should be communicated in an unconventional manner. Anything less isn't true to the spirit of the subject matter.

SUSAN: Ah, but I thought postmodernists didn't give a fig about truth.

STEPHEN: That's true.

SUSAN: And you've previously said that it's possible to write about the postmodern in a non-postmodern manner, even though it's not to your personal taste.

STEPHEN: That's true, too.

SUSAN: So, maybe there's a way round this.

STEPHEN: Oh yeah, what's that?

SUSAN: What if we simply talked it through. I'll ask you questions. You answer them as best you can, without compromising your postmodern integrity. And I'll get someone else to write it up in a conventional manner.

STEPHEN: Oh yeah, who's that?

SUSAN: A copywriter we have on retainer, Alan McSmithee.

STEPHEN: Oh yeah, I've heard of him.

SUSAN: That's settled then.

STEPHEN: Ah, but what about authorship? Who'll get credit for the chapter? You don't really expect me to tell you all I know about postmodern marketing, which could take the guts of 10 minutes, only to let someone else attach their name to it.

SUSAN: No, no, it'll be in your name, Stephen. Provided you can live with McSmithee writing it on your behalf.

STEPHEN: Sounds a bit unethical, Susan.

SUSAN: I didn't know you were big on ethics. You didn't used to be.

STEPHEN: No, I'm not. Ethics schmethics, I say.

SUSAN: So, what's the problem?

STEPHEN: The problem is I didn't write it, even if I agree with his interpretation of my interpretation of postmodern marketing. It's not exactly . . . um . . . authentic.

SUSAN: Ah, but almost everything's rewritten these days. Journals regularly rewrite manuscripts. Many management gurus, such as Gary Hamel and Tom Peters, openly acknowledge their reliance on copywriters. Ghost writing is big business. Teams of monkeys are typing as I speak. And anyway, I thought postmodernists didn't give a . . . er . . . monkeys for authenticity. I thought you lot thought plagiarism is okay. Fake is the new real, is it not?

STEPHEN: You seem to know an awful lot about postmodernism, Susan.

SUSAN: Yes, I tried reading one of your books once, Stephen.

Looks up, startled. Stares querulously at the telephone receiver.
Makes rude gesture in its general direction. Breathes deeply before replying.

STEPHEN: You're a Trojan, Suzy, that's what you are.

SUSAN: Look, I hate to rush you, compadre, but this is getting a bit tiresome. Can we cut the crap and shake a leg, or something?

STEPHEN: Well, perpetual deferral is prototypically postmodern, so I think we should string it out for a while longer. Don't you?

SUSAN: Ah, but I have a book to deliver. I haven't got all day. Let's get a move on, shall we?

STEPHEN: Okay, you incorrigible modernist, you. Ask what you will and I'll try to answer as honestly as I can. Which isn't very honest, let's be honest.

SUSAN: First things first. Can you think of a title?

STEPHEN: Certainly can.

SUSAN: That's a start. Do you mind telling me what it is?

STEPHEN: Not in the least.

SUSAN: Well?

STEPHEN: Hmmm, how's about 'Kotler ain't dead, baby, he's just havin' a break'?

SUSAN: No!

STEPHEN: 'The Cultural Contradictions of Kotlerism'?

SUSAN: No, nothing on the Venerable Phil.

STEPHEN: Let me see. What about 'One More Time, What is Postmodern Marketing'? And before you say anything, yes, the allusion to Michael Baker's oft-reprinted 'cri de marketing coeur' is quite deliberate. That's the kind of thing we postmoderns do, dropping smart-aleck hints of other works, be they academic articles, rock albums, classic movies or, in extremis, advertising slogans.

SUSAN: Nothing too highbrow, I see.

STEPHEN: Right. The postmodern is grounded in popular cultural forms like soap operas, video games, comic books and the World Wrestling Federation. Hell, we even have a special word for such misquoted quotations. Intertextuality. Or is it bricolage? Polysemy perhaps? Who knows? Pomo terms are interchangeable, inexplicable, incomprehensible . . .

SUSAN: You don't say.

STEPHEN: Oh yeah. It's great, isn't it? At one stage, I invented a postmodern lexiconometer.

SUSAN: A what?

STEPHEN: A postmodern lexiconometer. Basically, three columns of pretentious terms which can be combined in any order to produce a preposterously impenetrable postmodern phrase. Maybe we could include it in the chapter.

EXHIBIT 9.1: Patented postmodern phraseology producer

Actualize	Androcentric	Aphoria
Decentre	Discursive	Defamiliarize
Heterogeneity	Historicize	Hegemony
Hermeneutic	Heteroglossian	Hierarchical
Ideological	Intertextual	Indeterminacy
Interpretive	Iterative	Inherence
Monological	Metacriticism	Misprision
Patriarchy	Post-colonial	Phallogocentric
Polypony	Processual	Polyvalent
Subvert	Signifier	Semiosis
Theorize	Totality	Transcend
Transgressive	Transcode	Textual
Subjectivity	Subtext	Supplement
Valorize	Victimize	Value-free

SUSAN: I don't think so, Stephen.

STEPHEN: No, really, it's fun. Hyperreal Heteroglossian Hegemony. Polysemous, Patriarchal Praxis. Deconstructing Decentred Diacritics. Your readers'll love it!

SUSAN: Did you think of this all by yourself?

Looks at phone again. Silently mouths the words
'Did you think of this all by yourself?'.

STEPHEN: Come on, Susan. Get real. I'm not that clever. I stole it from someone. Can't remember who. But they're unlikely to complain, since plagiarism is part and parcel of the postmodern project.

SUSAN: Well, I don't think you'll have too many concerns on that score. Your intellectual property is quite safe from plagiarists, I would've thought.

STEPHEN: You were saying, Professor Hart . . . .

SUSAN: Now, now, don't get huffy with me.

STEPHEN: I'm not huffy!

SUSAN: Of course you're not. Tell you what, we'll allow you your Bakerlite title, plagiarized though it is.

STEPHEN: Alllll righty . . . .

SUSAN: Unless Michael objects. Then it's gotta go.

STEPHEN: Ah, but . . .

SUSAN: That's the deal. Take it or leave it.

STEPHEN: That's not very postmodern of you, Susan.

SUSAN: Look amigo, aside from the textual shenanigans, you still haven't told me what you mean by the postmodern, let alone postmodern marketing. What is it, *exactly*?

STEPHEN: Ah, now you've got me. I suppose it all depends, à la Wild Bill Clinton, on what you mean by *it*. Or is it *is*? That question mark is questionable too. And as for *exactly*, exactitude isn't exactly the kind of thing I specialize in.

SUSAN: Heaven help us!

STEPHEN: Not sure if I can swing that one, Susan.

SUSAN: Okay, let's take it one step at a time. Is postmodernism an *it*?

STEPHEN: Yes and no. It-ness implies something called postmodernism exists and that it can be identified, specified, set out and explained. Many postmodernists wouldn't accept this attempted categorization, however, because they believe the postmodern is fluid, intangible, inexplicable, unclassifiable, a polysemic linguistic sign that *it* doesn't somehow encapsulate. That said, the term is so ubiquitous and so widely discussed these days that, postmodern pedants notwithstanding, it is an *it*, yes. It has become an *it*, despite itself. If you see what I mean.

SUSAN: Sort of. What's the problem with *is*?

STEPHEN: It might be a *was*.

SUSAN: A *was*?

STEPHEN: Yup. The postmodern is passé. It's old hat. It has been. Postmodernism may be fairly new to marketing, but this stuff is 30 years old in the humanities.

SUSAN: Oh yes, what replaced it?

STEPHEN: Do you really want to know?

SUSAN: Perhaps not.

STEPHEN: Definitely not!

SUSAN: Moving swiftly on. What, pray, is your problem with the question mark?

STEPHEN: Nothing. I was wrong about that. The question mark is okay. The postmodern is essentially a series of questions rather than answers . . .

SUSAN: So, your questioning of the question mark was questionable?

STEPHEN: Exactly.

SUSAN: I thought exactitude was out, as well.

STEPHEN: Exactly! Do you want me to explain?

SUSAN: No, not just now. Let's go back to it-ness. You said it had become an it. What does postmodern marketing's it-ness consist of. What is, or was, *it?*

STEPHEN: The 4Ps.

SUSAN: The what? The 4Ps? Call me old-fashioned, but that's the modern marketing paradigm, surely. There's nothing postmodern about the 4Ps. I hate to break this to you, Stephen . . .

STEPHEN: Ah, but the postmodern 4Ps are different.

SUSAN: Really.

STEPHEN: Presentation. Practice. Periodization. Philosophy.

SUSAN: Right. Dare I ask you to elaborate?

STEPHEN: Sure. I've already covered 'presentation', the way in which postmodern marketing research is presented. Conventional modes of representation are out, unconventional forms of discourse are in.

Starts rummaging noisily underneath the desk.

SUSAN: Whatever you say. Good Lord, what's that dreadful racket?

STEPHEN: I'm getting out my bagpipes. I thought I'd skirl the story so far.

SUSAN: I'm all for unconventional discursive forms, Stephen, but we're a wee bit pushed for time. What does 'practice' consist of? That sounds fairly straightforward. Maybe there's something there we can construct a chapter around.

STEPHEN: You could be right. Practice basically refers to the fact that many of today's marketing practices are recognizably postmodern. Not everyone agrees of course, since the precise character of postmodernism is up for grabs and one person's PoMo is another person's NoNo. Nevertheless, according to Firat and Venkatesh, postmodern marketing consists of five key features – *hyperreality, fragmentation, reversed production and consumption, decentred subjects,* and *juxtaposition of opposites.*

SUSAN: Now we're getting somewhere. What is 'hyperreality'? Did you say 'fragmentation'? Can you explain 'reversed production and consumption'? Who 'decentred the subjects'? What's 'juxtaposition of opposites' when it's at home?

STEPHEN: Whoa! Hold your horses. Back up those bicuspids. I'm not going to explain all that.

SUSAN: What is your problem, *compadre?*

STEPHEN: If I try to explain 'hyperreality', 'fragmentation' and so forth, I'd have to include large chunks of text. Traditional text, I mean. Paragraphs, proper sentences and what have you. They'd completely ruin the dialogic form of this chapter.

SUSAN: There isn't going to be a dialogic form, Stephen. Give me a solid paragraph or two. You know it makes sense.

STEPHEN: No can do. No dialogue, no paragraphs, solid or otherwise. Sense doesn't come into it.

SUSAN: I can see that.

STEPHEN: Look, thanks for your call, Susan. Sorry we couldn't reach some sort of accommodation. Why don't you get in touch with Malcolm McDonald? He and his Cranfield cronies are planning to develop a postmodern marketing metric, I gather. Just what the world needs.

SUSAN: Hmmmm. What if we put the solid paragraphs in boxes, separate from the rest of the text? Casual readers can go straight to the boxes and get what they want without having to persevere with your ponderous, sorry pellucid, prose.

STEPHEN: I don't know. Postmodernists have an aversion to boxes. Smacks of pigeonholing, linearity, precision, *Marketing by Matrix*. Can't have that.

SUSAN: Ah, but we could call them something else. Tables? Figures? Exhibits?

STEPHEN: Exhibits might be okay, I suppose. Carries connotations of artistry, aesthetics, ostentatiousness. Yeah, I guess I could live with one or two of those.

SUSAN: Five, Stephen. You said Firat and Venkatesh identified five postmodern marketing practices.

STEPHEN: What, can your readers not read? Direct them to the original article in *JCR* and let them get on with it. What is this, *Deconstruction for Dummies*?

SUSAN: *By* dummies, if you ask me. Look, this book is supposed to be an anthology, an overview, a summary . . .

STEPHEN: A crib sheet for lazy bastards, you mean.

SUSAN: What, like the lazy bastards who won't write a proper chapter? I need five boxes.

STEPHEN: Exhibits. They're exhibits. Two's your lot.

SUSAN: Four.

STEPHEN: Three. That's my final offer. And don't even think of joining them up with arrows.

SUSAN: Done! Three boxes it is. Exhibits. Whatever. However, I want original material. I don't want a rehash of something you've published elsewhere.

STEPHEN: Everything I do is a rehash, Susan. Rehash Browns, that's me. Take it or leave it.

SUSAN: The publishers'll complain.

STEPHEN: No they won't. I've had lots of dealings with the slimy sods. As long as it isn't libellous, they couldn't care less.

SUSAN: Look, I don't have time for this. It's getting tiresome. Tell me about 'periodization', your third P.

STEPHEN: Now you're talkin'.

SUSAN: Oh, oh. Don't like the sound of that.

STEPHEN: Don't worry, Suzy, you'll love this one. For me, 'periodization' is the essence of the postmodern. Not everyone agrees, naturally, but what the hell do they know?

A student pokes her head around the open door of the office and knocks gently, only to be airily waved away with a 'today's tutorial is postponed' expression. She looks delighted and withdraws.

EXHIBIT 9.2: Hyperreality

Exemplified by the virtual worlds of cyberspace and the pseudo worlds of theme parks, hyperreality involves the creation of consumption sites that are more real than real. The distinction between reality and fantasy is momentarily blurred, as in the back lot tour of 'working' movie studios in Universal City, Los Angeles. In certain respects, indeed, hyperreality is *superior* to everyday reality, since the negative side of authentic consumption experiences (such as anti-tourist terrorism in Egypt, muggings in New York or dysentery in Delhi) magically disappears when such destinations are recreated in Las Vegas or Walt Disney World. Ironically, however, the alleged superiority of the fake is often based on an unwarranted stereotype of the real, and the reality of the fake – standing in line in Tokyo Disneyland, for example – may be much worse than anything the average visitor would actually experience in Egypt, New York, Delhi or wherever. But such is the cultural logic of postmodern marketing.

EXHIBIT 9.3: Fragmentation

Marketing in a postmodern world is unfailingly fast, furious, frenetic, frenzied, fleeting and fragmented. It is akin to zapping from channel to channel, or flicking through the pages of glossy magazines, in search of something worth watching, reading or buying. Shopping on speed. This disjointedness is partially attributable to the activities of marketers themselves, with their ceaseless proliferation of products, ever-burgeoning channels of distribution, increasingly compressed commercial breaks and apparent willingness to accept any form of payment from plastic cards to cowrie shells. (Presumably, plastic cowrie shell cards are waiting in the wings.) Marketing fragmentation, however, is also a response to the disconnected postmodern lifestyles, behaviours, moods, whims and vagaries of contemporary consumers. A product of profusion with a profusion of products, the postmodern consumer performs a host of roles, each with its requisite brand name array – wife and mother, career woman, sports enthusiast, fashion victim, culture vulture, hapless holidaymaker, websurfing Internet avatar and many, many more. Postmodern identities are fluid, so they say. Postmodern personae are proliferating, are they not? An off-the-shelf self is available in your favourite styles, colours, designs, fits and price points. Made-to-measure selves cost extra.

Susan: Are you going to enlighten me, at all?
Stephen: Well, periodization is apparent on a number of levels. First, there's the notion that we're living in a new era, the postmodern era. We have moved beyond modernity to a qualitatively different time, characterized by

---

EXHIBIT 9.4: Reversed production and consumption

This fragmented, hyperrealized, postmodern consumer, it must be stressed, is not the unwitting dupe of legend, who responds rat-like to environmental stimuli of Skinnerian caprice. Nor is the postmodern consumer transfixed, rabbit-like, in the headlights of multinational capital. Nor, for that matter, is he or she likely to be seduced by the sexual textual embeds of subliminal advertisers, though they might pretend to be. On the contrary, the very idea that consumers have something 'done' to them by marketers and advertisers no longer passes muster. Postmodern consumers, in fact, do things with marketing. Postmodern consumers are marketing literate. No matter how carefully developed and designed the marketing campaign, postmodern consumers will succeed in subverting it. Postmodern consumers are street-smart shoppers who are wise to the wiles of marketers, who are more than capable of dodging target marketing and who, as the recent 'spirit of '68' retro riots in Seattle, London, Davos and Genoa aptly demonstrate, are quite prepared to take control of 'their' brands, whilst denouncing the marketing malefactors who betrayed them.

---

indeterminacy, chaos, paradox, contradiction, fragmentation, hyperreality and all the rest. It's an epoch of computer-mediated infotainment, accelerating economic instabilities and impending environmental catastrophe.

SUSAN: Basically, fiddling the books while Rome burns.

STEPHEN: Something like that. Plus random acts of terrorism, deadly diseases caused by human irresponsibly, the ethical turmoil on the biotechnological frontier.

SUSAN: I thought the postmodern was supposed to be playful, ironic, fun . . . .

STEPHEN: After a fashion. It also laughs in the face of disaster, supposedly. It's closely associated with the idea of apocalypse. It maintains that the bad, old, modern dispensation has imploded. Hence, all the PoMo ruminations on the end of history, the end of philosophy, the end of society, the end of work, the end of the family, the end of innocence, the end of belief, the end of science, the end of organized religion, the end of humanism, the end of ecology, the end of capitalism, the end of the world. They say that if you want to sell lots of books these days, simply title your tome 'the end of something or other'.

SUSAN: The end of marketing?

STEPHEN: Ah, but that's been done already.

SUSAN: The end of postmodern marketing?

STEPHEN: Are you trying to tell me something?

SUSAN: Yes, get on with it!

STEPHEN: And then, of course, there's the idea of eternal recurrence. *Déjà vu* all over again. Old is the new new. Cyclical time is being recycled. Revivals, re-enactments, reconfigurations, relaunches, re-releases and all the rest are everywhere apparent. Old ads are being broadcast. Old products are being reissued. Old trade characters are being reanimated. Old distribution channels are being reopened. Old pricing strategies are being reconsidered. The cinemas are packing them in with remakes, sequels, and sequels of remakes like *The Mummy Returns*, to say nothing of historical spectaculars such as *Pearl Harbor* and postmodern period pieces akin to *Moulin Rouge*. Video rentals and sell through are equally retro-orientated, as are our television screens and theatres. Just consider *The Producers*, Broadway's biggest hit for decades. The music industry is retro a-go-go, moreover. Comebacks are two a penny. U2. Santana. Tom Jones. Aerosmith. ELO, for goodness sake! And then there's the plethora of new old products. The VW Beetle. Nike's Michael Jordan retro sneakers. The Chrysler P.T. Cruiser. Disney's Celebration. The Ford T-Bird. Restoration Hardware. The Jaguar S-series. Caffrey's Irish Ale. The new Mini. McDonald's 50s-style diners . . .

SUSAN: Okay, okay, okay. Don't get carried away. I get the picture. Whatever happened to the dialogic, by the way?

STEPHEN: Glad you interrupted, Sue. I wouldn't want this to turn into a proper scholarly discussion, let alone a solid paragraph.

SUSAN: You know, some readers might conclude that my interruption was deliberately staged. That it's nothing more than a crude rhetorical device to circumvent convention in an otherwise conventional adumbration of your argument.

STEPHEN: Adumbration? What kind of word is that? No one uses adumbration in everyday discourse. You're deliberately trying to suspend the suspension of disbelief, aren't you?

SUSAN: You're one to talk. How many people use words like everyday discourse in everyday discourse? And, as for suspending the suspension of disbelief, I mean, who really talks like that? This dialogue is almost postmodern in its inauthenticity.

STEPHEN: Nice one. Can I return to the monologue now?

SUSAN: Yep, I think the coast is clear.

STEPHEN: As I was saying, periodization is everywhere nowadays.

SUSAN: You're heavily into this retromarketing stuff, aren't you?

STEPHEN: Aye. I've just written a book on retro, though I don't want to mention it in case I'm accused of deliberate product placement.

SUSAN: Of being the Fay Weldon of marketing.

STEPHEN: Something like that.

SUSAN: What's the book called again?

STEPHEN: *Marketing – The Retro Revolution*. But I'd prefer not to draw attention to it. Selling under the guise of scholarship's a tad unseemly.

SUSAN: Who's the publisher?

STEPHEN: Sage. But really, Susan, it's not the done thing . . . .

SUSAN: How much does it cost?

STEPHEN: £19.99. However inspection copies are available, I'm led to believe.

SUSAN: You were saying?

STEPHEN: Sorry?

SUSAN: You were about to say something before the commercial break.

STEPHEN: Oh yes, periodization is everywhere nowadays.

SUSAN: You've told me that already.

STEPHEN: Only practising what I preach, Professor Hart.

SUSAN: God, this is getting tedious. What's Malcolm McDonald's number, again?

STEPHEN: Anyway, periodization is everywhere these days. According to the acerbic American comedian, George Carlin, the Western world is suffering from a debilitating disease called 'yestermania'. Its principal symptom is an unhealthy preoccupation with times past – sequels, reruns, remakes, reissues, recreations, re-enactments, adaptations, anniversaries, memorabilia, oldies radio and nostalgia record collections.

SUSAN: Excuse me, but since when did stand-up comedians become founts of scholarly knowledge?

STEPHEN: Since the postmodern turn. One of the key features of PoMo is that creative artists and works of art are considered more insightful than the findings of traditional research methods. This is true even of popular cultural art forms like stand-up comedy. It is especially true of popular culture art forms like stand-up comedy. I would argue that we can learn more about contemporary consumer society from Chuck Palahniuk, the author of *Fight Club* and *Choke*, than any number of discussion groups or questionnaire surveys. For example, I read an interview with him where he said, 'Art is a big pumped-up operatic version of real life; it's the lie that tells the truth better than the truth does'. That, to my mind, hits the nail on the head.

SUSAN: What's postmodern about that? We've heard variations of that argument since the Romantic movement of the nineteenth century, if not before.

STEPHEN: Right! The postmodern itself has been periodized. Postmodern ideas have been around for a very long time. PoMo is not new. Far from it.

SUSAN: So, it's the intellectual equivalent of new wine in old bottles?

STEPHEN: More like new old wine in new old bottles.

SUSAN: Whatever.

Long silence

SUSAN: That's it then? Your fourth P of philosophy is just a bunch of old ideas with a new name. Glad to hear it. I was a bit worried about the fourth P. I always thought postmodern philosophy was the hard part, a lot of stuff and nonsense about textuality, relativism and meaninglessness.

STEPHEN: Um . . . well . . . you see . . . there's more to it than conceptual recycling. Let me elaborate.

SUSAN: Well, I think I've heard enough to be getting along with. I'll have a word with Mr McSmithee and we'll take it from there. Perhaps we can just reference the rest.

STEPHEN: Ah, but then you'd be ignoring the most important stuff.

SUSAN: The tough stuff.

STEPHEN: The tough stuff that your readers really need to appreciate.

SUSAN: They won't read it anyway. They'll skip that bit. We can live without it.

STEPHEN: Yeah, but I thought you wanted a complete overview of postmodern marketing?

SUSAN: There is a limit, Stephen.

STEPHEN: Bear with me.

SUSAN: I know I'll regret this, but go ahead.

STEPHEN: I'll keep it short. The really important thing your readers have to understand is that postmodern philosophy is antifoundational. It rejects Enlightenment-inspired notions of truth, progress, rationality, rigour or, in marketing research terms, analysis, planning, implementation and control. It rejects the idea of marketing science, the search for analytical frameworks, general theories, meaningful models and all the rest. We all know these things are imperfect and deeply flawed, but we have hitherto worked on the assumption that we can improve on them, that progress will be made, that we can develop better concepts, theories or frameworks, provided we work hard enough and provided we bring additional methodological, mathematical and model-building brainpower to bear on the problem. Postmodern philosophy regards this as futile. It contends that we will never find a general theory, or an all-singing all-dancing framework, or even an agreed definition of marketing, branding, exchange, relationships or whatever. We can number-crunch till we are green in the face, but all we'll end up with is a lot more information and a lot less understanding.

SUSAN: So, we should just give up and go home?

STEPHEN: No, no, not at all.

SUSAN: What do you suggest we do instead of model building, hypothesis testing, theory development and the like?

STEPHEN: Hmmmm. Well, it depends on which particular postmodernist you talk to. Some say that the postmodern doesn't offer an alternative. It is simply a critique. It points out the problems with existing forms of understanding. That's all it does.

SUSAN: What use is that to anyone?

STEPHEN: Critique is vitally important. It gives a sense of perspective. It helps us stand back from what we're doing. It forces us to rethink our basic assumptions and bases for action. Nihilism has its place.

SUSAN: Ah, but if you don't offer an alternative, people'll stick with the devil they know.

STEPHEN: Yes, Susan, I agree with you there and some postmodernists have attempted to articulate an alternative.

SUSAN: Which is?

STEPHEN: Well, it sort of suggests a middle ground between the grand theories of modernity, the so-called metanarratives of progress, democracy, the good society etc., and the absolute negativity of the anti-modern wing of the postmodern movement.

SUSAN: And that means?

STEPHEN: It means a focus on petit narratives, storytelling, political interest groups, neo-tribalism, the quotidian, the ludic, the low brow, the ephemeral.

SUSAN: Sounds a bit like marketing to me.

Improvises stage directions in a desperate attempt to convince readers
that they're watching a play.

STEPHEN: Exactly. One of the most striking things about the postmodern turn is its preoccupation with matters commercial. Marketing, advertising, shopping centres, consumer behaviour and so forth are now regarded as legitimate topics of study by the wider academic community. Branding is no longer confined to the business school. Strategic plans are being dissected by sociologists and deconstructed by literary theorists. Hypermarkets are the haunt of historians. Consumers are the cargo cults of contemporary anthropology.

SUSAN: Well if that's the case, why are you asking us to abandon our intellectual birthright at a time when marketing's the 'in thing' academically?

STEPHEN: Marketing phenomena may be hot to trot but marketing research is regarded as a joke. It's considered the last bastion of scientism, the elephant's graveyard of positivism. Call it what you will.

SUSAN: That's just professional jealousy. These people resent the fact that business schools are burgeoning while their budgets are being cut.

STEPHEN: I think there's some truth in that, especially in the States where B-school salaries are much bigger than university norms. What's more some of the stuff the sociologists come up with is marketing 101. Ritzer's work springs immediately to mind. His ignorance of even the most basic marketing principles is mind-boggling. He would do well to cast his eye over Kotler . . . .

SUSAN: Steady on, Stephen. I never thought I'd see the day when you'd be recommending Kotler.

STEPHEN: Yeah, I can't believe I just said that. Anyway, notwithstanding petty university politics and academic one-upmanship, these exo-marketing marketing researchers, if I can call them that, have little or no time for mainstream marketing research. They regard us as apologists for multi-national capitalism, as part of the problem rather than the solution. And I think they've got a point.

SUSAN: So, what you're saying is that we're sitting on an intellectual goldmine but our conceptual picks and shovels are inadequate?

STEPHEN: You could put it like that. But it's not so much that our picks and shovels are substandard, it's that we're equipped with knives and forks. Plastic knives and forks. Meanwhile the claim jumpers are using dynamite. Their scholarly technology is far superior to ours.

SUSAN: That's depressing.

STEPHEN: It doesn't need to be. There're some excellent miners in the postmodern marketing community, trufflers of thought who are trying to articulate an alternative to the big science mindset that dominates our field. These people are into storytelling, ethnography, identity politics, semiotics, neotribalism, videography, subcultures and so forth. They may not be postmodernists in the strong sense, the nihilistic sense, the apocalyptic sense, but they are our best hope for the future by far. The marketing majority, the so-called mainstream, still regards them as the crazy gang and they haven't helped themselves in this regard, since they take pride in their heretical positioning. They're leather-jacketed, pony-tailed, cowboy-booted, middle-aged teenage rebels, basically. But the fact of the matter is that what they're doing is not only closer to the norms of contemporary social science, it's closer to what today's marketing practitioners want as well! Mainstream marketing research has almost nothing to say to managers and executives. The model builders are talking to themselves. They're onanists one and all.

SUSAN: Speak for yourself, Stephen.

STEPHEN: Ah, but you haven't heard the best bit, Susan.

SUSAN: I thought we had the best bit already.

STEPHEN: Oh yeah, right. Periodization's the best bit. I meant the ironic bit.

SUSAN: I thought it was all ironic.

STEPHEN: Well that's true. I mean the *really* ironic bit.

SUSAN: Will this take long?

STEPHEN: No, it's very simple. The irony is this. The other social sciences are already usurping our subject matter and they'll shortly be usurping our constituency of practitioners. If mainstream marketing research continues the way it's going, practitioners will turn to those social scientists, such as the unspeakable George Ritzer, who are spitting in our scholarly spittoon. And why shouldn't they? The exo-marketing expectorators, be they anthropologists or literary critics, offer insights that are better and more meaningful than ours. They work more cheaply than B school types, as well. Marketing practitioners are already disillusioned with the output of marketing academics. Why wouldn't they turn to someone with something different to say?

SUSAN: Ah, but I thought the sociologists and suchlike were opposed to money-grubbing capitalists?

STEPHEN: They are. At least in theory. They still quote *The Communist Manifesto* and condemn the fetishism of commodities.

SUSAN: We're okay, then?

STEPHEN: For the meantime. But it won't last. They'll be bought off too. Marx has already been outed as a capitalist and the Marxists will soon follow suit. You can tell from the way they write about marketplace phenomena. They're totally besotted with advertising agencies, shopping centres and suchlike. However, their training requires them to condemn the iniquities of the marketing system. All it needs is for someone to legitimize consorting with capitalists and then, to cite the hirsute one himself, 'all that is solid melts into air'.

SUSAN: That's a tad apocalyptic, isn't it?

STEPHEN: By Jove, I think she's got it!

SUSAN: Yes, I think I might just have got it, you patronizing, sexist sod.

STEPHEN: It's intertextual, Susan. *My Fair Lady* and all that.

SUSAN: My fair arse. Intertextual or not, it's still offensive.

STEPHEN: Ah, but it's only a little postmodern joke. Postmodern playfulness and all that.

SUSAN: It's still offensive, you condescending so and so.

STEPHEN: Sorry, Susan.

*Another student appears at the office door and is rewarded with a
'give me five minutes' signal. His face drops.*

SUSAN: Don't sorry me, sunshine. I may have got it, as you so elegantly observed, but I don't agree with it. You're seriously telling me that postmodern marketing involves (a) pretentious textual forms (b) a handful of traits like hyperreality and fragmentation, that were around long before the purported postmodern epoch (c) a preoccupation with the past that is again nothing new and (d) an anti-foundational philosophy that anticipates the overthrow of marketing by a bunch of smelly sociologists? Is that what you're saying?

STEPHEN: Pretty much. That's about it, yes.

SUSAN: And you expect me to include that lot in my new book?

STEPHEN: You did ask for a contribution. Chop chop, wasn't it?

SUSAN: Are you mad?

STEPHEN: That word has been used about me in the past.

SUSAN: Do you really think the publishers'll stand for it?

STEPHEN: What the hell they know?

SUSAN: Do you really think I'm going to ask McSmithee to write up this drivel?

STEPHEN: He's written worse.

SUSAN: Do you really think I have time to listen to any more of this pointless conversation?

STEPHEN: I guessed you were getting BT bonus points based on the length of the call.

SUSAN: God, I knew I should've e-mailed instead.

STEPHEN: E-mail. There's a thought! Maybe I should reframe this chapter as a series of e-mail exchanges.

SUSAN: What, you think I'm going through all this again?

STEPHEN: It's art, Susan.

SUSAN: That's not the word I'd use. It's close though.

STEPHEN: It's the lie that tells the truth better than the truth does. Would I lie to you?

SUSAN: Don't go there, sunshine.

STEPHEN: Your wish is my command.

SUSAN: Be careful what you wish for.

STEPHEN: I wish you'd allow me to do the chapter as a dialogue. A playlet, perhaps.

SUSAN: Not a chance . . . .

STEPHEN: Ah, but . . .

SUSAN: No way, Jose.

STEPHEN: Ah, but . . .

SUSAN: No buts about it.

Exit, stage left, pursued by publisher.

Marketing operations

PART 3

Marketing operations

CHAPTER 10

Market research and knowledge

Christine Ennew

Market research has a long history, perhaps more so than many other aspects of marketing. ESOMAR (the World Association of Opinion and Marketing Research Professionals) and the Market Research Society (UK) have both comfortably passed their 50th birthdays while their American counterpart, the Marketing Research Association is only two years away from that same milestone. The activity that they represent is, of course, much older. After all, the marketing process depends upon research and information, and implicit in every definition of marketing is the need to understand and be responsive to the external market environment. So it should probably not be surprising that the earliest recorded use of research to inform marketing decision-making dates back to 1879, while the first formal market research function was established in 1911 by Charles Parlin and the Curtis Publishing Company. From these early beginnings, market research developed rapidly in terms of the range of topics researched, the methods of data collection and the complexity of methods of analysis. Some of this development may be attributed to supply-side factors; the development of new statistical, interview and observation techniques served to increase the range of tools at the disposal of market researchers. Developments in technology (both hardware and software) reinforced these trends, making techniques that were once prohibitively expensive accessible to all. But the growth of market research is not down to supply-side factors alone. On the demand side, organizations have become increasingly information-hungry as they seek to compete in a rapidly changing and highly complex environment. Indeed, recent years have seen a growing recognition that organizational survival and success is heavily dependent on the ability to recognize and respond to changes in the environment – the processes of organizational learning (Argyris and Schon, 1978) and market orientation (Kohli and Jaworski, 1990). Market research serves as a source of the raw materials from which organizations may learn and as one of the building blocks of market orientation.

However, for much of its existence, market research has been treated almost as a distinct discipline, separate from but working alongside marketing. It is probably only in the last two decades or so that the strategic significance of market research and the importance of the information it generates has really come to the fore. Perhaps the simplest indicator of this is the growing interest in marketing information systems (MkiS) and marketing decision support systems (MDSS), both of which constitute standard components of any market research text and both of which emphasize the importance of integrating information from multiple sources. At the risk of overgeneralizing, historical perspectives on competitive success have tended to emphasize price-based competition or a focus on quality (Schnaars, 1998) but limits to declining costs and convergence in quality have meant that customer orientation, innovation, learning and knowledge have begun to take centre stage. In particular, the development of research in the area of market orientation, triggered by the seminal works of Kohli and Jaworski (1990), served to re-emphasize the importance of market research as one of the cornerstones of marketing. Subsequent research focusing on the growing interdependence between market orientation and learning orientation simply served to reinforce perceptions of the strategic significance of market research and the knowledge it generates (Sinkula, 1994).

As a consequence, market research appears to have moved away from being a simple support function and towards being an integral component of marketing strategy development. The purpose of the current chapter is to provide an overview of the nature and process of market research and to explore aspects of its evolution. The intention is to provide an overall perspective on the development of market research. This chapter does not aim to provide an explanation of how to do marketing research – there are already a vast range of books and articles that provide a comprehensive treatment of this topic (see, for example, Kumar, Aaker and Day, 2002; Webb, 1999; or Worcester and Downham, 1988). The chapter begins with a brief discussion of the nature and significance of market research and knowledge in order to provide a context for subsequent discussion. The next section examines the market research process very briefly and seeks to explores its evolution in terms of both theory and practice. The penultimate section examines the utilization of market research and seeks to highlight the factors that may encourage and inhibit the full and proper use of the knowledge generated through market research. The chapter closes with a section which provides conclusions relating to the current state of market research and identifies key challenges for the future.

The Nature and Significance of Market Knowledge

It is often helpful to begin a discussion with some definitions so that everyone can be clear about meanings. This chapter is concerned with market research and knowledge. The terms market research and marketing research are often used interchangeably, as are the terms market knowledge and market intelligence. For the purposes of the current chapter it is helpful to think of market (marketing) research as being concerned with the 'systematic collection, analysis and evaluation of information about specific aspects of marketing problems'. Market knowledge (intelligence) can then be thought of as the understanding, awareness and meanings that are created as a result of analysis and evaluation. In very simple terms, we might think of market research as being the input and market knowledge as the output. Obviously data may be collected, analyzed and evaluated without formal market research and the importance of informal data gathering should not be underestimated. Nevertheless, marketing research remains one of the major sources of marketing knowledge and intelligence and accounts for a significant component of marketing expenditures for many organizations.

Generating Knowledge

While market research is a major source of market knowledge and intelligence, the development of theory relating to learning organizations draws attention to other important and relevant sources of knowledge. In particular, there seems to be an emerging consensus that suggests that there may be four main sources of knowledge within organizations (see, for example, Garvin, 1993; Slater and Narver, 2000).

1 *Market-based knowledge*
   This refers to knowledge which arises from conventional market research based on primary and/or secondary data. Knowledge about customers, competitors, distributors and other key stakeholders is generated through the analysis of data collected through a variety of different methods (surveys, scanner data, focus groups, etc.). Research of this nature may be generated through an established in-house market research function or (and increasingly) through external specialists.

2 *Collaborative knowledge*
   Collaborative knowledge is knowledge generated from within networks through the interaction of individuals. It is based on the idea that individuals can and do learn from each other. In an increasingly complex environment, it becomes difficult for any one individual to have the depth of knowledge and experience to address a full range of business and marketing challenges. The existence of organizational networks provides a framework for interaction and the interaction between individuals with different knowledge sets has the potential to generate significant new understanding.

3 *Knowledge through experimentation*
   Information may arise as a consequence of experimentation. Experimentation essentially involves organizations trying out new ideas and observing and learning from the outcomes. It can be argued that getting ideas to market quickly and testing consumer response may be far more effective than detailed and long-winded processes of concept testing.

4 *Knowledge based on experience*
   Traditionally, learning through experience has been associated with production processes and the impact of experience on costs. Experience may be equally important from a marketing perspective, creating an opportunity for

organizations to learn about customers through frequent interactions, or learn about competitors through observation of strategic responses. One reason for the growing interest in relationship marketing stems from the opportunities it creates for organizations to learn from the experience of multiple interactions with consumers.

Slater and Narver (2000) argue that all four approaches to the generation of knowledge will be important in driving organizational performance. This chapter will focus specific attention on the first, namely conventional market research, not least because it continues to be the most visible as well as probably the single most important approach to knowledge generation.

Why Are Research and Knowledge Important?

The widespread use of phrases such as 'the knowledge economy' and the growing interest in 'knowledge management' signal the increased interest in the role of knowledge and learning as organizational assets which may serve as the building blocks for competitive advantage. From a marketing perspective, explicit recognition of the importance of information and its contribution to organizational performance originates in the work of Kohli and Jaworski (1990) and their definition of market orientation. Information generation is central to market orientation and market orientation in turn has a positive impact on business performance. As other chapters in this book have explained, the importance of market orientation as a determinant of performance has been extensively researched and a significant body of evidence suggests that a positive relationship does exist; furthermore, organizational learning also plays a significant role in driving organizational performance. Both processes are fundamentally dependent on market research. Research will contribute to these processes directly as an input to decision-making and in response to a specific and identified information need. Equally though research makes an important contribution through its impact on broader managerial understanding and awareness: some research does not address a specific issue but attempts more generally to aid understanding of the current and future market environment. Research and the resulting knowledge should generate better managerial decisions as a consequence of a superior level of understanding of the market places (market orientation), made by better informed managers who are acquiring new understanding and questioning existing perspectives on a continuing basis (organizational learning).

Having established what is meant by market research and knowledge, how it may be generated and why it is important, the chapter moves on to explore the processes by which market-based knowledge is generated and how that process may be changing.

The Evolution of the Market Research Process

In many senses, market research is fundamentally a practical subject. Text books, handbooks and courses on market research all tend to focus on the process of 'doing the research' with particular emphasis on the techniques of research design, measurement, data collection and data analysis. And yet, market research is heavily grounded in theory, or rather theories. For example, statistical theory underpins sampling processes and a range of analytic techniques. Similarly, epistemology guides many aspects of research design, while marketing theory, consumer theory and social psychology underpin both the approaches used to answer particular research questions and the way key constructs are measured. Finally, other more specialized market research problems may be guided by a variety of different aspects of social and cultural theory. Thus, market research can be thought of as highly practical but with a diversity of theoretical under-pinnings. As a subject area it will change and develop in response to changes in both theory and practice. In some areas of market research, the relevant aspects of theory have changed little (e.g., basic statistical theory, epistemology) and the subject has developed through changes in practice. In other areas, theoretical developments have been more significant (e.g., consumer theory, social and cultural theory) and market research has evolved through the interplay of theory and practice.

To explore the nature of market research and the way it has evolved, we will follow a conventional model for the market research process; i.e., one which breaks market research down into a series of discrete steps (see, for example, Kumar, Aaker and Day, 2002). In some senses, adopting this approach betrays the author's own philosophical perspective on the nature of research. More significantly perhaps, presenting research as a sequence of stages may create the illusion that the process itself is linear. No such illusion is intended. The research process is rarely linear and most practitioners would probably describe research as a complex, non-linear and interactive process. Increasingly we should recognize that market research is a process that may draw simultaneously on multiple data sources according to availability and that it continuously refines research questions through interactions with clients and feedback from initial data collection (Smith and Dexter, 2001). Notwithstanding this characterization of research, the 'sequence of stages' approach is adopted as a useful organizing framework. Each stage is introduced briefly in order to highlight the activities covered in that stage and then key developments in theory and practice are discussed.

Establish the Purpose of Research

Market research may be undertaken for a variety of needs, including immediate instrumental needs (answers to particular problems) as well as broader conceptual needs (enhancing understanding). Both types of research may be either exploratory, being concerned with generating preliminary insights about particular topics, or alternatively confirmatory and thus concerned with drawing more substantive conclusions. Although it is most commonly associated with customer research, market research also extends to competitors, channels, suppliers and a range of other relevant stakeholders.

The first step in any research process must be to identify the precise objectives for the research – what is the nature of the 'problem' under consideration, what questions are to be answered and what information is required? Superficially, defining the purpose of the research may seem straightforward, although as

Gibson (1998) points out, it requires careful thought, analysis and judgement. In some instances, the purpose of market research may be concerned with trying to understand gaps between desired and actual outcomes (e.g., research to help understand slow growth in sales). In other instances, the purpose may be to provide direct inputs to marketing decisions (e.g., researching new product concepts or segmentation). In yet other instances, research may be concerned with more general benchmarking and tracking activity (e.g., regular customer satisfaction surveys).

In some respects, the underlying purpose of market research will change little, if at all. Businesses have always needed research to help diagnose problems, to provide inputs to decision making and to track aspects of the external environment. For example, one of the earliest pieces of market research, carried out in 1879 by the advertising agency N.W. Ayer, was a simple survey to provide information to guide advertising decisions. Many modern day studies will have similar motivations. The only difference might lie in the complexity and sophistication of the techniques that are used. Thus, it could be argued that while the methods and techniques to generate answers may have changed, many of the underlying questions may remain similar. However, this may be too simplistic a view of market research questions. The questions that market research has to address are implicitly or explicitly dependent on a set of theories about the behaviour of the groups being researched and a set of beliefs about the nature of the external world (see for example the discussion in Carson *et al.*, 2001). To the extent that such theories and beliefs change and evolve then so will the nature of the questions that face market researchers.

To consider the impact of changes in theory on the specification of research questions it is instructive to consider the case of consumer research. Consumer research is probably the dominant form of market research. It can also be argued that consumer behaviour, and thus consumer theory, are the areas which have seen most development in theoretical terms. We can identify five different theoretical perspectives on the consumer. The traditional perspective on consumer behaviour has three basic theoretical perspectives; the information processing models which dominate textbook thinking about consumer behaviour, the behavioural perspective, and trait theory. Within the traditional perspective, consumer choice is essentially rational and deterministic and the consumer is largely passive, reacting and responding to marketing stimuli. In contrast, novel perspectives such as the interpretive and postmodern perspectives on consumer behaviour present a more complex, subjective and multifaceted view of consumer behaviour.

Traditionally, a large volume of consumer research has been predicated on the traditional perspective and has been dominated by information processing models, exploring links between attitudes and behaviour. Valentine and Gordon (2000) describe these consumers as 'statistical'; the consumer is 'a fact and as such is simplified, analysed, segmented and targeted' (p. 3). There is a long tradition of research dealing with consumer attitudes, predicated on a theoretical perspective in which attitudes predict intentions and intentions predict behaviour. Large-scale segmentation studies based around personality traits also reflect a more traditional perspective in which buying behaviour is seen to be the result of certain enduring features of an individual's personality. Research to develop segmentation systems such as VALS and PRIZM is founded on a belief in trait theory. The pre-eminence of these traditional perspectives has resulted in a dominant mode of enquiry in market research which focuses on a rational, goal-directed consumer whose decisions can be predicted through the identification and measurement of appropriate internal or external stimuli. In style, such research has been concerned with the identification patterns in attitudes and behaviour and the desire to aggregate – to identify aggregate groups of consumers or aggregate patterns of behaviour – to explore similarity rather than difference.

Newer perspectives on the consumer – predominantly those associated with interpretive or postmodern perspectives – imply a different way of thinking about consumers. These perspectives share a common view of the consumer as active rather than passive with the ability to construct their own subjective meaning rather than simply accept what is imposed by others. To Valentine and Gordon (2000), these newer perspectives require that we recognize the consumer as an extension of the person who is able to construct multiple meanings and identities through the process of consumption. In the interpretive perspective, considerable emphasis is placed on the importance of understanding consumers' constructed meanings of marketing actions. Brand researchers should recognize the brand as a living entity and an extension of the consumer, rather than just as an extension of the product. Since the brand is given meaning by the consumer, research questions need to shift away from the simple evaluation of brand features as independent components of the brand and move towards a more in-depth exploration of the meanings consumers ascribe to the brand as an entity.

In the postmodern perspective, the emphasis is on the symbolic, fragmented and subjective nature of consumption. Postmodern consumer research rejects the idea that consumers have well-defined needs and the idea that consumers can be understood in any objective sense. With its emphasis on multiple meanings and changing consumer identities, the postmodern perspective suggests not only different questions but also different methods of research including deconstruction and cognitive mapping. While it may be somewhat artful to argue that postmodern market research is impossible because the idea of a single representation of the subject being researched is inconsistent with the principles of postmodernism, such a perspective on consumers and society does have major implications for the nature and conduct of market research (Brown, 1995; Shankar and Patterson, 2001).

Although consumer theory has dominated the discussion thus far we should not exclude the impact of theoretical developments elsewhere in marketing and their implications for the nature of marketing research problems. Changing perspectives on the nature of competition and the growing interest in demand-side perspectives changes the issues that need to be addressed in competitor research. More generally, perhaps, the presence of marketing management as the dominant theoretical perspective (see, for example, Webster, 1992) and its emphasis on what marketers 'do' to customers to influence their behaviour underpins the long tradition of research dealing with the selection of appropriate levels for marketing mix variables (see, for example, Blamires, 1981). The belief that changes in the marketing mix will lead to changes in what and how much is bought provided the basis for studies to help identify optimal marketing decisions. To the extent that the traditional marketing management model is being challenged by more interactive, relationship-based theories of marketing, there will be future changes in the questions that market researchers must address.

The evolution of different theoretical perspectives on how consumers behave and how marketing works changes managers' and researchers' perceptions about the nature (or even existence) of cause and effect. These changes will directly affect the type of questions that market researchers will need to address. As subsequent sections will suggest, these changes will also have implications for the other stages in the research process.

Designing the Research Process

Once researchers have a clear idea of the purpose of the research, they must determine the best way to operationalize the research process; this requires a clear research design. The design of the research process is concerned with identifying the processes and methods to provide answers to the designated research questions. This process is often broken down into three stages:

1 *What data are required?*

   In broad terms, data may be primary or secondary and while the nature of the research questions will determine which type is more appropriate, it would be fair to say that most research will combine initial desk research and secondary data analysis with subsequent field work and primary data collection. The growth of the Internet in particular has dramatically increased the volume and variety of secondary data that is available, although not without raising questions as to its quality.

2 *What are the most appropriate sources?*

   Where secondary research is being used, data may be available internally or externally. Where primary research is planned, subjects must be selected for the research. This requires general consideration of the units of analysis as well as more specific considerations about sampling.

3 *How should the data be collected?*

   Traditionally, data collection can be one of three types: experimentation, observation and survey. First, experimentation is often used when the research question is concerned with a specific problem relating to the effect of a small number of marketing mix variables. This approach involves adjusting the levels of the variables that are of interest and monitoring consumer response. This monitoring would typically be accompanied by comparisons with a control group who may be located in a different geographic area or may be separated by time. Second, observation essentially involves watching consumer behaviour in a particular marketing situation and making inferences from the behaviour that is observed in relation to marketing stimuli. Third, surveys involve collecting information from the relevant individuals or organizations by directly asking questions on the issues of interest. Surveys were traditionally conducted by mail, telephone or in person, although there is a growing use of e-mail and websites as the basis for collecting survey data. The use of survey-based approaches to data collection can raise important issues about the processes of measuring the key concepts being investigated.

As explained in the previous section, changes in marketing and consumer theory have precipitated changes in the issues that may be of interest to market researchers. Changes in the questions that researchers ask will often require changes in the process of generating answers. For example, the traditional view of the brand as an extension of the product that could be decomposed into its constituent parts spawned questions about the management and assessment of brands that were commonly answered by large-scale quantitative surveys to measure consumer attitudes to elements of the brand. A switch towards a view of the brand as an extension of the consumer raised questions about the way in which the brand as an entity was perceived and the way it was changing. Such questions were more usefully addressed by qualitative and often projective techniques.

Developments in measurement theory (which may be attributable to marketing and/or psychology) have altered the way marketing concepts are operationalized for the purpose of market research. Largely as a consequence of the pioneering work of Churchill (1979) on scale development, researchers have a clearly defined and rigorous process for measuring marketing constructs. Moreover, with the appearance of collections of marketing scales (e g , Bruner and Hensel, 1996) a range of different measures have become widely accessible to researchers and the issue of scale development and the links between the nature of research questions and the desirable properties of scales continues to attract attention (see, for example, Flynn, 2001). In practical terms, there are indications of academically developed scales (SERVQUAL, for example) being utilized in commercial applications, a process which should enhance comparability and consistency. Moreover, the widespread availability of standardized questionnaires and measurement systems (see, for example, the question banks available at http://qb.soc.surrey.ac.uk/docs/home.htm) has encouraged a greater degree of standardization in data collection and this again facilitates more rigorous comparisons across research studies and over time.

Changes in the design of the market research process have also been driven by theoretical developments outside of marketing that have broadened the range of techniques available to researchers. The development of semiotics, for example, provided a new way of researching advertising and other related decisions (Harvey, 2001). At the opposite extreme, developments in time series analysis have had a major impact on approaches to forecasting.

Not all changes in the design of the market research process are theory driven, indeed, many of the most visible are probably related to changes in what is practical. Of particular significance here are developments in technology which have had a major impact on methods of data collection. Computer-aided data collection techniques have greatly increased the efficiency and accuracy of primary data collection, while bar code and smart card technology have enabled the capture of large volumes of data at point of sale. This in turn has enabled the construction of large-scale data warehouses which provide a valuable source of secondary data on consumer purchasing behaviour. More generally, the development of the Internet and developments in database technology have dramatically increased the range and variety of secondary data that is accessible cost effectively. Large volumes of syndicated research can be accessed directly and reports downloaded almost instantaneously. The development of data fusion (Baker,

Harris and O'Brien, 1989) has enabled the integration of proprietary and publicly available commercial databases to generate more comprehensive information sources.

ICT developments and particularly the Internet have also broadened the range of sources on which researchers may draw (Opperman, 1995). Geographical and temporal constraints can be eased, giving access to a much larger target population for either survey work, whether qualitative or quantitative. The potential for quick responses from Internet/web-based data collection is considerable, although there are many issues to do with sampling, response bias, availability and accuracy of sample frame and representativeness that remain unresolved. More significantly, perhaps, there are concerns over the accuracy of data captured by web-based surveys, with the eighth GVU Survey reporting that more than 40 per cent of the information collected via web questionnaires being inaccurate (Turban *et al.*, 2000). However, other studies suggest that consumers may be willing to reveal more and more detailed information in computer-based surveys (Moon, 2000). The value of the Internet is not limited to quantitative data collection. Feedback on online depth interviews has been positive (Curasi, 2001) although the value of online focus groups is still subject to some debate. Finally, online-based ethnographic studies are also under consideration (Kozinets, 2002).

Although web-based data collection is perhaps most commonly associated with survey or quasi-survey based methods of data collection, the features of the web allow other forms of data collection to take place. In particular, the use of cookies to track consumer movements between websites provides a novel form of observation. Similarly the ability to customize web interfaces and the nature of offers made to individual consumers provides a different medium for experimentation. The latter is not without problems though as Amazon found out when trialling different pricing policies for new and existing customers.

Implementing the Investigation

This is the process of actually carrying out the research. Implementation is always easier if the research process has been carefully and sensibly designed. Key to the implementation phase is the need to maintain good contact between the people doing the research, those managing it and those who will need to use it. Good communications should help to ensure that implementation problems are dealt with quickly and in a manner that is consistent with the client's requirements.

Changes in the implementation phase of the market research process largely reflect the chances that have occurred in relation to defining research questions and planning the research design. The development of new methods of data collection will create a need for staff to acquire new sets of skills – which may range from the use of computer-aided interviewing or web-based surveys through to the deconstruction of advertising material. Probably the most visible change in the implementation phase relates to data collection. Again, developments in ICT such as those described earlier have dramatically increased the speed, volume and accuracy of data collection and through improved communications, technology can ensure regular contact between the producers and the users of the research.

Analyzing Data

The implementation phase results in the collection of data. The analysis phase is then concerned with converting this data (whether qualitative or quantitative) into information. The results of the analysis will not solve the original problem but they will provide managers with the information they need to find answers to the original questions. Moreover, as the research process becomes a more integral part of the development of marketing strategies, increased emphasis is placed on the ability of market researchers to provide not just analysis but also advice on action points.

The degree of sophistication in data analysis will vary according to the problem under consideration. In some cases, data may be subject to highly complex statistical analysis. In other cases, the analysis may be very simple. Whatever type of analysis is used, it is important to remember that interpretation plays a key role at this stage. One potential source of bias may be that an individual analyst may be looking for patterns he or she expects to see rather than patterns which are actually there.

A major development with respect to the data analysis phase has been the ability to use a much wider range of techniques cost effectively. In the past decade a range of statistical tools that were once limited to the specialist have become very widely available and user friendly (Meidan and Moutinho, 1999). Computer processing capacity has enabled the processing of very large data sets and the development of a range of data-mining techniques has greatly facilitated the analysis of large-scale databases such as those associated with supermarket buying as recorded on loyalty cards. But developments are not just restricted to quantitative techniques. On the contrary, developments in tools for qualitative analysis have dramatically increased the productivity of researchers dealing primarily with focus groups or depth interviews.

Irrespective of the range and sophistication of the analytical techniques available, it is important to remember that the findings of any market research study depend on the quality of the data and the quality of the interpretation. When using market research to guide marketing decisions it is important that managers are comfortable with the quality and reliability of the data and the interpretation that is placed on the data. Interpretation in turn depends on the prevailing theoretical perspectives of those involved in the research – both researchers and those commissioning the research. As is explained later, these factors can have a significant impact on the extent to which market research is actually utilized.

Presenting Findings

Once the analysis is complete the findings must be presented to the client. Even when market research has been undertaken internally, the managers who requested the research would expect a presentation and report. Typically, the report will contain very detailed information often accompanied by extensive appendices. In contrast, the purpose of the presentation is to provide an overview of the key findings and issues that have emerged. As with the implementation phase, the final presentation phase has evolved but largely in practical terms as ICT developments have enabled increasingly sophisticated presentations.

The Utilization of Market Research

Thus far, this chapter has argued that market research and market knowledge have value and can contribute to enhanced organizational performance. It has also explored the process of doing market research and the ways in which that process is evolving. Implicit in this discussion has been the assumption that market research, once generated, will be utilized. Such an assumption may be unwise; indeed one reason why Kohli and Jaworoski (1990) conceptualize market orientation in terms of three elements (information generation, dissemination and responsiveness) is to highlight the importance of utilization.

Existing research would suggest that market research can be utilized in three different ways (Menon and Varadarajan, 1992; Slater and Narver, 2000). The instrumental and conceptual uses have been mentioned already; the third form of utilization is typically described as symbolic. Each of these will be considered briefly in turn.

- *Instrumental use*
  The *instrumental* use of marketing research is essentially a form of use where research is developed in order to solve a particular problem such as the decision to launch a new product, the pre-testing of an advertising campaign or the evaluation of customer satisfaction.

- *Conceptual use*
  Information may also be used *conceptually*; in this format the use of research results is rather more indirect than is the case with instrumental utilization and it may more usefully be conceptualized as developing the managerial knowledge base.

- *Symbolic use*
  Both the instrumental and conceptual use of marketing research imply using the research in a manner which is consistent with its intended purpose. However there are instances in which research findings may be distorted and/or used in a much more *symbolic* and political fashion. Such utilization may involve the partial or selective use of findings to support or legitimize a particular position or to justify actions taken for other reasons (Brown and Ennew, 1995). Often the failure to use market research in the way in which it was intended was attributed to a concern with trappings rather than substance (Ames, 1970) and a degree of uncertainty regarding the precise meaning of the marketing concept. Arguments about the symbolic use suggest that content may be deliberately ignored and form is used as a symbol to legitimize decisions which have already been taken or decisions which are taken for political rather than conventionally rational reasons. In these cases information is still utilized but not necessarily in the way that it was intended. While the ethical dimensions and practical merits of the use of information in this way may be subject to debate, for the

purposes of studying utilization it is important to recognize that this activity may coexist with other forms of utilization.

Early attempts to understand the utilization of information in organizations originated primarily within the information systems literature and adopted what was essentially a supply-side perspective. From this perspective, it was assumed that utilization would increase if the quality and quantity of marketing information also increased (see, for example, Buttery and Buttery, 1991; Higby and Farah, 1991); the prescription was simple – if suppliers could generate more and better information, organizations (consumers) would make more use of it. In essence this approach was a product orientation towards market knowledge. While clearly the quality of any information is an important issue and one which should not be disregarded, quality by itself will not increase utilization although poor quality may well reduce it.

In the 1980s, a more user-based perspective on marketing information utilization began to emerge to counterbalance the traditional producer-based perspective. Theoretical developments sought to identify the factors which were most likely to influence the extent to which a particular set of information was actually utilized. In one of the earlier studies, Deshpandé and Zaltman (1982; 1984) identified six sets of variables that were deemed to have an impact on the use of market research information. These were:

1 The purpose of the research project.
2 Organizational structure.
3 Research report characteristics.
4 The extent of surprise with results.
5 The life cycle of the product or service.
6 Interaction between managers and researchers.

In contrast to producer-based perspectives, this framework suggested that the quality of the information was only one of a range of factors that affected the utilization of that information. In attempting to evaluate this model empirically, Deshpandé and Zaltman focused on instrumental use only. Their results suggested that their framework was effective at explaining market research utilization from the perspectives of both managers (i.e., users) (Deshpandé and Zaltman, 1982) and researchers (i.e., producers) (Deshpandé and Zaltman, 1984).

Somewhat later, a more comprehensive model of market research utilization was developed by Menon and Varadarajan (1992) who attempted to integrate both producer and user perspectives and to examine all three forms of utilization. They suggest that the type and degree of information utilization will be affected by:

■ environmental factors

■ task complexity (i.e., task variability and task difficulty)

■ organizational factors (i.e., degree of organizational structure, information and innovation culture, internal and external communication flows)

- informational factors (cost of information, perceived credibility of information/knowledge, perceived usefulness of information/knowledge)
- individual factors (i.e., prior disposition)

While this framework is probably one of the most comprehensive models of market research utilization, it remains an essentially conceptual study. Moreover, Menon and Varadarajan (1992, p. 68) acknowledge that 'though we adopt an organizational perspective in the development of the conceptual model, the need to examine issues related to knowledge use from a micro perspective (i.e., cognitive processes of individual managers) should be recognized'. Other empirical evaluations of the ways in which marketing research is utilized and the factors which influence the utilization are few in number. Empirical evidence is primarily US-based while the number of studies conducted in Europe are limited or merely applied to one of the present frameworks (Diamantopoulos and Horncastle, 1997), or focused on a specific dimension of marketing activity such as exporting (see, for example, Souchon and Diamantopoulos, 1996).

This would suggest that the area of utilization requires further attention. After all, if market research and market knowledge have such a valuable contribution to make it would be wasteful to see resources devoted to the collection of information which is not used.

Conclusions

Market research has a long history and many aspects of modern market research would be familiar to many of the early practitioners. At the same time, the market research process has evolved over the century or so since it first really developed. Three key themes can be identified in this development process. The first is the move away from market research being seen as a discrete support activity and towards a recognition of the integral importance of information and knowledge in creating and maintaining a competitive market position. Second, with the market research function there has been a broadening out in terms of the types of issues that are subject to research. In particular, there are indications that the kind of questions that are being addressed by market researchers have expanded in a way which broadly mirrors the patterns of change and development in marketing theory. Third, developments in technology, both hardware and software, have greatly increased the type and volume of data that can be collected and analyzed. These same developments have also made available a wide range of more sophisticated methods of analysis.

Looking to the future, it is clear that there are a range of challenges that confront market researchers and the market research function. As marketing and consumer theory evolves, the perspectives on marketing issues may change. Nevertheless, individual researchers are often conditioned by their own traditions and assumptions. Learning to question these assumptions can be as important for marketing researchers as it is for managers within 'learning organizations'. The ability to be aware of and open to alternative conceptualizations has the potential to greatly increase understanding of the nature of consumer behaviour and marketing practice.

Many of the developments in relation to data collection can dramatically increase the volume and nature of data collected. This raises questions of how such data can or should be analyzed and the reliability and validity of data from different sources. Again, this suggests a growing need to challenge and question what may be presented as evidence for particular relationships. A further consequence of the range and variety of data collection methods is the growing concern about privacy and, in particular, the covert collection of data on consumers through the monitoring of web-based activity.

Finally, the issue of market research utilization remains controversial. Utilization is a complex social and economic process which is still only imperfectly understood. Nevertheless, at the heart of the market research process is the belief that information, when used for the purpose for which it was intended, can offer significant performance benefits for organizations. If this claim is to be believed, and there is evidence to support its validity, the realization of any benefits will depend upon the willingness of those who commission market research to use it in decision-making processes.

Market segmentation: Changes and challenges

Sally Dibb

Introduction[1]

In the 1960s and 1970s, Tesco targeted price-conscious grocery shoppers with a 'pile it high, sell it cheaply' trading philosophy created by founder Jack Cohen. The budget segment is no longer of interest to Tesco, and today the likes of Aldi, Netto and Kwik Save fight for leadership of this bottom end of the grocery supermarket sector. Tesco is now the overall market leader and ranks as one of the world's most successful retailers. Its strategy was devised in the early 1980s at a time when upscale Sainsbury's led the way. Tesco analyzed the customer needs, buying behaviour and expectations of not only its customers but of grocery shoppers in general. The company also examined macro consumer spending patterns, shopping habits, leisure trends, economic issues and the practices of the leading international retailers. The decision was made to leave behind the budget end of the market and to concentrate on delivering superior customer service, quality merchandise and the latest retailing concepts to a newly-defined priority target market. The target for Tesco was the growing number of affluent consumers seeking better quality merchandise in a customer-oriented in-store environment. By following this strategy, with new-look stores, better trained staff, more customer service, improved merchandise ranges and a new brand positioning, after a decade Tesco had caught up the market leader Sainsbury's. Now the company has left all competitors trailing in its wake.

The use of market segmentation, shrewd targeting and clear brand positioning have all been pivotal to this success. The role of these aspects of strategic marketing is still central to Tesco's business strategy, which is perhaps not surprising given the current CEO, Terry Leahy, was once a junior Tesco marketing executive. Tesco realized that e-commerce was on the horizon and decided to offer Tesco Direct, targeted at 'time-precious' consumers wishing to purchase Tesco products online. Other supermarket rivals have tried and failed to make e-tailing profitable. Tesco understood that only a specific subset of its customers desired to buy online and that its Tesco Direct proposition had to be carefully tailored to their needs and expectations with a user-friendly operating system and flexible home delivery. Whereas other e-tailers have struggled to cover their set-up costs, Tesco's web-based operation is already contributing to the company's profits owing to the target market strategy devised and effectively implemented by Tesco.

Market segmentation has proved to be highly beneficial for Tesco in other ways, too. Many retailers and service providers have developed loyalty cards, but Tesco's ClubCard is widely perceived to be one of the best. Not only does the ClubCard capture customer purchasing data, but the behind-the-scenes technology utilizes the resulting customer profile and purchasing data to group like-minded customers into tightly defined groups so that marketing propositions and communications can be carefully targeted. For example, new parents receive money-off vouchers for newborn baby products, plus pamphlets discussing baby care issues. Unlike certain competitors' loyalty card schemes, Tesco's sophisticated databases enable the offers to be modified as the baby grows older so that only relevant offers and information are mailed to the child's parents. Within the store, Tesco recognizes that some of its shoppers are more value conscious than others. In addition to its core range of manufacturer branded and own-label products, Tesco offers its own budget priced 'Value' range, with its distinctive blue, white and red packaging. For customers wishing to pamper themselves or cater for a special occasion, the deluxe, silver-packaged Tesco 'Finest' range offers high quality at a premium price. Even within its primary target market of more affluent and discerning grocery shoppers, Tesco has defined several market segments and appropriately specified marketing mixes.

The success of supermarket Tesco is based on being able to provide customers with the products and marketing programmes they desire. The use of market segmentation principles to guide its business strategy has helped Tesco to achieve this goal. This is because the retailer has recognized that the needs of all shoppers are not the same. The company's 'Value' and 'Finest' ranges are just two examples of how market segmentation has helped deal with this diversity. Tesco has also taken advantage of technological advances to market its offerings through entirely new channels. While the company recognizes that not everyone will want to shop over the Internet, by understanding its customer base Tesco has been able to develop a time-saving alternative for a segment of consumers whose lifestyles are particularly time pressured. Not all supermarkets that have pursued e-commerce opportunities have enjoyed Tesco's success, which is reaping the benefits of carefully implementing its strategy.

The aim of this chapter is to consider the application of market segmentation for businesses today. In particular, the focus is to examine the underlying rationale for market segmentation, the ways in which its use is changing and whether segmentation effectiveness can be assured. These issues, which are at the heart of today's thinking on market segmentation, are encapsulated in three fundamental questions that provide the framework for the chapter:

1 What evidence is there to support the use of a market segmentation approach?
2 What does the future hold for market segmentation?

3 What can businesses do to improve the chances of market segmentation success?

The chapter begins by explaining the concept of market segmentation and by considering the underlying rationale for its use. Next, the three stages of the market segmentation process are examined: segmenting, targeting and positioning. The discussion of segmenting – the grouping of customers with similar needs – involves reviewing different approaches to segmenting the consumer and business-to-business markets. This discussion is followed by a review of the targeting phase, which considers how many and which segments companies should target with their sales and marketing effort. An examination of positioning, the final stage of the market segmentation process, is next. Here the underlying rationale for positioning is explored and the positioning process examined. The next section reviews future trends for market segmentation, focusing on technological advance and the move towards the 'segment of one'. The final part of the chapter examines market segmentation success and explores what businesses can do to bring it about.

The Market Segmentation Concept

Market segmentation is the process by which customers in heterogeneous markets can be grouped into smaller more similar or homogeneous segments. Customers have different needs and wants and demand variety in the products and services they buy and use. This principle is at the heart of the market segmentation concept. In most circumstances, a mass marketing approach, involving the development of a single product and marketing programme for all customers, is inappropriate. Shampoo buyers expect to be offered a range of brands and product types so that they can purchase an offering that suits their hair type and hair washing needs. Children choosing breakfast cereals also have different preferences and desires that they assume will be satisfied when they visit their local Tesco or Sainsbury's store. Indeed, the diversity of products in today's supermarkets and other retail outlets is evidence of these expectations.

Despite the weight of customer expectations, it is rarely feasible for a business to satisfy all of the needs in the marketplace all of the time. Limits on financial and other resources constrain the variety that can be offered. Market segmentation helps balance customers' desire for variety with these resource constraints by encouraging businesses to focus their products and marketing programmes on certain groups of customers with specific needs. For example, a manufacturer producing frozen pasta meals is able to concentrate its efforts on developing its products for this format, rather than spreading its resources to include ambient and fresh offerings.

Segmentation Rationale and Benefits

Market segmentation is accepted to be a key element of the marketing discipline. This analytical process helps companies to put customers first, maximize resources and emphasize business strengths over rivals (Dibb and Simkin, 1996; Piercy,

2000; Piercy and Morgan, 1993). Businesses of all types, from confectionery manufacturers and hotel operators to car companies and industrial service suppliers, use market segmentation because they believe it will improve their marketing effectiveness and help maximize market opportunities. Despite its current popularity, market segmentation is not a new concept, with references going back nearly 50 years (e.g., Smith, 1956). The origins of the approach are in economic pricing theory, which suggests that maximum profits are generated when pricing levels discriminate between segments (Frank, Massy and Wind, 1972). Since this time, marketing's preoccupation with segmentation has grown, so that there are now more than 1600 academic references dealing with the topic (Wedel and Kamakura, 2000).

The rationale for adopting a market segmentation approach is well established with managers and in the marketing literature (Piercy, 2000; Weinstein, 1994). Customers demand variety: their product needs and buying behaviour are simply too diverse to be satisfied by a single product or service offering (Smith, 1956). Organizations that use market segmentation are able to deal with this heterogeneity in a resource-effective manner (Dibb and Simkin, 1996; Wind, 1978). This is because market segmentation works by grouping customers with similar needs and buying behaviours into segments. Products and marketing programmes can then be tailored to suit the needs of particular segments (Choffray and Lilien, 1980). As a result, marketers can on the one hand deal with the customer diversity, while on the other focus resources on the most attractive market areas (Beane and Ennis, 1987; Blattberg and Sen, 1976; Wind, 1978).

A wide range of reasons for using market segmentation has been reported (e.g., Weinstein, 1994).

- At the strategic level, market segmentation helps organizations decide where and how to compete, by helping identify the most profitable customers. For example, a regional contract cleaning company that has analyzed its customer segments might discover that its most profitable contracts are in the residential rather than the business market. This understanding will help the business decide where to compete in the future.

- At a tactical level, market segmentation drives businesses to deepen their customer understanding, so that a better understanding of needs and wants is achieved. This can lead to a better match between customer needs and the marketing programmes that are devised. Ultimately this should improve customer satisfaction levels and may enhance brand loyalty (McDonald and Dunbar, 1995).

- More effective resource allocation. Few companies have the resources to target 100 per cent of a market. Focusing on certain segments allows businesses to make the best of their resources.

- A better understanding of the competitive environment can be achieved because segmentation requires close scrutiny of rivals. Such additional insights can help companies develop and maintain a differential advantage or competitive edge over competing products and brands.

Although these benefits are widely regarded as substantive, many are essentially qualitative in character. There is relatively little quantifiable evidence of a direct link between market segmentation and business performance (Wedel and Kamakura, 2000). This is partly because of the difficulties in studying the impact of just one variable within the context of a complex business environment. Even so, the implication is that in justifying the use of market segmentation, managers need to be clear about the benefits on offer, especially since implementation costs can be high (Weinstein, 1994).

It is also important to consider that managers sometimes have problems putting market segmentation into practice (Dibb and Stern, 1995). The process can be complex and the fact that there is relatively little practical guidance on the practice of market segmentation exacerbates the problems (Dibb and Simkin, 1996; 2002; Hooley and Saunders, 1993). Even once the mechanics of the process have been handled, there can be difficulties with implementation (Webster, 1991). These concerns are addressed more fully in the final section of this chapter, where guidance for achieving market segmentation effectiveness is offered.

The Segmentation Process

As Figure 11.1 shows, the market segmentation process can be considered to consist of three stages. During the first stage – *segmenting* – customers are grouped on the basis of similar needs and buying behaviour so that the market is segmented. To achieve this, businesses must select an appropriate variable or combination of variables. For example, consumers differ in the degree to which they are health conscious. In some circumstances this behavioural characteristic can usefully be used for segmentation purposes. Food manufacturers such as Seeds of Change market products that are specifically targeted at those seeking organic offerings. The better marketers understand their customer base, the more likely they are to choose appropriate variables for segmenting the market.

---

(1) Segmenting
- Consider variables for segmenting the market
- Use the selected variables to group customers into segments
- Examine the profile of emerging segments
- Validate segments that emerge

(2) Targeting
- Select a targeting strategy
- Decide which and how many segments should be targeted

(3) Positioning
- Understand consumer perceptions
- Position product(s) in the minds of the targeted consumers
- Design an appropriate marketing mix and communicate the desired positioning

---

FIGURE 11.1 The segmentation process

The second stage – *targeting* – takes place once the segments have been identified. This is the point when decisions are made about which of the emerging segments should be targeted by the business. For most businesses, it is impossible to devote resources to all segments identified. Even the mighty Ford does not have models in every segment of the vehicle market. Instead, there must be a careful evaluation of the attractiveness of the different segment options. For example, animal tourist attraction Chester Zoo has a relatively small marketing budget, so careful management of resources is key. By appraising the relative attractiveness of different segments (educational trips, corporate events, visits by families, couples, etc.) the Zoo is better able to decide how to allocate this marketing spend (Dibb and Simkin, 2001).

During the final stage – *positioning* – the objective is to work out how to position the product or brand within the targeted segment(s). Once again, an excellent understanding of customer characteristics, perceptions and behaviour is imperative. A clear and unambiguous view of the needs and wants of targeted customers is vital to the development of a suitable product and marketing programme. When construction equipment manufacturer JCB developed a new range of skid steers, it used the results of detailed customer research to fine-tune the features of the product and to devise a suitable supporting marketing programme.

In the next few sections the different stages of the segmentation process are explored in more detail. As will become clear, technological advance is continuing to change how segmentation is applied and will play a major role in the future of the approach. These changes are described in a later section that considers current trends towards the so-called 'one-to-one' marketing and the 'segment of one'.

Stage 1: Segmenting

Segmenting involves aggregating customers with similar needs and/or buyer behaviour into more similar homogeneous groups or segments. The segmenting stage of market segmentation involves two basic steps. First, a variable or group of variables is used to aggregate customers with similar needs into segments. The variables or dimensions that are used for this purpose are often referred to as 'bases'. Many different base variables can be used and there is rarely one right way to segment a particular market. The key is to choose variables which make it possible to distinguish between customers' different product requirements. This section reviews base variables for consumer and business-to-business contexts.

Consumer Base Variables

In consumer markets the array of base variables includes simple characteristics, such as age, gender and occupation, through to more complex behavioural measures, such as attitudes towards the product and consumption patterns. A comprehensive listing of the variables available is given in Table 11.1. Here the base variables are divided into two types: those concerning basic customer characteristics and those that are product-related behavioural factors. The number of base variables that are used to generate segments varies in different

TABLE 11.1 Base variables for segmenting consumer markets

Basic customer characteristics[a]	Product-related behavioural characteristics
DEMOGRAPHICS Age/sex/family/race/religion The family lifecycle concept is an imaginative way of combining demographic variables.	**PURCHASE BEHAVIOUR** Customers for tinned foods, like baked beans, may be highly brand loyal to Heinz or HP, or may shop purely on the basis of price.
SOCIO-ECONOMICS Income/occupation/education/ social class Different income groups have different aspirations in terms of cars, housing, education, etc.	**PURCHASE OCCASION** A motorist making an emergency purchase of a replacement type, while on a trip far from home, is less likely to haggle about price than the customer who has a chance to 'shop around'.
	BENEFITS SOUGHT When customers buy toothpaste they seek different benefits: fresh breath and taste, or for others fluoride protection is the key.
GEOGRAPHIC LOCATION Country/region/type of urban area (conurbation/village)/type of housing (affluent suburbs/inner city).	**CONSUMPTION BEHAVIOUR AND USER STATUS** Examining consumption patterns can indicate where companies should be concentrating their efforts. Light or non-users are often neglected. The important question to ask is why consumption in these groups is low.
PERSONALITY, MOTIVES AND LIFESTYLE Holiday companies often use lifestyle to segment the market: young singles or tours catering especially for senior citizens or centres for young families.	**ATTITUDE TO PRODUCT** Different customers have different perceptions and preferences of products offered. Car manufacturers from Skoda to Porsche are in the business of designing cars to match customer preferences, changing perceptions as necessary.

Source: Dibb *et al.*, 2001.

Note: [a] Because of the ease with which information concerning basic customer characteristics can be obtained and measured, the use of these variables is widespread.

situations. Single variable segmentation – using just one variable to categorize customers – is obviously the most straightforward to perform. However, multi-variable segmentation – which applies a combination of variables – generally offers a greater level of precision in helping marketers to develop marketing programmes that satisfy customers within a particular segment. Examples of these approaches are described in the mini-cases below. The LEGO case illustrates how one company has used a simple segmentation approach, with children's age as the basis, to satisfy diverse needs in its market. The second mini-case, based on CACI, describes an altogether more complex segmentation approach based on lifestyle variables.

The use of segmentation approaches that combine geographic location and demographic variables is currently popular (Sleight, 1997). Known as *geodemographics*, this approach uses census data to categorize individuals according to where they live. The ability to target particular neighbourhoods through post-codes is attractive, not least because of the ease with which it can be applied. A number of geodemographic systems have been developed that help marketers understand the characteristics of target customers in different neighbourhoods. These include ACORN (A Classification of Residential Neighbourhoods) from the CACI Market Analysis Group, MOSAIC from Experien and SuperProfiles from CDMS. For example, the ACORN approach uses 79 variables to divide consumers into six different groups: thriving, expanding, rising, settling, aspiring, striving and unclassified. These categories are then further subdivided into 17 groups and 54 types. As the case below illustrates, geodemographics are now becoming even more sophisticated, with lifestyle variables being included in some classification schemes.

The potential downside of multivariable segmentation (using more than one variable) is that the greater the number of base variables applied, the larger is the number of emerging segments. If each segment requires a bespoke marketing mix, the resource implications can be considerable. However, as explained later, technological advance is making it easier to generate and serve more complex segmentation schemes and the trend is in this direction.

LEGO[2]

Most parents and children are familiar with the products of LEGO, the Danish toy business formed more than 60 years ago. Achieving a position among the world's top 10 toy manufacturers has been made possible by LEGO's ability to enchant children of all ages. To assist the process, LEGO has segmented the market, dividing its play materials on the basis of age.

Play materials 0–5 consists of LEGO PRIMO (sets of toys for children from birth to 36 months) and LEGO DUPLO which targets basic bricks and themed sets at children in the 18 month to six year old age group. Play materials 4–9 is aimed at an older age group. The traditional LEGO BASIC (basic building bricks plus extra pieces) and LEGO SYSTEM, which has more than 150 different sets based on a range of themes designed to appeal to boys, are familiar to most parents. Now this is supplemented with ZNAP, a construction system based on vehicles that can be transformed into something else. LEGO SCALA and LEGO SYSTEM Belville are aimed at girls and feature fairy tale, beach and horse-riding settings designed to appeal to girls' enjoyment of role-play situations. Play materials 7–16+ offers a range of LEGO TECHNIC products, based on a technical design and construction system and, more recently, LEGO MINDSTORMS. This is a totally new kind of system using a microcomputer which allows older children (and adults) to build robots that can really move.

CACI Lifestyles uk[3]

Lifestyles uk is CACI's lifestyle database which is designed to enable clients to target over 44 million consumers, analyzed by around 300 different lifestyle characteristics. These range from charity concerns, consumption patterns, financial matters, health and holidays, to household characteristics and personal information, newspaper readership, motoring and even pet ownership. A company can select a combination of these variables in order to identify potentially relevant consumers. These could be consumers with similar lifestyle traits to existing customers, or they could be consumers exhibiting a different lifestyle to enable the company to expand or diversify its customer base. For example, Home Service specializes in insurance products co-branded with electricity and water companies. The service recruits new members by direct mail and leaflet drops through letterboxes. Home Service has used CACI's Lifestyles uk database to profile existing customers of each of its core products. With these profiles, the full database of 44 million consumers has been screened to identify non-users who match the desired customer lifestyle characteristics.

Business-to-business Base Variables

Base variables for use in business-to-business markets, illustrated in Table 11.2, include simple characteristics such as the demographic profile of the business, through to more complex measures associated with the purchasing approach and characteristics of individuals in the buying centre. Some variables are more straightforward to use than others because they can be measured more easily and data on them are more readily available. Even so, it sometimes makes sense to use more complex variables, perhaps in combination with a simpler variable, because a more precise segment output may be achievable. For example, a paint manufacturer that segmented its customer base according to industry type introduced an additional segmentation variable relating to the purchasing behaviour of its customers. This change allowed the company's salesforce to be more responsive to variations in different business customers' buying patterns.

Just as in consumer markets, the key is to ensure that the variables chosen discriminate effectively between customers' needs and buyer behaviour. All too often there is a tendency in business markets to use simple-to-apply segmentation variables that do not satisfy this criterion. For instance, a leading US defence business utilizes its technical expertise with sensors, telecommunications and semiconductors in numerous non-defence markets. These range from hospital

TABLE 11.2 Business-to-business base variables[a]

Variables for segmenting business-to-business markets	
Personal characteristics of the buyers	Demographics, personality and lifestyles of those in the buying centre.
Situational factors	Urgency of purchase or size of order.
Purchasing approach	Buying centre structure, buying policies, balance of power amongst decision makers.
Operating variables	The technologies applied or the manner in which products are used.
Company demographics	Company age, location, industry, sector (SIC code), size, competitive set, etc. will alter product and purchasing requirements.

Note: [a] Variables at the foot of the table are the more straightforward to apply, becoming progressively more complex going up the table.

monitors, oil rig drill bits, alarm and fire detection systems, and radio communications, to the transportation industry. This definition of target markets in terms
of only customers' business sectors led to too many markets being pursued.
Analysis of currently successful customer accounts revealed that this company
was perceived to be a committed, helpful, knowledgeable and trusted supplier,
particularly by businesses with a naïve understanding of the technology they
were purchasing. The defence business used this partnership idea as a segmentation base to more narrowly define attractive customers and genuinely suitable
target market segments. The implication is that this business moved from a
simple demographic segmentation to one that was based on aspects of customer
buying behaviour.

Once the first segmenting step is complete and segments have been generated,
further efforts are needed to understand the characteristics of customers in the
emerging segments. The key is to develop as extensive and detailed a picture as
possible. This stage is known as *profiling* and uses descriptor variables. These
descriptors may include any of the customer characteristics or product-related
behavioural variables already described. For example, many banks are now
segmenting their personal banking customers on the basis of life cycle. Barclays
Life Changes service, which publishes a range of booklets designed to provide
financial advice for customers at turning points in their lives, is typical. With
brochures for those with a new baby, facing retirement, divorce and separation,
redundancy and for those facing disability, one objective is to inform customers
of relevant financial products. However, any bank attempting to market its
services to a segment defined on the basis of life cycle will also benefit from
understanding the detailed profile of those customers. For instance, a bank that is
developing pension products targeted at couples in their 40s who have started to
worry about retirement provision, will have a better chance of satisfying customer
needs if it develops a clear profile of those customers in terms of other variables.
The bank should, therefore, try to understand these customers' attitudes to
money, their other financial commitments, what retirement arrangements have
already been made, whether they are confident about handling their financial
commitments or whether they might require a good deal of guidance through the
process.

Many businesses deploying segmentation are initially uncertain of the relevant
base variables to use, or they have incomplete knowledge of the customers' needs
and buying characteristics. For these businesses, it is first necessary to develop the
required understanding of customer buying behaviour, often through in-depth
qualitative marketing research – focus or depth interviews – and then with
validatory quantitative analysis of more extensive survey data. Other organizations may already have such an understanding of these customer issues, but may
not have previously collected adequate data to objectively analyze customer
behaviour and determine customer segments. These organizations, too, must pull
together adequate, reliable and up-to-date marketing intelligence. Once the
relevant data on customer needs and buying behaviour are available, base
variables can be used to identify market segments, either qualitatively through
managers' discussions or preferably quantitatively using multivariate statistical

techniques. These include factor analysis, cluster analysis and conjoint techniques.

Essential Qualities for Effective Segments

Managers faced with implementing market segmentation often ask how they can assess the quality of a particular segmentation scheme. Most textbooks provide a simple checklist of quality criteria, stating that segments should be measurable, substantial, accessible, stable and usable. These criteria are based on a list devised by Kotler (1984) that has been modified by other authors over the years.

- *Measurable:* It should be possible to measure the size and market potential of segments. There are many examples where businesses have failed to adequately assess the potential size of new segments, sometimes with catastrophic consequences. When the children's drink Sunny Delight was first launched, demand exceeded expectations leading to shortages in the supermarkets.

- *Substantial:* The segment identified must be large enough to be viable, so that targeting it with products/services is a worthwhile marketing activity. A number of car manufacturers are currently investing in developing vehicles which run on more environmentally-friendly fuels such as electricity, liquid petroleum gas and hydrogen cells. Ford's all-electric concept car Think is one example. Although the environmental lobby has encouraged these developments, it is unclear whether a substantial enough market exists for these products at the current time. The car companies will be closely monitoring the situation so that the size of the potential market can be assessed.

- *Accessible:* Once a market segment is identified and its viability assured, it must be feasible to action a marketing programme with a finely-developed marketing mix aimed at targeted consumers. Sometimes, despite the fact that customers are sufficiently similar to be grouped together into a particular market segment, the similarities are not enough to enable a marketer to implement full marketing programmes. For example, a construction equipment manufacturer such as JCB, seeking to develop differentiated marketing offers for segments of customers, must understand the needs and buying patterns of customers in different segments. In addition, it must understand other things about the profile of customers in each segment. For instance, the company needs to understand the sector from which customers originate, the kinds of trade magazines they read, the exhibitions they attend and the events at which they like to be seen. This profiling information is vital to developing the marketing effort. Unfortunately, segmentation schemes do not always generate segments that have a sufficiently clear profile to achieve this.

- *Stable:* The stability of segments in the short, medium and long-term is not guaranteed. As customer needs and buyer behaviour change, so do the boundaries around segments. An assessment of a segment's viability, taking the competitive and marketing environment into consideration, is vital. Changing consumer attitudes towards the way food is produced created opportunities for manufacturers and retailers to develop lines of organic produce. The Enjoy range of food products from RHM is typical. However, entry into this part of the market is costly and time-consuming, so manufacturers and retailers need to have confidence in the long-term future of the segment.

- *Useful:* The generated segmentation output must provide clear benefits, resulting in a better relationship with targeted customers and sensible use of marketing and sales resources. The LEGO case reported above demonstrates a useful segmentation scheme, because the approach adopted has allowed the business to closely match the needs and wants of its targeted customers.

Once a company's marketers have identified market segments, they must move into the second phase of market segmentation and decide which segments should be targeted with sales and marketing resource.

Stage 2: Targeting

Targeting involves prioritizing the segment or combination of segments upon which a business is to focus its sales and marketing efforts. Even large organizations are rarely able to target all segments in the marketplace. During the targeting process, decisions are made about the segment or segments on which sales and marketing efforts are to be devoted. The targeting approach adopted will depend on an assessment of the attractiveness of particular segments during which a wide range of market, product and competitive factors will be considered. There will also be a systematic evaluation of company resources and capabilities. Once this process is complete, the organization will select the segments at which resources are to be aimed. Two fundamental questions are at the heart of the targeting approach adopted:

> *Question 1:* How many segments should the organization target with sales and marketing effort?
>
> *Question 2:* Which segments should be targeted by the organization (and what implications does this have for determining their attractiveness)?

How Many Segments to Target?

To answer the first question, organizations must decide about their broad targeting strategy. There are several possible options: a mass market or undifferentiated approach, a single segment strategy or a multisegment approach. Which is chosen will relate partly to the resources available and partly to the company's view of the marketplace and competitive environment.

- *Mass marketing strategy:* In this case, a single product/service concept is offered across most of the market segments in the market. This approach may be chosen because marketers feel there are relatively small differences in customer needs and buying behaviour across the market. Alternatively, the business might simply not have the resources to treat the segments separately or may not realize the benefits of market segmentation. Even though this approach may seem attractive in a resource sense, with the possibility of scale economies being achieved, the danger is that customers will be dissatisfied with what they are offered, as the marketing mix may be too generalized and unfocused. For example, the old-fashioned Costa Del Sol packaged holiday went into decline, forcing tour operators to launch a range of holidays targeted more closely at different segments – senior citizens, families, deluxe holiday seekers, clubbers, far from the crowd, etc.

- *Single segment strategy:* Organizations adopting this approach concentrate on a single segment with one product/service concept. There are obvious advantages for businesses with relatively constrained resources and the opportunity to specialize, but there are also risks with putting 'all eggs in one basket'. If the chosen segment declines for any reason, the financial strength of the business may be hit. Porsche only competes in the affluent high-performance sports car segment, which is prone to sales dips in times of economic recession.

- *Multisegment strategy:* This strategy involves targeting a different product/ service concept at each of a number of segments. This common approach allows the risk to be spread across a number of areas, but a considerable level of resource may be required to sustain all segments targeted. For example, Whitbread's luxury Marriott hotels are targeting a different segment of hotel visitors than the company's motel-style Travel Inn concept. This is reflected in the style of the marketing programme for each chain.

Which Segments to Target?

Once decisions have been made about the broad targeting strategy, the second targeting question must be addressed. This involves deciding which segments the organization should target and requires that the attractiveness of different segments be explored. When determining where to allocate resources, there is no substitute for systematically reviewing the attractiveness of different segment options. In a keynote article about the future of marketing, Doyle (1995) commented that, 'the strategic choice of markets and segments where the firm will compete, is an area which warrants particular attention'. There is also strong documented evidence to suggest that market attractiveness and business success are connected. A study by Chandler and Hanks (1994), based on 800 US manufacturing businesses, highlighted the links between perceived market attractiveness, resources and business success. Despite this evidence, it seems that practitioners have not always applied a sufficiently systematic approach to the problem (Plank, 1985, p. 89).

So what factors should be considered when assessing segment attractiveness? The following broad question areas are typical of those which marketing experts suggests should be posed:

- Does the company have knowledge of the market?
- Is this a market in which the company has existing marketing share?

- Does the company have required product expertise?
- What is the likelihood of production and marketing scale economies?
- What is the level and nature of the competition?
- Can customers' needs be easily met?
- What are the size, structure and likely segment growth?
- Does the company have adequate resources?
- What is the likely profitability and what market share gains are possible?

When British Airways launched EasyJet rival Go, it hoped to leverage its knowledge of the airline market, routes and infrastructure. The no-frills airline market proved more unfamiliar than British Airways expected, with the resulting sale of Go.

In practice, there are many different checklists available for assessing segment or market attractiveness (McDonald, 1995). In addition to what is available in the marketing literature, market attractiveness measures are discussed in the organizational behaviour, managerial economics, corporate strategy and financial management literatures. Table 11.3 provides a typical breakdown. Portfolio management models, such as the Directional Policy Matrix (DPM) also analyzes market attractiveness.

Marketing experts suggest that it is appropriate to adopt a balance of short and long-term criteria when reviewing the attractiveness of segments. Despite this, British businesses are sometimes accused of ignoring the long-term at the expense of criteria such as short-term profitability (Baker, Black and Hart, 1988; Simkin and Dibb, 1998). It seems that pressure to meet shareholder objectives may be partly to blame. By comparison, studies of Japanese companies have highlighted an emphasis on long-term growth and market share measures (Doyle, Saunders and Wong, 1986).

TABLE 11.3 Framework of segment attractiveness criteria

| | Market attractiveness factors | | |
Competitive factors	Economic and technological factors	Environmental factors	Market factors
Competitive intensity	Barriers to entry	Exposure to economic fluctuation	Size of segments
Quality of competition	Barriers to exit	Exposure to political and legal factors	Segment growth rate
Threat of substitution	Bargaining power of suppliers	Degree of regulation	Stage of industry evolution
Degree of differentiation	Level of technology utilization	Social acceptability and physical environmental impact	Predictability of demand
	Investment required	Natural forces	Price elasticity and sensitivity
	Margins available		Bargaining power of customers
	Likely technological change		Seasonality and cyclicality of demand
	Scale economies		Customers needs and ability to satisfy

Table 11.4 illustrates the results of a recent study of the attractiveness criteria used by UK businesses (Simkin and Dibb, 1998). With profitability cited overwhelmingly by large British businesses as the key criterion and variables such as market share appearing only in 11th place, it seems that concerns about the balance between short and long-term criteria may be well founded. However, some evidence of change was also unearthed by the study, which found that younger organizations were much more likely to apply long-term measures than those which were longer established.

It is important to stress the diversity of attractiveness measures that can be used. In different industries and contexts different combinations are appropriate. For example, a commercial vehicle manufacturer that uses achievable brand loyalty, financial contribution, market growth and competitive intensity as attractiveness measures has achieved a creditable mix of short and long-term variables that are appropriate to its market and situation. Meanwhile a bulk chemical supplier that uses customer fit, sales potential, financial value to the business and the desires of customers' customers, has chosen a different but equally suitable combination of variables. The key is to ensure that an appropriate mix of short and long-term variables is selected that are suitable for the particular company's circumstances, market conditions and strategic approach.

TABLE 11.4 UK business ranking of attractiveness criteria

Ranking	UK managers' attractiveness criteria	Overall measure
1	Profitability	41
2	Market growth	30
3	Market size	27
4=	Likely customer satisfaction	25
4=	Sales volume	25
6	Likelihood of sustainable differential advantage	23
7=	Ease of access of business	22
7=	Opportunities in the industry	22
9	Product differentiation	21
10	Competitive rivalry	18
11=	Market share	15
11=	Relative strengths in key functions	15
11=	Customers' price sensitivity	15
14	Customer image of company	14
15	Technological factors	7
16	Fit with business strategy	6
17	Stability of market	4
18=	Environmental factors	–3
18=	Threat of substitutes	–3
20	Barriers to entry	4
21	Negotiating power of buyers	–11
22	Ease of profiling customers	–13
23	Supplier power	–16

Source: Simkin and Dibb, 1998.

Note: The overall measure was obtained from a five-point Likert scale date. The measure was developed by allocating the following points to the scale: 1 = +2, 2 = +1, 3 = 0, 4 = –1, 5 = –2.

Positioning, the third phase of market segmentation, follows on from the segmenting and targeting phases. The positioning phase involves establishing a desirable product or brand image in the minds of targeted customers.

Stage 3: Positioning

Product or brand positioning concerns the decisions and activities that develop and maintain a company's product concept in the minds of target customers. Positioning is the final stage of the market segmentation process. At this point decisions are taken to determine how the product or service is to be positioned within the targeted segment. The key is to identify a place in the market amongst the array of existing brands (Ries and Trout, 1986; Trout and Rivkin, 1996). At the heart of any positioning are the perceptions which customers have about the product or brand. These perceptions must also be supported by the consumption experience. For example, the fine fragrances of Chanel have connotations of quality and expense and these characteristics are fundamental to the brand's positioning. It is only by ensuring that customers' expectations are met that Chanel is able to maintain this perception. This is because the positioning of a product is not sustainable when customer experiences contradict the image that is being created.

Positioning helps connect an organization's target market strategy with the marketing programmes that are developed. It concerns the product or brand image to be portrayed through the marketing programme. Indeed, positioning encompasses any and all decisions that shape the product or brand concept. Although the process starts with the product itself, positioning also involves how the product is styled, packaged, priced, promoted and distributed. Some managers associate positioning purely with marketing communications, believing that positioning begins and ends with advertising, direct marketing and other promotional activity. As is shown by the following example, this is far from the reality. In order to maintain the exclusivity which is synonymous with the brand, Rolex ensures that its watches are of the highest quality, premium priced, distributed through only a few retail outlets and advertized in publications associated with the rich and famous. This is because everything that is done to market Rolex products has repercussions for their positioning.

Positioning provides the opportunity for an organization to differentiate its product from others in the marketplace. This is sometimes referred to as 'market positioning'. It is clear that customers relate the positioning of a product or brand to their perceptions of competing offerings: a new mayonnaise is compared with Helmanns, tomato ketchup with Heinz and cola with Coca-Cola. The implication is that newly-positioned products should demonstrate how they are different from existing incumbents. In fact, positioning must do more than simply differentiate a product. It should also demonstrate to customers that there is an advantage in buying this product rather than another. The concept of differential advantage (sometimes also called competitive advantage, or a unique selling proposition (USP)) is therefore implicit in the positioning process. A differential advantage is something desired by targeted customers but unique to the product or marketing mix of one company. When a differential advantage exists, it should be reflected in the product's chosen positioning concept.

There are clear economic advantages for developing a distinctive positioning. Economic theory suggests that products that are distinct in ways that are attractive to customers become distanced from inferior substitutes that compete on the basis of price. This feature enables higher prices to be charged and can lead to greater profitability (Dickson, 1994). The economic advantages arise because of a strong relationship between effective differentiation and profit margin.

The positioning of a product or brand is affected by a number of constituents: customers, the product or brand itself, the company behind the brand, competitors and market conditions.

- *Customers:* Ultimately only they will decide how the product is perceived in the marketplace. This will be based partly on the communication and marketing surrounding the product, but also on their experiences of consumption and their perceptions of rivals' products.

- *The product or brand:* The tangible characteristics of the product must match up to the product concept that is being created.

- *The company behind the brand:* Customers expect a level of consistency between brands and the company behind them. In the 1980s the Trusthouse Forte (THF) brand was applied to a full range of hotels and catering outlets. Thus the THF brand appeared on everything from motorway service areas and motel-style accommodation through to the most luxurious of hotel outlets. This was potentially confusing for customers who had problems understanding precisely for what the brand stood.

- *The competition and market conditions:* Existing brands in the market affect the positioning that a product occupies. Businesses sometimes overlook the positioning of competing offers, whereas customers rarely do! Macro-environmental forces also have an impact. For example, terrorist atrocities have affected consumer perceptions of airline brands.

Understanding Consumer Perceptions

Consumer perceptions are pivotal to the positioning process. It is therefore no surprise that businesses go to considerable trouble to develop their understanding of these consumer feelings. Sometimes perceptual maps are developed to summarize the market and to draw out the relative positioning of competing brands. These maps, which are also sometimes referred to as positioning or product space maps, are a means of visually depicting customers' perceptions. The perceptual mapping technique is based on various subjective and mathematical approaches designed to depict relative positions of competing products, companies or brands. Developing a perceptual map requires that key product requirements be identified, through consumer research. For example, as Figure 11.2 shows, in the market for instant coffee dimensions such as taste and price are important to customers, and would be appropriate dimensions for a perceptual map. Once the dimensions have been identified, further customer research is needed to establish the relative merits of competing brands.

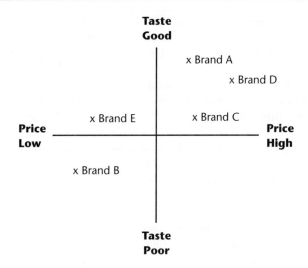

FIGURE 11.2 Perceptual map for instant coffee

By plotting customer views of the merits of competing brands, based on the chosen attributes, a visual representation of the marketplace can be created. Understanding the positionings on these maps helps marketers identify opportunities and develop suitable and effective marketing programmes to support products and services. A particular objective is to develop a positioning approach that differentiates the product or brand from others and avoids copying the existing positioning of competitors. In achieving this, it is important to also consider the fit with other products in the product line. Customers are likely to be more convinced by a positioning for a new product that is consistent with their expectations of the company producing it. When Toyota launched the Lexus brand, the company knew that it must provide a separate identity for the model and sell it through bespoke retail outlets. This was because customers did not associate Toyota cars with the kinds of up-scale values that the manufacturer was seeking to present through the Lexus range.

Perceptual tools designed to aid the positioning process must be based on the views of real customers. Sometimes marketers believe that they understand the market sufficiently to develop maps without recourse to customer views. This is often a mistake and may result in inappropriate marketing decisions being made. For example, managers at a plastics company supplying manufacturers of bathroom equipment were convinced that customers rated their plastics as the highest quality in the industry. This belief was based on research conducted some years earlier and was reflected throughout the organization's marketing and sales activity. When new research showed that customers' views had changed, the company had to adjust its marketing approach.

The Positioning Process

The following process describes the steps towards developing a product or brand positioning:

1 Define the segments in the relevant market. This may involve using a mix of published information and marketing research data. Most businesses have access to information about their industry and market place that can be used as a starting point. This can be supplemented as necessary with bespoke marketing research.

2 Decide on the segment(s) to be targeted. As explained earlier, a systematic process should be carried out to ensure that appropriate targeting decisions are made. This involves an analysis of company capabilities and resources and consideration of segment attractiveness.

3 Consider the needs, expectations and buying behaviour of target customers. Selecting an appropriate positioning will depend upon an accurate assessment of these criteria. In particular, the customers' product needs and benefits must be fully appreciated.

4 Check that the product matches the needs and expectations identified. Vital insights can be gained from marketing research that can help ensure a good fit with what customers really want.

5 Review the positioning and customer perceptions of all competing products in the chosen market segment(s). Perceptual mapping techniques can be used to assist the process.

6 Choose an image that differentiates the product from competing offerings. This positioning must closely match the requirements of target customers.

7 Communicate the positioning to customers, by telling them about the product and what it stands for. Although this mainly involves marketing communications and using the promotional mix, all aspects of the marketing mix must support the positioning. Thus the product should be appropriately priced, in suitable packaging, with the right kind of service package and distributed though appropriate channels or outlets. 'Positioning statements' or 'strap lines' may be part of the communications package, such as BMW's famous, 'The ultimate driving machine'.

Repositioning

Sometimes the positioning of a product or brand may need to be modified. The characteristics or expectations of the target market may have changed, or the emergence of a new competitor may be threatening existing players. Burger King, for example, based its positioning on the concept of total flexibility (you can have it anyway you want . . .), to hit out at the standard offerings of McDonald's. When faced with the need to review positioning, businesses have a variety of options (Doyle, 1998):

1 Introduce a new brand.
2 Change the existing brand.
3 Alter beliefs about the existing brands.
4 Alter beliefs about competing brands.
5 Alter attribute importance rates.
6 Introduce new or neglected attributes to find a new market segment.

Following bad publicity and a backlash from consumer groups, manufacturers of alcopops (flavoured alcoholic beverages) such as Hooper's Hooch repositioned their offerings so that they did not appeal so directly to teenagers. This involved a combination of modifying the packaging to appeal more to adults and altering beliefs about the products and who should enjoy them.

Getting positioning 'right' is essential, because once established it is extremely powerful and can be very difficult to change. Prior to the rebranding of Midland Bank to HSBC, managers at the high street bank expressed frustration that customers continued to use the positioning statement 'The Listening Bank'. Despite the fact that Midland had ditched the slogan, the words and sentiments continued to be etched on customers' minds. This illustrates the power of perceptions and helps explain why repositioning is so difficult and expensive to achieve. As a result, there are relatively few cases where a major shift in customer perceptions has been made. One example was the repositioning of carbonated soft drink Lucozade, which took the beverage from being a comforting energy builder for the sick to the modern sports drink of today. However, changes in positioning like this are expensive and hard to achieve. Considerable investment is usually needed in redesigning the product, any packaging and the marketing programme supporting it. It may take many years before targeted customers recognize the change. Even so, desirable results cannot be guaranteed. The stronger the existing positioning, the more difficult it is to achieve. For example, Volvo cars have become synonymous with safety. Although this has many advantages for the manufacturer, the downside has been that people also tended to brand the cars as 'tank-like'. Recently Volvo has engaged in a major marketing communications effort to portray its new models as more sporty and exciting. However, the company has endeavoured to link this with the strong connotations of safety for which its cars are known. For companies faced with the challenge of repositioning, it is simpler to develop an all-new brand for the existing product. This approach was adopted when fashion retailer Chelsea Man/ Chelsea Girl very successfully rebranded as River Island.

The previous three sections of this chapter have described the three stages of the market segmentation process, segmenting, targeting and positioning. However, the way in which market segmentation is applied is not static and it is important to address how the approach is changing. The next section considers how technological advance is providing new market segmentation opportunities and considers the approach's future.

Market Segmentation is Changing: Technology and One-to-one Marketing

One-to-one marketing, or the segment of one, involves bespoke marketing messages targeted at individual customers through a process of mass customization. Information about customers is the core ingredient for market segmentation. Rapid technological change, which is improving the capacity to collect, store and manipulate customer information, is therefore impacting upon how businesses approach segmentation and targeting (Postma, 1998). The outcome of these advances is that the potential for data collection is greater than ever. This information, which might include detailed insights into individuals' personal characteristics, behaviour, buying needs, desires and expectations, is essential to carrying out market segmentation. For many businesses, database improvements are providing access to a wider range of segmentation variables than previously possible (Wedel and Kamakura, 2000). This wider access has been accompanied by a trend towards more complex segmentation schemes using a greater number of variables. Yet easier access to data is not the only driver of change. Increasingly complex and varied customer lifestyles are also adding a new challenge for marketing. As Sheth, Sisodia and Sharma (2000, p. 58) explain, 'market diversity is increasing in both business and consumer markets (Sheth *et al.*, 1999). This diversity is generating market fragmentation and consequently mass market and segment marketing will become less effective and efficient'.

One outcome of this change is in consumer markets, where demographic shifts in lifestyle, income, ethnic group and age are increasing the diversity of customer needs and buying behaviour. Easier access to a wider range of behavioural variables than previously possible means that marketers can more readily handle these changes and need no longer rely so heavily on basic demographics. This has reopened the debate about the discriminatory power of different segmentation variables (Beane and Ennis, 1987; Belk, 1975; Dickson, 1982; Frank, Massy and Wind, 1972; Wedel and Kamakura, 2000). Many marketers apparently now prefer behavioural type segmentation variables, believing that characteristics relating to customers' moods and actions provide better insights into their buying preferences (Mitchell, 2000a).

Moving Towards the Segment of One

As a result of these technological advances, it is now technically feasible to capture information about and respond to the needs and wants of smaller and smaller segments. Businesses are no longer reliant on lists of target group characteristics. Instead, they are able to determine the actual preferences and consumption patterns of individual customers (Postma, 1998). Taken to the extreme, instead of dealing at the mass market or segment level, technology can be used to develop more responsive relationships with *individual* customers. This principle has been variously referred to as 'customer-centric marketing' (Sheth, Sisodia and Sharma, 2000), the 'segment of one' and 'one-to-one marketing' (Peppers and Rogers, 1993; 1999; Peppers, Rogers and Dorf, 1999).

The one-to-one approach relies on technology to develop adaptive, long-term relationships between customers and suppliers (Peppers and Rogers, 1999). According to Chaffey *et al.*, (2000, p. 290). One-to-one marketing, '. . . involves a company developing a long-term relationship with each customer in order to better understand that customer's needs and then deliver services that meet these individual needs'. This does not imply that each and every customer receives a completely customized offering. Instead, there is the notion of 'mass customization' (Gilmore and Pine, 1997) where marketers are able to, 'create an offering that customizes the product and/or some other element(s) of the marketing mix or standardize the offering' (Sheth, Sisodia and Sharma, 2000, p. 57).

Over time, the interactive abilities of the technology lead to a 'learning relationship' between customers and suppliers. The ongoing dialogue which ensues allows the business to continue to provide the desired product and service mix, thus enhancing customer retention and leading to repeated transactions over the lifetime of the relationship (Jenkinson, 1995; Shepard, 1995). For online service provider Amazon, the principles of one-to-one are an aid to retaining existing customers. The company achieves high levels of customer retention through its learning relationship, which builds a profile of each customer based on their previous purchases, credit card and delivery details. These data form the basis for smoothing subsequent interactions.

The foundations for one-to-one marketing are traceable to relationship marketing, direct/database marketing, and the services marketing area (Chaffey *et al.*, 2000; Meadows and Dibb, 1998; Müller and Halinen, 2000). In a technology context, the term customer relationship management (CRM) is often used almost interchangeably with relationship marketing. When the objectives of CRM are compared with the principles of one-to-one, it is not difficult to see why. Just as one-to-one marketing is concerned with developing relationships with the individual customer, CRM involves all activities undertaken to acquire, retain and maximize the value of these relationships. For example, Egg (Prudential's direct banking service), is using CRM principles to acquire customers and achieve growth. Egg is aimed at young professionals and better-off older people and is part of Prudential's strategy to broaden its range of distribution channels. Egg is seeking its share of this market through an offering that combines the benefits of a direct service with superior customer relationship management. By building a close relationship with customers, Egg claims to be able to build the necessary insights to provide each customer with an exclusively tailored service.

It is widely accepted that one-to-one involves a substantial injection of resources (Chaffey *et al.*, 2000). Concerns about the business case for one-to-one are being expressed by some marketing experts, who argue that the costs of one-to-one must be compensated for by long-term returns. Those who support one-to-one marketing counter by highlighting the value of customer relationships and suggesting that this can be further leveraged by focusing on high value customers (Zeithaml, 2000). Strong customer relationships have been shown to enhance customer retention rates. Research in the financial services sector indicates that businesses achieving a five per cent increase in retention of the best customers can enjoy a 60 per cent increase in profits over five years (Reichheld, 1993).

Once the appropriate systems are in place, the costs of maintaining customer relationships can be relatively small, reducing previous concerns about resourcing very small segments. Indeed, the depth of transactional and customer information provides the capability to measure the profitability of particular customer relationships. Pioneering work has been carried out in the financial services sector, where banks and credit card companies are learning to process transactional data so that robust estimates of customer profitability can be made (Bellis-Jones, 1989; Howell and Soucy, 1990; Storbacka, 1997; Shapiro and Bonoma, 1984). The following mini-case illustrates some of the ways in which HSBC has embraced the use of technology to refine its segmentation approach.

HSBC[4]

HSBC has recently announced the launch of its first premium global banking services aimed at personal customers. This development to the company's global brand, which is described on the HSBC website, is clearly centred on customer benefits (http://www.hsbc.com). The key aims of the new service are to provide high value personal customers with a tailored range of products and services which make full use of HSBC's formidable financial strength and global reach. The new service will have particular appeal to customers who travel frequently or work internationally. HSBC's branch and subsidiary network today spans 82 countries and territories worldwide and the HSBC Premier service will be accessible to customers in virtually every major city in the world.

There are a number of significant observations from this statement. The first is that HSBC is emphasizing that it is high value personal customers who will be offered a tailored range of products and services. These customers are apparently characterized according to behavioural dimensions as those travelling frequently or working internationally. It is also significant that HSBC stresses the appointment of a 'relationship manager' for each customer. This signals a focus on the 'life time value of the customer', with the company seeking to sell a range of appropriate products over an extended period. These concepts of high value customers and long-term relationships are central tenets of customer relationship management (Jenkinson, 1995; Müller and Halinen, 2000; Rapp and Collins, 1991).

Four Steps to One-to-one

Peppers and Rogers (1999) describe four steps for identifying the segment of one:

Step 1: Identify customers, by capturing and remembering customer details. To achieve the necessary understanding of customers, companies seeking to implement one-to-one must be able to capture, manage and analyze information of various types and from a variety of sources. The setup costs associated with this technical and managerial requirement may be considerable.

Step 2: Differentiate customers, by using the data collected to build a better understanding of individual characteristic, needs and buying behaviour. Building on the foundations of the first stage, the key is to identify customers that are loyal and seek long-term relationships, so that the marketing offer can be tailored to suit their needs. In this way, one-to-one allows businesses to capitalize on different levels of customer value by ploughing resources in the most profitable market areas (Blattberg and Deighton, 1996; Reichheld, 1993).

Step 3: Interact with customers, by 'capturing' each contact, in order to develop a learning relationship with individual customers. Learning relationships require ongoing interaction between customer and seller, so that every exchange continues from the point at which the last contact ended.

Step 4: Customize for customers, by using the information gained from learning relationships to demonstrate a lasting advantage. This means using the ongoing interaction to more explicitly meet a customer's needs. This is sometimes described as 'mass customization', where businesses are able to respond to the differences between customers, perhaps in terms of the bundling of marketing offers or in relation to the timing of a particular marketing approach. Amazon's Chief Executive refers to this concept as putting customers 'at the centre of their own universe' (Mitchell, 2000b, p. 28).

[handwritten margin note: Factors required for one-to-one be successful]

Progression through the one-to-one stages can be impeded in various ways. There may not be suitable technology in place. Even when this hurdle has been cleared, businesses may be unable to manipulate the data to identify high-value customers. Inflexible company culture or lack of strong leadership may inhibit required changes in the structure of the sales and marketing effort (Charan and Colvin, 1999; Sheth, Sisodia and Sharma, 2000). For example, a building society striving for a one-to-one approach, having invested in appropriate customer-facing systems, found that its existing pay and incentive structures were no longer appropriate. Instead of rewarding branch employees on the basis of the number of products sold, the company had to switch to incentives based on customer relationships and life-time value.

Later on, problems can arise if customers are unwilling to become involved in learning relationships. The key is to give customers a positive reason for engaging in this manner. For example, Egg justifies its need for ongoing customer information by explaining that the relationships that develop allow a greater responsiveness to customers' changing financial needs. As individuals encounter lifestyle changes, such as the birth of a baby or a house move, the company is ready to provide the required financial products.

The Future for the Segment of One?

The revolution in technology and data management suggests a secure future for one-to-one. There is no question that these developments have resulted in a more enlightened use of segmentation variables. It is equally clear that marketers in many sectors will continue to develop and exploit the opportunities on offer from interactive relationships. However, it is unlikely that one-to-one will replace traditional segmentation altogether. There are many contexts in which customers may resist technological interaction with suppliers. Indeed, some individuals may resist it altogether. Even in markets where the segment of one becomes the norm, the strategic role of segmentation may continue, with customer relationship management principles being used at a tactical level for interacting with individuals. In other words, traditional market segmentation will be used to subdivide customers into groups of like-minded people and customers, with one-to-one marketing programmes being deployed within prioritized target market segments.

Market Segmentation Problems

Although the rationale for market segmentation is widely accepted, there is strong evidence that practitioners can have difficulties putting it into practice (Dibb and Simkin, 2002; Hooley, 1980; Littler, 1992). Problems can arise for various reasons and can crop up at any point in the segmentation process. In some circumstances, these difficulties are sufficiently severe that the segmentation process completely breaks down. Segmentation failure is believed to have occurred in situations where the process fails to yield a solution that can be implemented. Operational constraints, poor managerial understanding of segmentation principles and resource problems are just some of the problem areas which have been blamed (Doyle, Saunders and Wong, 1986; Hooley, 1980; Plank, 1985). Some authors also apportion responsibility to the marketing literature, which they say offers relatively little guidance on implementation and making segmentation work (Dibb, 1999; Saunders, 1987).

Relatively little research has directly addressed what it is that makes market segmentation succeed or fail (Dibb, 1998). This may be partly due to the difficulty in establishing quantifiable evidence of the link between the use of market segmentation and measurable business performance. There is, however, rather more in the way of anecdotal evidence of the advantages accruing from a segmentation approach. As Table 11.5 shows, a number of qualitative success factors have been identified.

Some of these success factors relate to the organization's infrastructure, while others are concerned with how the segmentation process is carried out and implemented. This further supports the fact that barriers to market segmentation can occur at any point in the market segmentation process, from even before the analysis takes place right through to the implementation phase. For example, a business supplying animal feed to retail pet stores and supermarkets may be discouraged from carrying out a segmentation analysis because it does not have access to appropriate data or suitably qualified personnel to undertake the work. Another company might proceed with a segmentation project only to find that there are too few customers in the segments or that the segments identified are inherently unstable. For another organization, there may be targeting problems because members of a segment which demonstrates similar product needs and buying behaviour do not have a distinctive demographic profile. This might prevent the implementation of a suitable marketing programme.

TABLE 11.5 Market segmentation success factors

- Commitment and involvement of senior managers
- Personnel with appropriate skills
- Readiness to respond to market changes
- Creative thinking
- Clearly-defined objectives
- Well-designed planning
- Careful organization of the process and its implementation
- Carefully designed research
- Good quality, up-front data collection
- Appropriate choice of segmentation bases
- Clear implementation and tracking

Sources: Brown, Shivishankar and Brucker, 1989; Coles and Culley, 1986; Dibb, 1998; Engle *et al.*, 1972; Haley, 1984; Weinstein, 1987; 1994.

The implication is that managers need practical guidance to overcome the various barriers that might be encountered. Businesses investing heavily in segmentation have the expectation that the literature will provide detailed, step-by-step guidance on implementing the approach. The following questions, gleaned from a study of managers in a multinational industrial chemicals business, are typical of those posed by managers encountering segmentation for the first time (Dibb, 1998):

- What should I do with the data? Do I need a statistics expert?
- What variables should I use to segment my market?
- How will I know if I have used the right variables?
- How will I know if I have reached a sensible solution with robust segments?
- What do I do with the segments once I have them?
- How will I know if my segmentation is effective?
- When will I need to change or update the segmentation?

In practice, marketers tasked with carrying out segmentation analysis are often surprised by the dearth of practical guidance on offer. Perhaps this is also why some managers prefer to trust their instincts about how the market is structured rather than engage in a more systematic segmentation analysis. Bonoma and Shapiro (1984) had the following comment to make:

> Though a wide variety of segmentation schemes has been proposed since Smith (1956) first argued for the advantages of market segmentation, managers have not been offered guidelines for how to choose segments, analyse serving costs, or monitor resulting customer groups in a way that allows simplicity of choice and clarity of results. Consequently, in many businesses only the most simple and intuitive segmentation attempts are made.
>
> (p. 257)

Unfortunately, since this quote made in the mid 1980s, little additional applied guidance has emerged in the literature regarding market segmentation.

Reviewing market segmentation barriers shows that they occur at different points in the market segmentation process (Dibb and Simkin, 2001). Infrastructure barriers prevent the segmentation process being started, process barriers may inhibit the segmenting, targeting and positioning steps, while implementation barriers might prevent the segments being operationalized.

Diagnosing Market Segmentation Barriers

Infrastructure barriers

Unsuitable or inflexible aspects of an organization's infrastructure can hinder the implementation of segmentation. The potential barriers include organizational structure, corporate culture, inadequate data or systems, financial resources, technical resources or people issues. This last category can be especially problematic. Successful segmentation requires suitably skilled and experienced individuals. Seniority within the management structure and the ability to communicate across functions are also important because of the far-reaching changes that might result from segmentation analysis. One study indicates that commitment from senior management improves the prospects for segmentation because future objectives are more likely to be set at the segment level (Dibb, 1999).

Poor managerial understanding of segmentation principles has been frequently cited as a cause of segmentation failure. This can take various guises. Some companies erroneously see segmentation as an operational tool for dividing the market into more convenient parts. The resulting 'segments' may simply delineate customers into sectors on the basis of product markets that may not have homogeneous needs and buying behaviour. An example might be an accountancy company that created segments solely on the basis of billing amount. Inexperienced managers might also lose sight of the long-term strategic importance of segmentation, viewing the approach as a mechanism for delivering short-term tactical benefits. In these cases, there may be little sense of why segmentation is being carried out at all and the result can be inconsistencies in the marketing offer and programmes supporting it. The fact that market segmentation is often regarded as a market analysis rather than a strategic tool might also be to blame. Some experts believe that this is because companies often consider the development and resourcing of segments as separate activities (Claycamp and Massy, 1968; Green and Carmone, 1970; Wensley, 1981).

Process barriers

These are concerned with any factors that might disrupt the segmenting, targeting, and positioning process. The questions posed by managers, listed earlier, indicate that at the start of the process there is an anxiety to understand what factors might contribute to a successful outcome. During the segmentation analysis itself, at the culmination of the segmenting stage, there is a desire to understand the qualities of the emerging segments. Once the output has been agreed, guidance on judging segment attractiveness is needed so that appropriate targeting and positioning decisions can be made. This is where attractiveness criteria, such as those described in the targeting section of this chapter, are applied.

The need to understand segmentation success factors may be particularly strong at the outset of the segmentation process. It is, therefore, disappointing that the marketing literature is poorly developed in this area. Once the process is underway, other difficulties come to the fore. The segmenting stage may be disrupted by insufficient or inappropriate data, because managers lack the appropriate analytical skills or simply because inappropriate base variables have been used. Problems can also arise during the targeting stage, perhaps because an unsuitable list of attractiveness criteria has been used. Once the target segment selection has been completed, there may be problems with positioning, which may be balked by poor quality customer and competitive data, or inadequate capabilities regarding marketing communications.

As explained earlier, the literature offers some guidance for managers as they progress through the market segmentation process. This is in the form of segment criteria which provide a simple measure of the 'validity' of emerging segments, allowing a basic assessment of a particular scheme to be made. However, while many marketers are now familiar with Kotler's (1984) original statement that segments should be *measurable*, *accessible*, *substantial*, and *actionable*, it is curious that implementation guidance has not become altogether more sophisticated.

Implementation barriers

Businesses engaging in segmentation analysis will inevitably have resource constraints and will also be limited by a variety of operational and practical factors (Dibb and Simkin, 1997; Young, Ott and Feigin, 1978). This area has not received much attention in the segmentation literature (Beane and Ennis, 1987; Chéron and Kleinschmidt, 1985; Dibb and Simkin, 2002; Plank, 1985; Wind, 1978). Even worse, much of what is written seems to assume that businesses carrying out segmentation are unconstrained and can simply dispose of their existing segmentation schemes and start afresh. This is often far from the reality.

Some of the constraints on implementation are the same as those cited under infrastructure barriers. These include restrictions relating to industry structure and distribution channels, such as in the car industry, where there are accepted norms about different categories of car engine size and EU regulations guide the business practises of dealerships. Organizational structure issues may also limit implementation. Businesses may, for example, be reluctant to enforce a segmentation approach that requires a restructuring of the sales force or of the distribution network. There may also be cultural problems to overcome if implementation involves other substantive changes to company structure or working practises.

The following mini-case illustrates the infrastructure, process and implementation barriers faced by a regional electricity company (REC) as it tried to come to terms with its newly competitive markets.

Regional Electricity Companies[5]

Up until the 1990s, most of Britain's utility companies were state-owned. When the government decided that the regional electricity providers must operate in a competitive environment, customers were able for the first time to 'shop around' for their electricity. This was a major cultural change for the Regional Electricity Companies (RECs); instead of guaranteed custom from those living in their region, they now had to compete for customers all over the country. This meant they must decide which customers to target, in what parts of the country, with what proposition and through what distribution channels. A particular concern was to identify those customers who were most likely to switch providers. With this in mind, one of the RECs undertook a major market segmentation programme, involving a substantive marketing research exercise.

As the REC tried to implement the required programme of data collection, analysis and strategy development, it encountered a number of serious barriers. At the infrastructure level the business had very limited marketing expertise – no surprise given the REC had not previously traded in a competitive market. There was also a very poor understanding of market segmentation principles, which meant that the business had to 'buy in' consultancy expertise. This lack of expertise continued to cause problems throughout the segmentation process and implementation. While the process was underway, managers were frequently unsure how to progress or what decisions to take. During implementation, there were not enough marketing personnel or marketing resources to action the identified segments. The fact that market segmentation was misunderstood also meant that there was little incentive to overcome the difficulties.

Treating the Barriers

Various steps can be taken to treat market segmentation barriers. To avoid infrastructure difficulties, businesses prior to commencing a market segmentation programme must ensure that the required marketing intelligence, skilled personnel and resources are in place. Dealing with segmentation process barriers requires that a logical sequence of activities is followed so that the necessary data collection, analysis and strategic thinking are carried out. This will only be possible if the business has personnel with the required market segmentation expertise. Once the market segmentation process has started, managers must be ready to share the output with colleagues so that implementation barriers can be avoided. Adequate marketing budgets must be provided to facilitate the segmentation process and the implementation of its recommendations. Table 11.6 illustrates the diagnosis and treatment of market segmentation barriers in more detail.

Concluding Comments

This chapter aimed to address three fundamental questions. First, what evidence is there to support the use of a market segmentation approach? Second, what does the future hold for market segmentation? Finally, what can businesses do to improve the chances of market segmentation success?

Market Segmentation: The Evidence

The rationale for applying market segmentation is well established in the marketing literature. It is suggested that businesses pursuing a market segmentation strategy enjoy more effective resource allocation, have a better customer and competitor understanding and can more easily decide where and how to compete. At a tactical level this enables a better fit between customer needs and the marketing programmes that are devised. However, although these benefits are generally considered to be substantive, the difficulty quantifying the link between market segmentation and business performance means that the available evidence is qualitative. Indeed, it has even been suggested that the benefits of market segmentation arise primarily because the technique forces businesses through a systematic process of data collection, analysis and strategic consideration, rather than directly from the process itself. The segmentation process *per se* encourages a thorough appraisal of the market place and emerging opportunities.

The implication is that businesses must be completely clear about their rationale for using market segmentation and equally certain about the benefits available to them. This is made even more desirable by the considerable costs that may be associated with pursuing a segmentation approach. It is self-evident that developing bespoke marketing programmes for different market segments is likely to require more resources than a mass marketing approach. Businesses investing

TABLE 11.6 Diagnosing and treating key segmentation barriers

	Infrastructure	Segmentation process	Implementation
Diagnosis	1. No MIS in place 2. No culture of data collection 3. Weak channels of inter/intrafunctional communication 4. Company inflexible and resistant to new ideas 5. Poor senior management involvement in marketing initiatives 6. Lack of customer focus 7. Lack of marketing expertise and marketing function 8. Poor understanding of underlying segmentation rationale and scale of impact 9. No provision for resourcing analysis and strategic thinking	1. Inadequate marketing data to identify segmentation bases 2. Poor commitment to sharing of data and ideas 3. Inadequate interfunctional/site buy-in 4. Insufficient suitable marketing personnel 5. Inadequate budget to undertake segmentation 6. Poor understanding/misuse of the basic segmentation process 7. Poor appreciation of fit with corporate strategic planning 8. Insufficient analytical marketing skills	1. Ineffective internal/external communication of segment solution 2. Inadequate senior managerial involvement in segment roll out 3. Insufficient conviction or skills to operationalize segmentation scheme 4. Unclear demarcation of responsibility for implementation 5. Inadequate/poor alignment of budgeting/resourcing for implementation 6. Insufficient time allowed to roll out segment solution 7. Poor fit between tactical marketing programmes and segment solution 8. Inflexibility and/or product focus in the distribution system 9. Resistance to modifying organizational culture/structure/distribution
Treatment	Prior to undertaking segmentation: • Conduct review of available marketing intelligence • Identify relevant skills and personnel • Ensure senior management participation • Plan and facilitate channels of communication • Earmark required resources • Instigate internal orientation of segmentation principles and programme	During the segmentation process: • Specify sequential steps for segmentation process • Identify skill gaps. Seek external advice and training • Prioritize information gaps. Collect data. Create/update MIS • Instigate regular internal debriefs of data and ideas • Review ongoing fit with corporate strategy	Facilitate implementation: • Identify key internal and external audiences • Prepare internal champion-led marketing programme to communicate segment solution to audiences • Facilitate necessary changes to organizational culture/structure/distribution • Reallocate personnel and resources to fit segmentation solution • Specify schedule and responsibilities to roll out segment solutions • Instigate mechanism for monitoring segment roll out

Source: Dibb and Simkin, 2002.

heavily in a segmentation programme might, therefore, reasonably expect quantitative evidence of the effectiveness. As yet, rather little direct evidence is available, suggesting a need for more research providing quantifiable evidence of the impact and effectiveness of segmentation. More work also needs to be done to better understand the nature and role of success factors in segmentation. Nevertheless, practitioners such as Tesco's marketers are convinced of the merits of a market segmentation approach.

Market Segmentation: The Future

The role customer information plays in the market segmentation process is irrefutable. Today's technological advances are improving business's capacity to collect, store and manipulate customer information and these, in turn, are impacting upon how market segmentation and targeting are used. As the potential for data collection and manipulation grows, managers are gaining access to a wider range of segmentation variables than ever before. In some sectors, this change is leading towards increasingly complex market segmentation schemes using more variables than previously. At the same time, customers' lifestyles are becoming more complex and varied, providing a range of new marketing opportunities.

These changes mean that it has become technically possible to respond to the needs of smaller and smaller segments. Taken to its logical conclusions, the technology can even be used to develop more responsive relationships with the 'segment of one'. The use of 'one-to-one' marketing, which relies on building deep, long-term and adaptive relationships between customers and their suppliers, is already becoming a way of life in some sectors. However, there is no evidence that this new kind of market segmentation will replace traditional approaches. Many customers will continue to resist the kind of technological interaction that is at the heart of 'one-to-one' marketing. Even in contexts where the approach becomes established, there will continue to be a strategic role for market segmentation, with one-to-one being applied at a tactical level within priority target markets.

Market Segmentation: Achieving Success

Whether or not a market segmentation process is successful depends greatly on the nature of any barriers or implementation problems faced. There is no questioning the potential complexities of the market segmentation process or the difficulties that can arise with organizational infrastructure, the process itself, and the implementation phase. The fact that these problems are comparatively neglected by much of the academic literature does not help. However, there is evidence that with careful planning, steps can be taken to minimize the scale of these difficulties.

Proactively dealing with the causes of potential infrastructure, process and implementation barriers helps minimize the likelihood of market segmentation breakdown. Many of these obstacles can be handled by judicious planning at the very outset of the market segmentation process. This might involve ensuring necessary resources and suitably skilled and motivated staff are in place, auditing the availability of data, checking that senior management is prepared to drive the initiative and making sure that the results of the exercise are regularly communicated around the organization. Once the market segmentation process is underway, the emphasis shifts to checking that the approach is systematic, so that the necessary analysis and strategic thinking are carried out. Finally, implementation becomes the focus, so that any required change in organizational culture, structure and distribution can be facilitated. This requires the identification of suitable company champions, earmarking of key internal and external audiences, and schedules and responsibilities identified for roll out of the market segmentation solution.

Notes

1 *Sources*: Sally Dibb and Lyndon Simkin (2001) *Marketing Briefs: A Revision and Study Guide.* Oxford: Butterworth-Heinemann; www.tesco.co.uk; *Tesco Marketing Materials* (2001) Amanda Wilkinson, 'Retailers are doing it for themselves', *Marketing Week*, September 27 2001, pp. 19–20.
2 *Sources*: Adapted from Sally Dibb and Lyndon Simkin (2001) *Marketing Briefs: A Revision and Study Guide.* Oxford: Butterworth-Heinemann; LEGO: www.lego.com.
3 *Sources*: Adapted from CACI website, Lifestyles UK, CACI 1997; Sally Dibb, Lyndon Simkin, William Pride and O.C. Ferrell (2001) *Marketing: Concepts and Strategies.* Boston: Houghton Mifflin; *Marketing Systems Today* (1998) 13(1), 11.
4 *Source*: http://www.hsbc.com
5 *Source*: Sally Dibb and Lyndon Simkin (2002) 'Market segmentation: Diagnosing and treating the barriers', *Industrial Marketing Management*.

CHAPTER 12

New product development: A marketing agenda for change

Nikolaos Tzokas, Susan Hart and Michael Saren

Research into new product development (NPD) takes place within many different intellectual and functional domains, including marketing, technology management, R&D strategy, business policy, production and operations management, design, engineering design and innovation management, to name but a few. Accordingly, this research is published in a wide array of learned journals, for example, *The Journal of Product Innovation Management*, *Technovation*, *Policy Studies*, *R&D Management*, *The Journal of Marketing*, *The Journal of Marketing Research*, *Design Studies*, and *The Journal of Operations Management*. While both the above lists are not in any way definitive, it is not surprising that there is a huge variety of topics covered, from different organizational and disciplinary perspectives which are not traditionally related to marketing. That said, for NPD to be successful, its goal is to reach customers with benefits that match their needs and wants, and reviewing NPD research and writing focused on the centrality of customers is the focus of this chapter. The chapter traces changes in the treatment of NPD across several disciplinary boundaries, with a constant focus on 'the customer'.

The chapter begins by reviewing the new product success and failure (S/F) literature and articulating the case that to create new products that customers want to buy requires firms to develop capability in the acquisition and management of market information. It then goes on to examine the range of influences on the market information capabilities, organizing them into two major groups: task and non-task. The discussion of the task factors integrates previous research into new product development with research on innovation and blends in further themes from manufacturing and engineering management. Discussion of the non-task factors is organized into three levels: organizational, group and individual. The chapter concludes by constructing a conceptual framework for the study of market information capability in NPD and considers potential paths for future research.

The Contribution of Market Information to NPD Success

The development of customer-relevant product advantages is a recurrent prerequisite for new product success in the literature (Cooper, 1979; Cooper and Kleinschmidt, 1994; Link, 1987; Maidique and Zirger, 1984; Mayers and Marquis, 1969; Rothwell *et al.*, 1974). This requires that customer information be fed into the development process, yet there is little empirical research which has examined *what* information is required, *when* it is required and *how* it can be used during the various *activities* of the NPD process, and thus fails to add to our understanding of how to integrate the 'voice of the customer' into the NPD process.

From a normative point of view, the NPD process is comprised of multiple, overlapping and iterative stages, whose final output (the new product) is dependent upon both technical and marketing input (Hart and Baker, 1994; Saren, 1994; Souder and Moenaert, 1992; Takeuchi and Nonaka, 1986). The form of this input is largely information. Both technical and market-based information are constantly refined as the process evolves from a new product idea to a physical product which displays, in the case of success, product advantages perceived by its target market. In addition, the NPD process has been described as a sequence of information processing activities (Allen, 1985; de Meyer, 1985; Moenaert *et al.*, 1992). The more effective those information processing activities, the greater the achievement of the new product success factors. We contend that the importance of market information goes further than its ability to attune the developers' to the 'voice of the customer'. Several other critical success factors can be viewed as requiring market information processing activities, as summarized in Table 12.1.

These factors are derived from a broadly-based body of literature whose diversity in both conceptual and methodological terms has been noted by recent reviews (Craig and Hart, 1992; Montoya-Weiss and Calantone, 1994). Each of the success factors implies the integration of certain market information elements; examples are given in Table 12.1. Yet, these elements implied by success factors have not been previously suggested, let alone researched. This may seem surprising, given that the NPD process is often viewed as one of uncertainty reduction, wherein information is generated and used to reduce the uncertainties germane to the process (Allen, 1985; de Meyer, 1985). However, defining market information is far from clear-cut, whilst operationalizing the activities associated with its collection and use has only been rarely attempted, mostly without due recognition of adjacent disciplines (Moorman, 1993). Below we explore the nature of market information, tracing changes in its treatment in the various salient literatures.

What is Market Information?

In order to examine the nature and role of market information, it is first necessary to define what is meant by the term. Most marketing and marketing research

TABLE 12.1 The role of market information in achieving critical success factors

Success factor	Studies citing importance	Operationalization of success factors	Expected market information elements
		STRATEGIC SUCCESS FACTORS	
Product advantage	Cooper, 1994; Cooper and Kleinschmidt, 1987; 1991	• Excellent relative product quality in comparison to competitive offerings • Good value for money (perceived by the customer) • Excellence in meeting customer needs • Inclusion of benefits perceived by the customer as useful • Benefits which are obvious to the customer • Superior price/performance characteristics • Unique attributes	• Customer perceptions of competitive offerings • Technological dimensions of competitive offerings • Customer perceptions of new product's attributes and benefits • Feedback from customers after trial • Feedback on customer understanding of the message • Perceptual maps, based on customer data • Technical specifications • Product design information • Attributes and features specifications
Well-specified protocol	As above; Rothwell, 1977; Rothwell et al., 1974; Rubenstein et al., 1976	Firm's knowledge and understanding, prior to development of: • The target market; • Customer needs, wants, preferences; • The product concept; and • Product specifications and requirements	Research information detailing: • Market demographics/psychographics • Customer needs, wants and preferences • Technical specifications • Product design information • Attributes and features specifications (prior to development)
Market attractiveness	Maidique and Zirger, 1984	• High growth rates • High market need for product type • Stability of demand • Relative price insensitivity • High trial of new products	• Economic market data • Economic trends • Level of employment • Income levels • Inflation rates
Top management support	McDonough and Leifer, 1986; Ramanujam and Mensch, 1985	• Levels of risk aversion • Aspects of corporate culture	• Risk involved • Identification of product champions • Power and influence distribution among managers
Synergy/familiarity	Maidique and Zirger, 1984; Rothwell et al., 1974	• Knowledge of technology • Relevance to other projects • Access to scientific institutes and laboratories	• Extent of new knowledge involved • Technology centres where knowledge resides • Key scientists • Technological networks of firms

TABLE 12.1 The role of market information in achieving critical success factors *continued*

Success factor	Studies citing importance	Operationalization of success factors	Expected market information elements
		DEVELOPMENT PROCESS ISSUES	
Proficiency of pre-development activities	Cooper, 1994; Cooper and Kleinschmidt, 1987; 1991; Rubenstein et al., 1976; Voss, 1985	• Proficiency of concept screening • Preliminary market and technical assessment • Preliminary business analysis • Preliminary technical assessment	• Research on customer perceptions, gap analysis, needs analysis, concept tests • Market size potential, market segments • Technical feasibility, preliminary costs • Market size, like price, profit, break-even, etc.
Proficiency of marketing activities	Cooper, 1979; Link, 1987; Maidique and Zirger, 1984; Roberts and Burke, 1974; Rothwell et al., 1974	• Proficiency of concept • Product and market tests • Service • Advertising • Distribution • Elements of market launch	• Market information for the acceptance of alternative product concepts or designs • Customer preference data • Market profile information • Information concerning the distribution channels of interest
Proficiency of technological activities	Maidique and Zirger, 1984; Rothwell et al., 1974	• Proficiency in physical product development • In-house and in-use test iterations • Trial production runs • Technology acquisition	• Technical solutions to functional and marketing problems • Technical information on test performance • Information on production costs and problems • Information on suppliers' developments and adjacent technologies
Integration of R&D and marketing	Gupta and Wilemon, 1990; Maidique and Zirger, 1984; Rochford and Rudelius, 1992; Rubenstein et al., 1976; Takeuchi and Nonaka, 1986	• Amount of information shared • Agreement on decision-making authority • Functional involvement at each stage	• Relevance • Novelty • Credibility • Comprehensibility of information • Timeousness of information provision • Timeousness of information exchange
Speed in development	Cooper and Kleinschmidt, 1994; Dumaine, 1991; Takeuchi and Nonaka, 1986	• Time-to-market • Product launched on schedule • No. of competitors on market at time of launch	• Competitive information

texts have already made a distinction between market and marketing information (Tull and Hawkins, 1992). The former relates to information describing the market only, whilst the latter refers to information concerning the marketing activities of the firm, their impact on and interaction with the market, and their effectiveness in achieving marketing objectives. Others, however, use 'market information' to cover a broad array of issues, including the dominant economic characteristics of an industry, factors determining competitive success, industry prospects for profitability, etc. (Marty, 1994; Moorman, 1993). In this case, market information might be fed into a firm from a variety of sources, both internal and external. In detailing how market information should be collated internally, Kohli and Jaworski (1990) suggest that information can and should be generated in departments throughout the organization and is not the exclusive responsibility of a marketing department (Daft and Weick, 1984; Webster 1988). Following on from this point, these horizontal, interdepartmental flows of market information may also be formal or informal (Sandell, 1995). Developments in the literature on the market orientation of firms suggest that too much attention to customer and immediate market information only may be characterized as narrow and myopic (Day, 1994; Sinkula, 1994; Slater and Narver, 1995). The implication, therefore, is to change the interpretation of market information from one residing in any one department to one which embraces organizational breadth and which is not tied to any one function within an organization.

This interpretation, however, brings conceptual problems which traditional research in marketing has only hesitantly approached. For market information capability to integrate successfully the voice of the customer into NPD, processes are required to make sense of different functions' 'thought worlds' (Dougherty, 1992). As Leonard-Barton (1991) states, 'individuals have to learn to communicate, during the act of innovation, about how their diverse bits of know-how and know-why can be embodied and synthesized in a single new product' (p. 61). Incorporation of these notions requires the integration of literature describing capabilities in general and marketing capabilities in particular.

Capabilities are a capacity to deploy resources by integrating knowledge, business processes and organizational learning (Mahoney and Panadian, 1992). Capabilities are lodged in knowledge distributed among four distinct dimensions: accumulated knowledge and skills based on experience; knowledge embedded in technical systems and databases; formal and informal management systems to create and control knowledge; and as a part of organizational cognition (Day, 1994). Day also classifies three types of capabilities: outside-in; inside-out; and spanning skills to unite the two. Therefore capabilities may be external or internal. This is a most interesting concept for NPD, since no research has looked at how these categories of capability affect the task of integrating the voice of the customer into new products. These we call 'market information capabilities' which are not delineated in terms of any particular function and which refer equally to what is known through experience or history. This view resonates with Day's (1994) recommendation that, among other things, the 'market sensing' capability of a firm depends on its ability to keep an 'open-minded inquiry'; i.e., taking information from many sources simultaneously on multiple dimensions.

Moreover, the organizational learning literature has contributed to this subject and posits that market information processing is a function of what the organization has learned previously, in terms of both facts about its relevant markets and its particular way of acquiring, distributing, interpreting and storing information, whether that be formal or informal (Daft and Weick, 1984; Huber, 1991; Levitt and March, 1988; Sinkula, 1994). The work of Moorman (1993) had developed these themes further, describing four key processes associated with market information: information acquisition; information transmission; conceptual utilization; and instrumental utilization. Acquisition refers to the collection of primary or secondary data from organizational stakeholders, either formally or informally. Information transmission refers to the degree to which the information is diffused among relevant users, conceptual utilization refers to the indirect use of information, which is seen as conceptual or affective components of use, while instrumental utilization refers to the extent to which market information is applied and influences decisions.

To date, much research associated with customer-relevance in NPD has focused on mechanisms that might be used (new product departments or committees, new venture teams, new product champions or R&D departments, for example). A change in approach that is suggested in the above, namely the development of market information capability, is implicit in much of the traditional literature but not addressed explicitly. In order to examine what a 'market information capability' might be in this context, the next section of the chapter deals with those factors which influence the extent and nature of market information capability in NPD. To organize these influencing factors, we have borrowed from another sphere of marketing literature, namely, organizational buying behaviour, which develops a catalogue of task and non-task influencers. Task influencers are those factors which relate directly to the nature of the immediate product development. Non-task influencers are enduring factors, permeating the whole organizational fabric. They affect market information capability in every product development project, because they are germane to an individual involved with the development project, or the team handling the development project, or indeed are conditions underlying the organization as a whole which affect every development project. (Ozanne and Churchill, 1971; Wind and Cardozo, 1974). In the next section, both sets of factors are examined.

Market Information in NPD and Task-related Factors: New Product Strategy (Protocol)

Much research in the 1980s and 1990s stressed the importance of strategic new product decisions which set the parameters within which a new product will be developed. These decisions refer typically to the way in which a new product, once launched, will compete in its category: as a first entry into a market; as a cost-reduced version of extant products; or as an innovative and unique solution to a customer problem (Cooper, 1993; Crawford, 1994; Nystrom, 1979). Decisions such as these are frequently related to the firms' familiarity with the product or technology under development, indeed the level of newness in product development is an important but neglected issue in NPD research. In their meta-analytic review of NPD success literature, Montoya-Weiss and Calantone (1994) show that a minority of studies incorporate the level of technological newness as an influencing factor in the types of NPD process undertaken by companies. The work by Cooper and Kleinschmidt (1991) found that both high and low levels of innovativeness were associated with different factors typically influencing product success. These results were later confirmed in a replication study in the chemical industry (Cooper and Kleinschmidt, 1993). Similarly, Griffin (1993) found that the greater the levels of newness in the product being developed, the longer the development time, particularly in the early stages of the NPD process. These results lend face validity to the propositions espoused by Cooper and Kleinschmidt (1991) that newness in the project requires greater levels of development work, including attention to market information collection. Further, as Griffin (1993) notes, 'additional insights on better managing projects can be gained by capturing supplementary data for those projects, for example, number and timing of market research studies' (1993, p. 124). Thus the strategy of the NPD (in terms of newness) seems to have a moderating effect on the type of information sought and the processes involved. Although there has been no research into these phenomena to date, the foregoing discussion suggests that the organization will be more adept at processing market information which is in line with its current operations, and therefore, its past learning. Some evidence for this suggestion exists in the shift in emphasis toward successive generations of new products, with the lifecycle of any one 'version' assuming less importance (Glazer, 1991).

A number of typologies, based on the newness of the product, exist in the literature; for example, evolutionary/revolutionary innovations (Cohn and Turyn, 1984), radical/incremental (Dewar and Dutton, 1986), continuous/discontinuous innovations (Robertson, 1967), the Booz Allen and Hamilton (1982) empirically-based typology of new product introductions, and Johne's (1994) routine, extended, radical and new style product development. Johne (1994) has expounded the view that the types of market information – termed market listening – may have different components depending on the type of product development being pursued. Combining the conceptual views of Ansoff (1979), Booz Allen and Hamilton (1982) and Cardozo et al. (1993), Johne developed a typology of product development newness, depicted in Figure 12.1, wherein he argues for different types of market listening. Using this typology, Johne (1994) argues that *routine product development* requires routine feedback from the external market in the form of sales representative reports, published market reports and market trend information. In addition, specific research surveys will be undertaken to fine tune the development decisions. Internal market information is supplied regarding relevant technologies which might be incorporated into existing products. *Extended product development*, developing old products for new markets or market segments, requires extra external market information which focuses on likely demand – since the markets and market need at which the development is aimed is, in this case, current. *Radical product development* consists of developing products with new attributes, predominantly for existing target markets, and requires gathering external market information with particular reference to competitive product attributes, buyer needs, importances of the needs and preferences, and market perceptions. *New style product*

NEWNESS OF THE CUSTOMER BASE		
	Low	High
P R O D U C T **N E W N E S S**	**Radical product development** NPD aimed at the existing customer base.	**New style product development** NPD aimed at extending the customer base.
	Routine product development Old product development (OPD) aimed at the existing customer base.	**Extended product development** Old product development (OPD) aimed at extending the customer base.

FIGURE 12.1 Product market newness in NPD

development, the development of radically new products for gaining access to new customer groups, requires external market information which addresses macro-market trends. Techniques such as problem, activity and scenario analysis might well be important, especially in the initial stages of the NPD process.

Given the different market information requirements of various types of NPD, it follows that the market information capabilities required for a radical new product development are likely to be very different from those required by routine product development, where there is, indeed, greater familiarity with the market and technology behind the product.

Whilst the newness of the NPD project, both in terms of market and product, is directly related to the amount of uncertainty, and therefore information require-ments in the process, almost all the conceptualizations of that process suggest that it is one of uncertainty reduction. That being so, it is necessary to consider the implications of the NPD activities throughout the process for market informa-tion capability.

Types of Information and the Different Stages of the NPD Process

The NPD process has often been viewed as one in which uncertainties are inherent (Goldhar, Bragaw and Schwartz, 1976; More, 1985; Rothwell and Robert-son, 1973; Souder and Moenaert, 1992). These uncertainties require information inputs, which are then converted by the players involved in each activity into information outputs, which are deemed to reduce uncertainty if the process is to proceed further (Bonnet, 1986; Moenaert and Souder, 1990).

Research has suggested that uncertainty is a function of task variability and task analyzability (Daft and Weick, 1984; Souder and Moenaert, 1992; Victor and

Blackburn, 1987). By applying this perspective to the NPD process, it has been argued that task variability describes the amount of new uncertainty that emerges throughout the process, and that task analyzability describes the amount of procedures available to reduce the emerging uncertainty. As explained above, the NPD process is one of incremental uncertainty reduction, so the amount of task variability and analyzability will change over the duration of the project. In his study of software development at ICL, Hauptman (1986) described a taxonomy of information types for innovation which relates well to uncertainty reduction as defined by task variability and task analyzability (Souder and Moenaert, 1992). The taxonomy posits two types of information, *innovative* and *coordinative*. Innovative information is that which solves problems occurring during the NPD process, and coordinative information concerns the identification and scheduling of tasks and outputs throughout the NPD process. Thus, innovative information is suggested to be more appropriate in uncertainty reduction to decrease task variability, and coordinative information is more appropriate to increase task analyzability. This taxonomy is a useful way of capturing the different types of market information required as inputs to the NPD process at various stages. It does not, however, explicitly capture the decision 'gates' that occur (Cooper, 1993). In order to relate the type of information to the types of decisions for which it might be appropriate, it is necessary to examine in greater detail the process of NPD.

The NPD process is one where each of a series of development phases is followed by an evaluation phase, with each evaluation being followed by a 'decision gate' where the decision to continue or stop the development is taken (go/no go). In line with recent thinking, these stages are iteratively overlapping and the gates are 'fuzzy' (Cooper, 1994; Griffin, 1997).

During the pre-development activities, which tend to occur at the preliminary stages of the NPD process, where, as yet, there is no specific concept which could be evaluated by customers, strategic market information is required (market/customer trends, need assessments, perceptual maps, and so on). The types of market research study delivering information for these needs is known as 'exploratory' (Kinnear and Taylor, 1991; Leonard-Barton, 1991; Ortt and Schoormans, 1993; Tull and Hawkins, 1992). Exploratory research can be classified as either innovative or coordinative. For example, exploratory research such as purchase or consumption trends might be intended for reducing uncertainty about the potential target market for a developing product, in which case it would be classified as innovative. On the other hand, exploratory research describing usage problems with a particular product category will give an indication of the magnitude of the development task required to solve those problems, in which case the information is coordinative.

As the development process proceeds, the effectiveness of marketing research is related to the extent to which it provides specific methods for reducing more specific points of uncertainty. This kind of research is generally described as 'confirmatory' (Kinnear and Taylor, 1991; Tull and Hawkins, 1992).

If the market information provided is too specific (i.e., confirmatory/coordinative) early in the NPD process, there is a greater risk that the basis for development is ignorant of market trends, competitive strengths or weaknesses perceived by the market, or market needs. On the other hand, if market information continues to identify new uncertainties throughout the later stages of the NPD process, there is a risk that the development will become caught in a cycle of information-gathering activity which results in 'drowning in information, but starving for knowledge'.

The activities associated with the development of new products address different problems and face different constraints which further complicates their implications for market information capability. Reitman (1965) suggested that task structure can be defined as a continuum, with well-structured (defined) problems having a few open constraints and ill-structured problems having many. (This is reminiscent of the concepts of variability and analyzability.) Adding structure to a problem requires information, which can be drawn from existing knowledge or by acquiring additional contextual information, or a combination of the two.

In the context of NPD, this emphasizes the effect of the newness of the NPD project and the particular stage of the process in determining the structure of the problem, and therefore the required market information capability. For example, the most uncertain activity of any new product development is likely to be idea generation, but idea generation for new products in new markets is likely to be more uncertain than where the development is essentially a modification of a product aimed at a market where the company is already active. Therefore, each activity or task has inherent characteristics which require different levels of knowledge and information. The work of Shanteau (1992) on the theory of expert competence sheds light on these complexities by showing task characteristics which are associated with good or poor performance by experts. This is reproduced in Table 12.2.

From this table, it can be seen that certain characteristics of tasks enhance or impede an expert's performance and, further, these task characteristics can be related to the very issues of newness and NPD activity discussed above. This is graphically represented in Figure 12.2.

For example, decision aids such as computer launch simulations are widely available for product modifications but are rare where new technologies/products are concerned. Similarly, with modifications there are fewer excuses for errors,

TABLE 12.2 Task characteristics

Good performance	Poor performance
Static stimuli	Dynamic stimuli
Decisions about things	Decisions about behavior
Experts agree on stimuli	Experts disagree on stimuli
More predictable problems	Less predictable problems
Some errors expected	Few errors expected
Repetitive tasks	Unique tasks
Feedback available	Feedback unavailable
Objective analysis available	Subjective analysis only
Problem decomposable	Problem not decomposable
Decision aids common	Decision aids rare

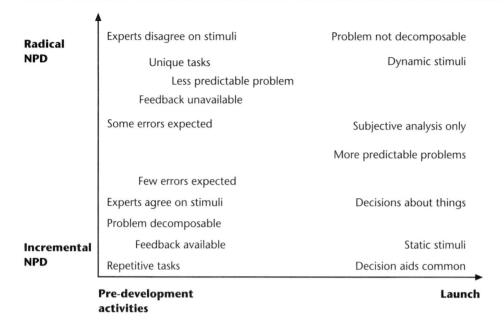

Radical NPD

Experts disagree on stimuli

Problem not decomposable

Unique tasks

Dynamic stimuli

Less predictable problem

Feedback unavailable

Some errors expected

Subjective analysis only

More predictable problems

Few errors expected

Experts agree on stimuli

Decisions about things

Problem decomposable

Incremental NPD

Feedback available

Static stimuli

Repetitive tasks

Decision aids common

Pre-development activities

Launch

FIGURE 12.2 Task characteristics and newness of NPD activities

due to familiarity, than is the case with radical innovation. Therefore, character-istics inherent in the detail of the various NPD tasks, together with the overall strategic direction of the development are likely to influence not only the requirement of market information capability, but also the extent to which that capability can affect the outcome of the project.

The final task influence on market information capability relates to the group of people whose responsibility it is to develop and launch the new product.

The Influence of the Team on Market Information Capabilities

Teams have long been an interest of researchers in NPD, often focusing on different dimensions such as team formulation, teamwork and communication. In this section two dimensions are explored, namely the *coordination mechanisms* of the NPD project and its *composition*. The organizational mechanism for new product development has been called the 'project organizational structure' (Craig and Hart, 1992). Speaking of structure we use Olson, Walker and Ruekert's (1995) conceptualization whereby structure is the formal design of roles and admin-istrative mechanisms to control and integrate work activities and resource flow (including information). The NPD process requires the flow of information which resides in different functional areas of the firm but also outside the firm (e.g., customers, market, technology centres). In other words, the locus of the informa-tion and its 'stickiness' (von Hippel, 1995) determines whether or not the firm is capable of using specific information, irrespectively of its perceived utility. A composition which allows access to the different loci of the information during the NPD process is expected to enhance the market information capability of the firm.

Although such compositions provide efficiencies in the use of information from diverse sources, they create problems of interaction and coordination of the individuals involved in the NPD process, which in turn can block the use of information. The structural constructs of formalization and centralization have been suggested in the past as mechanisms for coping with such problems and the relative debate has produced two opposite views. One is represented by the ideas of Burns and Stalker (1961) and Lawrence and Lorsch (1967) whereby a mechanistic system is most appropriate for firms operating under stable conditions; in contrast an 'organic' system is most appropriate for firms operating in a less stable environment where the need for additional information and interpersonal communication is very important during task execution. Evidence in support of their view is provided by Galbraith (1986) who observed that as the level of task uncertainty increases, the amount of information to be found and processed by decision makers increases too. He postulated that changes in the organizational structure of firms represent the strategic efforts of firms for processing information. Therefore a mechanistic structure is implemented because tasks are routine and predictable, while an organic structure is used when the level of uncertainty is higher and the mechanistic rules and procedures cannot cope with the demands of this situation. Mintzberg (1983) subscribed to the view that 'although we can characterize certain organizations as bureaucratic or organic overall, none is uniformly so across its entire range of activities' (p. 37). The differences between the organization as a whole and its sub-units were appreciated by Holbek (1988) and were attributed by him to the efforts of organizations to make use of the advantages of organicity and bureaucracy for the initiation and implementation stages of innovations respectively. Holbek postulated that the dilemma between bureaucracy and organicity is faced by organizations through solutions involving differentiation in time, differentiation in space and hybrid solutions (i.e., balanced differentiation in space and time). Furthermore, he suggested that in order to gain better insights into the problem of this organizational dilemma, 'measurement of organicity or bureaucracy must be made for the relevant organization units, as well as for the organization as a whole' (p. 274).

What is clear from these developments is that market information capability is directly influenced by the NPD coordination mechanism used. Recently, Olson, Walker and Ruekert (1995) have provided a list of nine types of coordination mechanisms which are part of a continuum, ranging from bureaucratic controls (hierarchical, mechanistic) to design centres (participative, organic); i.e., bureaucratic controls, individual liaisons, temporary task forces, integrating managers, matrix structures, design teams, and design centres. However, they acknowledged that the different coordination mechanisms are not totally independent from each other. In addition, by concentrating on structural (task) matters to the detriment of the non-structural, non-task elements of team dynamics, an important source of variability across structures is completely missed. It is to these non-task factors that we now turn.

Market Information Capability and Non-Task Related Factors: The Organizational Level

Strategy-making Process Capability and Market Information Capability

The main role of market information as discussed in this chapter is to inform and support strategies of the firm. Therefore, what drives the collection, dissemination and use of market information can be attributed, partly, to the strategic-making process of the firm. This brings into the discussion the strategy and strategy-making modes of the organization. Recent advances in the strategic literature view organizational effectiveness as a result of the firm's ability to master and employ a multiplicity of strategies and strategic modes, e.g., command, symbolic, rational, transactive and generative, although each of these modes demands the mastery of seemingly contradictory or paradoxical organizational skills (Bourgois and Eisenhardt, 1988; Hart, 1992; Hart and Banbury, 1994; Quinn, 1988). Drawing an analogy here, it can be suggested that much like organizational effectiveness, success in NPD requires the simultaneous mastery of seemingly contradictory or paradoxical organizational skills such as decisiveness and reflectiveness, broad vision and attention to detail, bold moves and incremental adjustments, customer orientation and attention to competitive moves, technological advances and resource constraints, timely NPD and completion of all the key activities in the NPD process. Therefore NPD strategies that combine discrepant or paradoxical organizational processes lead to success (Nonaka, 1988; Quinn, 1988). Since different strategic modes at the organizational and NPD level have different requirements for market information, they give rise to complex market information systems (collection: dissemination and use) which in turn are difficult to imitate. In other words, the market information capability of the firm is enhanced, thus becoming a core competence of the organization. As such we expect to find a higher market information capability in organizations that exhibit a high strategic process capability.

Organizational Learning Process Capability and Market Information Capability

Market information capability, as defined in the present chapter, also fits well with the concept of organizational learning (OL). Since the seminal work of Argyris and Shon (1978), OL has been viewed as a recurrent feature of successful organization (see Chapter 5). Recent advances in this field have produced useful typologies of OL in terms of types of learning, which can also be viewed in terms of types of knowledge that it is produced within the organization, and processes of learning (Shrivastava, 1983). Whereas in the past a distinction was made between organizations that can learn and those that cannot learn, today it is acknowledged that learning occurs in all organizations; the main difference, however, lies in the mode of learning which is favoured by the organization as a whole. In terms of OL processes Huber (1991) suggested that OL is composed of at least four processes; namely, knowledge acquisition, information distribution, information interpretation and organizational memory. Similarly, Sinkula (1994) and Slater and Narver (1995) view OL as a three-stage process that includes information acquisition, information dissemination and shared interpretation. As far as types or styles of OL is concerned Argyris and Shon (1978) have distinguished OL between single-loop and double-loop, of which, Senge (1990) suggested a difference between adaptive and generative learning, and Shrivastava (1983) proposed six different styles namely, one-man institution, mythological, information seeking, participative, formal management and bureaucratic learning. Underlying all these different types and processes of learning are different types of knowledge that are produced within organizations. These have been distinguished by Collins (1993) to embrained, embodied, encultured, embedded and encoded knowledge, whereas somewhat similar typologies have been produced in the field of organizational memory (Day and Nedungadi, 1994; Despande, Farley and Webster, 1993; Sinkula, 1994). In an attempt to integrate the literature on knowledge and OL Blackler (1995) has produced a typology of organizations and knowledge types based on whether the emphasis placed by the organization is on contributions of key individuals or collective endeavour and whether the focus of the organization is on familiar problems or novel problem. As such he produced four different types; namely, expert-dependent organizations which capitalize on the embodied competencies of key members, knowledge-routinized organizations which capitalize on technologies, rules and procedures, symbolic analyst-dependent organizations which capitalize on the embrained skills of key members, and communication intensive organizations which place their emphasis on the encultured knowledge and collective understanding. Blackler (1995) continues, suggesting that despite the usefulness of his typology, knowledge remains problematic. Capitalizing on activity theory he draws a distinction between knowledge and knowing and conceptualizes knowing as a phenomenon within organizations which is mediated, situated, provisional, pragmatic and contested. His ideas reinforce prescriptions for moving away from simple descriptions of what organizations know or what kind of knowledge resides within organizations, to rich studies of how the process of knowing is achieved in the organization. In terms of our discussion this is extremely important since organizational success in the NPD area is associated with the ability of the firm to perform well both in familiar and novel product/ market situations. This means that for an organization to succeed in its many and different NPD efforts it should be able to master and mobilize knowledge and knowing procedures that may seem paradoxical or inconsistent.

The next section focuses on the team level and investigates how it affects the market information capability of the firm.

The Team Level

One of the key changes over the years of research in NPD is the shift from a broad acceptance of NPD as a linear process, to one that comprises non-discrete and non-sequential complex streams of activities (Kanter, 1988; Schroeder *et al.*, 1989), characterized by dynamic decision tasks. Dynamic decision tasks indicate situations where the decisions made at time t alter the state of the system and thus the information upon which decisions in time $t+1$ are based (Diehl and Sterman, 1995). Decision tasks in the NPD process exhibit an additional form of dynamism in that decisions made in one area of the NPD process or the firm (e.g., capital investment in machinery and equipment, and marketing decisions with regard to the characteristics of the product), condition decisions to be made in other areas (e.g., engineering and R&D).

The main reason underlying the use of group rather than individual decision-making units in dynamic and complex managerial processes, such as NPD, is that groups, through deliberation and discussion, can broaden the knowledge base which is applied to the process and hence make more informed decisions than any one individual can. Yet, in marketing, little work has addressed the phenomena that occur within the group as it deliberates. This is in sharp contrast with other fields of organizational and human enquiry (such as psychology, organizational psychology, social psychology and decision making) and corroborates criticism for the apparent reluctance of marketing researchers to make creative use of advances and changes in fields different than mainstream marketing. Nevertheless, this is not to say that advances in the latter fields have thoroughly addressed all the problems related to group decision making. For example Svenson (1996) maintains that the vast majority of researchers have treated the decision-making process as referring to choices between alternatives with goal conflicts. However, she continues, in real-life decision-making the search and creation of decision alternatives plays a significant role in the success of the process, yet almost no decision research has treated this problem. Arguably the NPD process, viewed as a group decision-making process, falls in the latter category. Decision processes oriented towards evaluating alternatives with goal conflicts have been characterized as 'alternative-focused thinking', whereas those oriented to searching and creating decision alternatives have been characterized as 'value-focused thinking' (e.g., Keeney, 1992; Mintzberg, Raisinghani and Thoret, 1976).

Having said that, research on strategic decision making has shown that much of the discussion within groups is used to promote existing preferences and exert conformity pressures and power on others (McGrath, 1984; Parks and Cowlin, 1996). On the same lines Levine, Rescnick and Higgins (1993) maintain that social factors that arise during the group processes are important elements in the success of the collaborative efforts.

These issues are relevant to our discussion of market information capability since as Brown and Starkey (1994) suggest, information and communication phenomena are surface manifestations of complex configurations of deeply felt beliefs, values and attitudes (p. 808). These beliefs, values and attitudes can be attributed, to a certain extent, to the organization and the dynamics of the team in which individuals participate. Brown and Starkey (1994) found, in their case study of team decision making, subcultures which differed radically from each other competed for status, power and resources with each other and invested the cultural fabric of the organization with considerable conflict and political tension. Yet, others have postulated that a level of organizational, as opposed to personal, conflict is necessary within groups and organizations since it promotes discussion and deliberation (Eisenhardt, Kahwajy and Bourgeois, 1997). In addition, post-decision consolidation within groups has been suggested as a factor which adds to the quality of the decision making, implementation and enhancement of group and individual learning (Svenson, 1996). Consolidation, in turn, is enhanced by the speed and accuracy of the decision information feedback (Svenson and Malmsten, 1996). However, a note of caution should be inserted here since according to Diehl and Sterman (1995):

> people generally adopt an event-based, 'open-loop' view of causality, ignore feedback processes, fail to appreciate time delays between action and response and in the reporting of information, do not understand stock and flows, and are insensitive to nonlinearities which may alter the strengths of different feedback loops as a system evolves.
> (p. 198)

They call this phenomenon 'misperception' of feedback.

The discussion above leads us to the conclusion that information acquisition, transmission and use is enhanced by group processes that promote organizational conflict, deliberation, post-decision consolidation and feedback. Nevertheless, it must be stated here that excessive levels of the above processes, e.g. conflict, will harm the decision-making abilities of the group by creating unnecessary delays and political tension. On the same line of reasoning, task-related factors may be at work, thus conditioning the required levels of deliberation, consolidation and feedback. For example, excessive deliberation on a rather familiar problem will create delays, and time pressures on NPD tasks might reduce the time available for consolidation and feedback.

The Individual Level

The NPD's traditional call for 'proficiency' in the NPD process fits well with the notion of 'expertise' in psychology and decision-making literature. Research on experts and expertise in these fields has produced conflicting results. More specifically, in decision-making research (DMR), experts' deficiencies have been reported in almost every type of decision analysis. However, in the cognitive psychology field experts always have outperformed novices in every aspect of cognitive functioning, from memory and learning to problem solving and reasoning (Anderson, 1981). In order to resolve this conundrum Shanteau (1992) has proposed the theory of expert competence (TEC) where he suggests that the performance of experts is contingent upon a number of factors. These are as follows:

(a) *Domain knowledge.* This includes not only textbook knowledge but knowledge gained from experience in working on real problems. Research in this area has shown that experts develop a 'case-based reasoning' enhanced by the use of 'contextual' information and the ability to organize vast amounts of information in a convenient way.

(b) *Psychological traits.* These traits include self-confidence, excellent communication skills, the ability to adapt to new situations, and a clear sense of responsibility. According to Shanteau (1992), for a person to be accepted as an expert it is necessary to act like one.

(c) *Cognitive skills.* Experts have highly-developed attention abilities, a sense of what is relevant, the ability to identify exceptions to rules and the capability of working effectively under stress.

(d) *Decision strategies*. Although many strategies are unique to given domains, there are several that are widely used. They include making use of dynamic feedback, relying on decision aids, decomposing complex decision problems and pre-thinking solutions to tough situations.

(e) *Task characteristics*. This is an overlooked factor even in psychology. According to Shanteau (1992) the task characteristics determine whether it is possible for experts to behave competently or not. Since task characteristics have been discussed earlier in this paper, they are omitted from the present discussion.

Although the above characteristics refer to experts in general,[1] they can be used for understanding the relationship between individuals and market information capability within the NPD area of organizations. More specifically, the theory of expert competence can be used to give greater form and substance to the concept of market information capability. In terms of substance, the TEC directs us to conclude that market information should include domain-specific and contextual information organized in a way that links them to past cases (domain knowledge, and cognitive skills): it should abide to rigorous scientific rules for its collection and organization; should be communicated throughout the organization; is invested with responsibility and accountability (psychological traits); is up-to date and flexible (cognitive skills); allows for dynamic feedback; and collects and reports information which is aligned to the requirements of decision aids. In terms of form, the people responsible for the systematic collection, organization and distribution of market information should develop an understanding of the problems faced by the different constituencies they serve within the organization; the same degree of understanding should permeate those who make use of market information in their decision-making process. Underlying this process is an understanding of the history of the organization and its evolutionary processes (domain knowledge and cognitive skills). People involved with the collection, organization and distribution of information within the firm should have the necessary background knowledge and education for doing so, as well as the necessary responsibility and accountability (psychological traits); They should develop an understanding of the decision strategies used within the firm and be able to align their efforts with the requirement of each strategy (decision strategies).

These ideas consolidate what has been debated earlier in this chapter and begin to set an agenda of non-task, individual-related factors which can be used as criteria against which existing research can be evaluated and new directions outlined. For example, although functional integration has been put forward as a necessary condition for sharing of information and knowledge among individuals, a greater proportion of the literature examines only the integration between the R&D and marketing departments of the firm during the NPD process (Gupta and Wilemon, 1990). The integration of these functions with others in the firm, which are also implicated in the NPD process, e.g., manufacturing, accounting and finance, sales and public relations, hardly figures in the literature.

Two further factors which operate at the individual level are also relevant to the development of an organization's market information capability: goal orientation and employee socialization.

According to Dweck's (1986) motivational theory the goals that the individuals pursue in their work influence the framework they use for their interpretation of different events and situations as well as their reaction to outcomes. She identified two types of goal orientation; namely learning and performance goal orientation. Individuals exhibiting a learning orientation approach are given tasks with the aim to increase their understanding of novel issues and enhance their competence in undertaking this task, thus promoting 'mastery-oriented' responses to given tasks. They are favourably disposed towards experimentation and they view failure as part of their learning process. In contrast, performance-oriented individuals are characterized by an avoidance of challenging tasks, a preference of familiar activities and ones that they have performed well in the past so as to avoid negative judgements of their competence, and when faced with failure they attribute it to low ability, loose interest and they may seek to withdraw from the task entirely (Button, Mathieu and Zajac, 1996; Dweck and Leggett, 1988; Elliot and Dweck, 1988). For our discussion, since the market information capability is inherently a learning exercise, we expect individuals involved in the NPD with a learning orientation to seek, disseminate and use market information to a greater extent than performance-oriented individuals do.

That said, market information capability has to be viewed as an organization-wide capability. Wind and Mahajan (1997) state that despite the existence of firms with total commitment to innovation, the vast majority give little attention to the role of marketing research and modelling in creating a total organizational commitment to innovation. They go on to suggest the need to instil a firm appreciation of the value of marketing research and the need to build and nurture marketing research and modelling competencies. Their ideas support our views for the creation of an organization-wide culture that appreciates the value of market information and motivates individuals to collect, distribute and use market information in order to tune their research and development efforts to the voice of the customer, thus creating an organization-wide market information capability. The latter could be seen as related to the organizational socialization of the individuals. Organizational socialization has been perceived as an inherently learning process through which knowledge and competence is transferred between the different generation of managers and other employees within the firm (Feldman, 1976; Hall, 1987; Schein, 1968; Van Maanen and Schein, 1979). According to Louis (1980) the process of organizational socialization imbues employees with the culture and values of the organization and provides them with the necessary technical and interpersonal competence to achieve what is expected of them and to interact with other individuals in the organization. Since the creation of a market-information capability, from an individuals' perspective, requires significant domain and contextual knowledge, as well as the ability to engage in a dialogue and information exchange with other individuals, it would lead to the conclusion that market information capability of the firm will, to a large extent, be related to individuals' organizational socialization.

Figure 12.3 summarizes the content of the chapter and sets out the inter-relationships among the key sets of issues.

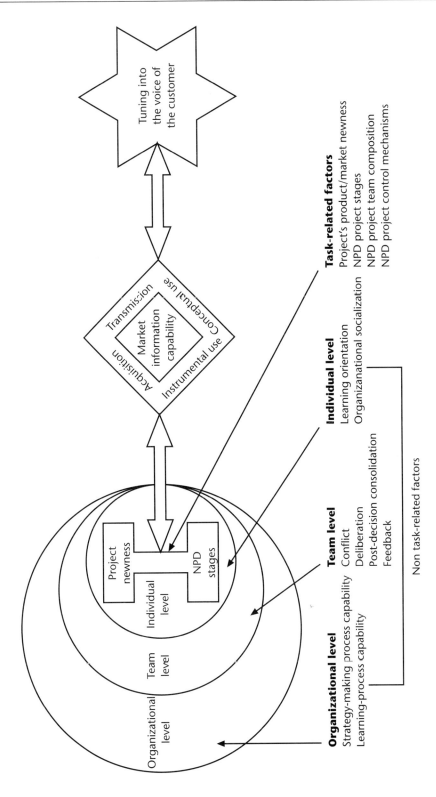

FIGURE 12.3 Conceptual framework

Conclusion

This chapter has outlined a changed conceptualization of the issues vital to understanding how a customer's perspective might be infused into the NPD process. Unlike early views of NPD, where the customer is seldom represented, or represented by an assumption that market research will supply the necessary inputs, this chapter has attempted to take on board the organization-wide, team-related and individual factors that might impede a firm's ability to get the 'voice of the customer' embedded into its NPD processes. Moreover, working through the more recent themes to have appeared across a wide variety of disciplines, the chapter has presented a view of NPD which underlines the changes in thinking that have threaded through a wide and often fragmented literature that have profound implications for how researchers in marketing might approach the topic of NPD.

Note

1 We acknowledge here that the more abstract notion of expertise lies not only in the minds of experts but also in expert systems; i.e., systems of knowledge creation, manifestation and use which consist of both people, artefacts, routines and processes.

CHAPTER 13

Marketing communications changes

[handwritten: Threat to mass comms / future of comms.]

Martin Evans

It could be argued that nearly all marketing activity is 'communications' so to tackle this area in one relatively short chapter requires some focusing. In this spirit, the chapter will explore what the writer believes to be the most significant development in marketing over the last couple of decades (and which is set to continue). That is, the brave new world of data-driven organization–customer interaction. The role and nature of the evolution of this is changing marketing communications, marketing more generally, markets, marketing communicators themselves, and even society, forever. If you think this is exaggeration, read on!

In short, marketing communications is being forced to be more accountable and the data-driven approach facilitates (to various degrees in practice) the ability to 'count them out and count them back in again'. The old criticism of mass media advertising usually attributed to Lord Leverhulme, that nobody could tell him which half of his advertising spend was wasted, is probably somewhat unfair to modern advertising effectiveness researchers. But the difficulties involved with quantifying the contribution of traditional mass media promotional approaches to profit has not helped satisfy the accountability criterion.

Every contact with the customer can be an opportunity for data-driven marketing communications to gather more data. This is manifested in the lists of target prospects that a marketing communicator can purchase from list brokers. A list of, for example, prospects in the gardening market might have been compiled from the following sorts of sources:

- Subscribers to gardening magazines;
- Purchases of gardening products via mail or via the Internet;
- Entrants to competitions for products in this market;
- Respondents to lifestyle surveys who claim to have an interest in gardening;
- Visitors to certain gardens or 'heritage' sites;
and so on.

The result is that marketing communications are increasingly being targeted at named individuals rather than at anonymized segments. Response and other personalized data is being mined in increasingly sophisticated ways, and 'new' marketing metrics are being used to calculate the allowable costs of communications campaigns and to identify those customers who are more likely to contribute most to profit. This itself has spawned an entire new marketing paradigm – the 'relational' one. Without data the precise profile characteristics and transactional history of nature of named customers would not be known and it is upon this 'biography' (Evans, 1999) that relational campaigns are based. New communications media facilitate more interactive organization–customer contact. These include the Internet, telephony and computer technology, and a recent phenomenon has been the convergence of these within, for example, mobile telephones which can access the Internet and which make two-way interaction possible. Marketers, for example, being able to physically locate these telephones via satellite tracking in order to send personalized advertising messages to those who have shown a propensity to buy from store X when they are actually passing store X.

Marketing communicators are being equally affected in a number of ways. First there is the personal dilemma over what, at the extreme, some might see as 'pestering' their best customers for even more purchases and the deselection of those customers who contribute less, all based on understanding the 'buying biography' of named customers. Also, however, few marketers are properly equipped to deal with data-driven marketing communications (Evans *et al.*, 2002). Marketers in the marketing communications arena especially, might have excellent skills in terms of dealing with the media and clients or with the creative side of advertising, but they can rarely bridge the skills gap between understanding segmentation (for example) in strategic and tactical terms on the one hand, and on the other the data mining and other communications metrics for planning, implementing and evaluating data-driven marketing communications campaigns.

Markets are clearly being affected in that the explosion of contact media hinted at above means consumers expect more direct and instant responses from organizations. The nature of some of these media, such as the Internet, means that customers can have greater control of the communications process. They can search across different suppliers, often across national boundaries, for prices, availability and service features, and can be less reliant upon mass media advertisements for information. Other issues, however, affect customers, not least the trade-off between divulging their personal details and transaction patterns against the type of personalized targeting of communications outlined above.

First there is physical privacy, which is when a customer feels they are receiving too many marketing communications. Earlier eras would have held debates over the intrusion of mass media marketing communications via TV and outdoor advertising but now we see concerns over the physical amount of marketing communications addressed to named individuals via the mail, phone (and text messaging) and the Internet. But information privacy is perhaps the major issue in terms of wider social implications, and refers to the ability of individuals to determine the nature and extent of information about them being communicated to others (Westin, 1992). The dilemma is one of balancing consumers' rights to control access to their personal information and companies' rights to information access for business purposes. This is different from earlier concerns over advertising, which were more related to a sort of popularist subconscious brainwashing as exemplified by Vance Packard's book *The Hidden Persuaders* (1957) that attacked mass media advertising in the 1950s. Now, we see social concerns over unknown people accessing personal details and sharing them with other unknown people.

It is interesting, though, to go back in time again and remember a prediction from Shubik (1967):

> [T]he computer and modern data processing provide the refinement – the means to treat individuals as individuals rather than parts of a large aggregate. . . . [T]he treatment of an individual as an individual will not be an unmixed blessing. Problems concerning the protection of privacy will be large.

This is not a misprint – it *was* 1967.

So, with this as the backdrop to the chapter, the first area to be explored is the nature and evolution of data-driven organization–customer interaction itself.

The New Marketing Communications

Data-driven Organization–Customer (Relational?) Interaction

The use of the national census in many countries was a watershed for marketing communications and heralded a shift in both practice and theory. The census, of course, led to geodemographic systems and was a major catalyst in providing alternatives to anonymized market research samples. Instead we have data from all households. The further fusion of geodemographics with personalized data from lifestyle surveys and from transactional data provides what marketers are taking to be a buying 'biography' of customers, and from this they think they can develop relationships with customers (Evans, 1999).

The 'new' approach claims to change the paradigm from a focus on one-off exchanges to one in which exchanges trace back to previous interactions and reflect an ongoing process. This in turn can lead to increased satisfaction for the customer as well as for the company.

The main operationalizing of relationship marketing is via data-driven marketing communications, because this provides the means to identify and track individual customers and their buying behaviour, calculate 'lifetime' value, and generate personalized marketing communications.

But the more conceptual underpinning of relationship marketing communications involves trust, commitment, mutual benefit, adaptation and regard for privacy (O'Malley, Patterson and Evans, 1999). However, marketing communicators are not overly concerned with inviting customers to establish mutual relationships. Consider the following advice to business:

> [R]elationship marketing . . . requires a two-way flow of information. This does not mean that the customer has to give you this information willingly, or even knowingly. You can use scanners to capture information, you can gather telephone numbers,

conduct surveys, supply warranty cards, and use a data overlay from outside databases to combine factors about lifestyle, demographics, geographics, psychographics, and customer purchases'.

(Schultz, Tannenaum and Lauterborn, 1993)

This, probably commonplace view, would define relationship marketing as an oxymoron.

Tesco, in the UK, has analyzed its loyalty card data and it has been reported that mining the mountain of transactional data from its 10 million Clubcard users, it has identified 100,000 different segments, each targeted with a different set of money-off vouchers via a customer magazine (Marsh, 2001). A similar example is provided by Tower Records. This company has segmented its customer database and e-mails offers to selected targets, and 'out of every 10,000 e-mails sent, no more than three people receive the same offer' (Marsh, 2001).

The 'personalized' approach to relational marketing communications, however, might experience future flack. Digital printing technology, for example, allows personalization to a higher degree. 'You can personalize page by page, it's easy to put a name anywhere throughout the copy' (Arnold, 2002). A development of this in the US was an apparently handwritten mailing targeted at members of a particular health care segment. So convincing was this that over 150 people complained on the basis that it looked like a friend writing to them telling them they needed to lose weight (Rubach, 2002).

Technology will also facilitate more examples of personalized targeting of segments. It is possible to target an individualized TV message, analogous to personalized mailing, to a unique address via fibre optic cable (Channel 4, 1990).

Communications Knowledge Management and Integration

In practice, the underpinning of the operationalizing of organization–customer relationship marketing communications does not always go beyond data mining, which is used to identify and classify customer segments for differential targeting. It is unfortunate that many companies see a software package as all that is required. If the management of this resulting knowledge is not integrated and shared across relevant organizational functions, there is little chance of there being sustainable relational marketing. 'Knowledge management', as it is often termed, is a framework for moving data-driven marketing to a more strategic position. This is an approach that shifts the narrower relationship marketing toward intra- and inter-company networks within the broader customer relationship marketing (CRM) paradigm.

The marketing communicator needs to be less insulated from other functions and even from the informational advantages and consequences of data shared with other organizations. For example, Depres and Chauvel (2000) distil literature from academics, consultants and practitioners on this issue and demonstrate (Figure 13.1) how (vertical axis) information can be transferred from the individual across groups (e.g., the marketing communications function) and to the organization (other functions, even outside the marketing function). The horizontal axis in Figure 13.1 provides a 'process' that essentially reinforces the importance of 'sharing'. A simple practical example will help here. In a research project into the use of multi-step flows of communication in the motor market,

Context

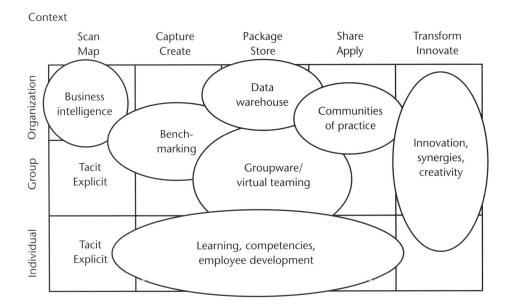

Source: Depres and Chauvel (2000)

FIGURE 13.1 Knowledge management

Evans and Fill (2000) found that motor company public relations (PR) managers make heavy use of motoring journalists as opinion formers (attempts are made to influence what these journalists say about new cars) but they are less able to make use of opinion leaders amongst car buyers. The problem is one of identifying these and then targeting them. However, the research revealed that in many of these companies there is also a database marketing communications department that records details of those who have purchased a new car early in its lifecycle. These 'earlier adopters' include a high proportion of opinion leaders. But the worrying part of the research was that the PR managers usually claimed that this database was not shared with them and that marketing and PR are 'separate'!

This chapter has to focus because of space, so we will not explore the intricacies of integrated marketing communications in the era of shared and 'managed' communications knowledge, but the above clearly raises the issue. Many marketing communications agencies are claiming to be able to offer integration of different promotional approaches (for example, Figure 13.2) but a somewhat cynical note has to be sounded because there is little evidence of this being more than rhetoric.

Is the Data-driven, Relational Communications Approach Less Insightful?

Transactional and profiling data provides valuable information on who is buying what, when, how and where, but it is market research that can get beneath the surface even further and discover the 'why' of behaviour.

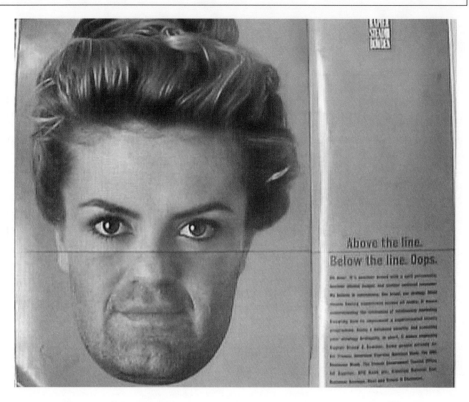

FIGURE 13.2 Dis-integrated marketing communications

So, something more affective is needed. Needs and benefits sought by customers are not always considered to be as important as 'behaviour'. Some organizations are rejecting the more affective research in favour of purely behavioural data. For example, the JIGSAW consortium, composed of Unilever, Kimberley Clark and Cadbury Schweppes, has been pooling transactional data on their respective customers in order to grow product categories and to combat the power of intermediary retailers. This consortium has decided not to use attitudinal customer data any more and base their marketing communications decisions on the massive amount of behavioural transactional data they, collectively, possess.

An interesting reinforcement of the problem raised here comes from a UK Chartered Institute of Marketing project (CIM, 2001) into the effects of technology on marketing and marketers. In this, marketers' commitment to understanding customers in the new era was explored and 'data' of the sort discussed above was often seen to be more important than qualitative understanding:

> I've been going to these groups for 20 years . . . the number of occasions to which the director of marketing has turned up to these groups you can count on one hand. . . . Therefore when a marketing director gets to present to the board, does he really know as much as the sales director sitting next to him? Very likely not.
>
> Consultant, FMCG sector (CIM, 2001)

Mitchell (2001) recently quoted a director of one of the largest retailers in UK:

We've given up trying to understand our customers ... helping us cut a lot of complexity from our business. The academic's instinct is to gather a large amount of information, formulate a theory and apply it to a situation. ... [This] creates waste in the form of the wrong information at the wrong time, leading to the wrong decisions ... or ... fruitless attempts to predict or alter customer behaviour.'

The favoured approach by this company, 'sense and respond' (Haeckel, 2001) is to react quickly on the basis of customer contact via call centres, the Internet, interactive digital TV and infomediaries. This is understandable in the current context of pressure to achieve short-term profit in order to provide shareholder value. However it can lead to a subordination of the key components of the marketing concept itself, namely customer satisfaction and *any* customer understanding, other than what can be gleaned and inferred from, for example, tracking transactional data. Indeed, CRM has been manifested not in shared and managed customer knowledge across a learning organization, but rather as the purchase of a software package.

'Behaviour' is not a surrogate for measures of satisfying customer needs. Gofton (2001), for example, reports that the UK consultancy firm, Qci, found that few organizations distinguish between the satisfaction levels of their most and least valuable segments: 'Only 16% [of the 51 blue chip companies interviewed] understand what the main drivers of loyalty are ... 30% never look at this and only half carry out some research to identify loyalty'. Indeed a study amongst pharmaceutical companies found that when asked what the key challenges are for the introduction of CRM, only 6.5 per cent of the issues mentioned related to improving customer satisfaction (Clegg, 2001). The implications of the above, then, are that purely behavioural response does not necessarily equate with an *understanding* of consumers. Taking this further, if the 'behavioural' responders become the central focus then aren't we storing up trouble for the future in attending less to why the others are non responders?

A related issue concerns another consequence of the new marketing communications being 'measurable'. The marketing communications industry is able to conduct experiments (tests) by selecting samples for different lists or different 'creatives' and monitoring response rates in order to identify the better performing approaches. In a research project (Evans, O'Malley and Patterson, 1997) some qualitative groups of older women declared that they received substantial quantities of direct mail communications on behalf of charities. They also said that this was not 'junk mail' because it was of interest to them – the matching of 'causes' with their own interests was very accurate. They were so moved by the direct mailing that they felt it important to donate – and they did just this. As far as the 'new marketing communicator' is concerned this 'response' reinforces the donors' status on the database and they will be targeted again – and probably by related charities who are likely to share lists.

The point, though, is that the women went on to say that they were barely able to afford to donate, but felt they 'had to' and were almost in tears over the issue. The reaction of a senior marketing communicator whose agency specializes in charity communications was 'but it worked' – such reliance on mechanistic testing at the expense of more insightful research is submitted here as being an issue that the industry would do well to address. Although this targeting might work in the short term, what additional problems might be being stored up for the future – not only when the 'targets' decide 'enough is enough' and refuse to donate anymore and bin all subsequent mailings – or if they merely spread ill will about the charities' marketing communications approach?

The point, then, is that the new marketing communications has much to gain from turning to more traditional market research – not as a substitute for the highly measurable and accountable testing methodology, but to create a valuable *Pyschological insight* 'gestalt' (Evans and Middleton, 1998).

All in all, then, there are some concerns over the practicalities and operationalizing of relational marketing communications. It is surely the case that the data-driven approach will continue but will this lead to true organization–customer relationships rather than just repeated exchange interactions? Even by 2001 there were signs that the bubble might have burst: 'corporate disillusionment and downright hostility to the whole CRM bandwagon is reaching feverpitch' (Mitchell, 2001a). Perhaps marketing communicators should be more honest; they want to track customer spending in order to target people with what would be hoped would be offers more likely to produce a purchase response. The problem with the 'r' word is that it has too many associations with human relationships, but organization–customer interaction is not the same (O'Malley and Tynan, 1999).

Another rather cynical note comes from research by Kennedy and Ehrenberg (2000) who suggest, with reference to 'brands' that 'good old-fashioned mass marketing approaches to branding are what have made brands'. Could this bring further doubt onto the sustainability of the (psuedo) relational paradigm for marketing communications?

The 'New Marketing Communications' Metrics

Data-driven marketing communications is easy enough to conceptualize but it is absolutely essential that its practicalities are understood by marketing communicators – otherwise it will not be the *marketing* communicators who will be employed in marketing communications!

This section, then, demonstrates some of the 'metrics' involved, by working through a typical sequence in a hypothetical case study.

A financial services company markets several financial service products and wants to identify new segments within its existing customer base for a cross-selling strategy. It wants to cross-sell Account Type A to those who have already purchased Account Type B. Through the application of data mining/CRM[1] software the company can easily identify those customers who have already purchased various of the company's products.

The company could target all of these who have *not* bought 'A' but this would undervalue customer and transactional data as an asset. In addition, the company would also want the highest return on marketing investment. It is increasingly important to be accountable in terms of return on investment (ROI). Instead, the company could use this software to interrogate existing customers who have both A and B accounts. Data mining can identify what makes these customers different from others and what makes them more or less likely to take both products. Transactional data can also be analyzed for recency, frequency and monetary value (RFM) and long time value (LTV) analyses. These are two important metrics

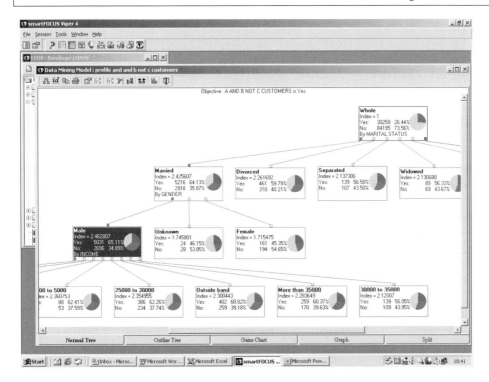

FIGURE 13.3 Example of VIPER CRM software   © Smartfocus

in data-driven marketing and many software packages, such as the one demonstrated here, include algorithms for these further metrics. The results might show that the 'best' existing A and B account holding customers come mainly from areas classified as blue collar owners, high income families, suburban semi's, and low rise council MOSAIC groups, income over £35,000, married, and aged in the 40–60 band.

However, the fullest benefit from existing customer data comes from looking at all of the attributes together. The easiest way to achieve this is via CHAID, which in this case is an integral component of the software being used and of most similar packages. Here, (Figure 13.3) various customer and transactional attributes have been investigated to see which best explain what characterizes customers who have both accounts A and B. A tree structure represents different 'hot' and 'cold' branches through the data. Each branch represents a different level of importance in explaining who the A and B customers are. Each attribute is assessed and the most important or 'significant' forms the first split. Taking the entire customer base in this instance, 26.44 per cent of all customers have both A and B accounts.

By following the 'hottest branch' the company can understand which characteristics are possessed by those customers who have purchased both A and B account types. Further branches of the CHAID tree might cascade down to even more segments, based on whichever variables prove to be significant. Space prevents showing further stages here, but assume the analysis produced 60 target segments. Each of these would have significant and different characteristics. Targeting could be done on a 'test' basis in which a sample from each might be targeted and those with better response rates could then be targeted with the full 'roll-out' campaign. Also, each could be targeted with different treatments, according to whatever gender, age, marital status or geodemographic character-istic might underpin the 'creative'.

The discussion above probably gives the impression that we have moved to one-to-one relationship marketing communications but this is far from the truth. Dibb explores aspects of this and points out that 'at the heart of segmentation strategy is the notion that customers will allow themselves to be managed' (Dibb, 2001). Indeed the use of the word 'management' in CRM might signal that 'relationship management' is an oxymoron. It implies power and that that power is one way. For customers to be 'locked in' to an air miles loyalty scheme, for example, might be music to the ears of the data-driven marketing communicator, but do all customers appreciate being 'locked in'?

Such data analysis as has been outlined above can lead to individuals being targeted but not necessarily *as individuals*. The CHAID example demonstrated that although individual data was processed, the resulting segments are still aggregates even if their constituent members are targeted by name and address, and probably with different styles of offer from those in other segments (such as in the Tesco example cited earlier).

There are, however, two paradoxes that emerge from this. First, the data-driven approach to marketing communications is, as has been shown, focusing in on itself. That is, there is a trend to using personalized data for targeting communica-tions at the expense of more traditional (especially qualitative) market research. As discussed earlier, marketing communicators might be missing out on richer insights into their targets. The second paradox is that marketing communicators themselves are often not equipped for the new role in which they now find themselves. More specifically, the 'traditional' marketing communicator is not especially numerate and would not always be able to speak the same language as those dealing with the data mining of the above example, never mind be able to do it themselves.

This brings us to the next issue, the implications of the 'new marketing communications' for 'the new marketing communicator'.

The New Marketing Communicator

Carson (1999) interviewed a group of leading US marketing practitioners and concluded that analytical skills and statistics topped the list of 'areas in which their education was lacking'. So strong is the issue that it could even be described as a fairly universal 'skills gap' amongst marketing communicators. The CIM (2001) research mentioned earlier brings disquieting news:

> Marketers should develop IT/new technology skills – (maybe via 'junior mentors' – younger people who are 'IT savvy' and who can educate their senior colleagues). We cannot influence the development and usage of IT within companies unless we know something about it.
>
> Senior manager, financial services multinational

[k]now how to do the numbers and prove their financial contribution to the bottom line.

Senior manager, financial services multinational

Before you address e skills we need to address more basic problems: do marketing people understand money? Cash flow? ROI? These are rhetorical questions to which the answer is 'no'.

How many times have marketers actually got outside their comfort zone and really got their hands dirty with this new technology? Unless you know how difficult it actually is, it's easy to under-estimate the time and effort in getting these things off the ground. I know because I've been a one-man band for the last ten years, but most marketers just hand over a brief to IT. And then when IT turn round and say no, marketers don't know enough to challenge it.

Consultant, strategic branding

This is important, and marketing communications academics themselves should also take this on board because it has implications for their own course design and delivery. As marketing communications is increasingly driven by marketing databases and strives to achieve a degree of personalized and interactive customer (relationship?) management, marketing communications students would benefit from being able to deal with customer modelling and database analysis. Many marketing communications courses are strong on advertising, branding, creatives and media selection, but unless the new accountability metrics are taken on board the next generation of marketing communicators will not be sufficiently equipped for their roles. Indeed, we are already seeing non marketers taking over some of this ground and marketers losing, for example, control of websites as reported by the CIM (October 2001).

The 'new marketing communications' brings further consequences, beyond marketing communications, so the next area of discussion concerns markets and the implications of the above developments for both customers and for society in a wider context.

Markets and Social Impact

Who Controls Organization–Customer Communication?

New communications media and technology is facilitating different forms of organization–customer interaction. The Internet, interactive digital TV and mobile telephony are examples of media that are changing how customers deal with organizations and vice versa.

One important issue concerns the shift of control from marketer to customer. Traditional models of e-commerce, for example, are the conventional business-to-business and business-to-consumer. However, as consumers band together in loose but cooperative buying groups, they begin to wrest greater levels of control over the buying process, and at the same time engage with marketing communicators even more, hence the consumer-to-business model. The consumer-to-consumer 'community' model is relatively new but is a powerful example of control shifts toward the consumer and could facilitate a greater degree of (mutual) relationship building than other models.

> Cyberspace has become a new kind of social terrain, crowded with '*virtual communities*', in which people come together for sexual flirtation, business, idle gossip, spiritual exploration, psychological support, political action, intellectual discourse on all kinds of subjects – the whole range of human interests and needs.
>
> (Anderson, 1999)

Rheingold (1993) has observed that:

> [T]he future of the Net is connected to the future of community, democracy, education, science, and intellectual life – some of the human institutions people hold most dear, whether or not they know or care about the future of computer technology.

It seems clear then that marketing communications is moving in a rather more sophisticated and eclectic direction than was the case in previous eras.

These new strategic models are having an impact in leading edge sectors, one of which is music. One respondent to the CIM (2001) project who knew this sector well, succinctly summarized the issues that are likely to be noticed across many sectors:

> The product can be delivered electronically;
> Consumers can 'do it for themselves', so C2C power shifts may take place;
> It's an entertainment sector, so there's plenty of chance for chat rooms to flourish;
> The fragmentation of the music sector into segments plays to the web's strengths of multiple linkages;
> With fragmentation comes a need to gather data so that you know what the degree of fragmentation is;
> Affiliate group marketing has already been shown to be successful.
>
> (Respondent to *Marketing Trends Survey*, CIM, 2001)

But marketing communicators must not only recognize this but also be able to implement strategy: 'Differentiation is not through strategy but through implementation. . . . The companies that are doing this have such different abilities to execute all this . . . the ones who are executing are so far ahead of the ones who aren't . . .' (executive consultant, IT sector, CIM, 2001).

The implications for marketing communications, here, include the importance of exploring the ramifications of *management by customers* rather than the *management of customers* and the importance of not merely devising strategies but focusing on implementation issues. This is not the only issue for marketing communicators and their markets. Earlier sections explored the trend (based on data-driven communications) to relational communications. Customers are also not always convinced by this, however, as reported by Evans, O'Malley and Patterson (2001a). Consumer quotes, such as the following, reflect this: 'I don't mind companies knowing more about me but that bit about meeting your needs is a load of bullshit'; 'They target what *they* think you are interested in'. That research concluded that many consumers are cynical and critical of marketing communications which they consider to be frivolous, insulting, intrusive and/or generally inappropriate (Evans, O'Malley and Patterson, 2001a).

New Marketing Communications and Privacy Issues

This moves us to a key issue that should come to the reader at this stage as no great surprise. Data itself is increasingly 'personal' and this raises privacy issues, as mentioned at the beginning of the chapter.

Take the first mentioned catalyst, the census. Names and addresses cannot be revealed from the census, but a link via the postal code system with the electoral roll means that it is possible to identify individual households and their characteristics. One of the current debates (at the time of writing) is between the Information Commissioner's position that the electoral role was not collected for marketing purposes and should not therefore be used in this way, and on the other hand the marketing industry, which argues for freedom in its use. Although the electoral roll is rarely used as a list in itself, it is used as the base for virtually every targeting tool, and geodemographics started this process. One concern of the Information Commissioner is that some people may disenfranchise themselves by not registering for fear of being over-targeted by marketers. A legal case has already brought this to a head. In November 2001 a member of the public won his case against Wakefield Council after that Council had not been able to confirm that his electoral roll data (name and address) would not be supplied to third parties without his consent, such as marketers (Acland, 2001). Having said this it is likely that an opt out option will be added to the electoral roll and this should help to alleviate privacy concerns, at the same time as shifting the marketing communications paradigm in yet another direction; 'permission marketing'. Perhaps customers will give permission to specific organizations to use their details for specified purposes.

The previously mentioned strategic alliance consortia approach between companies, in order to broaden the relationship concept beyond organization–customer interaction to wider networks, has further social implications. If 'opt out' boxes are not ticked, this will allow companies to use personal data 'within the group'. Do all customers know that 'the group' might not be merely 'the brand' they have just purchased (with which they might indeed like to have some sort of interactive exchange) but rather it is several multinational conglomerates (with whom they might not)?

The sharing of data has other implications. Mail Marketing for example is sharing some of its lists with Infocore, a US list company (Wood, 1998). However, the European Data Protection Directive prevents all member countries from exporting personal information to countries that do not have adequate data protection, and this includes the US in the view of the EU. As the Information Commissioner has said, 'businesses exporting data must be satisfied that they comply with the law – otherwise I will simply prevent the activity' (France, 1998)

Another data source being used comes from the sky. In the UK an aerial photographic census is being created (Anon, 1999). Simmons Aerofilms and the National Remote Sensing Centre will be 'married with other data sets such as Census information and demographic details' (Stannard, 1999). Some people might see this as an uncontrollable invasion of privacy.

The possible acquisition of genetic data is another potential concern (Specter, 1999) and perhaps even more serious ethical issues are likely to need addressing here. The accessing of individual medical records might be considered to be an invasion of privacy if what is thought to be confidential between doctor and patient is shared across financial services companies. In a survey of 3000 UK households, three quarters were against genetic tests for insurance underwriting, 85 per cent against insurance companies rejecting applicants on this basis and 78 per cent against insurance companies charging higher premiums on the basis of genetic tests. Indeed, 68 per cent of the sample thought that this use of genetic data should be prohibited by law (Borna and Avila, 1999). Introna and Powlouda (1999) report that medics have expressed concern over this trend. The logical extension of the scenario is that those who don't need insuring will be insured and the rest will be excluded.

Another consideration is that data fusion itself has been assessed as 'not containing much in the way of internal validity checks, creating the real possibility that decisions will be made using a fused database which does not represent reality' (Jephcott and Bock, 1998). So, all of the above might lead to a kind of 'future shock' if the resulting targeting is based upon flawed analysis.

A further area of relevance to any wider social responsibility of (data-driven) marketing communications, is the purchase of marketing data by government departments. CACI, for example, have an entire department dealing exclusively with government contracts for ACORN and related products. Geodemographic systems use an increasing range of financial data sources to overlay census, housing and demographic data, and the resulting 'financial' ACORN and MOSAIC products can easily be seen to be of potential value to the Inland Revenue (for example) to check financial details and trends against tax returns from those they want to investigate further. The UK Inland Revenue is also able to access individualized transaction data from supermarket loyalty schemes for those cases of potential tax fraud that it investigates (Key, 2000). Claimed levels of poverty on the tax return can be compared with actual purchase behaviour. Would consumers be so willing to sign up for these schemes if this was known?

The UK government has been interested in loyalty scheme data for another purpose. The idea was to track consumers' food consumption patterns with a view to assessing the impact of genetically modified foods (Hansard, 1999; Parker, 1999). Is this the point beyond which the use of personal data, supposedly for marketing communications purposes, becomes unacceptable – or is it entirely justified to use such data to investigate a serious health issue of public concern?

The LTV and RFM analysis discussed earlier can lead to those customers who are not considered to be strong contributors to the company being deselected. They would not be sent relevant offers or, in the case of financial services, for example, they would be offered accounts which require higher initial deposits than they can afford. Indeed the Halifax bank was discovered, via a flip chart left in an hotel room after a company training session, to refuse to allow certain groups of people to be customers at all (Mackintosh, 2002).

There are signs that the problem has been recognized by government; it has set up a social exclusion department and is concerned about banks closing branches in favour of direct approaches because of potential exclusion effects within some sections of the community. In the US the Community Reinvestment Act is supposed to prevent banks from closing in poor neighbourhoods, so perhaps there are signs of the tide turning with respect to these sorts of wider social responsibility issues, but at a political rather than marketing level. There are doubts about the likely outcome, though. Political lobbying by companies via public relations and the 'political donation' system, to influence competition and other legislation in companies' favour, is often more powerful and decisive.

The above discussion of how marketers are using data and perhaps verging on abusing it, in some cases, suggests a reciprocal cynicism on the part of some marketing communicators. Consider marketers' reactions to issues that have been suggested in this paper as being not only important, but which might even offer relational opportunities if they are addressed positively. The following are headlines in *Precision Marketing* between November 2001 and February 2002:

Uproar across industry as decision favours privacy
(Precision Marketing, November 2001)
DMA poised to fight electoral roll ruling
(Precision Marketing, December 2001)
Industry bodies slam new SMS Preference Service
(Precision Marketing, January 2001)
Net industry in Uproar as EU plans to abolish Cookies
(Precision Marketing, November 2001)

The new marketing communications, then, raises concerns over not only the cynicism of customers toward marketing communicators but also of marketing communicators toward their customers, despite their claims of developing relationships with them.

Conclusions

So, where does all this take us? First, marketing communications has changed forever. It is increasingly data driven. This is because of pressures for it to be more accountable and because technology has provided appropriate metrics, via, for example, database technology.

Technology has also provided new means for organization–customer interaction and this is manifested in new models of marketing communications, some of which are increasingly shifting the locus of control in the communications process toward the customer. This is another manifestation of significant change in marketing communications, which in previous eras was based on marketer-to-customer contact via, for example, mass media advertising and personal selling. Now, the customer can 'surf the net' for their own best deals and can share experiences with other (anonymous) consumers, whether this be positive or negative 'word of mouth' communications.

Furthermore, by over-relying on response rates and testing the new marketing communications is in danger of being accused of short-termism because the reasons behind 'response' or 'non response' are not being studied as fully as the mere fact of response or non response. Even the Institute of Direct Marketing itself can be criticized here – in a recent mailing to its members it stated 'we've been accused . . . of drowning the marketing profession in mailings, inserts and leaflets, too many of them looking interchangeable . . . [but] the programme always made its response targets' (Smith, 1997).

Marketing communicators require new skills to keep up with new forms of communicating with their customers and to cope with the new communications metrics. This is a major issue and it is suggested that a significant skills gap exists in this respect.

It is also suggested that marketing communications needs to address the following social responsibility issues (Evans, 2000) in terms of their morality:

- Data collected for social purposes that are used in the domain of database marketing (e.g., census data and medical details)
- Data for marketing purposes that go to the state (e.g. some marketing-compiled financial and loyalty card data to the Inland Revenue
- Data for marketing purposes being potentially accessed for criminal use
- Exclusion based on RFM analysis and implications of this for disadvantaged consumers and the 'societal marketing concept' (Lavidge, 1970; Lazer, 1969).

So, on the one hand, there are arguments for *wider* social responsibilities of marketing communications to be taken on board and on the other hand there are increasing pragmatic pressures for marketing communicators to *narrow* their focus on short-term profits and shareholders and perhaps for them to rather cynically reject social concerns. The latter probably makes the former too much of a romantic fantasy.

Note

1. Thanks to Smartfocus for providing this example of their VIPER CRM software.

CHAPTER 14

'Customer-led' strategic Internet marketing

Jim Hamill and Alan Stevenson

Something to think about . . .

Companies in all industries today are faced with rising customer disloyalty and shrinking margins. But some companies are enjoying surprising successes by focusing on individual customers, using technology to create long-term, individualised, one-to-one relationships.

(Peppers, Rogers and Dorf, 1999b)

Everyday, all around the world, managers worry about the declining loyalty of their customers. Customers are being wooed ever more feverishly by competitors offering better prices, better deals – a process that has dramatically accelerated with the growth of the Internet. As customers become more interactive with the companies they buy from, business success hinges increasingly on creating long-term, profitable, 'one-to-one' customer relationships.

(Peppers and Rogers, 1997)

What's the secret of a successful e-business initiative? What's the winning formula? You guessed it. It starts by focusing on your existing customers, figuring out what they want and need and how you can make life easier for them. Then you can expand your efforts to reel in prospective customers . . . closing the sale and cementing a profitable, long-term relationship becomes a snap, because you have already made it easy for customers to do business with you.

(Seybold, 1998)

Most managers and companies have heard the wakeup call, and they believe that customer centricity is the key to success in the future. The hard part now is becoming fluent in alternative thinking, strategies, and tactics – breaking away from the responses and policies that our parents and grandparents taught us for the past 100 years.

(Newell, 2000)

The first challenge of the twenty-first century is to master the changes that come with customers being in control. Each company needs to develop an unprecedented degree of flexibility in order to offer customers what they want, when and how they want it. Companies that manage this transition effectively will thrive; those that don't will fail. . . . Customer differentiation is the key to success in the twenty-first century.

(Nykamp, 2001)

We are entering a new and critical period in the evolution of the Internet as a strategic business tool – a customer-led phase. Companies who learn how to use interactive technology for building strong one-to-one customer relationships will create new opportunities for achieving customer differentiation and sustained competitive advantage. While information technology facilitates cost effective relationship building, adopting a customer-focussed approach to e-business is not a technology issue. First and foremost, it is about accepting customer dominance and implementing innovative approaches to sales, marketing and overall corporate strategy. Adopting a customer-led approach requires high levels of senior executive vision, insight and leadership and a total transformation of the organisation around the customer. Customer-led represents a paradigm shift from more traditional exchange based transactions.

(Hamill, forthcoming)

Over the last two decades, innovative companies have moved from supplying markets to serving market segments, then to serving individual customers, one-at-a-time. The traditional marketing mix elements of product, price, promotion and place (the 4Ps) can no longer be relied on to provide long-term competitive advantage. The 4Ps have been replaced by the 4Cs of relationship marketing – Customer needs and wants; Costs; Convenience; and Communication. Customer differentiation has become the key to sustaining long-term competitive advantage.

(Horovitz, 2000)

The major premise of this chapter is that we are entering a new and critical phase in the evolution of the Internet as a strategic marketing tool – a 'customer-led' phase.

As shown in Figure 14.1, a combination of market, customer, economic and technology 'drivers' have shifted the balance of power from suppliers to customers. In an era of customer dominance, competitive advantage based on costs or product/service differentiation is no longer enough. 'Customer differentiation' has become the key to achieving sustained competitiveness and profitability and this requires new organizational 'mindsets' supported by innovative 'customer-led' sales and marketing strategies.

The ultimate objective of being customer-led is to identify, acquire, retain and grow 'quality' customers; with the interactive power of Internet technology providing companies (regardless of size) with a cost-effective channel for building strong 'one-to-one' customer relationships. The main focus of the chapter is the way in which the Internet can be used as an integral part of a multi-channel customer-led sales and marketing strategy to achieve quality customer recruitment, retention and growth. The three main sections of the chapter cover:

- Being customer-led – what is it?, and perhaps more importantly, what it is not
- Business benefits of being customer-led
- Developing and implementing customer-led Internet marketing strategies

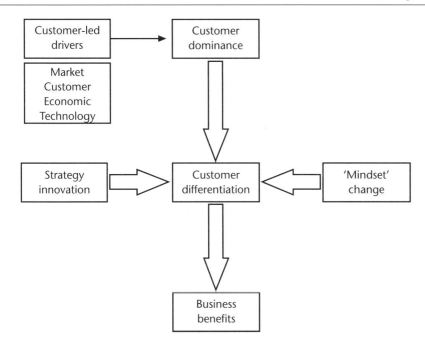

FIGURE 14.1 The foundations of 'being customer-led'

'Being Customer-led' – What Is It? Why Is It So Important?

In an era of rising customer expectations, intense global competitive rivalry, price wars, declining margins, lower customer switching costs, etc., traditional approaches to sales and marketing are no longer sufficient. New innovative customer-led approaches are required to achieve sustained customer and competitive advantage.

According to Nykamp (2001) the *customer differential* represents a new level of competitive differentiation through building impermeable customer relationships. Building on the pioneering work of Peppers and Rogers (1997) and others (Newell, 2000; Seybold, 1998), it is becoming increasingly recognized that there will be winners and losers in e-business. Winners will be those who fully utilize the power of Internet technology for building close one-to-one relationships with their most valuable and most growable customers. The ultimate objective of being customer-led is to identify, acquire, retain and grow 'quality' customers. It is the quality of a company's customer base; the strength of the relationship it has with them; and its ability to leverage up and cross-selling opportunities with quality customers that provide a sustained source of competitive advantage and long-term profitability.

For many companies, being customer-led represents a radical departure from traditional approaches to sales and marketing and a new organizational 'mindset' is often required. At the outset, therefore, it is important to provide a clear explanation of what the concept of 'being customer-led' actually means, what it is not, and why it has become so important.

It is particularly important to distinguish the concept of 'being customer-led' from the more widely used term Customer Relationship Management (CRM). Many companies have responded to the growing power of customers by implementing expensive CRM systems, yet the evidence suggests that most of these have not produced a return on investment. The main reason for CRM failure has been the fact that most projects have been technology driven rather than 'customer-led'.

To a large extent, the term CRM has been hijacked by software vendors promising instant 'out-of-the-box' solutions to complex strategic, organizational and human resource issues. While technology has a very important role to play in building customer relationships, there is no simple 'out-of-a-box' solution. Being customer-led is not about software, database marketing, loyalty programmes, customer bribes or hard selling. It is about building strong one-to-one relationships with 'quality' customers, achieving customer loyalty and maximizing customer lifetime earnings. The core of a customer-led strategy is organizational re-engineering towards satisfying the needs of 'quality' customers on a highly customized and personalized basis. There is a huge difference between paying lip service to the concept of being customer-led and building an integrated customer-led organization.

From the growing literature in this area, we can identify 10 key characteristics of being customer-led and these are listed below:

1. *Focus on quality customers not markets.* Over the last two decades, innovative companies have moved from supplying markets to serving market segments, then to serving individual customers, one at a time. The ultimate purpose of being customer-led is to identify, acquire, retain and grow quality customers; i.e., 'strategically significant', 'most valuable' and 'most growable' customers. This allows more targeted and cost-effective sales and marketing by concentrating limited resources on the 20 per cent of customers who contribute 80 per cent of profits, rather than dissipating resources on 'below zero' customers.

2. *Focus on one-to-one relationships.* The essence of being customer-led is the establishment of strong one-to-one relationships with 'quality' customers and achieving sustained competitive advantage through building customer learning and the delivery of individualized, personalized and customized products, services, support, etc.. Building learning relationships increases customer retention and loyalty, maximizes up and cross-selling opportunities, and helps to erect barriers to competitive entry. Being customer-led requires a focus on the total customer experience (not just the 4Ps) and a mindset shift from being a supplier of products to a supplier of total customer solutions.

3. *Lifetime value and short-term selling.* By delivering exceptional customer value, erecting barriers to competitive entry, and maximizing up and cross-selling opportunities, being customer-led maximizes the lifetime value of the customer relationship as well as increasing short-term sales opportunities through highly targeted and focused marketing efforts. It is much more profitable to up and cross sell to existing quality customers than it is to be constantly recruiting new low value customers.

4. *A 'win-win' situation.* Customer-led strategies are not implemented for philanthropic reasons. It is a 'win-win' relationship that seeks to maximize the long-term value of the relationship for both the customer and the company.

5. *Information technology is a necessary but not a sufficient condition.* Effective use of information technology and information systems is critical to the successful implementation of a customer-led strategy where integration is required between front end customer acquisition and retention technology and back office operational and management systems. On its own, however, technology is a necessary but not a sufficient condition.

6. *Being customer-led requires an integrated and coordinated organizational approach.* Being customer-led is too important to be left to the marketing people and requires the total commitment of all levels in the organization. Creating, communicating and delivering value to selected customers requires a cross-functional and integrated organizational approach driven by a customer-led organizational culture.

7. *Requires new business metrics and performance measures.* Appropriate customer-led performance measures need to be agreed and put in place. Sales staff and channel partners should be rewarded for customer retention and loyalty, as well as for short-term selling.

8. *Being customer-led has become critical due to the dynamic changes taking place the global business environment.* As a consequence of deregulation, globalization; the end of 'mass marketing', rising customer expectations and choice, increased competition; technology and communication improvements, lower switching costs, etc., companies can no longer compete on the basis of product/price alone. Achieving customer differentiation is the key to competitive success in the twenty-first century (Nykamp, 2001).

9. *Being customer-led requires strategic planning.* Successful customer-led strategies should be based on sound analysis (customer mapping – see later in this chapter) and the coordination of strategies covering all customer touch points as part of an integrated and coordinated multi-channel approach to customer relationship building. It requires high level, senior executive '360 vision' combined with clear strategies and action plans to get there. Strategy and action should involve the integration and co-ordination of culture, people, processes, systems and technology to deliver exceptional levels of customer service, personalized and customized to the needs of individual customers.

10. *Customer-led should drive the business.* Being customer-led focuses on key mission critical questions such as 'who should we serve?'; 'what should we serve to them?'; and 'how should we serve them?'. It is important, therefore, that the customer focus is positioned at the forefront of the strategic process around which the business is organized. Customer-led decisions will impact on all functional areas of activity including marketing, but also operations, sales, customer service, HR, R&D and finance, as well as IT. Customer-led requires a cross-functional, customer-focused business strategy and organization.

'Being Customer-led': Business Benefits

Companies do not become customer-led because they are nice (although this helps) or because they want to be popular (a pleasant side effect). There are major bottom line business benefits to be derived. Before exploring the strategic role of Internet marketing in achieving 'quality' customer recruitment, retention and growth, the main business benefits of being a customer-led organization are summarized below.

Being customer-led will allow companies to:

- Concentrate their marketing and sales efforts on 'quality' customers; i.e. high value or high growth potential customers
- Build learning relationships with 'quality' customers to better service their emerging needs and wants through highly-customized and personalized products and services
- Maximize 'quality' customer retention and loyalty
- Maximize customer up and cross-selling opportunities
- Maximize customer profitability and lifetime value
- Acquire new 'quality' customers more easily because the company has 'got it right' for existing customers
- Improve value delivery to key customers
- Achieve cost savings and improved marketing/sales efficiency through targeting limited resources on 'quality' customers (actual and potential)
- Build a sustained competitive advantage through customer differentiation
- Erect barriers to competitive entry

The ultimate objective of being customer-led is to maximize the lifetime profitability of loyal, 'quality' customers. A major theme in the literature in this area is that the annual profitability from 'quality' customers increases substantially through the relationship lifecycle due to lower customer acquisition costs, customer referrals, price premiums (loyal customers will pay higher prices for quality service), lower customer servicing costs, and so on. It is much more profitable to build relationships with your most valuable and most growable customers than it is to be constantly recruiting new customers – many of whom may be 'below zero' customers, i.e., customer acquisition costs may exceed customer value contribution. This link between customer loyalty and customer profitability has recently been questioned in an article in the *Harvard Business Review* by Reinartz and Kumar (2002).

Developing and Implementing 'Customer-led' Internet Marketing Strategies

Used effectively, the Internet can provide companies with a low cost communications channel for identifying, acquiring, retaining and growing 'quality' customers. Getting there, however, is no easy task and requires high level, senior

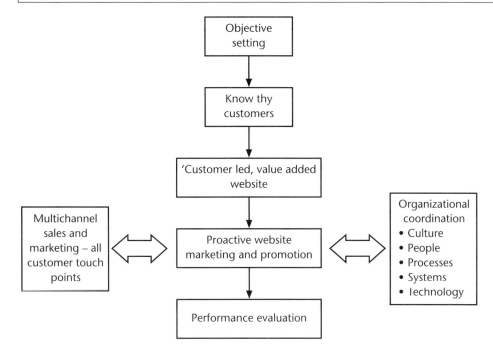

FIGURE 14.2 'Customer led' strategic Internet marketing

executive '360 vision' supported by clear Internet marketing strategies and action plans.

Based on our knowledge of the growing literature in this area, and our extensive experience in providing 'best practice' consultancy advice to companies over the last five years, we would identify five key stages in the development and implementation of effective customer-led Internet marketing strategies as shown in Figure 14.2.

Stage 1: Agreeing Customer-led Objectives and Performance Measures

In too many companies, e-business has been technology rather than customer-driven. However, technology is simply the enabler that allows customer-led objectives to be achieved in a cost effective manner.

The starting point in developing effective customer-led Internet marketing strategies is to establish the main business objectives to be achieved. These need to be agreed by the senior management team and communicated throughout the organization to achieve 'buy-in' and support.

Effective use of Internet technology for sales and marketing can provide a wide range of 'bottom line' business benefits. To illustrate the range of benefits that can be derived from effective customer-led Internet marketing, Figure 14.3 summarizes the main strategic objectives underlying two of our most recent consultancy assignments.

(a) **Teco Information Systems Europe Ltd** is the European sales and marketing office of the Teco Group of Taiwan – a global high-technology company with interests across a broad spectrum of technology-based industries. The Manchester office is responsible for all Europe, Middle East and Africa (EMEA) sales and marketing for the following product lines:

- display products (monitors, plasma, LCDs, CRTs, flat CRTs);
- optical storage products (CD-Roms, DVDs);
- Windows-based terminals (stand alone, incorporated into LCDs);
- imaging products (scanners, digital cameras).

The company operates through a network of distributors (65) and value added resellers (10,000) throughout the EMEA region and is the exclusive European distributor of the Relisys brand. A major part of the company's strategy is: 'To grow Relisys into a leading brand name throughout EMEA; to ensure consistency of branding across all marketing materials; and to deliver high quality products, services and customer care throughout EMEA'.

The new website will play a critical role in helping to promote the Relisys brand internationally; strengthening the reseller network; and supporting the relationship with existing customers. Following detailed discussions with Teco's senior management team, five main strategic objectives were identified for the new site:

1. To provide high level customer support and value to distributors, resellers and end users.
2. Use of the website to market and promote the Relisys brand and to recruit additional 'quality' resellers.
3. To increase sales and rationalize the sales ordering process through e-commerce.
4. To build strong 'one-to-one' relationships with distributors, resellers and consumers through the provision of online technical support, up- and cross-selling.
5. To achieve cost and efficiency savings through faster information and communication flows, reducing the sales cycle and automating technical support and customer service.

Specific objectives to be achieved are:

- To better support existing customers, especially 'most valuable' and 'most growable' customers.
- To provide 24/7 online customer service and technical support.
- To strengthen one-to-one relationships with existing customers through the development of a password-protected distributor/reseller extranet.
- To exploit customer up-selling and cross-selling opportunities.
- To establish a differentiated competitive advantage through utilizing Internet technology to deliver exceptional levels of customer service.
- To enhance the international visibility, image and reputation of the company in the EMEA region.
- To make it easy for new and existing customers to find information about the product range and to do business with the company.
- To develop an online sales channel through the website to support offline activities.
- To provide an interactive channel for dealing with new customer enquiries.
- To provide detailed product information to existing and potential customers in a user-friendly manner; presented in both technical and non-technical formats.
- To provide accurate and timely information on site visitors through detailed analysis of log statistics.
- To ensure that the site captures visitor information as the starting point in developing an e-CRM strategy.
- To reduce operating costs.
- To lay the foundations for future developments of an integrated e-business strategy at Teco.

FIGURE 14.3 Strategic Internet marketing – objectives

(b) Vatentex (not the company's real name) is a supplier of specialist software to the power and electricity utility industries. While operating in a niche market, potential customers are global in scope. The company's new website has both short and medium-to-longer term objectives.

The most immediate objective of the new site is to support the global sales and marketing effort. Medium-to-longer term, and as the global customer base expands, the company will begin utilizing Internet technology for supporting the customer relationship; aimed at delivering high levels of customer service while at the same time controlling customer service costs as the global client base expands.

From a sales and marketing perspective, the most immediate objectives to be achieved from the new website and supporting Internet marketing strategy are:

- To support the global sales and marketing effort.
- to enhance the global visibility, image and reputation of the company.
- To build global brand identity and ensure brand consistency.
- To make it easy for new/potential customers to find information about the company, its products and services, and to to do business with the company.
- To develop an online global sales and marketing communications channel to support offline activities.
- To provide an interactive channel for dealing with new customer enquiries.
- To build a database of customer enquiries to assist future marketing efforts.

Overall, the main objective of the new website – from a sales and marketing perspective – is to identify, acquire and retain quality customers; i.e. 'most valuable' and 'most growable' customers. Medium-to-longer term, and as the customer base grows, the site should be expanded to become a web-enabled customer support centre providing high-level support and value to existing customers at low costs.

Specific objectives to be achieved as the site develops over time include:

- To control customer support costs as the global customer base expands.
- To ensure high-level customer support and service, especially to 'most valuable' and 'most growable' customers, supported by Internet technology.
- To provide 24/7 online customer service and technical support.
- To build strong 'one-to-one' customer relationships, loyalty and retention.
- To exploit customer up- and cross-selling opportunities.
- To build learning relationships with key customers supported by Internet technology.
- To achieve customer differentiation and erect barriers to competitive entry.

FIGURE 14.3   Strategic Internet marketing – objectives *concluded*

Stage 2: 'Know Thy Customers' – Customer Mapping

You cannot build a relationship with someone you don't understand! The foundation of a successful customer-led Internet marketing strategy is to 'know your customers'. Customer profiling, knowledge and understanding are critical for building highly-targeted Internet-supported sales and marketing programmes.

There are four main stages involved in 'customer mapping':

- *Customer identification and segmentation.* Segmentation of customers (actual and potential) into groups with similar needs and wants.

Customer identification and segmentation	Customer ranking	Customer understanding and learning	Website personalization/ customization
Segmentation of customers into groups with similar needs and wants – should include actual and potential.	Ranking of different customer groups in terms of their relative value to the comany in order that resources can be targeted on 'quality customers'.	Development of learning relatinships with 'quality' customer groups as a basis for 'one-to one' marketing.	Personalization/ customization of the company's website for different customer groups.

Begin with the customer to ensure that strategy is customer led NOT technology driven

FIGURE 14.4 Customer mapping

- *Customer understanding and learning.* Development of customer profiles, knowledge and understanding as the basis for highly-targeted sales and marketing strategies.
- *Customer ranking.* Identification of 'most valuable' and 'most growable' customers in order that limited marketing resources can be targeted on customers and prospects providing the greatest value to the company.
- *Personalization and customization.* Personalization and customization of the company's website for different customer groups.

Customer mapping will ensure that e-initiatives are led by the needs and wants of different customer groups as shown in Figure 14.4, rather than being technology driven; and will form the basis for highly-targeted Internet marketing strategies.

Stages 3 and 4: Internet Marketing and Promotion

For any company, there are two main components of an effective Internet marketing and promotion strategy:

(a) The development of a customer-led, value-added website.
(b) Proactive marketing and promotion of the site to achieve agreed business objectives.

A. Website development

According to Siegel (1999), most companies build their websites from the inside out rather than from the outside in. In other words, most company websites are introvert rather than extrovert sites reflecting the organizational structure and existing product range of the company. This inevitably leads to the creation of 'brochure ware' sites. According to the author, websites should be built from the outside in; i.e., built around customer groups as shown in Figure 14.5.

The introvert website

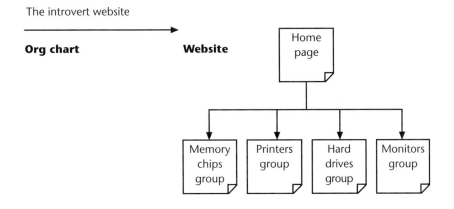

The extrovert website

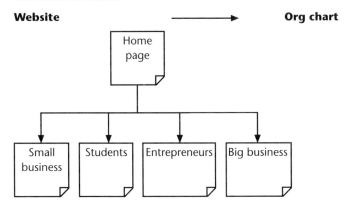

Source: Adapted from Seigel (1999)

FIGURE 14.5 Introvert and extrovert websites

Based on our extensive experience in this area, we have developed a list of 10 main criteria for assessing website quality and value and this is shown in Table 14.1.

B. Proactive website marketing and promotion

Having a website, even one that follows 'best practice' principles as discussed above, is not enough. A 'build it and they will come' approach will not work on the Internet. Websites need to be proactively marketed and promoted in order to succeed.

In all the hype surrounding the dot.coms and e-commerce, many companies have lost sight of the fact that there are only three key questions that need to be addressed in developing an effective website marketing and promotion strategy:

1. Who are we targeting?
2. Where do we find them on the Internet?

TABLE 14.1 Characteristics of a good business website

	Characteristic	Comments
1	Clear strategic objectives	Does the site have clear strategic objectives? Has site design, development, content, etc. been driven by these objectives? Is the ongoing performance of the site monitored against strategic objectives? How does the site fit with other communications channels used to achieve strategic objectives? Is it part of a multi-channel customer communications strategy?
2	Customer led rather than product driven	Is the site customer led rather than product driven? Is site content driven by the needs and wants of different customer groups? Has a 'customer mapping exercise' been undertaken? Are there different sections of the site for different customer/user groups?
3	Value added content updated on a regular basis	Does the site provide value added content? How do we measure and assess the value of site content? Do we monitor content value on an ongoing basis? Is content customized and personalized for different customer/user groups? Is content updated on a regular basis?
4	Content management	Is the website dynamic rather than static? Is it database driven? Does it have an easy to use content management system to ensure that site content is kept relevant and up-to-date?
5	Data quality management	What organizational processes have been put in place to ensure that content is regularly updated? Does the organization have a data quality management programme? Is there effective integration of culture, people, processes, systems and technology?
6	Professional design and usability	Is the site professionally designed projecting a consistent corporate image and identity? Has usability been tested? Does it meet legislative standards?
7	High interactivity; high functionality	How interactive and functional is the site? What improvements can be made in this area? Can customers/users contact the right person through your site using whatever channel they wish, e.g. e-mail, form-based, phone, call back, etc. or are they restricted to e-mailing the webmaster? Do you encourage customer feedback through the site? Can customers talk to each other through forums? Does it provide self-service customer support?
8	Easy to navigate; quick to download	Can site users 'find what they are looking for' quickly and easily? Is the site easy to navigate and quick to download? Is usability tested on an ongoing basis?
9	e-Communications strategy	What use is made of e-communications to support the site? Does the organization have an e-communications strategy?
10	Effective Internet marketing	How well is the site marketed and promoted? Is there a comprehensive strategic Internet marketing plan in place?

3. How best can we communicate our message to them, globally and at low costs?

Answering these three questions will ensure highly-targeted and focused sales and marketing messages; i.e., the 'right' message is delivered to the 'right' people at the 'right' time in the 'right' place using the 'right' e-communications channel.

There are a wide range of methods available to companies for marketing and promoting their websites including:

- search engine positioning strategies
- log file analysis and evaluation
- directory listings
- banner advertising
- B2B hubs
- sig.files
- e-mail-based marketing
- effective use of newsgroups and discussion forums
- integration of online and offline marketing

Search engine positioning strategies. An effective search engine positioning strategy should comprise six main elements:

1. Search engine optimization
   It is important that website coding is optimized for effective search engine registration. This requires the appropriate use of key words in the title, meta and alt tags and in the core text of the site. Different keywords, title, meta and alt tags should be used in different sections of the site reflecting different product and application categories and target customers.
2. Search engine registration
   Websites should be registered with all of the leading search engines and re-registered at least on a monthly basis. In addition to registering the homepage, individual sections of the site covering different product lines and customer groups should be registered separately.
3. Keyword purchasing
   Some search engines have introduced a keyword buying policy ensuring a top search position for agreed keywords, paid for on a cost per thousand basis. Companies should compare the costs and associated benefits of buying selected keywords to help market and promote their websites.
4. Web position monitoring
   The position of a website on the search engines can change over time. Web position software should be used, at least on a quarterly basis, to monitor the position of the site on the leading engines and adjustments made to the registration process, and to the coding of the site, where appropriate. This is critical as the position of a site on the engines can vary at very short notice. Strategic re-coding of the site should also take place as a result of new product launches and new strategic objectives.

5. Keyword adjustments
   As above.
6. Re-registration of the site
   Needs to be done on an ongoing basis, at least once per month, taking into account feedback from the web position reports.

Log file analysis and evaluation. Log file statistics can provide companies with invaluable marketing information concerning site visitors and their behaviour on the site. Web Trends Software should be used to present this information in an easy to evaluate format. Using Web Trends, log files can track the demographics of website visitors and provide valuable information concerning how visitors find the site, search engine performance, keywords used, geographical distribution of site visitors, average length of time spent on the site, most and least popular pages, error logs, etc. Log files should be analyzed and evaluated at least on a monthly basis and appropriate recommendations made for improvements.

Directory links. One of the most cost effective ways of driving traffic to a company's site is to establish strategic links to related websites. The number of links established will also help to improve the site's ranking on the search engines and it is important to establish as many relevant web links as possible. Part of the marketing strategy implementation should include the identification of appropriate links and contact with site owners re-listing.

Banner advertising. Evidence shows that the click-through rate on banner advertising can be as low as two per cent and there is growing disillusionment with this form of Internet marketing. However, advertising fees are falling and highly targeted/focused advertising on the right websites can still be very effective in building global brand identity. Companies need to evaluate the benefits and costs of banner advertising compared to the other forms of Internet marketing being discussed here.

B2B hubs. Business-to-business portals or 'hub' websites have been one of the fastest growing areas of activity on the Internet. For B2B companies, strategic use of such hubs can be one of the most cost effective ways of achieving a highly-targeted and focused global marketing message. There are a number of hub websites covering most industrial sectors.

Sig.files. Companies should introduce standardized sig.file policies to ensure that all outgoing e-mail provides 'free' website marketing and promotion.

E-mail marketing. E-mail newsletters, and e-mail new product announcements, etc. can provide a very effective, low-cost channel for maintaining ongoing communications with actual and potential customers.

Effective use of newsgroups and discussion forums. Doing business on the Internet is about relationship building and one-to-one marketing. There are a large number of newsgroups and discussion forums that can provide companies with qualitative research into their target markets and customer behaviour. Monitoring and participating in relevant newsgroups and forums can provide companies with a low-cost platform for building global brand identity. Note: In using both e-mail marketing and newsgroups/forums, it is critical that companies follow best practice 'netiquette'.

Integration of online and offline marketing. Online and offline marketing should be coordinated and integrated to ensure a consistent brand identity.

Stage 5: Performance Evaluation

Companies should measure the performance of their websites on a regular, ongoing basis. The main performance indicators include:

- Number and quality of visitors to the site and trends over time
- Impact on corporate image and reputation
- Number of sales enquiries
- Sector and geographical distribution of enquiries
- Increase in the number and quality of customers
- Increase in sales, directly and indirectly
- Improved communications with partner organizations and the establishment of one-to-one relationships
- Size/quality of your e-mail mailing list
- Cost savings through greater use of electronic communications
- e-Commerce sales, where appropriate

Overcoming the Risk of Failure

It is an accepted (but regrettable) fact that the track record of software systems/database development projects is not particularly impressive. Evidence shows a high incidence of projects being delivered late, over budget or failing to meet user requirements.

The main reasons for failure include poor planning and incomplete requirements specification, failure to anticipate risks, inappropriate development methodology, and poor database design. Major risks include:

- Requirement risks – failure to clearly specify core business objectives and requirements
- Systems risks – failure to adequately evaluate current systems and processes and how these will impact on new developments
- Technology risks – relating to choice of IT infrastructure, especially integration issues with existing legacy systems
- Skills risks – failure to take adequate account of staff IT skills and training requirements
- People risks – failure to take adequate account of new working practices and the cultural/human resource impact of new IT/IS, and problems overcoming resistance to change.

While the above relates mainly to large software development projects, there are similar risks involved in web development and Internet marketing projects. Many websites are delivered late or over budget and do not achieve agreed strategic objectives. Many companies have been disappointed with the return on investment from their Internet marketing activities.

TABLE 14.2 The website development and strategic Internet marketing project life cycle

	Lifecycle stage	Comment
Stage 1	Customer mapping	Identification of needs and wants of different customer groups.
Stage 2	Customer segmentation	Segmentation of customers into different groups as a basis for website customization and personalization.
Stage 3	Business needs and objectives	A clear statement of core business objectives to be achieved and business requirements from the website/Internet marketing plan.
Stage 4	Requirement and risk analysis	Detailed systems requirement and risk analysis – should be customer focused, including internal customers/users.
Stage 5	Design	Agree design, content, structure, navigation, etc. of the new site.
Stage 6	Construction	Prototyping and iterative development of the site.
Stage 7	Implementation	Full implementation including integration of IS and IT.
Stage 8	Testing and delivery	For different user groups.
Stage 10	Documentation and ongoing maintenance of the site	Ensure that detailed documentation is kept. Ongoing maintenance.
Stage 11	Implementation of the supporting website marketing and promotion strategy	Search engine positioning strategy, log file analysis, directory listing, e-mail communications strategy, B2B hubs, etc.
Stage 12	Performance evaluation	Ongoing, including regular performance checks.

To improve the overall performance and effectiveness of Internet marketing, companies need to plan and manage their online activities well. Our recommended approach is to borrow 'best practice' project management methodologies from the software engineering profession and to adapt and apply these to website development and Internet marketing activities. One such framework is shown in Table 14.2.

Conclusions

Used effectively, the Internet can provide a low cost 'gateway' to global markets even for small and medium-sized enterprises. Getting there, however, is no easy task and requires high level, strategic vision supported by effective planning, management and implementation skills. As we move away from the hype and hysteria surrounding the dot.coms, there is a growing realization that the real power of Internet technology is its ability to provide a low-cost channel for building strong one-to-one relationships with high value customers. It is the companies who fully utilize the interactive power of Internet technology for supporting the customer relationship who will be the real winners in e-business.

CHAPTER 15

Measuring marketing performance

Tim Ambler and Stefano Puntoni

Marketers have long striven to show the importance of their perspective and how marketing contributes to the achievement of company goals. Financial evaluation does not necessarily provide a solution and the pressure to justify marketing investment has intensified with the increase of alternatives, such as e-commerce, knowledge management and technology, and the new focus on shareholder value.

Reflecting the increase in the requests for accountability of marketing activities within firms, the measurement of marketing performance is receiving growing attention from both academics and practitioners (e.g. Clark, 1999; Marketing Science Institute, 2000; Marketing Week, 2001; Moorman and Rust, 1999; Schultz, 2000; Shaw and Mazur, 1997). Even though the importance of measuring performance is widely acknowledged it is surprising the limited attention that such a topic has received until recently in the field of marketing.[1]

Management needs to measure the 'success' or 'failure' of marketing initiatives. Measurement has traditionally focused on macro-level financial indicators such sales and sales growth (Clark, 1999). This may be explained in part by the difficulty in relating marketing activities to long-term effects (Dekimpe and Hanssens, 1995) and in separating and quantifying marketing effects and operations from those of other functions of the firms (Bonoma and Clark, 1988). An added obstacle is the challenge in defining and correlating intermediate data, such as customer attitudes, with performance. Many businesses find it problematic to measure even relatively quantitative behaviors such as customer retention, and the inevitable result is that many companies have been unwilling to expend the time, energy and resources to do it effectively (Ambler, 2000). Fortunately, this seems to be changing. New measures are appearing, such as balanced scorecards, customer satisfaction measures, process metrics and activity-based costing. The US Institute of Management Accountants report the growing use of non-financial measures (IMA, 1993; 1995; 1996). The Marketing Science Institute has raised marketing metrics to become its leading capital research project (Marketing Science Institute, 2000).

This chapter describes UK company practice and provides a framework which enables marketers to compare their own metrics and marketing performance review processes. The goal of the chapter is to offer a picture of emerging perspectives and issues in the area of performance measurement. The biggest obstacle to measuring marketing performance is the assessment of the marketing asset (which we call 'brand equity') (Marketing Leadership Council, 2001).

We distinguish between marketing in the holistic, company-wide sense (Webster, 1992), the functional activities conducted by professional marketers, and also the budgetary sense (the costs charged to marketing). The first of these is dominant and concerns immediate customers as well as end users and competitors. The assessment of particular aspects of the mix, such as advertising, can be seen within the context of company-wide marketing. Furthermore, the importance of different components of the mix depends on sector and environmental context.

Managers are forced by time, financial constraints and environmental uncertainty to take a partial view of their environment (Day and Nedungadi, 1994). The goals they select reflect such a partial view and, even when they are not part of an explicit strategy, can still be inferred by what managers measure. Thus metrics do not provide only guidelines for change. Metrics have implications beyond their 'accounting' meaning because they are evidence of what each company considers important, reflecting priorities and both the explicit and implicit strategies that drive companies.

This chapter is structured as follows. We review theoretical principles and findings from the literature. We then discuss the recent empirical research into current practice. After speculating about emerging trends and where research is needed, we draw some conclusions.

Theoretical Background

The marketing performance literature has been criticized for its limited diagnostic power (Day and Wensley, 1988), its focus on the short term (Dekimpe and Hanssens, 1995; 1999), the excessive number of different measures and the related difficulty of comparison (Clark, 1999), and the dependence of the perceived performance on the set of indicators chosen (Murphy, Trailer and Hill, 1996). 'Perhaps no other concept in marketing's short history has proven as stubbornly resistant to conceptualization, definition, or application as that of marketing performance' (Bonoma and Clark, 1988, p. 1).

The first part of this review identifies four theoretical perspectives which we integrate into a single framework. The second part focuses on managerial practice, in particular, the evolution from financial to non-financial measures. The third reviews the measurement of the intangible marketing asset, 'brand equity'.

Theoretical Foundations of Performance Assessment

This section reviews reasons why top management would seek to quantify marketing performance. The first explanation, control theory, posits that management has a strategy and a known set of intermediary stages with which actual performance can be compared. Like the navigators of old, captains of business can both monitor and improve progress by minimizing variances.

A second explanation is provided by agency theory. Agents, whether middle managers reporting to their seniors or directors reporting to shareholders, provide information to principals to provide reassurance that they are behaving in the interest of principals. This takes two forms: marketing behaviors, e.g. marketing investment; and outcomes, e.g. sales.

A third explanation is provided by institutional theory which suggests that metrics will be selected, or perhaps evolve, according to the cultural norms of businesses and the sectors within which they operate.

Orientation theory suggests that the choice of metrics will be influenced by the way top management perceives its business. A more market-oriented business is likely to seek more market metrics.

These four theories overlap but one conclusion is that metrics are important not just for the information they contain but for their portrayal of what top management considers important.

Control theory

The monitoring of the results derived by marketing activities provides the informational means to ensure that 'planned marketing activities produce desired results', as stated by Jaworski (1988, p. 24) in his definition of marketing control. The perceived effectiveness of marketing actions is dependent upon the control model adopted within the firm, as well as upon the effectual implementation of such model as 'marketing managers can learn to improve performance by altering the utility levels associated with marketing control variables' (Fraser and Hite, 1988, p. 97).

Thus managers seek to enhance performance by identifying performance predictors, modeling the relationships between the predictors and performance and then monitoring the predictors. These mental models may not be explicit.

Marketing control plays an essential role towards the end of an efficient implementation of marketing strategies (Noble and Mokwa, 1999). Indeed, 'an organization can tolerate a work force with highly diverse goals if a precise evaluation system exists' (Eisenhardt, 1985, p. 135). The literature dedicated to marketing control however is fragmentary and agreement on a theoretical framework is lacking (Jaworski, 1988; Jaworski, Stathakopolous and Krishnan, 1993; Merchant, 1988). The two principal dimensions of marketing control are outcome versus behavior-based forms of control and the degree of formality of marketing controls (Anderson and Oliver, 1987; Celly and Frazier, 1996; Eisenhardt, 1985; Jaworski, 1988; Jaworski and MacInnis, 1989; Jaworski, Stathakopoulos and Krishnan, 1993; Ouchi, 1979).

Outcome-based controls emphasize 'bottom line'[2] results whereas behavior-based controls emphasize 'tasks and activities' that in turn are expected to be related to bottom-line results (Celly and Frazier, 1996). Outcome-based controls require little monitoring, little managerial direction and are characterized by objective measures of outcomes, whereas behavior-based controls require considerable monitoring, high levels of managerial direction, and subjective and complex evaluations (Krafft, 1999; Oliver and Anderson, 1994).

Outcome versus behavior-based forms of control have been particularly investigated in the study of sales control systems (e.g., Anderson and Oliver, 1987; Babakus *et al.*, 1996; Cravens *et al.*, 1993; Krafft, 1999; Oliver and Anderson, 1994). Scholars identified a variety of factors influencing the reliance of a firm on one or the other form of control. In particular outcome observability, nature of the task, environmental uncertainty, size of the firm, and organizational culture have been indicated as important determinants of the type of control implemented within an organization (Anderson and Oliver, 1987; Krafft, 1999; Oliver and Anderson, 1994; Ouchi, 1979).

Formal controls require written, management-initiated mechanisms that influence the probability that employees or groups will behave in ways that support the stated marketing objectives, e.g. marketing plans. Informal controls refer typically to worker-initiated mechanisms that influence the behavior of individuals or groups in marketing units (Jaworski, 1988). Within a company, formal and informal control tend to vary according to the position of the unit to be controlled in the knowledge flow network of the firm (Gupta and Govindarajan, 1991). The control system heavily influences the working environment. For example, the use of formal controls – financial, quantitative measures, i.e. 'budget-constrained style' controls – have been found to increase tension and damage relations between subordinates and superiors (e.g., Jaworski, 1988; Jaworski and McInnis, 1989).

In Jaworski's (1988) initial formulation, formal and informal controls were treated as exclusive classes. Later, however, Jaworski acknowledged that these two types of control could coexist (Jaworski, Stathakopoulos and Krishnan, 1993). Four general control typologies are generated according to the level of reliance on formal and informal controls. The 'clan system' relies more on informal that on formal controls, whereas the opposite is true for the 'bureaucratic system'. When reliance is high on both forms of control Jaworski, Stathakopoulos and Krishnan (1993) define the 'high control system', as opposed to the 'low control system' deriving from low reliance on both types of controls.

Marketing metrics can be both formal, e.g. as part of the routine reporting to the top executive committee, or informal, where market or marketing behavior information is provided without direct comparison with expectations.

Agency theory

Agency theory was developed in the field of financial economics and the original formulation was aimed at the study of ownership structure (Jensen and Meckling, 1976). The focus of the theory is on the principal–agent contractual relationship where the principal has delegated work to the agent. Uncertainty arises between the outcome and what is postulated by the contract. Such uncertainty has three potential sources. The first concerns adverse selection – the misinterpretation of the ability of the agent. The second is moral hazard by the part of the agent, called self-interest. Moreover, agency theory assumes that outcomes are partly due to environmental factors beyond the control of both principal and agent (Fama and Jensen, 1983). A third source of uncertainty is therefore related to the environment. Problems connected to adverse selection are usually referred to as 'pre-contractual problems' whereas problems related to moral hazard are referred to as 'post-contractual problems' (Bergen, Dutta and Walker, 1992).

In the field of marketing, agency theory has been applied to a variety of settings such as salesforce management, channel coordination and competitive signaling (see Bergen, Dutta and Walker, 1992 for a review). However, few studies investigate marketing information disclosure from an agency theory perspective.

Managers expend considerable sums on a variety of communications to reduce agency costs associated with information asymmetry (Fama, 1980; Fama and Jensen, 1983; Jensen and Meckling, 1976). The theory 'emphasizes the need for measurability of performance and for performance criteria that employees can influence' (Eisenhardt, 1988, p. 489). Agency theory takes a rational, economic perspective of how information will be transmitted vertically within the organization: information that is positive for the agent will be communicated to the principal to the extent that the gain obtained from its disclosure does not exceed the costs of obtaining and disseminating it. Agency theory predicts that in the absence of costs, managers will fully disclose all their information (Grossman, 1981; Ross, 1979). However, information asymmetries between marketing groups and top management provide the former with degrees of freedom on the information to be disclosed. Such opportunity may in turn translate into a distorted informational flow.

Agency theory is related to control theory because 'agency theory looks at the relative merits of behavior-based contracts . . . vis-à-vis outcome-based contracts . . . as a means of efficiently ensuring the fidelity of the agents' (Nilakant and Rao, 1994, p. 653). Both forms of marketing control decrease the chances for the agent to behave opportunistically and therefore provide the instrument for the principal to make sure that the agent will act in the principal's interest (Eisenhardt, 1989). This suggests a link between the type of control implemented within a firm and the relationship existing between principal and agent: 'for control mechanisms to achieve the intended performance, due consideration must be given to the nature of the principal–agent relationship and the structure within which this relationship is embedded' (Aulakh and Gencturk, 2000, p. 523). According to agency theory, the greater the difficulty of effectively measuring marketing performance, the greater should be the efficiency of behavior-based forms of control compared to outcome-based forms of control.

The application of agency theory to internal marketing metrics assumes the existence of a separate group of marketing specialists who control market(ing) information. This is not always the case.

Institutional theory

Institutional theory (Meyer and Rowan, 1977) postulates that organizational action is mainly driven by cultural values and by the history of the specific company, as well as by those of its industry sector. In this framework, organizational actions reflect imitative forces and traditions, even in the presence of major changes in job content and technology (Eisenhardt, 1988; Zucker, 1987). According to the institutional perspective, organizational practices are legitimated by the environment (Tolbert and Zucker, 1983). According to Meyer and Rowan (1977):

> [O]rganizations are driven to incorporate the practices and procedures defined by prevailing rationalized concepts of organizational work and institutionalized in society.

Organizations that do so increase their legitimacy and their survival prospects, independent of the immediate efficacy of the acquired practices and procedures.

(p. 340)

Thus marketing information disclosure to top management can be predicted from 'perceptions of legitimate behavior derived from cultural values, industry tradition, firm history, popular management folklore and the like' (Eisenhardt, 1988, p. 492).

Institutional theory provides an essentially social view of metrics selection (e.g. Brown, 1999). Dearborn and Simon (1958) demonstrated that 'functional conditioning' is an important predictor of executives' behaviour; i.e., that executives generally perceive those aspects of a situation that relate to the activities and goal of their department. This 'selective attention' has consequences for information gathering and use. The selection of the type of measure employed to assess competitive advantage and evaluate the effectiveness of marketing activities depends in fact on the manager's 'view of the world' (Day and Nedungadi, 1994).

Different epistemic perspectives, i.e. ideas about the nature of knowledge, are shaped by the unique characteristics of each human being and his or her social environment. As a consequence, managers have different and sometimes divergent ideas of which is the best way to obtain new knowledge. Moorman and Zaltman (1985) draw attention to the relevance of social construction in the definition of reality used by different 'epistemic communities'. They suggest that:

> [O]ur aims or purposes of inquiry are shaped by the methods we use and the assumptions we make about the nature of the facts and the phenomena they relate to also shape our selection of methods and even our aim. Similarly, our methods influence our aims as well as our assumptions about the factual nature of the phenomena we are concerned with.

> (Moorman and Zaltman, 1985, p. 312)

Selective attention to a part of a stimulus may reflect a deliberate ignoring of the remainder as irrelevant to the subject's motives, or consist of a learned response stemming from some past history of reinforcement (Dearborn and Simon, 1958).

Chattopadhyay et al. (1999) carried out an extensive study to determine the factors that influence the way executives think. They conclude that 'executives' beliefs are clearly influenced to a greater extent by the beliefs of other members of the upper-echelon team than by their past and current functional experience' (p. 781). As a result of social desirability factors and political issues, the set of marketing metrics selected by a company therefore tends to reflect the intended subjective performance ('what the Board wants') that may in some cases be different from objective performance ('comparable information with competitors and/or information required by external stakeholders').

Orientation

The extent to which top management is interested in assessing marketing, or market performance, may be explained by the extent to which they are market-oriented (Day, 1994a; Jaworski and Kohli, 1993; Kohli and Jaworski, 1990; Narver and Slater, 1990). Market-driven firms need to gather and disseminate market intelligence within the organization (Day, 1994b; Kohli and Jaworski, 1990; Slater and Narver, 1995). Various perspectives contribute to explain the vertical flow of market-related information within the firm. Managers are forced by time, financial constraints and environmental uncertainty to take a partial view of their environment (Day and Nedungadi, 1994). Thus the metrics they select reflect such a partial view and strategy can perhaps be inferred from what managers measure.

The final theoretical perspective concerns the relationship and the balance of power between functions within the firm (Fisher, Maltz and Jaworski, 1997; Homburg, Workman and Krohmer, 1999; Sarin and Mahajan, 2001; Workman, 1993). Dawes, Lee and Dowling (1998) and Fisher *et al.* (1997) empirically showed that information control is linked intimately with influence and power. Marketing literature has long recognized the relevance of the process of information dissemination within the organization in the study of the behavior of the marketing group (e.g., Dawes, Lee and Dowling, 1998; Fisher *et al.*, 1997; Glazer, 1991; Hartline, Maxham and McKee, 2000; Homburg, Workman and Krohmer, 1999; Jaworski and MacInnis, 1989; Kohli and Jaworski, 1990; Moorman 1995; Moorman, Zaltman and Deshpandé, 1992). The results of these studies indicate the effect of political issues on the flow of information from the marketing group to the top management and relate this discussion to the stream of research devoted to corporate culture and to its influence on marketing actions (Deshpandé, Farley and Webster, 1993; Deshpandé and Webster, 1989; Dunn, Norburn and Birley, 1994; Homburg and Pflesser, 2000; Moorman, 1995).

Organizational culture has been defined as 'the pattern of shared values and beliefs that helps individuals understand organizational functioning and thus provide them norms for behavior in the organization' (Deshpandé and Webster, 1989, p. 4). One of the main features of a market-oriented organizational culture is the presence of organization-wide norms for market orientation (Homburg and Pflesser, 2000). These norms will shape in turn the dynamics of information disclosure to the top management as well as the content of such information. This point of view substantiates the perspective advocated by institutional theory.

Discussion of Theoretical Perspectives

These four theoretical perspectives overlap to some degree. Control and agency theories are two rational approaches to metrics selection but the latter is only relevant where a separate marketing function determines the metrics to be presented to top management. Institutional and orientation theories are more experiential and imply that metrics selection will be driven by social factors within the firm and the industry sector. None of these theories has much to contribute to which individual metrics will be chosen, except for market orientation which would relatively prefer external customer and competitor market to internal, e.g. financial, metrics. This will be tested later in this chapter.

Managerial Practice

We now turn to the analysis of the evolution of marketing performance assessment in practice and the benchmarks with which they are compared. Control theory suggests that the metrics are only as useful as the variances are actionable. In other words, unless management is able to identify whether performance is on course or in which respects and how far it is off course, they will not be able to take appropriate decisions.

Metrics evolution

Success measures can be classified broadly as either financial or non-financial (Buckley *et al.*, 1988; Frazier and Howell, 1982). Early work in firm-level measurement of marketing performance focused on financial measures: profit, sales and cash flow (Day and Fahey, 1988; Feder, 1965; Sevin, 1965).

Many authors criticized the only use of financial indicators in determining marketing performance (Bhargava, Dubelaar and Ramaswani, 1994; Chakravarthy, 1986; Eccles, 1991). Accounting measures are in the main short-term and take little account of the value to the firm of long-term customer preference, or the marketing investment which created it. For example, Chakravarthy (1986) wrote: 'accounting-measure-of-performance record only the history of a firm. Monitoring a firm's strategy requires measures that can also capture its potential for performance in the future' (p. 444). For many corporations, such as Coca-Cola, intangible assets have become more significant than tangible assets (Standard and Poor, 1996). Financial performance measures are therefore necessary but not sufficient in defining overall business performance and an exclusive use of financial measures may actually undermine long-term performance (Collins and Porras, 1995).

In the 1980s, market share gained popularity as a strong predictor of cash flow and profitability (e.g. Buzzell and Gale, 1987). Over the past decade, other non-financial measures such as customer satisfaction (e.g. Ittner and Larcker, 1998; Szymaski and Henard, 2001), customer loyalty (Dick and Basu, 1994), and brand equity (see Keller, 1998 for review) have attracted wide attention. Ittner and Larcker (1998) found that 'the relationship between customer satisfaction and future accounting performance generally is positive and statistical[ly] significant' (p. 2).

Clark (1999), in his history of marketing performance measures, showed how traditional financial measures (profit, sales, cash flow) expanded to a range of non-financial (market share, quality, customer satisfaction, loyalty, brand equity), input (marketing audit, implementation and orientation) and output (marketing audit, efficiency/effectiveness, multivariate analysis) measures. As a consequence, the number and variety of measures has risen: Meyer (1998) suggests that 'firms are swamped with measures' (p. xvi) and that some have over 100 metrics. This variety makes comparison difficult between results of different studies (Murphy, Trailer and Hill, 1996). A literature search of five leading marketing journals yielded 19 different measures of marketing 'success', the most recurrent among which were sales, market share, profit contribution, and purchase intention (Ambler and Kokkinaki, 1997).

The general pattern of evolution of marketing metrics appears to be:

- Little awareness of the need for marketing metrics at top executive level.
- Seeking the solution exclusively from financial metrics.
- Broadening the portfolio with a miscellany of non-financial metrics.
- Finding some rationale(s) to reduce the number of metrics to a manageable set of about 25 or less, e.g. Unilever (1998).

Benchmarks

Two kinds of benchmarks are required for the valid assessment of performance: internal benchmarks (e.g. plans) reveal the extent to which management's own expectations and goals are met; external benchmarks (e.g. competitive, market) provide a more neutral perspective which also takes into account environmental and market factors (Ambler and Kokkinaki, 1997).

In addition to internal and external benchmarks, performance assessment for any period requires adjustment for the effects brought forward from past, and carried forward for future, periods. Some advertising effects take more than one year to decay and therefore affects the following financial year (Assmus, Farley and Lehmann, 1984).

Brand Equity

The need for valid benchmark comparisons indicates the need for assessing short-term performance on a like-for-like basis. In accounting terms, aligning the period's inputs and outcomes requires their adjustment for the state of the marketing asset, i.e. the benefits created by marketing which have yet to reach the firm's profit and loss account, at the beginning and end of the period in question.

Intangible assets are in fact a significant determinant of business performance (Jacobson, 1990). If a firm has built up large intangible assets it can expect a continuing flow of sales and profits without further investment, at least for a time. Thus the intangible assets provide, in theory, a possible way to reconcile short and long-term performance.

Brand equity (Aaker, 1991; 1996) is a widely-used term for the intangible marketing asset. Srivastava and Shocker (1991) define brand equity as:

> [A] set of associations and behaviors on the part of a brand's customers, channel members and parent corporation that permits the brand to earn greater volume or greater margins than it could without the brand name and that gives a strong, sustainable and differential advantage
>
> (p. 5)

Brand equity stems from the confidence that consumers place in one brand relative to its competitors. This confidence translates into consumer loyalty and their willingness to pay a premium price for the brand and/or willingness to continue to purchase. Brand equity provides a way to assess the evolution of the brand over time and to measure the effectiveness of marketing performance.

Building brand equity 'provides sustainable competitive advantage because it creates meaningful competitive barriers' (Yoo, Donthu and Lee, 2000, p. 208), including the opportunity for successful extensions, resilience against competitors' promotional pressures, and creation of barriers to competitive entry

(Farquhar, 1989; Keller, 1993). The literature indicates three main methods of measuring brand equity: non-financial measures, brand valuation and consumer utility.

Non-financial measures are of two types: consumer behavioral measures, such as loyalty and market share, and 'intermediate' measures such as awareness and intention to purchase (e.g. Keller, 1993; Park and Srinivasan, 1994). For example, Keller (1993) defines customer-based brand equity as 'the differential effect of brand knowledge on consumer response to the marketing of the brand' (p. 8) to distinguish the analysis of brand equity carried out by focusing on consumer intermediates to that carried out by focusing on its financial outcome. Keller distinguishes between two components of customer-based brand equity: brand awareness and brand image. The first is related to the ability of the consumer to identify the brand, the second is instead connected to the perceptions held about the brand, expressed in terms of product-related attributes.

Agarwal and Rao (1996) found that ten popular brand equity measures (such as perceptions and attitudes, preferences, choice intentions, and actual choice) were convergent. Perceptions, preference and intentions (five in all) predicted market share but the wider range of brand equity may still be necessary to explain behavior. In other words, the extent of covariance was not enough to allow measures to be dropped altogether. 'It may not be necessary to subject respondents to difficult questions in order to obtain accurate measures of brand equity. Simple appropriately worded single-item scales may do just as well' (Agarwal and Rao, 1996, p. 246). Customer-based measures, however, are limited by the inability of a consumer survey to elicit accurate information about the store environment in terms of prices and promotions of different brands (Park and Srinivasan, 1994).

The second, financial, perspective (e.g. Simon and Sullivan, 1993) can be used to value the brand at the beginning and end of each period and the difference used to adjust the short-term performance (e.g. profits). For this reason it is attractive to financially-oriented firms. The leading analysis of the relationship between stock market prices and brand value has been carried out by Simon and Sullivan (1993) who separated the value of brand equity from the value of the firm's other assets. The result is an estimate of brand equity that is based on the financial market evaluation of the firm's future cash flow. The estimate of brand equity is obtained from the firm's intangible assets as a difference between the financial market value of the firm and the value of its tangible assets. The main advantage of the financial approach is providing measures that are future-oriented, compared to customer-based measures that reflect the effectiveness of the marketing activities carried out by the firm in the past. The financial approach is based on the future value of the present level of brand equity because current stock returns are driven by expectation about the future based on current information (Lane and Jacobson, 1995).

Kerin and Sethuraman (1998) underline the link between stock market prices and a firm's intangible assets: 'From a financial perspective, tangible wealth emanated from the incremental capitalized earnings and cash flows achieved by linking a successful, established brand name to a product or service' (p. 260).

Of the various ways of valuing brands, discounted cash flow is the most frequently used (Arthur Andersen, 1992; Perrier, 1997). Ambler and Barwise

(1998) claim that brand valuation is flawed for the purpose of assessing marketing performance.

A third approach takes a utility perspective and infers the value of brand equity from consumers' choices by formulating assumptions about the structure of the utility function at the individual level (Guadagni and Little, 1983; Kamakura and Russell, 1993; Swain *et al.*, 1993). Its major strength is the use of actual purchase behavior. However, the specification of the utility function is weak: 'our measure of intangible value is a residual and is conditioned on both the validity of the overall Brand Value measure and on the particular objective measures of physical features used' (Kamakura and Russell, 1993, p. 20).

Swain *et al.* (1993), however, use:

> [T]he entire utility value attributed to a brand as a basis for measuring equity, whereas [*Kamakura and Russell*] use a specific part of the utility function, reflecting their definition that brand equity is the 'additional utility not explained by measured attributes'.
>
> (p. 42)

This choice is motivated by the fact that 'the effect of brand equity occurs throughout the components of the utility function, and hence any measure of brand equity should be based on total utility' (Swain *et al.*, 1993, p. 42). They obtain a measure of brand equity, called equalization price, by comparing the estimated utility with the utility obtained by the same set of brands in a hypothetical referential market in which there is no market differentiation.

Lassar, Mittal and Sharma (1995) suggest that brand equity is the outcome of consumer perceptions rather than of objective indicators. A measure of brand equity is therefore related to financial results, not because of its absolute value, but because of its value in relation to competition.

While there are various ways to measure brand equity, we conclude that quantifying the increase or decline in this intangible asset is a crucial part of assessing marketing performance since without that, short-term results can present a biased picture.

Theoretical Framework

The concept of marketing adopted within an organization affects the kind of measurement system implemented for determining performance (Dunn, Norburn and Birley, 1994; Jaworski, 1988; Moorman, 1995; Ruekert, 1992; Webster, 1992). The set of metrics reviewed by top management should ideally be both necessary and sufficient, and also consistent across financial periods and across business functions since they are both formed by, and part of, the firm's culture and internal understanding. Since they will also be mindful of tracking progress relative to competitors, sector considerations, i.e. the metrics generally used in that sector, will be a factor (institutional theory).

From a control theoretic point of view, metrics can be seen as indicating progress towards objectives. As such, a set of metrics always concerns effectiveness, but not necessarily efficiency. 'The greater the consistency between each control and the stated marketing objective, the greater the likelihood of attaining the marketing objective' (Jaworski, 1988, p. 32).

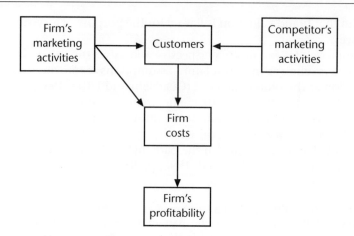

FIGURE 15.1 Basic model

The corporate objectives are taken to be the 'bottom line' in the sense of profitability. Marketing in the holistic sense used here (Webster, 1992) is thus the activities undertaken by the company to convert the customer into shareholder cash (profits if not dividends). Figure 15.1 provides the basic model showing cash flow from customer to the firm's profitability.

The discussion of brand equity would indicate that, conceptually, we can assess marketing performance from the profitability in the period together with the change in brand equity – primarily customer-based brand equity since most practitioners would not include employees and other stakeholder-based brand equity in a marketing assessment.

Since customer memories cannot be directly accessed, we opt for the first of the three approaches discussed above since that includes the other two. In other words, we will accept in principle financial (including brand valuation) and non-financial measures, both intermediate and behavioral. Furthermore, the competitive nature of the market can be recognized by accepting both absolute measures, e.g. customer satisfaction, and relative measures, e.g. satisfaction as a per cent of that held by the leading competitor. Relative may be to one or more competitors or relative to the whole market.

Of course this catholic acceptance of measures is subject to our definition of metrics: top management must be using some, probably implicit, process to reduce the possible measures to the necessary and sufficient (in their view) set of metrics. Thus metrics may be derived according to control and/or institutional and/or orientation theories. We are excluding only agency theory on the basis that we do not wish to limit our study to companies with separate marketing departments.

Figure 15.2 develops the basic model in order to separate out brand equity effects in two ways: the immediate (trade) customer is distinguished from the end user (consumer). This distinction applies to most business (including business to business where the user is not usually the buyer) but not necessarily in retailing. Secondly, intermediate effects are separated from consumer behavior.

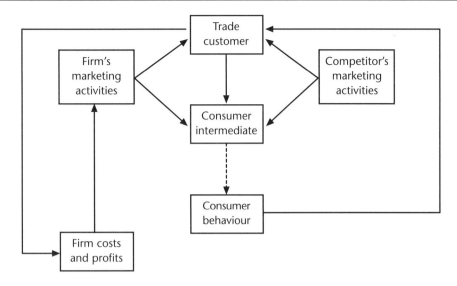

FIGURE 15.2 Generalized model of cash flows

Thus marketing activities impact both trade customers and consumers at the intermediate, or 'in-the-head', level. These in turn interact and result in consumer usage. Cash flows from consumer to trade customer to the financial results (both costs and profits) but these also fund the marketing activities.

Figure 15.2 also provides a conceptual framework for assembling marketing performance metrics:

- The short-term metrics are supplied by the inputs (marketing activities, such as share of voice) and the outputs (the financial results, such as sales and profit contribution).

- The brand equity asset, changes in which are needed to adjust the short-term perspective, are provided by the status of the three boxes in the central column: trade customer and consumer intermediate and behavior.

Thus a metrics system can itself be assessed by its fit with this framework and the comparison of those metrics as follows:

- Control theory suggests that metrics should be compared with management expectations, e.g. a formal marketing plan.

- Market orientation would imply that the metrics should be compared with competitor performance.

- Finally, the short-term results should be adjusted by changes in brand equity as noted above.

This framework is now used to structure the findings from three stages of data gathering. The first was qualitative (in-depth interviews with British managers) and the next two were quantitative. The former used the framework in Figure

15.2 to group metrics together and the second quantified usage of individual metrics. The goal was to establish current business practice both as the basis for further research and for managers to benchmark their firms' processes.

Discussion of Current Practice

In this section of the chapter we will discuss and compare the results provided by recent descriptions of company practice (Davidson, 1999; Kokkinaki and Ambler, 1999; Marketing Leadership Council, 2001; Riley and Ambler, 2000). The three studies were conducted in the UK and the fourth in the USA.

On the basis of previous literature, of existing research among analysts and shareholders and of the analysis of a limited number of company reports, Davidson (1999) develops two lists of metrics. From an initial list of 47 metrics he developed arguments for his most valuable 10 metrics. The four criteria for the selection of the short list were importance to analysts, practical ability to report, importance to management, and economic importance. Table 15.1 presents Davidson's shorter list.

Davidson (1999) points out the change brought to company reporting by the inclusion of 'non-tangible measures'. 'If company reporting metrics focus more strongly on activity that influences future success, managers may give these areas more attention. . . . Such a change could make companies more customer and future driven' (p. 771).

Kokkinaki and Ambler (1999) investigate the issue of measuring marketing performance taking a different approach from Davidson (1999): they used primary data to determine current practice. The research was composed of two stages. After six pilot interviews with chief executives and senior marketers of UK firms, the first stage of the research consisted of 44 in-depth interviews with marketing and finance managers from various sectors – mainly consumer goods and services. On the basis of the findings of this study, a survey instrument was constructed which gathered data on orientation and metrics, grouped according to the categories shown in Table 15.2.

The framework in Figure 15.2 matched the way respondents grouped metrics, except for innovation. This was considered an important category but the

---

TABLE 15.1 The 10 most valuable metrics according to Davidson (1999)

Metric

- Market trend
- Market share
- Major brand trends
- Customer retention levels
- New products/services in the past five years as a percentage of sales
- Unit volume trend (per cent)
- R&D as a percentage of sales
- Capex as a percentage of sales
- Marketing as a percentage of sales
- Distribution trend (per cent)

TABLE 15.2 Importance of measure categories for assessing performance

	Mean	t^a	df	Sig. t
Financial	6.51	–	–	–
Direct customer	5.53	−14.90	499	0.000
Competitive	5.42	−16.78	523	0.000
Consumer intermediate	5.42	−15.60	515	0.000
Consumer behavior	5.38	−15.60	522	0.000
Innovativeness	5.04	20.13	524	0.000

Source: Kokkinaki and Ambler, 1999.
Note: [a] *t*-tests refer to the comparisons between financial measures and each of the other categories.

metrics, e.g. the proportion of sales represented by products launched in the last three years, did not fit the framework; i.e., financial, competitive, trade customer, consumer intermediate and behavior. Accordingly this category was added to the framework in Table 15.2. Financial measures were reported as being seen by top management as significantly more important than all other categories.

According to the study, plans provide the most frequent benchmarks of financial and innovativeness measures, in those cases where such measures are used. Market share apart, it appears that internal (plan) and external benchmarks are routinely used only by the minority of respondent firms.

As far as the marketing asset is concerned, 62.2 per cent of the respondents reported the use of some term to describe the concept. The most common terms are brand equity (32.5 per cent of those who reported a term), reputation (19.6 per cent), brand strength (8.8 per cent), brand value (8.2 per cent) and brand health (6.9 per cent). Moreover, only 24.9 per cent of the firms regularly (yearly or more) value the marketing asset financially, whereas 41 per cent of them regularly quantify it in other ways, e.g. through customer/consumer-based measures. These findings suggest that a minority of companies (37 per cent of the total sample) quantify their marketing assets, using any formulation, on a regular basis.

Our conceptual framework suggested that the marketing performance assessment system could be tested with three criteria: comparisons with both internal (plan) and external (competitor) performance benchmarks, adjusted by changes in the marketing asset. Kokkinaki and Ambler (1999) suggest that less than one quarter of UK firms could meet all three criteria. Of course, these data merely indicate that they have the measures available for such comparisons, not that they necessarily make them.

Concerning orientation, Kokkinaki and Ambler's (1999) results showed that customer orientation did not influence the regularity of tracking of financial and competitive measures, but that the regularity of collection of competitor measures was influenced by competitor orientation. The relationship between orientation and measure importance is less clear. Customer orientation was positively related with the importance attached to most measures, except financial and competitive measures. Competitor orientation also influenced the importance of competitor measures, but it was also a significant predictor of the importance attached to measures related to consumer behavior, consumer thoughts and feelings, and innovativeness.

Riley and Ambler (2000) take a perspective more similar to that of Davidson (1999) as they explored how firms assess their marketing performance, together with differences by industry sector and firm size. They were concerned with marketing metrics that reflect both common usage and best practice. Using survey methodology (a telephone survey was conducted of 200 UK marketing or finance senior executives with an additional 31 survey instruments completed at the pilot stage), content validity and scale purification techniques, 54 measures originally identified were reduced to a common practice list of 19 metrics on the basis of top management review and perceived importance for assessing performance.

Respondents were asked to indicate the importance of each measure for assessing the overall marketing performance of the business and the highest level of routine review of this metric within the firm. Table 15.3 ranks the top 15 (> 62 per cent usage) metrics by frequency of use, compared with the frequency that it was rated as 'very important' and the frequency that it reached the top level of management. In line with Kokkinaki and Ambler's (1999) results, most firms rely primarily on internally-generated financial figures to assess their marketing performance.

As far as industry differences are concerned, consumer goods industries consistently rated metrics highly, both in terms of importance and level of review, whereas business-to-business services consistently ranks them lowly on both counts. It is probably fair to deduce that consumer goods are the most, and business-to-business services the least, market-oriented sectors.

TABLE 15.3 Ranking of marketing metrics

Metric	% claiming to use measure	% of firms rating as very important	% claimed to reach top level	Pearson correlation between level and importance
1. Profit/profitability	92	80	71	0.719**
2. Sales, value and/or volume	91	71	65	0.758**
3. Gross margin	81	66	58	0.827**
4. Awareness	78	28	29	0.732**
5. Market share (volume or value)	78	37	34	0.727**
6. Number of new products	73	18	19	0.859**
7. Relative price (SOM value/ volume)	70	36	33	0.735**
8. Number of consumer complaints/ level of dissatisfaction)	69	45	31	0.802**
9. Consumer satisfaction	68	48	37	0.815**
10. Distribution/availability	66	18	11	0.900**
11. Total number of customers	66	24	23	0.812**
12. Marketing spend	65	39	46	0.849**
13. Perceived quality/esteem	64	37	32	0.783**
14. Loyalty/retention	64	47	34	0.830**
15. Relative perceived quality	63	39	30	0.814**

Note: $n = 231$, **$p < 0.01$.

Considering the two columns in Table 15.3 reporting level of review and importance it can be seen that 19 items match. These 19 metrics could be considered as the primary general metrics: awareness, perceived quality, consumer satisfaction, relevance to consumer, perceived differentiation, brand/product knowledge, number of new customers, loyalty/retention, conversions, (trade) customer satisfaction, number of complaints, relative consumer satisfaction, perceived quality, number of new products, revenue of new products, margin of new products, sales, gross margins and profitability.

While this list is well distributed over the framework in Figure 15.2 above it is perhaps surprising that market share and relative price are omitted. Subsequent practitioner discussions have informally suggested that in many sectors these metrics are uncertain. For example, in financial services the basis for calculating relative price was not known.

Table 15.4 contains a comparison of the long list of metrics selected by Davidson (1999) and that selected by Riley and Ambler (2000). The table shows considerable overlapping.[3]

The first row in the table above shows that 18 of the 46 metrics were common. The following rows indicate the reasons why the metrics in Davidson's list were not included in Riley and Ambler's (2000).

The fourth (US) study was a survey conducted amongst their members by the Marketing Leadership Council (2001). By far the greatest pressure for improved marketing metrics (66 per cent compared with 22 per cent for the next reason) was the need to demonstrate the financial impact of marketing. 71 per cent considered that the topic was more important than it had been a year before. This confirms the Marketing Science Institute's (2000) decision to keep marketing metrics at the top of their priorities.

The use of metrics across different sectors is shown in Table 15.5. This shows a consistent number of metrics across sectors at around 21 but the expected variation in selected due to sector factors.

The majority (63 per cent) of respondents were dissatisfied with their marketing metrics, the largest problem being the difficulty of measuring brand equity (49 per cent). Lack of data (58 per cent), inconsistency over time (52 per cent) and lack of expertise (50 per cent) were cited as the main reasons.

TABLE 15.4 Comparison of metrics selected by Davidson (1999) and by Riley and Ambler (2000)

Metric name	Number of metrics
Used in both studies	18
Diagnostics	4
Trends (derivatives)	4
Composites	6
General business measures outside what is generally seen as 'marketing', e.g. logistics, R&D and employee issues	10
Others	4
Total	46

TABLE 15.5 Metric usage reported by the Marketing Leadership Council (2001)

Metric	B2B	B2B hi tech	B2C direct	B2C telecoms	B2C indirect	Packaged goods	Pharma	Total (%)
Market share	100.0	100.0	77.0	100.0	100.0	92.0	100.0	93.3
Sales revenue	81.0	100.0	81.0	100.0	95.0	100.0	100.0	89.5
Market growth	85.0	70.0	65.0	100.0	90.0	92.0	80.0	80.8
Satisfaction	85.0	80.0	85.0	80.0	55.0	67.0	40.0	74.3
Price level	77.0	90.0	69.0	100.0	60.0	75.0	80.0	74.0
Market size	77.0	60.0	58.0	80.0	80.0	92.0	80.0	73.2
Aided awareness	62.0	60.0	69.0	100.0	90.0	75.0	80.0	73.1
Overall awareness	65.0	60.0	69.0	100.0	85.0	67.0	80.0	72.0
Unit volume	65.0	70.0	73.0	100.0	70.0	83.0	60.0	72.0
Sales by channel	69.0	70.0	65.0	100.0	75.0	83.0	60.0	71.9
Unaided awareness	62.0	60.0	65.0	80.0	90.0	75.0	80.0	71.2
Market share by segment	65.0	70.0	58.0	60.0	80.0	75.0	80.0	68.3
Customer complaints	50.0	50.0	73.0	60.0	55.0	75.0	20.0	58.6
Customer preference	58.0	50.0	62.0	60.0	65.0	58.0	20.0	57.8
Perceived quality	62.0	60.0	65.0	60.0	50.0	67.0	–	57.8
Customer service levels	50.0	50.0	58.0	40.0	60.0	83.0	40.0	56.8
Number of customers	50.0	40.0	81.0	80.0	40.0	42.0	40.0	54.9
Number of new customers	50.0	30.0	73.0	80.0	50.0	50.0	40.0	54.8
Perceived value	42.0	60.0	46.0	40.0	60.0	58.0	40.0	49.8
Attitude	46.0	60.0	39.0	20.0	60.0	58.0	60.0	49.1
Purchase intent	46.0	60.0	42.0	40.0	55.0	67.0	20.0	49.0
Brand equity	39.0	40.0	42.0	40.0	65.0	67.0	40.0	48.2
Likelihood to recommend	50.0	60.0	54.0	40.0	40.0	33.0	20.0	46.2
Recall of brand attributes	35.0	40.0	42.0	60.0	60.0	42.0	60.0	45.3
Churn rate	39.0	40.0	73.0	100.0	20.0	33.0	–	44.3
Customer profitability	35.0	30.0	46.0	60.0	45.0	50.0	40.0	42.4
Brand value	31.0	40.0	42.0	40.0	60.0	42.0	40.0	42.3
No. products per customer	19.0	10.0	62.0	60.0	45.0	50.0	20.0	39.5
Customer gross margin	35.0	30.0	46.0	40.0	40.0	42.0	20.0	38.6
Percentage of sales at discount	35.0	30.0	19.0	40.0	50.0	50.0	80.0	37.5
Price premium/discount	27.0	20.0	27.0	20.0	50.0	58.0	40.0	34.6
No. transactions per customer	12.0	10.0	46.0	20.0	45.0	42.0	40.0	31.8
Inclusion in consideration set	19.0	30.0	31.0	20.0	40.0	42.0	20.0	29.8
Customer acquisition cost	23.0	20.0	50.0	60.0	20.0	17.0	20.0	29.8
Average discount provided	27.0	30.0	15.0	20.0	35.0	42.0	60.0	28.8
Share of wallet	27.0	20.0	39.0	20.0	20.0	33.0	–	27.0
Cost to serve per customer	19.0	10.0	39.0	40.0	25.0	25.0	20.0	26.0
Price elasticity	15.0	–	27.0	40.0	30.0	50.0	–	24.0
Weight ratio (heavy/light users)	4.0	–	27.0	20.0	30.0	50.0	40.0	22.2
Customer lifetime value	12.0	10.0	35.0	40.0	10.0	8.0	–	17.5
n =	26.0	10.0	26.0	5.0	20.0	12.0	5.0	104.0
Mean	45.8	46.9	52.7	57.7	54.0	56.6	49.0	52.7
Av. measures per company	18.3	17.8	21.1	23.1	21.6	22.7	17.2	21.1

Future Research

The research reported above gives a good picture of the metrics in use and some of the problem areas. Metrics are becoming a major focus of attention, driven by the demands of top management to show evidence of achievement – preferably in financial terms. Whilst there are concerns with the methodology and therefore the validity and reliability of these findings the larger issues concern association between measurement and performance and the means by which metrics are selected and how they are used, i.e. metrics process.

Theory and strategic factors indicate that there can be no set of metrics which suits all firms. Contextual determinants include the sector, the size and age of the business, and the rate of change of the firms' commercial environment. To the extent that metrics represent milestones on the firm's chosen strategic path, the metrics will vary accordingly. In particular each firm will have, explicitly or implicitly, a mental model linking the use of resources with performance. Within that brand equity can be seen as a reservoir of unrealized cash flow. It grows during the good times and acts to support profits in more difficult times, and especially when marketing budgets are cut. Further research is needed to match metrics with these models and particularly the contributions made by the different elements of the marketing mix.

As discussed above, evidence seems to suggest that the evolution of marketing performance consciousness follows a sequence from non awareness to scientific assessment (Kokkinaki and Ambler, 1999). Further research is needed to provide empirical support to this evolutionary perspective on the measurement of marketing performance. It is possible that metrics follow marketing development but at some distance.

Examples are customer relationship management (CRM) and e-business metrics, a topic that is becoming increasingly important (Marketing Science Institute, 2000; Mohammed *et al.*, 2001). Even though some analytic instruments developed for the analysis of offline environments are likely to provide useful suggestions, the development of an efficient system of online metrics requires the development of an entire new set of tools. Novak and Hoffman (1996) compiled a list of online metrics. This includes: visitor metrics, exposure metrics (e.g., number of times a banner is downloaded), reach and frequency metrics, duration time metrics (such as stickiness, the length of time a visitor spends on a website), etc.. However, popular online metrics such as click-through, reach and overall traffic do not measure the effectiveness of online marketing activities. These measures implicitly assume a definition of the effect of advertising only in terms of instant response, ignoring subtler and longer-term effects such as branding (Fattah, 2000). A new set of metrics seems therefore necessary to understand properly the effectiveness of online marketing activities. Yahoo! provides a service called 'Buzz' which tracks searches made by Internet users on Yahoo!'s directory service. This tool makes it possible not only to measure trends and to understand consumer response but also to monitor competition.

Part of the difficulty in these emerging activities is that terms need to be defined and broadly agreed before metrics can become widespread. Cutler and Sterne (2000), who surveyed e-metrics usage, state: 'while the industry at large is struggling with a common vernacular to compare one company's Web site with another, most firms are having trouble trying to communicate internally' (p. 15). And the rate of change means that most companies lack the staff, resources and expertise to cope with the volume of data available from their systems. Much the same could be said of CRM.

For companies that operate both offline and online another problem is how to integrate offline and online data and how to interpret online metrics. For example, excessive focus on profitability may be causing traditional retailers to miss nearly two-thirds of the value that their websites create (Media Metrix, 2001). Sales and profitability measures of websites do not consider the purchase intent generated through the website that will cause an increase in the sales of offline channels, an effect that Media Metrix defines as 'transactional benefits'.

Conclusions

The marketing literature has underestimated the importance of measuring marketing performance for the attainment of good marketing practice. This paper has summarized the current state of the art. Firstly, a literature review was provided to explain the ecology in which the performance assessment is carried out and the changes witnessed recently in marketing performance evaluation. Secondly, a framework was proposed to provide the structural reference for the analysis of current practice. The schema was organized around six measurement categories: (1) financial; (2) competitive arena – measures relative to a competitor or the whole market; (3) consumer behavior; (4) consumer intermediate – thoughts and feelings; (5) direct trade customer; and (6) innovation. Thirdly, the results of empirical studies attempting to describe company practice were discussed. The goal was to offer a picture of current practice. Finally, managerial implications and directions for future research have been included.

Marketing discourages short-termism and has lacked the ability to account for its actions partly due to the difficulty of bridging accounting periods. Brand equity, in theory, provides that bridge but practitioners are wrestling with satisfactory ways to measure it. If the asset has grown, the short-term profits are understated and vice versa. Marketing metrics provide the diagnosis. The dilemma for the marketing manager is that 'only short-term results of marketing actions are readily observable, yet short-term profit maximization is not the best paradigm for allocating resources' (Dekimpe and Hanssens, 1999, p. 397).

The inherent problem of associating marketing expenditures with performance leads to the notion shared by many executives that marketing expenditures are costs rather than investments. As a consequence, to a greater extent than other expenditures, the marketing budget is seen as discretionary. Kotler (2000), for example, underlines that financial executives generally think that 'marketing executives ask for substantial budgets for advertising, sales promotions, and sales force, without being able to prove how much revenue these expenditures will produce' (p. 692).

In today's market, companies face growing competition and deal with more knowledgeable and aware consumers. Markets are characterized by an abundance of products but a limited shelf space. Companies can choose between an increasing number of communication channels, e.g. the Internet, but the consumer attention span is limited. Information technology makes it possible to cross geographical and cultural boundaries in a way unthinkable just a couple of decades ago. All these factors put an even greater pressure on firms to build and maintain strong brands. In this scenario, such an important tool as metrics towards the goal of an efficient allocation of marketing resources cannot be overlooked.

Digital navigation was slow to evolve in shipping and we should not expect the idea of steering a firm by numbers to be any more immediate. In the first place destinations were in sight and responses, whether to the tiller or sales efforts, were quickly apparent. Helmsmen learned to avoid under- or over-correction by trial and error. Captains of businesses and ships today have charge of large and complex enterprises with destinations beyond sight and struggle to stay above ever more turbulent waters. To these managers, the advantage of withdrawing from hands-on control to the study of positional metrics is not as obvious as future generations may think.

Notes

1. 'Performance' here is used conventionally to mean the financial results from business activities (e.g. sales, profits, increase in shareholder value), not the activities themselves.
2. 'Bottom line' usually means net profits but may alternatively mean whatever ultimate goal the company seeks.
3. The 'other' category in Table 15.4 indicates measures that were not excluded by Riley and Ambler's (2000) methodology of selection, even though they were included in Davidson's (1999) list. These metrics were: recommend to a friend, number of marketing awards, advertising as a percentage of sales, and brand preference.

References

Chapter 2

Aggarwal, R. and Soenen, L. (1989) 'Managing persistent real changes in currency values: The role of multinational operating strategies'. *Columbia Journal of World Business*, 23(3), 45–58.

Ali, A., Krapfel, R. Jr. and LaBahn, D. (1995) 'Product innovativeness and entry strategy: Impact on cycle time and break-even time'. *Journal of Product Innovation Management*, 12, 54–69.

Baden-Fuller, C. and Stopford, J. (1991) 'Globalization frustrated: The case of white goods'. *Strategic Management Journal*, 12, 493–507.

Bagwell, K. and Staiger, R. (1998) 'Will preferential agreements undermine the multilateral trading system?' *Economic Journal*, 108, 1162–82.

Baldwin, R. (1990) 'On the microeconomics of the European Monetary Union'. *European Economy*, 'Special Issue on the Economics of EMU', 44, 234–70.

Berry, M., Dimitratos, P. and McDermott, M. (2002) 'Globalisation and the smaller firm: Reconcilable notions?' In F. McDonald, H. Tüselmann and C. Wheeler (eds), *International Business: Adjusting to New Challenges and Opportunities*. Basingstoke: Palgrave.

Bhagwati, J. (1991) *The World Trading System at Risk*. New York: Princeton University Press.

Bhagwati, J. (1993) 'Regionalism and multilateralism: An overview'. In J. De Melo and A. Panagariya (eds), *New Dimensions in Regional Integration*. Cambridge: Cambridge University Press.

Brealey, R. (2001) 'The Asian crisis: Lessons for crisis management and prevention'. In M. Czinkota and I. Ronkainen (eds), *Best Practice in International Business*. Fort Worth: Harcourt College Publishers/Thomson Learning.

Brewer, T.L. and Young, S. (2000a) *The Multilateral Investment System and Multinational Enterprises*. Oxford: Oxford University Press.

Brewer, T.L. and Young, S. (2000b) 'The world trade organization: Global rule-maker?' In N. Hood and S. Young (eds), *The Globalization of Multinational Enterprise Activity and Economic Development*. Basingstoke: Macmillan.

De Grauwe, P. (1998) *The Economics of Monetary Integration*. Oxford: Oxford University Press.

Dicken, P. (1992) *Global Shift*, 2nd ed. London: Sage/Paul Chapman.

Dimitratos, P. (2001) 'The difference between internationalization and globalization: What is its significance for the modern firm'. Οικονομικά Χρονικά *(Economic Annals)*, April–May, 30–31 (in Greek).

Dornbusch, R. (2001) 'A primer on emerging market crises'. www.stern.nyu.edu/globalmacro

Dunning, J.H. (1995) 'Reappraising the eclectic paradigm in an age of alliance capitalism'. *Journal of International Business Studies*, 26, 461–91.

Dunning, J.H. (2000) 'Globalization and the theory of MNE activity'. In N. Hood and S. Young (eds), *The Globalization of Multinational Enterprise Activity and Economic Development*. Basingstoke: Macmillan.

Dyer, B., Gupta, A.K. and Wilemon, D. (1999) 'What first-to-market companies do differently'. *Research Technology Management*, 42(2), 15–21.

Eichengreen, B. (1998) *Globalizing Capital: A History of the International Monetary System*. Princeton, NJ: Princeton University Press.

Eichengreen, B. (1999) *Towards a New International Financial Architecture: A Practical Post-Asia Agenda*. Washington, DC: Institute of International Economics.

Either, W. (1998) 'The new regionalism'. *Economic Journal*, 108, 1149–61.

El Agraa, M. (1997) *Economic Integration Worldwide*. London: Macmillan.

Emerson, M., Gros, D., Italianer, A., Pisani-Ferry, J. and Reichenbach, H. (1992) *One Market, One Money*. Oxford: Oxford University Press.

Frankel, J. (1997) *Regional Trading Blocs in the World Economic System*. Washington, DC: Institute of International Economics.

Giddens, A. (1999) *Runaway World: How Globalization is Reshaping our Lives*. London: Routledge.

Gros, D. and Thygesen, N. (1998) *European Monetary Integration*, 2nd ed. London: Addison Wesley Longman.

Henning, C. (1997) 'Cooperating with European Monetary Union'. *Policy Analysis in International Economics* No. 49. Washington, DC: Institute of International Economics.

Hood, N. and Peters, E. (2000) 'Globalization, corporate strategies and business services'. In N. Hood and S. Young (eds), *The Globalization of Multinational Enterprise Activity and Economic Development*. Basingstoke: Macmillan.

Hood, S. and Young, S. (2000a) 'Globalization, multinational enterprises and economic development'. In N. Hood and S. Young (eds), *The Globalization of Multinational Enterprise Activity and Economic Development*. Basingstoke: Macmillan.

Hood, N. and Young, S. (2000b) 'Globalization and economic development: Overview and conclusions'. In N. Hood and S. Young (eds), *The Globalization of Multinational Enterprise Activity and Economic Development*. Basingstoke: Macmillan.

ILO (International Labour Office) (2000a) *Tripartite Declaration of Principles Concerning Multinational Enterprises and Social Policy*. Geneva: ILO.

ILO (2000b) *7th Survey Analysis (1996–1999) of the Tripartite Declaration*. Geneva: ILO.

ILO (2000c) *International Programme on the Elimination of Child Labour: IPEC*. Geneva: ILO.

IMF (International Monetary Fund) (2000) *Annual Report – Making the Global Economy Work for All*.

Johanson, J. and Vahlne, J.-E. (1977) 'The internationalization process of the firm: A model of knowledge development and increasing foreign market commitments'. *Journal of International Business Studies*, 8(1), 23–32.

Johanson, J. and Vahlne, J.-E. (1990) 'The mechanism of internationalisation'. *International Marketing Review* 7(4), 11–24.

Johanson, J. and Wiedersheim-Paul, F. (1975) 'The internationalization of the firm: Four Swedish cases'. *Journal of Management Studies*, 12, 305–22.

Julien, P.-A. (1996) 'Globalization: Different types of small firm behaviour'. *Entrepreneurship and Regional Development*, 8(1), 57–74.

Knight, G.A. and Cavusgil, S.T. (1996) 'The born global firm: A challenge to traditional internationalization theory'. *Advances in International Marketing*, 8. Greenwich, CT: JAI Press.

Krugman, P. (1999a) 'Analytical after thoughts on the Asian crisis'. www.wws.princeton.edu/~pkrugman/

Krugman, P. (1999b) 'Don't laugh at me, Argentina: Serious lessons from a silly crisis'. www.wws.princeton.edu/~pkrugman/

Kumar, V. and Nagpal, A. (2001) 'Segmenting global markets: Look before you leap'. *Marketing Research*, 13(1), 8–13.

Levitt, T. (1983) 'The globalization of markets'. *Harvard Business Review*, 61(3), 92–102.

Madsen, T.K. and Servais, P. (1997) 'The internationalization of born globals: An evolutionary process'. *International Business Review*, 6, 561–83.

Makhija, M.V., Kim, K. and Williamson, S.D. (1997) 'Measuring globalization of industries using a national industry approach: Empirical evidence across five countries and over time'. *Journal of International Business Studies*, 28, 679–710.

Marks, M.L. and Mirvis, P.H. (2001) 'Making mergers and acquisitions work: Strategic and psychological preparation'. *Academy of Management Executive*, 15(2), 80–92.

Micklethwait, J. and Wooldridge, A. (2000) *The Future Perfect*. London: Heinemann.

Mirza, H. (2000) 'The globalization of business and East Asian developing-country multi-nationals'. In N. Hood and S. Young (eds), *The Globalization of Multinational Enterprise Activity and Economic Development*. Basingstoke: Macmillan.

Moffett, M. and Yeung, B. (1999) 'Financial management, international'. In R. Tung (ed), *The Handbook of International Business*. London: Thomson Learning.

Morrison, A.J., Ricks, D.A. and Roth, K. (1991) 'Globalization versus regionalization: Which way for the multinational?' *Organizational Dynamics*, 19(3), 17–29.

Naisbitt, J. (1994) *Global Paradox*. London: Nicholas Brealey.

OECD (Organisation for Economic Cooperation and Development) (1992) *Technology and the Economy: The Key Relationships*. Paris: OECD.

OECD (1997) *Globalisation and Small and Medium Enterprises*, 1, Synthesis Report. Paris: OECD.

OECD (1999) *Session on Globalisation – Manual on Globalisation Indicators*. Paris: OECD.

OECD (2000) *The OECD Guidelines for Multinational Enterprises*. Paris: OECD.

Ohmae, K. (1985) *Triad Power: The Coming Shape of Global Competition*. New York: The Free Press.

Ohmae, K. (1990) *The Borderless World*. New York: Harper Collins.

Porter, M.E. (1987) 'From competitive advantage to corporate strategy'. *Harvard Business Review*, 68(3), 79–61.

Prasad, S. (1999) 'Globalisation of smaller firms: Field notes on processes'. *Small Business Economics*, 13(1), 1–7.

Radelet, S. and Sachs, J. (1998) 'The East Asian financial crisis: Diagnosis, remedies and prospects'. *Brookings Papers on Economic Activity*, 1. Washington, DC.

Rennie, M.W. (1993) 'Born Global'. *McKinsey Quarterly*, 4, 45–52.

Rodrik, D. (1997) 'Has globalization gone too far?' *California Management Review*, 39(3), 29–53.

Rondinelli, D.A. and Behrmann, J.N. (2000) 'The promises and pains of globalization'. *Global Focus*, 12(1), 3–15.

Roth, K. (1992) 'International configuration and coordination archetypes for medium-sized firms in global industries'. *Journal of International Business Studies*, 23, 533–49.

Rugman, A. (2000) *The End of Globalisation*. London: Random House.

Schott, J. (2001) *Prospects for Free Trade in the Americas*. Washington, DC: Institute of International Economics.

Scollay, R. and Gilbert, J. (2001) *Trading Arrangements in the Asia Pacific*. Washington, DC: Institute of International Economics.

Simon, H. (1996) *Hidden Champions*. Boston: Harvard Business School Press.

Stajkovic, A. and Luthans, F. (2001) 'Business ethics across cultures: A social cognitive model'. In M. Czinkota and I. Ronkainen (eds), *Best Practice in International Business*. Fort Worth: Harcourt College Publishers/Thomson Learning.

Stiglitz, J. (2000) 'What I learned at the world economic crisis'. *The New Republic*, 17 April, 5–8.

Storey, D. (1994) *Understanding the Small Firm Business Sector*. London: Thomson Learning.

Thomson Mergers and Acquisitions Report (0000). www.mareport.com/mar/News Update. html

Trebilcock, M. and Howse, R. (1999) *The Regulation of International Trade*. London: Routledge.

United Nations (1995) *World Investment Report 1994: Transnational Corporations, Employment and the Workplace*. New York: United Nations.

UN Division for Sustainable Development (1999) *Agenda 21 for CSD*. New York: United Nations.

Voudouris, I., Lioukas, S., Makridakis, S. and Spanos, Y. (2000) 'Greek hidden champions: Lessons from small, little-known firms in Greece'. *European Management Journal*, 18, 663–74.

Williamson, J. (1999) 'Crawling bands or monetary bands: How to manage exchange rates in a world of capital markets'. *International Economics Policy Briefs*, No. 99–3. Washington, DC: Institute of International Economics.

Yip, G.S. (1989) 'Global strategy . . . in a world of nations'. *Sloan Management Review*, 31(1), 29–41.

Young, S. (2001) 'What do researchers know about the global business environment?' *International Marketing Review*, 18(2), 120–29.

Young, S., Slow, J. and Hood, N. (2000) 'Globalization and the growth of small and non-dominant firms: Case evidence from Scotland'. In N. Hood and S. Young (eds), *The Globalization of Multinational Enterprise Activity and Economic Development*. Basingstoke: Macmillan.

Chapter 3

Albrecht, K. and Zemke, R. (1985) *Service America! Doing Business in the New Economy*. New York: Warner Books.

Anderson, E., Fornell, C. and Lehmann, D. (1994) 'Customer satisfaction, market share and profitability: Findings from Sweden', *Journal of Marketing* 58 (July), 53–66.

Anderson, E.W. and Mittal, V. (2000) 'Strengthening the satisfaction-profit chain', *Journal of Service Research*, 3(2), 107–20.

Baker, M. (2000) *Marketing Strategy and Management*, 3rd ed. London: Macmillan.

Baudrillard, J. (1981) *For a Critique of the Political Economy of the Sign*. St Louis: Telos.

Baudrillard, J. (1988) *Selected Writings*. Oxford: Polity Press.

Bauman, Z. (1992) *Intimations of Postmodernity*. London: Routledge.

Beckman, S., Christensen, A.S. and Christensen, A.G. (2001) 'Myths of nature and environmentally responsible behaviours: An exploratory study', *Rethinking European Marketing Proceedings of the 30th EMAC Conference* (May). Norway.

Belk, R.W. (1995) *Collecting in a Consumer Society*. London: Routledge.

Belk, R.W., Wallendorf, M. and Sherry, J.F. (1989) 'The sacred and the profane in consumer behaviour: Theodicy on the odyssy', *Journal of Consumer Research*, 16 (June), 1–38.

Bennett, R. (1997) 'Anger, catharsis, and purchasing behaviour following aggressive customer complaints', *Journal of Consumer Marketing*, 14(2).

Bergadaa, M. (1990) 'The role of time in the action of the consumer', *Journal of Consumer Research*, 17 (Dec), 289–302.

Berger, P. (1966) 'Identity as a problem in the sociology of knowledge', *European Journal of Sociology*, 7, 105–15.

Berry, L. (1995) *On Great Service: A Framework for Action*. New York: Free Press.

Bitner, M.J., Booms, B.H. and Mohr, L.A. (1994) 'Critical service encounters: The employee's viewpoint', *Journal of Marketing*, 58 (Oct), 95–106.

Bloemers, R., Magnomi, F. and Peters, M. (2001) 'Paying a green premium', *The McKinsey Quarterly*, Summer, p. 15.

Boedecker, M. (1995) 'New-type and traditional shoppers: A comparison of two major consumer groups', *International Journal of Retail and Distribution Management*, 23(3), 17–26.

Brosnan, M. (1998) *Technophobia: The Psychological Impact of Information Technology*. London: Routledge.

Buttle, F. (1996) 'SERVQUAL: Review, critique, research agenda', *European Journal of Marketing*, 30(1).

Byrne, D. (1999) *Social Exclusion*. Buckingham: Open University Press.

Campbell, C. (1989) *The Romantic Ethic and the Spirit of Modern Consumerism*. Oxford: Blackwell Publishers.

Catterall, M., Maclaren, P. and Stevens, L. (2000) *Marketing and Feminism*. London: Routledge.

Celsi, R., Randall, R. and Leigh, T. (1993) 'An exploration of high risk leisure consumption through ski-diving', *Journal of Consumer Research*, vo (June), 1–23.

Chuckman, J.W. (1990) 'The environment and the economy: Aspects from an industry point of view', *Vital Speeches*, 56(21), 569–82.

Churchill, G. and Surprenant, C. (1982) 'An investigation into the determinants of customer satisfaction', *Journal of Marketing Research*, 19 (Nov), 491–504.

Coiera, E. (1996) 'The Internet's challenge to health care provision', *British Medical Journal*, 312, 3–4.

Cook, D.L. and Coupey, E. (1998) 'Consumer behaviour and unresolved regulatory issues in electronic marketing', *Journal of Business Research*, 41, 231–38.

Corrigan, P. (1997) *The Sociology of Consumption*. London: Sage.

Cova, B. (1997) 'Community and consumption: Towards a definition of the linking value of product or service', *European Journal of Marketing*, 31(3–4).

Cummins, S. and Macintyre, S. (1999) 'The location of food stores in urban areas: A case study in Glasgow', *British Food Journal*, 101(7), 545–53.

Davidson, M. (1992) *The Consumerist Manifesto: Advertising in Post Modern Times*. London: Routledge.

Debord, G. (1977) *The Society of the Spectacle*. Detroit: Red and Black.

de Simone, L.D. and Popoff, F. (1997) *EcoEfficiency: The Business Link to Sustainable Development*. Cambridge: The MIT Press.

Dion, K., Bersshied, E. and Walster, E. (1972) 'What is beautiful is good', *Journal of Personality and Social Psychology*, 24(3), 285–90.

Dittmar, H. (1992) *The Social Psychology of Material Possessions*. Hemel Hempstead: Harvester.

Docscha, S. and Ozanne, J. (2000) 'Marketing and the divided self: Healing the nature/woman separation'. In M. Catterall, P. Maclaren and L. Stevens (eds), *Marketing and Feminism*. London: Routledge.

Douglas, M. and Isherwood, B. (1979) *The World of Goods*. London: Routledge.

Eccles, S. and Woodruffe-Burton, H. (2000) 'Off to the shops: Why do we *really* go shopping?'. In M. Catterall, P. Maclaren, and L. Stevens (eds), *Marketing and Feminism*. London: Routledge.

Elliot, R. (1999) 'Symbolic meaning and post-modern consumer culture'. In D. Brownie, M. Saren, R. Wensley and R. Whittington (eds), *Rethinking Marketing: Towards Critical Marketing Accountings*. London: Sage.

Elliot, R., Eccles, S. and Gournay, K. (1996) 'Revenge, existential choice and addictive consumption', *Psychology and Marketing*, 13(8), 753–68.

Eysenbach, G. and Diepgen, T.L. (1998) 'Towards quality management of medical information on the Internet: Evaluation, labelling and filtering of information', *British Medical Journal*, 317, 1496–502.

Fiske, J. (1989) 'Commodities and culture'. In *Understanding Popular Culture*. London: Unwin Hyman.

Fornell, C. and Wernerfelt, B. (1988) 'A model for customer complaint management', *Marketing Science*, 7 (Summer), 271–86.

Fuat Firat, A. (1995) 'Consumer culture or culture consumed'. In J.A. Costa and G. Bamossy (eds), *Marketing in a Multicultural World*. California: Sage.

Fuat Firat, A., Dholakia, N. and Venkatesh, A. (1995) 'Marketing in a postmodern world', *European Journal of Marketing*, 29(1), 40–56.

Gabaix, X. and Laibson, D. (2000) 'A boundedly rational decision algorithm', *American Economic Review*, 90 (May) 433–38.

Gabriel, Y. and Lang, T. (1995) *The Unmanageable Consumer: Contemporary Consumption and its Fragmentation*. London: Sage Publications.

Goffman, E. (1959) *The Presentation of Self in Everyday Life*. Garden City, NY: Doubleday.

Golding, P. and Murdock, G. (1996) 'Culture, communications and political ecomony'. In J. Curran and M. Gurevitch (eds), *Mass Media and Society*. London: Arnold, pp. 11–30.

Goulding, C. (2000) 'The commodification of the past, postmodern pastiche and the search for authentic experiences at contemporary heritage attractions', *European Journal of Marketing*, 34(7), 835–53.

Gray, R. (2000) 'The changing face of women', *Marketing*, (May), 34–35.

Grogan, S. (1999) *Body Image: Understanding Body Dissatisfaction in Men, Women and Children*. London: Routledge.

Gummesson, E. (1998) 'Implementation requires a relationship marketing paradigm', *Journal of the Academy of Marketing Sciences*, 26 (Summer), 242–49.

Hart, G. (1998) 'The future's not what it once was', *Grocer*, 221 (April 11), 56.

Heskett, J.L., Jones, T.O., Loveman, G.W., Sasser, W.E. and Schlesinger, L.A. (1994) 'Putting the service-profit chain to work', *Harvard Business Review*, (March–April), 164–74.

Hibbert, S., Hogg, G. and Quinn, T. (2002) 'Consumer response to social entrepreneurship: The Big Issue in Scotland', *Journal of Nonprofit and Voluntary Sector Marketing*.

Hirshman, E. (1993) 'Ideology in consumer research, 1980 and 1990: A Marxist and feminist critique', *Journal of Consumer Research*, 19(4), 537–35.

Hogg, G. and Moore, C. (2001) *Banking for Young Professionals*, unpublished research report.

Hogg, M. and Michell, P. (1996) 'Identity, self and consumption: A conceptual framework', *Journal of Marketing Management*, 12, 629–44.

Holbrook, M. (1999) 'Commentary on reframing consumers'. In D. Brownie, M. Saren, R. Wensley and R. Whittington (eds), *Rethinking Marketing: Towards Critical Marketing Accountings*. London: Sage.

Holbrook, M. and Hirschman, E. (1982) 'The experiential aspects of consumption: Consumer feelings, fantasies and fun', *Journal of Consumer Research*, 9 (Sept), 132–40.

Howard, J. and Sheth, J. (1969) *The Theory of Buyer Behaviour*. New York: Wiley.

Howard, M. (2001) '21st-century consumer society', *Journal of Consumer Behaviour*, 1(1), 94–101.

Hunt, S. and Menon, A. (1993) 'Is it metaphor at work or is it metaphors, theories and models at work?'. In G. Laurent, G. Lilien and B. Pras (eds), *Research Traditions in Marketing*. Boston: Kluwer, pp. 426–32.

Iacobucci, D., Grayson, K. and Ostrom, A. (1994) 'Customer satisfaction fables', *Sloan Management Review*, 35 (Summer), 93–96.

Jacoby, J., Speller, D. and Kohn, C. (1974) 'Brand choice behaviour as a function of information overload', *Journal of Marketing Research*, (11), 63–69.

Jadad, A. (1998) 'Promoting partnerships: challenges for the internet age', *British Medical Journal*, 319, 761–64.

Jones, T.O. and Sasser Jr., W.E. (1995) 'Why satisfied customers defect', *Harvard Business Review*, November/December, 88–99.

Karakaya, F. and Charlton, E. (2001) 'Electronic commerce: current and future practices', *Managerial Finance*, 27(7), 42–53.

Kaufman, C., Lane, P. and Linquist, J. (1991) 'Exploring more than 24 hours a day: Polychronic time use', *Journal of Consumer Research*, 18 (December), 392–401.

Keaney, M. (1999) 'Are patients really consumers?', *International Journal of Social Economics*, 26(5), 695–706.

Kilbourne, W.E. and Beckmann, S. (1998) 'Review and critical assessment of research on marketing and the environment', *Journal of Marketing Management*, 14(6), 513–32.

Kirkpatrick, D. (1990) 'Environmentalism', *Fortune*, February 12, 44–51.

Knights, D. and Odih, P. (1999) It's a matter of time: The significance of the women's market in consumption'. In D. Brownie, M. Saren, R. Wensley and R. Whittington (eds), *Rethinking Marketing: Towards Critical Marketing Accountings*. London: Sage.

Kress, K., Ozawa, N. and Schmid, G. (2000) 'The new consumer emerges', *Strategy and Leadership*, 28(5) Sept/Oct, 4–7.

Laermans, R. (1993) 'Learning to consumer: Early department stores and the shaping of modern consumer culture', *Theory Culture and Society*, 10(4), 79–102.

Laroche, M., Saad, G., Cleveland, M. and Brown, E. (2000) 'Gender differences in information search strategies for a Christmas gift', *Journal of Consumer Marketing*, 17(6), 500–24.

Lee, M. (2000) *The Consumer Society Reader*. Oxford: Blackwell.

Levitt, T. (1960) 'Marketing myopia', *Harvard Business Review*, (July/Aug), 45–56.

Loewenstein, G. (2001) 'The creative destruction of decision research', *Journal of Consumer Research*, 28(3), 499–505.

Lovelock, C. (1994) *Product Plus: How Product + Service = Competitive Advantage*. New York: McGraw-Hill.

Mazur, L. (2002) 'Internet has put convenience on consumer's list', *Marketing*, 10 (Jan) 16.

McCracken, G. (1988) *Culture and Consumption: New Approaches to the Symbolic Character of Consumer Goods and Activities*. Bloomington: Indiana University Press.

McDaniel, S.W. and Rylander, D.H. (1993) 'Strategic green marketing', *Journal of Consumer Marketing*, 10(3), 4–10.

McGrath, M.A., Sherry, J. and Heisley, D. (1993) 'An ethnographic study of an urban periodic marketplace: lessons from the Midville Farmers Market', *Journal of Retailing*, 69(3).

McKendrick, N., Brewer, J. and Plumb, J.H. (1982) *The Birth of a Consumer Society: The Commercialisation of Eighteenth–Century England*. London: Europa Pubs.

Miller, D., Jackson, P., Thrift, N., Holbrook, B. and Rowlands, M. (1998) *Shopping, Place and Identity*. London: Routledge.

Mintel (2000) *2020 Vision: Tomorrow's Consumer*. Mintel International Group Ltd.

Moore, C., Doyle, S. and Thomson, E. (2001) 'Til shopping us do part – the service requirements of divorced male fashion shoppers', *International Journal of Retail and Distribution Management*.

Mukerji, C. (1983) *From Graven Images: Patterns of Modern Materialism*. New York: Columbia University Press.

Muniz Jr, A. and O'Guinn, T. (2001) 'Brand community', *Journal of Consumer Research*, 27 (March), 412–32.

Nava, M. (1996) 'Modernity's disavowal: women and the department store', *Modern Times: Reflections on a Century of English Modernity*. London: Routledge.

Nicosia, F. (1966) *Consumer Decision Processes: Marketing and Advertising Implications*. Englewood Cliffs: Prentice Hall.

O'Guinn, T. and Faber, R. (1989) 'Compulsive buying: a phenomenological exploration', *Journal of Consumer Research*, 16(2), 147–57.

Oliver, R.L. (1993) 'A conceptual model of service quality and service satisfaction: compatible goals, different concepts'. In S. Brown, T. Swartz and Bowen (eds), *Advances in Services Marketing and Management Volume 2*. JAI Press, pp. 65–85.

Otnes, C. and McGrath, M.A. (2001) 'Perceptions and realities of male shopping behaviour', *Journal of Retailing*, 77, 111–37.

Ottman, J. (1998) *Green Marketing: Opportunities for Innovation*. Lincolnwood: NTC Business Books.

Palmer, A. (2002) 'The role of selfishness in buyer–seller relationships', *Marketing Intelligence and Planning*, 20(1), 22–27.

Peters, T. and Waterman, R. (1982) *In Search of Excellence*. New York: Harper Row.

Popcorn, F. (2001) *Eve-olution: The Eight Truths of Marketing to Women*. London: Harper Collins.

Quazi, A. (2002) 'Managerial views of consumerism: A two-country comparison', *European Journal of Marketing*, 36(1/2), 36–50.

Reichheld, F.F. and Teal, T. (1996) *The Loyalty Effect: The Hidden Force behind Growth, Profits, and Lasting Value*. Boston, MA: Harvard Business School Press.

Ridderstrale, J. and Nordstrom, K. (2000) *Funky Business*. London: Pearson.

Roberts, J.A. (1996) 'Green consumers in the 1990s: profiles and implications for advertising', *Journal of Business Research*, 26(2), 217–31.

Roper Organisation (1990) 'The environment: Public attitudes and individual behaviour'. In A. Iyer and B. Banerjee (1993) 'Anatomy of green advertising', *Advances in Consumer Research*, 20, 494–501.

Ross, L. and Nisbett, R. (1991) *The Person and the Situation: Perspectives of Social Psychology*. Philadelphia: Temple University Press.

Rust, R.T., Zahorik, A.J. and Keiningham, T.L. (1995) 'Return on quality (ROQ): Making service quality financially accountable', *Journal of Marketing*, 59 (April), 58–70.

Sampson, P. (1993) 'A better way to measure brand image', *Admap*, 27(7) (July–Aug), 19–24.

Schiffman, L.G., Kanuk, L.L. (2000) *Consumer Behaviour*. USA: Prentice Hall.

Schouten, J.W. and Alexander, J. (1995) 'Subcultures of consumption: An ethnography of the new bikers', *Journal of Consumer Research*, 22 (June), 43–52.

Shaw, D. and Clarke, I. (1999) 'Belief formation in ethical consumer groups: An exploratory study', *Marketing Intelligence and Planning*, 17(2).

Slater, D. (1997) *Consumer Culture and Modernity*. Cambridge: Polity Press.

Solomon, M., Bamossy, G. and Askegaard, S. (1999) *Consumer Behaviour: A European Perspective*. London: Prentice Hall.

South, S.J. and Spitze, G. (1994) 'Housework in marital and non-marital households', *American Sociology Review*, 59 (June), 327–47.

Stevenson, I. (1998) 'Report – digital television', referenced in *Clicks and Mortar Report of the Retail e-commerce Task Force of the Retail and Consumer Services Foresight Panel, 2000*. Department of Trade and Industry.

Sturrock, F. and Pioch, E. (1998) 'Making himself attractive: The growing consumption of grooming products', *Marketing Intelligence and Planning*, 16(5), 337–43.

Underhill, P. (1999) *Why We Buy: The Science of Shopping*. London: Orion Business.

Veblen, T. (1899/1925) *The Theory of the Leisure Classes: An Economic Study of Institutions*. London: Allen and Unwin.

Ward, M. and Lee, M. (2000) 'Internet shopping, consumer search and product branding', *Journal of Product and Brand Management*, 9(1), 6–20.

Watt, G. (2001) 'Policies to tackle social exclusion', *British Medical Journal*, 323, 7306, 00 (July 28), 175–76.

Watt, G. and Ecob, R. (2000) 'Analysis of falling mortality rates in Edinburgh and Glasgow', *Public Health Medicine*, 22, 330–6.

Which? Online Annual Survey (1998) http://www.which.com/nonsub/speacial/ipsurvey

Wilson, A. (1994) *Emancipating the Professions*. Chichester: John Wiley and Sons.

Woodruffe, H. (1997a) 'Eschatology, promise, hope: the utopian vision of consumer', *European Journal of Marketing*, 31(9/10), 667–76.

Woodruffe, H.R. (1997b) 'Compensatory consumption (or why women go shopping when they are fed-up?)', *Marketing Intelligence and Planning*, 15(7), 325–34.

Yu, Y.-T. and Dean, A. (2001) 'The contribution of emotional satisfaction to consumer loyalty', *International Journal of Service Industry Management*, 12(3).

Zeithaml, V., Parasuraman, A. and Berry, L. (1990) *Delivering Quality Service*. New York: Collier Macmillan.

Further reading

BBC (1995) *People and Programmes: BBC Radio and Television for and Age of Choice*. London: British Broadcasting Corporation.

Bouchet, D. (1995) 'Marketing and the redefinition of ethnicity'. In J.A. Costa and G. Bamossy (eds), *Marketing in a Multicultural World*. California: Sage.

Clicks and Mortar: Report of the Retail e-commerce Task Force of the Retail and Consumer Services Foresight Panel (2000). Department of Trade and Industry.

Dholakia, R.R., Pederson, B. and Hikmet, N. (1995) 'Married males and shopping – are they sleeping partners?', *International Journal of Retail and Distribution Management*, 23(3), 27–33.

Foxall, G.R., Goldsmith, R.E. and Brown, S. (1998) *Consumer Psychology*. London: Thomson Learning.

Laing, A. and Hogg, G. (2002) Political exhortation, patient expectation and professional execution: perspectives on the consumerisation of healthcare, *British Journal of Management*.

Mintel (2001) *British Lifestyles 2001*. Mintel International Group Ltd.

Chapter 4

Camuffo, A., Romano, P. and Vinelli, A. (2001) 'Back to the future: Benetton transforms its global network', *MIT Sloan Management Review*, Fall, 46–52.

Christopher, M. (1997) *Marketing Logistics*. Oxford: Butterworth-Heineman.

Christopher, M. and Peck, H. (1998) 'Fashion Logistics'. In J. Fernie and L. Sparks (eds), *Logistics and Retail Management*. London: Kogan Page.

Coopers & Lybrand (1996) *European Value Chain Analysis Study – Final Report*. Utrecht: ECR Europe.

Cox, A. (1996) 'Relationship competence and strategic procurement management. Towards an entrepreneurial and contractual theory of the firm', *European Journal of Purchasing and Supply Management*, 2(1), 57–70.

Department of Trade & Industry (DTI) (2001) *@ Your Home, New Markets for Customer Service and Delivery*, Retail Logistics Task Force. London: Foresight.

Fernie, J. (1990) *Retail Distribution Management*. London: Kogan Page.

Fernie, J., Pfab, F. and Marchant, C. (2000) 'Retail grocery logistics in the UK', *International Journal of Logistics Management*, 11(2): 83–90.

Fernie, J. and Sparks, L. (1998) *Logistics and Retail Management*. London: Kogan Page.

Fiddis, C. (1997) *Manufacturer–Retailer Relationships in the Food and Drink Industry. Strategies and Tactics in the Battle for Power*, FT Retail and Consumer Publishing. London: Pearson Professional.

Harrison, A., Christopher, M. and van Hoek, R. (1999) *Creating the Agile Supply Chain*. Corby: Institute of Logistics and Transport.

Kurt Salmon Associates (1993) *Efficient Consumer Value in the Supply Chain*. Washington DC: Kurt Salmon.

Laseter, T., Houston, P., Ching, A., Byrne, S., Turner, M. and Devendran, A. (2000) 'The last mile to nowhere', *Strategy & Business*, 20 (September).

McKinnon, A.C. (1989) *Physical Distribution Systems*. London: Routledge.

Porter, M. (1985) *Competitive Advantage: Creating and Sustaining Superior Performance*. New York: Free Press.

Punakivi, M. and Saranen, J. (2001) 'Identifying the success factors in e-grocery home delivery', *International Journal of Retail & Distribution Management*, 29(4), 427–39.

Punakivi, M. and Tanskanen, K. (2002) 'Increasing the cost efficiency of e-fulfilment using shared reception boxes', *International Journal of Retail & Distribution Management*, 30, forthcoming.

Punakivi, M., Yrjola, H. and Holmstrom, J. (2001) 'Solving the last mile issue: Reception box or delivery box', *International Journal of Physical Distribution and Logistics Management*, 31(6), 427–39.

Ring, L.J. and Tigert, D.J. (2001) 'Viewpoint: the decline and fall of Internet grocery retailers', *International Journal of Retail & Distribution Management*, 29(6), 266–73.

Verdict Research (2000) *Electronic Shopping, UK*. London: Verdict.

Williamson, O.E. (1979) 'Transaction cost economics: The governance of contractural relations', *Journal of Law and Economics*, 22 (October), 223–61.

Womack, J.P., Jones, D. and Roos, D. (1990) *The Machine that Changed the World: The Story of Lean Production*. New York: Harper-Collins.

Further reading

Ford, D. (2001) *Understanding Business Marketing & Purchasing: Interaction, Relationships, Networks*, 3rd ed. London: Thomson Learning.

Slack, N., Chambers, S., Harland, S. C., Harrison, A. and Johnson, R. (1988) *Operations Management* (2nd ed.). London: Pitman Publishing.

Yryola, M., Tanskanen, K. and Holmstron, J. (2002) 'The way to profitable Internet grocery retailing – 6 lessons learned', *International Journal of Retail & Distribution Management*, 30, forthcoming.

Chapter 5

Ackoff, R.L. (1999) *Recreating the Corporation: A Design of Organizations for the 21st Century*. London: Oxford University Press.

Addelson, M. (2001) 'What is a Learning Organization', online copy of a series of perspectives on organizational learning available at: www.psol.gmu.edu/psol/perspectives.nsf

Adler, P.S. and Cole, R.E. (1993) 'Designed for learning: a tale of two auto plants', *Sloan Management Review*, 34 (Spring), 85–94.

Alderson, W. and Cox, R. (1948) 'Towards a theory of marketing', *Journal of Marketing*, 13 (October), 137–52.

Anderson, P.F. (1982) 'Marketing, strategic planning and the theory of the firm', *Journal of Marketing*, 46 (Spring), 15–26.

Argyris, C. and Schön, D.A. (1978) *Organizational Learning: A Theory of Action Perspective*. Reading, MA: Addison-Wesley.

Atuahene-Gima, K. (1996) 'An exploratory analysis of the impact of market orientation on new product performance', *Journal of Product Innovation Management*, 12, 275–93.

Bacharach, S.B. (1989) 'Organizational theories: some criteria for evaluation', *Academy of Management Review*, 14(4), 496–515.

Bagozzi, R.P. (1984) 'A prospectus for theory construction in marketing', *Journal of Marketing*, 48 (Winter), 11–29.

Baker, W.E. and Sinkula, J.M. (1999a) 'Learning orientation, market orientation and innovation: integrating and extending models of organizational performance', *Journal of Market Focused Management*, 4, 295–308.

Baker, W.E. and Sinkula, J.M. (1999b) 'The synergistic effect of market orientation and learning orientation on organizational performance', *Journal of the Academy of Marketing Science*, 27(4), 411–27.

Barney, J.B. (1991) 'Firm resources and sustained competitive advantage', *Journal of Management*, 17, 99–120.

Bartels, R. (1951) 'Can marketing be a science?', *Journal of Marketing*, 15 (January), 319–28.

Bartels, R. (1974) 'The identity crisis in marketing', *Journal of Marketing*, 38 (October), 73–76.

Beeby, M. and Booth, C. (2000) 'Networks and inter-organisational learning: A critical review', *The Learning Organisation*, 7(2), 75–88.

Bentley, K. (1990) 'A discussion of the link between one organization's style and structure and its connection with its market', *Journal of Product Innovation Management*, 7, 19–37.

Bharadwaj, S.G., Varadarajan, P.R. and Fahy, J. (1993) 'Sustainable competitive advantage in service industries: A conceptual model and research propositions', *Journal of Marketing*, 57 (October), 83–99.

Bogner, W.C. and Barr, P.S. (2000) 'Making sense in hypercompetitive environments: A cognitive explanation for the persistence of high velocity competition', *Organisation Science*, 11(2), 212–26.

Boussouara, M. and Deakins, D. (1999) 'Market-based learning, entrepreneurship and the high-technology small firm', *International Journal of Entrepreneurial Behaviour and Research*, 5(4), 204–23.

Brews, P.J. and Hunt, M.R. (1999) 'Learning to plan and planning to learn: Resolving the planning school/learning school debate', *Strategic Management Journal*, 20, 889–913.

Cangelosi, V.E. and Dill, W.R. (1965) 'Organizational learning: Observations toward a theory', *Administrative Science Quarterly*, 10(2), 175–203.

Caplan, N., Morrison, A. and Stambaugh, R.J. (1975) *The Use of Social Science Knowledge in Policy Decisions at the National Level*. Ann Arbor, Mi: Institute for Social Science Research.

Cartwright, T.J. (1991) 'Planning and chaos theory', *Journal of the American Planning Association*, 57(1), 44–56.

Chaston, I., Badger, B. and Sadler-Smith, E. (2000) 'Organizational learning style and competences: A comparative investigation of relationship and transactionally-oriented small UK manufacturing firms, *European Journal of Marketing*, 34(5/6), 625–40.

Cohen, B. (1980) *Developing Sociological Knowledge: Theory and Method*. Englewood Cliffs, NJ: Prentice-Hall.

Cohen, M.D. and Levinthal, D.A. (1990) 'Absorptive capacity: A new perspective on learning and innovation', *Administrative Science Quarterly*, 35, 128–52.

Cohen, M.D. and Sproull, L.S. (1991) 'Organisational learning', *Organisation Science*, 2(1), ii–iv.

Courtney, H., Kirkland, J. and Viguerie, P. (1997) 'Strategy under uncertainty', *Harvard Business Review*, 75 (November–December), 67–79.

Crossan, M.M., Lane, H.W. and White, R.E. (1999) 'An organizational learning framework: From intuition to institution', *Academy of Management Review*, 24(3), 522–37.

Cummings, T.G. and Worley, C.G. (1997) *Organisational Development and Change*. Cincinnati, OH: South-Western College Publishing.

Cyert, R.M. and March, J.G. (1963) *A Behavioural Theory of the Firm*. Englewood Cliffs, NJ: Prentice-Hall.

Daft, R.M. and Weick, K.E. (1984) 'Toward a Model of Organizations as Interpretation Systems', *Academy of Management Review*, 9 (April), 284–95.

Damanpour, F. (1991) 'Organizational innovation: A meta-analysis of effects of determinants and moderators', *Academy of Management Journal*, 34 (September), 555–90.

Davenport, T.H. and Prusak, L. (2000) *Working Knowledge: How Organizations Manage What They Know*. Boston, MA: Harvard Business School Press.

Day, G.S. (1994a) 'The capabilities of market-driven organisations', *Journal of Marketing*, 58 (October), 37–52.

Day, G.S. (1994b) 'Continuous learning about markets', *California Management Review*, 36(Summer): 9–31.

Day, G.S. (1997) 'Aligning the organization to the market'. In D.R. Lehman and K.E. Jocz (eds), *Reflections on the Future of Marketing*. Cambridge, MA: Marketing Science Institute, pp. 67–93.

Day, G.S. and Nedungadi, P. (1994), 'Managerial representations of competitive advantage', *Journal of Marketing*, 58 (April), 31–44.

Day, G.S. and Wensley, R. (1983) 'Marketing theory with a strategic orientation', *Journal of Marketing*, 47 (Fall), 79–89.

Dean, J.W. and Sharfman, M.P. (1993) 'Procedural rationality in the decision making process', *Journal of Management Studies*, 30(4), 587–610.

DeCarolis, D.M. and Deeds, D.L. (1999) 'The impact of stocks and flows of organizational knowledge on firm performance: An empirical investigation of the biotechnology industry', *Strategic Management Journal*, 20, 953–68.

Deligönül, Z.S. and Çavuşgil, S.T. (1997) 'Does the comparative advantage theory of competition really replace the neoclassical theory of perfect competition', *Journal of Marketing*, 61 (October), 65–73.

Deshpandé, R. (1983) 'Paradigms lost: On theory and method in research in marketing', *Journal of Marketing*, 47 (Fall), 101–10.

Deshpandé, R. Farley, J.U. and Webster, F.E. (1993) 'Corporate culture, customer orientation and innovativeness in Japanese firms: a quadrad analysis', *Journal of Marketing*, 55(1), 23–73.

Deshpandé, R. and Webster, F.E. (1989) 'Organizational culture and marketing: Defining the research agenda', *Journal of Marketing*, 53, 3–15.

Deshpandé, R. and Zaltman, G. (1982) 'Factors affecting the use of market research information: A path analysis', *Journal of Marketing Research*, 19 (February), 14–31.

DiBella, A.J. (1995) 'Developing learning organizations: A matter of perspective', paper presented at the *Academy of Management Conference*, Vancouver.

Dickson, P.R. (1996) 'The static and dynamic mechanics of competition: A comment on Hunt and Morgan's comparative advantage theory', *Journal of Marketing*, 60 (October), 102–06.

Dickson, P.R., Farris, P.W. and Verbeke, W.J.M.I. (2001) 'Dynamic strategic thinking', *Journal of the Academy of Marketing Science*, 29(3), 216–37.

Dixon, N. (1994) *The Organisational Learning Cycle: How We Can Learn Collectively*. Maidenhead: McGraw-Hill.

Dodgson, M. (1993) 'Organisational learning: A review of some literatures', *Organisation Studies*, 14(3), 375–94.

Dubin, R. (1978) *Theory Building*. New York: The Free Press.

Easley, R.W., Madden, C.S. and Dunn, M.G. (2000) 'Conducting marketing science: The role of replication in the research process', *Journal of Business Research*, 48, 83–92.

Easterby-Smith, M. (1997) 'Disciplines of organisational learning: Contributions and critiques', *Human Relations*, 50(9), 1085–1113.

Edmondson, A.C. (1996) 'Learning from mistakes is easier said than done: Group and organizational influences on the detection and correction of human error', *Journal of Applied Behavioural Science*, 32(1), 5–28.

Fiol, C.M. and Lyles, M.A. (1985) 'Organisational learning', *Academy of Management Review*, 10(4), 803–13.

Garvin, D.A. (1993) 'Building a learning organisation', *Harvard Business Review*, 71 (July–August), 78–91.

Gerbing, D.W., Hamilton, J.G. and Freeman, E.B. (1994) 'A large-scale second-order structural equation model of the influence of management participation on organisational planning benefits', *Journal of Management*, 20(4), 859–85.

Gherardi, S. (1999) 'Learning as problem driven or learning in the face of mystery?', *Organisation Studies*, Winter.

Goh, S. and Richards, G. (1997) 'Benchmarking the learning capability of organisations', *European Management Journal*, 15(5), 575–83.

Goll, I. and Rasheed, A.M.A. (1997) 'Rational decision making and firm performance: The moderating role of environment', *Strategic Management Journal*, 18, 583–91.

Grant, R.M. (1996a) 'Prospering in dynamically-competitive environments: Organisational capability as knowledge integration', *Organisation Science*, 7, 375–87.

Grant, R.M. (1996b) 'Toward a knowledge-based theory of the firm', *Strategic Management Journal*, 17 (Special Issue), 109–22.

Greenley, G.E. (1995) 'Market orientation and company performance: Empirical evidence from UK companies', *British Journal of Management*, 6, 1–13.

Gummesson, E. (2001) 'Are current research approaches in marketing leading us astray', *Marketing Theory*, 1(1), 27–48.

Halbert, M. (1964) 'The Requirements for Theory in Marketing'. In R. Cox, W. Alderson and S.J. Shapiro (eds), *Theory in Marketing*. Homewood, Il: Irwin, 17–36.

Hamel, G. and Prahalad, C.K. (1994) *Competing for the Future*. Boston, Ma: Harvard Business School Press.

Handy, C. (1990) *The Age of Unreason*. Boston, MA: Harvard Business School Press.

Hansen, M.T., Nohria, N. and Tierney, T. (1999) 'What's your strategy for managing knowledge?' *Harvard Business Review*, 77 (March–April), 106–16.

Hart, S. (1992) 'An integrative framework for strategy making processes', *Academy of Management Review*, 17, 327–51.

Harvey, C. and Denton, J. (1999) 'To come of age: The antecedents of organisational learning', *Journal of Management Studies*, 36(7), 897–916.

Hedberg, B. (1981) 'How organisations learn and unlearn'. In P.C. Nystrom and W.H. Starbuck (eds), *Handbook of Organisational Design*. London: Oxford University Press, 8–27.

Homburg, C., Workman, J.P. and Jensen, O. (2000) 'Fundamental changes in marketing organisation: The movement toward a customer-focused organisational structure', *Journal of the Academy of Marketing Science*, 28(4), 459–78.

Homburg, C., Workman, J.P. and Krohmer, H. (1999) 'Marketing's influence within the firm', *Journal of Marketing*, 63 (April), 1–17.

Houston, F.S. (1986) 'The marketing concept: What it is and what it is not', *Journal of Marketing*, 50, 81–87.

Howard, D.G., Savins, D.M., Howell, W. and Ryans, J.K. (1991) 'The evolution of marketing theory in the United States and Europe', *European Journal of Marketing*, 25(2), 7–16.

Hubbard, R., Vetter, D.E. and Little, E.L. (1998) 'Replication in strategic management: Scientific testing for validity, generalisability and usefulness', *Strategic Management Journal*, 19, 243–54.

Huber, G.P. (1991) 'Organisational learning: The contributing processes and the literatures', *Organisation Science*, 2, 88–115.

Hunt, S.D. (1983) *Marketing Theory: The Philosophy of Marketing Science*. Homewood, Il: Irwin.

Hunt, S.D. (1990) 'Truth in marketing theory and research', *Journal of Marketing*, 54 (July), 1–15.

Hunt, S.D. and Lambe, C.J. (2000) 'Marketing's contribution to business strategy formation: Market orientation, relationship marketing and resource advantage theory', *International Journal of Management Reviews*, 2(1), 17–43.

Hunt, S.D. and Morgan, R.M. (1995) 'The comparative advantage theory of competition', *Journal of Marketing*, 59 (April), 1–15.

Hunt, S.D. and Morgan, R.M. (1997) 'Resource-advantage theory: A snake swallowing its tail or a general theory of competition', *Journal of Marketing*, 61 (October), 74–82.

Hurley, R.F. and Hult, G.T.M. (1998) 'Innovation, market orientation and organisational learning: An integration and empirical examination', *Journal of Marketing*, 62 (July), 42–54.

Jackson, S. and Schuler, R.L. (2001) 'Turning knowledge into business', *Financial Times*, 'Mastering Management' supplement, January 15, 12–13.

Jaworski, B.J. and Kohli, A.K. (1993) 'Market orientation: Antecedents and consequences', *Journal of Marketing*, 57(3), 53–70.

Jaworski, B.J. and Kohli, A.K. (1996) 'Market orientation: Review, refinement and roadmap', *Journal of Market Focused Management*, 1(2), 119–35.

Jones, A.M. and Hendry, C. (1994) 'The learning organisation: Adult learning and organisational transformation', *British Journal of Management*, 5, 153–62.

Kelley, D. and Amburgey, T.L. (1991) 'Organisational inertia and momentum: A dynamic model of strategic change', *Academy of Management Journal*, 34(3), 591–612.

Khanna, T., Gulati, R. and Nohria, N. (1998) 'The dynamics of learning alliances: Competition, cooperation and relative scope', *Strategic Management Journal*, 19, 193–210.

Kilmann, R.H. (1996) 'Management learning organisations: Enhancing business education for the 21st century', *Management Learning*, 27(2), 203–38.

Kluge, J., Stein, W. and Licht, T. (2001) *Knowledge Unplugged: The McKinsey & Company Global Survey on Knowledge Management*. New York: Palgrave.

Kock, N.F., McQueen, R.J. and Corner, J.L. (1997) 'The nature of data, information and knowledge exchanges in business processes: Implications for process improvement and organisational learning', *The Learning Organisation*, 4(2), 70–80.

Kohli, A.K. and Jaworski, B.J. (1990) 'Market orientation: The construct, research propositions and management implications', *Journal of Marketing*, 52(2), 1–18.

Kohli, A.K., Jaworski, B.J. and Kumar, A. (1993) 'MARKOR: A measure of market orientation', *Journal of Marketing Research*, 30 (November), 467–77.

Kolb, D.A. (1984) *Experiential Learning: Experience as the Source of Learning and Development*. Englewood Cliffs, NJ: Prentice-Hall.

Kyriakopoulos, K. (2000) *The Market Orientation of Cooperative Organisations*. The Netherlands: The Netherlands Institute for Cooperative Entrepreneurship, Nyenrode University.

Levitt, B. and March, J.G. (1988) 'Organisational Learning', *Annual Review of Sociology*, 14: 319–40.

Lei, D., Hitt, M.A. and Bettis, R. (1996) 'Dynamic core competence through meta-learning and strategic context', *Journal of Management*, 22(4), 549–69.

Li, T. and Calantone, R. (1998) 'The impact of market knowledge competence on new product advantage: Conceptualisation and empirical examination', *Journal of Marketing*, 62 (October), 13–29.

Li, T., Nicholls, J.A.F. and Roslow, S. (1999) 'The relationship between market-driven learning and new product success in export markets', *International Marketing Review*, 16(6), 476–503.

Lukas, B.A., Hult, G.T.M. and Ferrell, O.C. (1996) 'A theoretical perspective of the antecedents and consequences of organisational learning in marketing channels', *Journal of Business Research*, 36, 233–44.

Lyles, M.A. and Lenz, R.T. (1982) 'Managing the planning process: A field study of the human side of planning', *Strategic Management Journal*, 3, 105–18.

Malhotra, Y. (1996) 'Organisational learning and learning organisations: An overview', online copy available at: www.brint.com/papers/orglrng.htm

Marketing Science Institute (1998) *Research Priorities 1998–2000*. Cambridge, MA: Marketing Science Institute.

McKean, J. (1999) *Information Masters: Secrets of the Customer Race*. Chichester: Wiley.

McKenna, R. (1991) 'Marketing is everything', *Harvard Business Review*, 69, January–February), 65–79.

McNaughton, R., Osborne, P., Morgan, R.E. and Kutwaroo, G. (2001) 'Market orientation and firm value,' *Journal of Marketing Management*, 17(5–6), 521–42.

Menon, A. and Varadarajan, P.R. (1992) 'A model of market knowledge use within firms', *Journal of Marketing*, 56 (October), 53–71.

Miner, A.S. and Mezias, S.J. (1996) 'Ugly duckling no more: Pasts and futures of organisational learning research', *Organisation Science*, 7(1), 88–99.

Moorman, C. (1995) 'Organisational market information processes: Cultural antecedents and new product outcomes', *Journal of Marketing Research*, 32 (August), 318–35.

Moorman, C., Kyriakopoulos, K. and Wallman, J.P. (2000) 'Market learning in organisations: A typology and propositions', working paper, Fuqua School of Business, Duke University, Durham, NC.

Moorman, C. and Rust, R.T. (1999) 'The role of marketing', *Journal of Marketing*, 63, Special Issue, 180–97.

Morgan, R.E. and Chimhanzi, J. (2001) 'Dimensions of organisational learning and business performance: Cognitive and behavioural perspectives'. In E. Harlan, H. Spotts, L.

Meadows and S.M. Smith (eds), *On Global Marketing Issues at The Turn of the Millennium*, Proceedings of the Tenth Biennial Academy of Marketing Science World Congress, University of Miami. Miami, Fl.

Morgan, R.E. and Hunt, S.D. (2002) 'Determining marketing strategy: A cybernetic systems approach to scenario planning', *European Journal of Marketing*, forthcoming.

Morgan, R.E., Katsikeas, C.S and Appiah-Adu, K. (1998) 'Market orientation and organisational learning capabilities', *Journal of Marketing Management*, 14, 353–81.

Morgan, R.E., McGuinness, A. and Thorpe, E.R. (2000) 'The contribution of marketing to business strategy formation: A perspective on business performance gains,' *Journal of Strategic Marketing*, 8, 341–62.

Morgan, R.E. and Strong, C.A. (1998) 'Market orientation and dimensions of strategic orientation', *European Journal of Marketing*, 32(11/12), 1051–73.

Morgan, R.E. and Turnell, C.R. (2001) 'Market-based organisational learning: Business performance gains in financial services organisations', working paper, School of Management and Business, University of Wales Aberystwyth, Aberystwyth.

Mutch, A. (1999) 'Critical realism, managers and information', *British Journal of Management*, 10, 323–33.

Narver, J.C. and Slater, S.F. (1990) 'The effect of a market orientation on business profitability', *Journal of Marketing*, 52(3), 20–35.

Nonaka, I. (1994) 'A dynamic theory of organisational knowledge creation', *Organisation Science*, 5, 14–37.

Nonaka, I. (1996) 'The knowledge creating company'. In K. Starkey (ed.), *How Organisations Learn*. London: Thomson Learning, 18–42.

Pelham, A. and Wilson, D.T. (1996) 'A longitudinal study of the impact of market structure, firm structure, strategy and market orientation culture on dimensions of performance', *Journal of the Academy of Marketing Science*, 24, 27–43.

Pfeffer, J. and Salancik, G.R. (1978) *The External Control of Organisations: A Resource Dependence Perspective*. New York: Harper and Row.

Polito, A. (1995) 'Toward an interdisciplinary theory of organisational learning', unpublished paper, Department of Management, Terry College of Business, University of Georgia, Atlanta, Ga.

Popper, M. and Lipshitz, R. (2000) 'Organisational learning: Mechanisms, culture and feasibility', *Management Learning*, 3(2), 181–96.

Priem, R.L., Rasheed, A.M.A. and Kotulic, A.G. (1995) 'Rationality in strategic decision processes, environmental dynamism and firm performance', *Journal of Management*, 21, 913–29.

Probst, G., Raub, S. and Romhardt, K. (2000) *Managing Knowledge: Building Blocks for Success*. New York: Wiley.

Quinn, J.B. (1980) *Strategies for Change: Logical Incrementalism*. Homewood, IL: Irwin.

Ramanujam, V. and Venkatraman, N. (1987) 'Planning system characteristics and planning effectiveness', *Strategic Management Journal*, 8, 453–68.

Reichardt, C.S. and Cook, T.D. (1979) 'Beyond qualitative versus quantitative methods'. In T.D. Cook and C.S. Reichardt (eds), *Qualitative and Quantitative Methods in Evaluation Research*. Beverly Hills, Ca: Sage, pp. 7–32.

Rubinstein, M.F. and Firstenberg, I.R. (1999) *The Minding Organisation: Bring the Future to the Present and Turn Creative Ideas into Business Solutions*. New York: Wiley.

Ruekert, R.W. (1992) 'Developing a market orientation: An organisational strategy perspective', *International Journal of Research in Marketing*, 9, 225–45.

Schein, E.H. (1996) 'Culture: The missing concept in organisation studies', *Administrative Science Quarterly*, 41, 229–40.

Schwenk, C. (1995) 'Strategic decision making', *Journal of Management*, 21(3), 471–93.

Senge, P.M. (1990) *The Fifth Discipline: The Art and Practice of the Learning Organisation*. New York: Doubleday/Currency.

Senge, P.M., Roberts, C., Ross, R., Smith, B. and Kleiner, A. (1995) *The Fifth Discipline Fieldbook: Strategies for Building Learning Organisations*. New York: Doubleday Dell.

Sheth, J.G., Gardner, D.M. and Garrett, D.E. (1988) *Marketing Theory: Evolution and Evaluation*. New York: John Wiley and Sons.

Sinkula, J.M. (1994) 'Market information processing and organisational learning', *Journal of Marketing*, 58 (January), 35–45.

Sinkula, J.M., Baker, W.E. and Noordewier, T. (1997) 'A framework for market-based organisational learning: Linking values, knowledge and behaviour', *Journal of the Academy of Marketing Science*, 25(4), 305–18.

Slater, S.F. and Narver, J.C. (1994) 'Does competitive environment moderate the market orientation-performance relationship', *Journal of Marketing*, 58 (January), 46–55.

Slater, S.F. and Narver, J.C. (1995) 'Market orientation and the learning organisation', *Journal of Marketing*, 59 (July), 63–74.

Slocum, J.W., McGill, M. and Lei, D.T. (1994) 'The new learning strategy: Anytime, anywhere, anyplace', *Organisational Dynamics*, 23(2), 33–47.

Spender, J.-C. and Grant, R.M. (1996) 'Knowledge and the firm: overview', *Strategic Management Journal*, 17 (Winter special issue), 5–9.

Sugarman, B. (2001) 'The learning organisation and organisational learning: New roles for workers, managers, trainers and consultants', online copy available at: www.lesley.edu/faculty/sugarman

Sujan, H., Weitz, B. and Kumar, N. (1994) 'Learning orientation, working smart and effective selling', *Journal of Marketing*, 58(3), 39–52.

Ulrich, D. and Lake, D. (1990) *Organisational Capability*. New York: Wiley.

Van den Bosch, F.A.J., Volberda, H.W. and de Boer, M. (1999) 'Coevolution of firm absorptive capacity and knowledge environment: Organisational forms and combinative capabilities', *Organisation Science*, 10(5), 551–68.

Varadarjan, P.R. (1999) 'Strategy content and process perspectives revisited', *Journal of the Academy of Marketing Science*, 27 (Winter), 88–100.

Varadarajan, P.R. and Clark, T. (1994) 'Delineating the scope of corporate, business and marketing strategy', *Journal of Business Research*, 31(2–3), 93–105.

Varadarjan, P.R. and Jayachandran, S. (1999) 'Marketing strategy: An assessment of the state of the field and outlook', *Journal of the Academy of Marketing Science*, 28 (Spring), 120–43.

Vorhies, D.W. (1998) 'An investigation of the factors leading to the development of marketing capabilities and organisational effectiveness', *Journal of Strategic Marketing*, 6, 3–23.

Walsh, J.P. (1995) 'Managerial and organisational cognition: Notes from a trip down Memory Lane', *Organisation Science*, 6 (May–June), 280–320.

Williamson, O.E. (1975) *Markets and Hierarchies: Analysis and Anti-Trust Implications*. New York: Free Press.

Winter, S.G. (1987) 'Knowledge and competence as strategic assets'. In D. Teece (ed.), *The Competitive Challenge*. Cambridge, MA: Ballinger, pp. 159–84.

Winter, S.G. (2000) 'The satisficing principle in capability learning', *Strategic Management Journal*, 21, 981–96.

Workman, J.P., Homburg, C. and Gruner, K. (1998) 'Marketing organisation: An integrative framework of dimensions and determinants', *Journal of Marketing*, 62 (July), 21–41.

Zinkhan, G.M. (1999) 'Interdisciplinary contributions to marketing thought', *Journal of Market Focused Management*, 4, 289–94.

Zinkhan, G.M. and Hirschheim, R. (1992) 'Truth in marketing theory and research: An alternative perspective', *Journal of Marketing*, 56 (April), 80–88.

Chapter 6

Baker, T.L., Simpson, P.M. and Siguaw, J.A. (1999) 'The impact of suppliers' perceptions of reseller market orientation on key relationship constructs', *Journal of the Academy of Marketing Science*, 27(1), 50–57.

Balakrishnan, S. (1996) 'Benefits of customer and competitive orientations in industrial markets', *Industrial Marketing Management*, 25, 257–69.

Bhuian, S.N. (1998) 'An empirical examination of market orientation in Saudi Arabian manufacturing companies', *Journal of Business Research*, 43(1), 13–25.

Cadogan, J.W. and Diamantopoulos, A. (1995) 'Narver & Slater, Kohli & Jaworski and the market orientation construct: Integration and internationalization', *Journal of Strategic Marketing*, 3(1), 41–60.

Cadogan, J.W., Diamantopoulos, A. and de Mortanges, C.P. (1999) 'A measure of export market orientation: Scale development and cross-cultural validation', *Journal of International Business Studies*, 30(4), 689–707.

Cadogan, J.W., Diamantopoulos, A. and Siguaw, J.A. (2002a) 'Export market-orientated activities: Their antecedents and performance consequences', *Journal of International Business Studies*, 33(3), 615–26.

Cadogan, J.W., Paul, N., Salminen, R.T., Puumalainen, K. and Sundqvist, S. (2001), 'Key antecedents to "export" market-oriented behaviors: A cross-national empirical examination', *International Journal of Research in Marketing*, 18(3), 261–82.

Cadogan, J.W., Sundqvist, S., Salminen, R.T. and Puumalainen, K. (2002b) 'Market-oriented behavior: Comparing service with product exporters', *European Journal of Marketing*, 36(9/10), 1076–102.

Churchill Jr, G.A. (1979) 'A paradigm for developing better measures of marketing constructs', *Journal of Marketing Research*, 16 (February), 64–73.

Dawes, J.G. (2000) 'Market orientation, production focus, and company ROI', *Advances in International Marketing*, Supplement 1, 3–14.

Day, G.S. (1999) 'Misconceptions about marketing', *Journal of Market Focused Management*, 4(1), 5–16.

Day, G.S. and Wensley, R. (1988) 'Assessing advantage: A framework for diagnosing competitive superiority', *Journal of Marketing*, 52 (April), 1–20.

Deng, S. and Dart, J. (1994), 'Measuring market orientation: A multi-factor, multi-item approach', *Journal of Marketing Management*, 10(8), 725–42.

Deshpandé, R., Farley, J.U. and Webster, F.E. (1993) 'Corporate culture, customer orientation, and innovativeness in Japanese firms: A quadrad analysis', *Journal of Marketing*, 57 (January), 23–37.

Deshpandé, R. and Webster, F.E. (1989) 'Organizational culture and marketing: Defining the research agenda', *Journal of Marketing*, 53 (January), 3–15.

Diamantopoulos, A. and Cadogan, J.W. (1996) 'Internationalizing the market orientation construct: an in-depth interview approach', *Journal of Strategic Marketing*, 4(1), 23–52.

Diamantopoulos, A. and Hart, S. (1993) 'Linking market orientation and company performance: Preliminary evidence on Kohli and Jaworski's framework', *Journal of Strategic Marketing*, 1, 93–121.

Dobni, C.B. and Luffman, G. (2000) 'Market orientation and market strategy profiling: An empirical test of environment-behaviour-action coalignment and its performance implications', *Management Decision*, 38(8), 503–19.

Dreher, A. (1994) 'Marketing orientation: How to grasp the phenomenon.' In M. Baker (ed.), *Perspectives on Marketing Management*, 4. Chichester: John Wiley & Sons, 149–70.

Edwards, J.R. and Bagozzi, R.P. (2000) 'On the nature and direction of relationships between constructs and measures', *Psychological Methods*, 5(2), 155–74.

Farrell, M.A. (2000) 'Developing a market-oriented learning organisation', *Australian Journal of Management*, 25(2), 201–22.

Felton, A.P. (1959) 'Making the marketing concept work', *Harvard Business Review*, 37 (July–August), 55–65.

Gatignon, H. and Xuereb, J.-M. (1997) 'Strategic orientation of the firm and new product performance', *Journal of Marketing Research*, 34 (February), 77–90.

Gray, B., Matear, S., Boshoff, C. and Matheson, P. (1998) 'Developing a better measure of market orientation', *European Journal of Marketing*, 32(9/10), 884–903.

Greenley, G.E. (1995a) 'Market orientation and company performance: Empirical evidence from UK companies', *British Journal of Management*, 6(1), 1–13.

Greenley, Gordon E. (1995b) 'Forms of market orientation in UK companies', *Journal of Management Studies*, 32(1), 47–66.

Greenley, G.E. and Foxall, G.R. (1998) 'External moderation of associations among stakeholder orientations and company performance', *International Journal of Research in Marketing*, 15(1), 51–69.

Han, J.K., Kim, N. and Srivastava, R.K. (1998) 'Market orientation and organizational performance: Is innovation a missing link?', *Journal of Marketing*, 62 (October), 30–45.

Harris, L.C. (1998) 'Cultural domination: The key to market-oriented culture?', *European Journal of Marketing*, 32(3/4), 354–73.

Harris, L.C. (1999) 'Barriers to developing market orientation', *Journal of Applied Management Studies*, 8(1), 85–101.

Harris, L.C. and Ogbonna, E. (2000) 'The response of front-line employees to market-oriented culture change', *European Journal of Marketing*, 34(2/4), 318–40.

Homburg, C. and Pflesser, C. (2000) 'A multiple-layer model of market-oriented organizational culture: Measurement issues and performance outcomes', *Journal of Marketing Research*, 37 (November), 449–62.

Hooley, G., Fahy, J., Cox, T., Beracs, J., Fonfara, K. and Snoj, B. (1999) 'Marketing capabilities and firm performance: A hierarchical model', *Journal of Market Focused Management*, 4(3), 259–78.

Hooley, G.J., Lynch, J.E. and Shepherd, J. (1990) 'The marketing concept: Putting the theory into practice', *European Journal of Marketing*, 24(9), 7–23.

Hooley, G.J. and Newcomb, J.R. (1983) 'Ailing British exports: Symptoms, causes and cures', *The Quarterly Review of Marketing*, 8(4), 15–22.

Hunt, S.D. and Morgan, R.M. (1995) 'The comparative advantage theory of marketing', *Journal of Marketing*, 59 (April), 1–15.

Jaworski, B.J. and Kohli, A.J. (1993), 'Market orientation: Antecedents and consequences', *Journal of Marketing*, 57 (July), 53–70.

Jaworski, B.J. and Kohli, A.K. (1996) 'Market orientation: Review, refinement, roadmap', *Journal of Market Focused Management*, 1(2), 119–35.

Kennedy, K.N., Lassk, F.G. and Goolsby, J.R. (2002) 'Customer mind-set of employees throughout the organization', *Journal of the Academy of Marketing Science*, 30(2), 159–71.

Kohli, A.K. and Jaworski, B.J. (1990) 'Market orientation: The construct, research propositions and managerial implications', *Journal of Marketing*, 54 (April), 1–18.

Kohli, A.K., Jaworski, B.J. and Kumar, A. (1993) 'MARKOR: A measure of market orientation', *Journal of Marketing Research*, 30 (November), 467–77.

Kumar, K., Subramanian, R. and Yauger, C. (1998) 'Examining the market orientation-performance relationship: A context-specific study', *Journal of Management*, 24(2), 201–33.

Kwon, Y.-C. and Hu, M.Y. (2000) 'Market orientation among small Korean exporters', *International Business Review*, 9(1), 61–75.

Lado, N., Maydeu-Olivares, A. and Rivera, J. (1998) 'Measuring market orientation in several populations: A structural equations model', *European Journal of Marketing*, 32(1/2), 23–39.

Lafferty, B.A. and Hult, G.T.M. (2001) 'A synthesis of contemporary market orientation perspectives', *European Journal of Marketing*, 35(1/2), 92–109.

Langerak, F. (2001) 'Effects of market orientation on the behaviors of salespersons and purchasers, channel relationships, and performance of manufacturers', *International Journal of Research in Marketing*, 18(3), 221–34.

Levitt, T. (1969) *The Marketing Mode*. New York: McGraw-Hill Book Company.

Lings, I.N. (2002) 'Internal market orientation: Construct and consequences', *Journal of Business Research*, 55 (in press).

Lukas, B.A. and Ferrell, O.C. (2000) 'The effect of market orientation on product innovation', *Journal of the Academy of Marketing Science*, 28(2), 239–47.

Mavondo, F.T. and Conduit, J. (2000) 'Construct validity of market orientation: Do people in different industries share the same meaning?', *Advances in International Marketing*, Supplement, 1, 29–44.

Matsuno, K., Mentzer, J.T. and Rentz, J.O. (2000) 'A refinement and validation of the MARKOR scale', *Journal of the Academy of Marketing Science*, 28(4), 527–39.

Narver, J.C. and Slater, S.F. (1990) 'The effect of market orientation on business profitability', *Journal of Marketing*, 54 (October), 20–35.

Oczkowski, E. and Farrell, M.A. (1998) 'An examination of the form of market orientation in Australian companies', *Australasian Marketing Journal*, 6(2), 3–12.

Pitt, L., Caruana, A. and Berthon, P.R. (1996) 'Market orientation and business performance: Some European evidence', *International Marketing Review*, 13(1), 5–18.

Prasad, V., Kanti, K., Ramamurthy, and Naidu, G.M. (2001) 'The influence of internet-marketing integration on marketing competencies and export performance', *Journal of International Marketing*, 9(4), 82–110.

Pulendran, S. and Speed, R. (1996) 'Planning and doing: The relationship between marketing planning styles and market orientation', *Journal of Marketing Management*, 12(1), 53–68.

Pulendran, S., Speed, R. and Widing II, R.E. (2000) 'The antecedents and consequences of market orientation in Australia', *Australian Journal of Management*, 25(2), 119–43.

Raju, P.S., Lonial, S.C. and Gupta, Y.P. (1995) 'Market orientation and performance in the hospital industry', *Journal of Health Care Marketing*, 15(4), 34–41.

Rose, G.M. and Shoham, A. (2002) 'Export performance and market orientation: Establishing an empirical link', *Journal of Business Research*, 55(3), 217–25.

Ruekert, R.W. (1992) 'Developing a market orientation: An organizational strategy perspective', *International Journal of Research in Marketing*, 9(3), 225–46.

Shapiro, B.P. (1988) 'What the hell is "market oriented"?', *Harvard Business Review*, 66 (November–December), 119–25.

Siguaw, J.A., Brown, G. and Widing II, R.E. (1994) 'The influence of the market orientation of the firm on sales force behavior and attitudes', *Journal of Marketing Research*, 31 (February), 106–116.

Slater, S.F. and Narver, J.C. (1994) 'Does competitive environment moderate the market orientation–performance relationship', *Journal of Marketing*, 58 (January), 46–55.

Slater, S.F. and Narver, J.C. (1995) 'Market orientation and the learning organization', *Journal of Marketing*, 59 (July), 63–74.

Slater, S.F. and Narver, J.C. (1996) 'Competitive strategy in the market-focused business', *Journal of Market Focused Management*, 1(2), 159–74.

Slater, S.F. and Narver, J.C. (2000) 'The positive effect of a market orientation on business profitability: A balanced replication', *Journal of Business Research*, 48(1), 69–73.

Steinman, C., Deshpandé, R. and Farley, J.U. (2000), 'Beyond market orientation: When customers and suppliers disagree', *Journal of the Academy of Marketing Science*, 28(1), 109–19.

Strieter, J.C., Celuch, K.G. and Kasouf, C.J. (1999) 'Market-oriented behaviors within organizations: An individual-level perspective', *Journal of Marketing Theory and Practice*, 7 (Spring), 16–27.

Thirkell, P.C. and Ramadhani, D. (1998) 'Export performance: Success determinants for New Zealand manufacturing exporters', *European Journal of Marketing*, 32(9/10), 813–29.

Uncles, M. (2000) 'Market orientation', *Australian Journal of Management*, 25(2), i–ix.

Van Egeren, M. and O'Connor, S. (1998) 'Drivers of market orientation and performance in service firms', *Journal of Services Marketing*, 12(1), 39–58.

Vorhies, D.W. and Harker, M. (2000) 'The capabilities and performance advantages of market-driven firms: An empirical investigation', *Australian Journal of Management*, 25(2), 145–71.

Webster, C. (1995) 'Marketing culture and marketing effectiveness in service firms', *Journal of Services Marketing*, 9(2), 6–21.

Webster Jr, F.E. (1992) 'The changing role of marketing in the corporation', *Journal of Marketing*, 56 (October), 1–17.

Wong, V. and Saunders, J. (1993) 'Business orientations and corporate success', *Journal of Strategic Marketing*, 1(1), 20–40.

Chapter 7

Aaker, D.A. (1997) 'Discovering brand magic: The hardness of the softer side of branding', *International Journal of Advertising*, 16, 199–210.

Alvesson, M. (1994) 'Critical theory and consumer marketing', *Scandinavian Journal of Management*, 10(3), 291–313.

Ambler, T. (1999) 'Editorial: rewards from brand-customer relationships', *Journal of Brand Management*, 6(6), 364–66.

Anderson, J.C. and Narus, J.A. (1984) 'A model of the distributor's perspective of distributor-manufacturer working relationships', *Journal of Marketing*, 48 (Fall), 62–74.

Bagozzi, R. (1995) 'Reflections on relationship marketing in consumer markets', *Journal of the Academy of Marketing Science*, 23(4), 272–77.

Barnes, J. and Howlett, D. (1998) 'Predictors of equity in relationships between financial services providers and retail customers', *International Journal of Bank Marketing*, 16(1), 15–23.

Barnes, J.G. (1994) 'Close to the customer: But is it really a relationship', *Journal of Marketing Management*, 10, 561–70.

Barnes, J.G. (1995) 'Establishing relationships – getting closer to the customer may be more difficult than you think', *Irish Marketing Review*, 8, 107–16.

Barnes, J.G. (1997) 'Closeness, strength, and satisfaction: Examining the nature of relationships between providers of financial services and their retail customers', *Psychology and Marketing*, 14(8), 765–90.

Bendapudi, N. and Berry, L.L. (1997) 'Customers motivation for maintaining relationships with service providers', *Journal of Retailing*, 73 (Spring), 15–37.

Berry, L.L. (1983) 'Relationship marketing'. In L.L. Berry, G.L. Shostack and G.D. Upah (eds), *Perspectives on Services Marketing*. Chicago: American Marketing Association, pp. 25–28.

Berry, L.L. (1995) 'Relationship marketing of services – growing interest, emerging perspectives', *Journal of the Academy of Marketing Science*, 23(4), 236–45.

Berry, L.L. and Parasuraman, A. (1991) *Marketing Services – Competition Through Quality*. New York: The Free Press.

Bitner, M.J. (1995) 'Building service relationships: It's all about promises', *Journal of the Academy of Marketing Science*, 23(4), 236–45.

Blackston, M. (1992) 'Observations: Building brand equity by managing the brand's relationships', *Journal of Advertising Research*, May/June, 79–83.

Blattberg, R.C. and Deighton, J. (1991) 'Interactive marketing: Exploiting the age of addressability', *Sloan Management Review*, Fall, 5–14.

Booms, B.H. and Bitner, M.J. (1981) 'Marketing strategies and organisational structures for service firms'. In J.H. Donnelly and W.R. George (eds), *Marketing of Services*. Chicago: American Marketing Association.

Borys, B. and Jemison, D.B. (1989) 'Hybrid arrangements as strategic: Theoretical issues in organisational combinations', *Academy of Management Review*, 14(2), 234–40.

Bowen, J.T. and Shoemaker, S. (1998) 'Loyalty: A strategic commitment', *Cornell Hotel & Restaurant Administration Quarterly*, February, 39(1), 12–24.

Buchanan, R. and Gilles, C.S. (1990) 'Value managed relationships: The key to customer retention and profitability', *European Management Journal*, 8(4), 523–26.

Butler, J.K. (1991) 'Toward understanding and measuring conditions of trust: Evolution of a conditions of trust inventory', *Journal of Management*, 17(3), 643–63.

Christy, R., Oliver. G. and Penn, J. (1996) 'Relationship marketing in consumer markets', *Journal of Marketing Management*, 12, 175–87.

Colgate, M. and Stewart, K. (1998) 'The challenge of relationships in services – a New Zealand study', *International Journal of Service Industry Management*, 9(5), 454–68.

Copulsky, J.R. and Wolf, M.J. (1990) 'Relationship marketing: Positioning for the future', *Journal of Business Strategy*, July/August, 16–26.

Creed, D.W.E. and Miles, R.E. (1996) 'Trust in organisations: A conceptual framework linking organisational forms, managerial philosophies, and the opportunity cost of controls'. In R.M. Kramer and T.R. Tyler (eds), *Trust in Organisations: Frontiers of Theory and Research*. California: Sage Publications.

Crosby, L.A., Evans, K.R. and Cowles, D. (1990) 'Relationship quality in services selling: An interpersonal influence perspective', *Journal of Marketing*, 54 (July), 68–81.

Crosby, L.A. and Stephens, N. (1987) 'Effect of relationship marketing on satisfaction, retention, and prices in the life insurance industry', *Journal of Marketing Research*, XXIV (November), 404–11.

Czepiel, J.A. (1990) 'Service encounters and service relationships: Implications for research', *Journal of Business Research*, 20 (July/August), 16–26.

De Wulf, K., Odekerken-Schroder, G. and Iacobucci, D. (2001) 'Investments in consumer relationships: A cross-country and cross-industry exploration', *Journal of Marketing*, 65 (October), 33–50.

Desmond, J. (1997) 'Marketing and the war machine', *Marketing Intelligence and Planning*, 15(7), 338–51.

Dick, A.S. and Basu, K. (1994) 'Customer loyalty: Toward an integrated framework', *Journal of the Academy of Marketing Science*, 22(2), 99–113.

Dowling, G.R. and Uncles, M. (1997) 'Do customer loyalty programmes really work?', *Sloan Management Review*, Summer, 71–82.

Duncan, T. and Moriarty, S.E. (1998) 'The role of relationship quality in the stratification of vendors as perceived by customers', *Journal of the Academy of Marketing Science*, 26(2), 128–42.

Dwyer, F.R., Schurr, P.H. and Oh, S. (1987) 'Developing buyer–seller relationships', *Journal of Marketing*, 51 (April), 11–27.

Evans, M. (1998) 'From 1086 and 1984: Direct marketing into the millennium', *Marketing Intelligence and Planning*, 16(1), 56–67.

Evans, M., O'Malley, L. and Patterson, M. (1996) 'Direct marketing communications in the UK: A study of growth, past, present and future', *Journal of Marketing Communications*, 2, 51–65.

Fitchett, J.A. and McDonagh, P. (2000) 'A citizen's critique of relationship marketing in risk society', *Journal of Marketing Strategy*, 8(2), 209–22.

Ford, D. (1980) 'The development of buyer–seller relationships in industrial markets', *European Journal of Marketing*, 14(5/6), 339–54.

Ford, D. (1997) *Understanding Business Markets: Interaction, Relationships, Networks*, 2nd edn. London: Academic Press, Harcourt Brace and Co.

Fournier S., Dobscha, S. and Mick, D.G. (1998) 'Preventing the premature death of relationship marketing', *Harvard Business Review*, January–February, 42–51.

Gambetta, D. (1988) 'Can we trust trust?' In D. Gambetta (ed.), *Trust: Making and Breaking Co-operative Relations*. Oxford: Basil Blackwell.

Geyskens, I., Steenkamp, E.M.J.-B., Schear, L.K. and Kumar, N. (1996) 'The effects of trust and interdependence on relationship commitment: A trans-Atlantic study', *International Journal of Research in Marketing*, 13, 303–17.

Gordon, I. (2000) 'Organising for relationship marketing'. In J.N. Sheth and A. Parvatiyar (eds), *Handbook of Relationship Marketing*, Thousand Oaks, CA: Sage, pp. 505–23.

Gordon, M.E., McKeage, K. and Fox, M.A. (1998) 'Relationship marketing effectiveness: The role of involvement', *Psychology and Marketing*, 15(5), 443–59.

Grönroos, C. (1978) 'A service-orientated approach to marketing of services', *European Journal of Marketing*, 12(8), 588–601.

Grönroos, C. (1983) *Strategic Management and Marketing in the Service Sector*. Cambridge, MA: Marketing Science Institute.

Grönroos, C. (1990) 'Relationship approach to marketing in service contexts: The marketing and organisational behaviour interface', *Journal of Business Research*, 20 (January), 3–11.

Grönroos, C. (1994) 'From marketing mix to relationship marketing: Towards a paradigm shift in marketing', *Management Decision*, 32(2), 4–20.

Grönroos, C. (1995) 'Relationship marketing: The strategy continuum', *Journal of the Academy of Marketing Science*, 23(4), 252–54.

Grönroos, C. (1996) 'Relationship marketing: Strategic and tactical implications', *Management Decision*, 34(3), 5–14.

Gummesson, E. (1987) 'The new marketing – developing long-term interactive relationships', *Long Range Planning*, 20, 10–20.

Gummesson, E. (1994) 'Making relationship marketing operational', *International Journal of Service Industry Management*, 5(5), 5–20.

Gundlach, G.T. and Murphy, P.E. (1993) 'Ethical and legal foundations of relational marketing exchanges', *Journal of Marketing*, 57 (October), 35–46.

Gwinner, K.P., Gremier, D.D. and Bitner, M.J. (1998) 'Relational benefits in services industries: The customer's perspective', *Journal of the Academy of Marketing Science*, 26(2), 101–14.

Håkansson, H. (1982) *International Marketing and Purchasing of Industrial Goods*. New York: Wiley.

Harris, L.C., O'Malley, L. and Patterson, M. (2002) 'Relationship marketing in professional services: Understanding attraction in the legal sector'.

Holmlund, M. and Knock, S. (1996) 'Relationship marketing: The importance of customer-perceived service quality in retail banking', *The Service Industries Journal*, 16(3), 287–304.

Hunt, S.D. and Menon, A. (1995) 'Metaphors and competitive advantage: Evaluating the use of metaphors in theories of competitive strategy', *Journal of Business Research*, 33, 81–90.

Jackson, B.B. (1985) *Winning and Keeping Industrial Customers*. Lexington, Ma: Lexington Books.

Levitt, T. (1983) *The Marketing Imagination*. New York: The Free Press.

Lovelock, C.H. (1983) 'Classifying services to gain strategic marketing insights', *Journal of Marketing*, 47 (Summer), 9–20.

Macneil, I.R. (1980) *The New Social Contract: An Inquiry into Modern Contractual Relations*. New Haven, CT: Yale University Press.

Management Services (2000) 'Customer complaints "top 10 taboos" revealed in survey', *Management Services*, Aug, 9–11.

McCall, M. (1966) 'Courtship as social exchange: Some historical comparisons'. In B. Farber (ed.), *Kinship and Family Organisation*. New York: John Wiley & Sons Inc, pp. 190–210.

McKenna, R. (1991) *Relationship Marketing: Successful Strategies For The Age of the Customer*. Reading, MA: Addison-Wesley.

Morgan, R.M. and Hunt, S.D. (1994) 'The commitment-trust theory of relationship marketing', *Journal of Marketing*, 58 (July), 20–38.

O'Brien, L. and Jones, C. (1995) 'Do rewards really create loyalty?', *Harvard Business Review*, May–June, 75–82.

O'Malley, L. (1998) 'Can loyalty schemes really build loyalty', *Marketing Intelligence and Planning*, 16(1), 58–67.

O'Malley, L. and Mitussis, D. (2002) 'Relationships and technology: Strategic implications', *Journal of Strategic Marketing*, forthcoming.

O'Malley, L. and Patterson, M. (1998) 'Vanishing point: The mix management paradigm reviewed', *Journal of Marketing Management*, 14(8), 829–52.

O'Malley, L., Patterson, M. and Evans, M.J. (1997) 'Intimacy or intrusion: The privacy dilemma for relationship marketing in consumer markets', *Journal of Marketing Management*, 13(6), 541–60.

O'Malley, L. and A. Prothero (2003) 'Beyond the frills of relationship marketing', *Journal of Business Research*, forthcoming.

O'Malley, L. and Tynan, C. (1999) 'The utility of the relationship metaphor in consumer markets: A critical evaluation', *Journal of Marketing Management*, 15, 487–602.

O'Malley, L. and Tynan, C. (2000) 'Relationship marketing in consumer markets: Rhetoric or reality?', *European Journal of Marketing*, 34(7), 797–815.

O'Malley, L. and Tynan, C.T. (2001) 'Reframing relationship marketing for consumer markets', *Interactive Marketing*, 2(3), 240–46.

Palmer, A. (1996) 'Integrating brand development and relationship marketing', *Journal of Retailing and Consumer Services*, 3(4), 351–57.

Patterson, M., O'Malley, L., Evans, M.J. (1997) 'Database marketing: Investigating privacy concerns', *Journal of Marketing Communications*, 3(3), 151–74.

Peterson, R.A. (1995) 'Relationship marketing and the consumer', *Journal of the Academy of Marketing Science*, 23(4), 278–81.

Petrof, J.V. (1997) 'Relationship marketing: The wheel reinvented', *Business Horizons*, 40(6), November/December, 26–31.

Pine II, J.B., Peppers, D. and Rogers, M. (1995) 'Do you want to keep your customers forever?', *Harvard Business Review*, March–April, 103–14.

Price, L.L., Arnould, E.J. and Tierney, P. (1995) 'Going to extremes: Managing service encounters and assessing provider performance', *Journal of Marketing*, 59 (April), 83–97.

Reichheld, F.F., and Sasser Jr, E.W. (1990) 'Zero defections: Quality comes to services', *Harvard Business Review*, 69 (September–October), 105–11.

Rowe, G.W. and Barnes, J.G. (1998) 'Relationship marketing and sustained competitive advantage', *Journal of Market Focused Management*, 2, 281–97.

Schurr, P.H. and Ozanne, J. (1985) 'Influences on exchange processes: Buyer's preconceptions of a seller's trustworthiness and bargaining toughness', *Journal of Consumer Research*, 11 (March), 939–53.

Shani, D. and Chalasani, S. (1992) 'Exploiting niches using relationship marketing', *Journal of Business Strategy*, 6(4), 43–52.

Sheaves, D.E. and Barnes, J.G. (1996) 'The fundamentals of relationships: An exploration of the concept to guide marketing implementation', *Advances in Services Marketing and Management*, 5, 215–45.

Sheth, J.N. and Parvatiyar, A. (1995) 'Relationship marketing in consumer markets: Antecedents and consequences', *Journal of the Academy of Marketing Science*, 23(4), 255–71.

Shostack, L.G. (1977) 'Breaking free from product marketing', *Journal of Marketing*, 45 (April), 73–80.

Sisodia, R.S. and Wolfe, D.B. (2000) 'Information technology; its role in building, maintaining and enhancing relationships'. In J.N. Sheth and A. Parvatiyar (eds), *Handbook of Relationship Marketing*. Thousand Oaks, CA: Sage, pp. 525–63.

Smith, W. and Higgins, M. (2000) 'Reconsidering the relationship analogy', *Journal of Marketing Management*, 16(1–3), 81–93.

Solomon, M.R., Suprenant, C., Czepiel, J.A. and Gutman, E.G. (1985) 'A role theory perspective on dyadic interactions: The service encounter', *Journal of Marketing*, 49 (Winter), 99–111.

Spekman, R.E. (1988) 'Strategic supplier selection: Understanding long-term buyer relationships', *Business Horizons*, 31(4), 75–81.

Stone, M., Woodcock, N. and Wilson, M. (1996) 'Managing the change from marketing planning to customer relationship management', *Long Range Planning*, 29(5), 675–83.

Turnbull, P.W. (1979) 'Role of personal contacts in industrial export marketing', *Scandinavian Journal of Management*, 7, 325–39.

Tyler, T.R. and Kramer, R.M. (1996) 'Whither trust'. In R.M. Kramer and T.R. Tyler (eds), *Trust in Organisations: Frontiers of Theory and Research*. California: Sage, pp. 1–15.

Tzokas, N. and Saren, M. (1997) 'Building relationship platforms in consumer markets: A value chain approach', *Journal of Strategic Marketing*, 5(2), 105–20.

Webster, F.E. (1992) 'The changing role of marketing in the corporation', *Journal of Marketing*, 56 (October), 1–17.

Wilson, D.T. (1995) 'An integrated model of buyer-seller relationships', *Journal of the Academy of Marketing Science*, 23(4), 335–45.

Chapter 8

Abecassis, C., Caby, L. and Jaeger, C. (2000) 'IT and coordination modes: The case of the garment industry in France and the US', *Journal of Marketing Management*, 16(5), June, 425–48.

Aldrich, H.E. (1987) 'The impact of social networks on business founding and profit: A longitudinal study'. In *Frontiers of Entrepreneurship Research*. Wellesley, MA: Babson College.

Aldrich, H. and Zimmer, C. (1986) 'Entrepreneurship through social networks'. In D.L. Sexton and R.W. Wilson (eds), *The Art and Science of Entrepreneurship*. Ballinger, MA: Babson College, pp. 154–67.

Anderson, E. and Weitz, B. (1992) 'The use of pledges to build and sustain commitment in distribution channels', *Journal of Marketing Channels*, 29, 18–43.

Anderson, H., Havila, V. and Salmi, A. (2001) 'Can you buy a business relationship?: On the importance of customer and supplier relationships in acquisitions', *Industrial Marketing Management*, 30, 575–86.

Auster, E. (1990) 'The interorganisational environment: Network theory, tools and applications'. In F. Williamson and D. Gibson (eds), *Technology Transfer: A Communication Perspective*. Sage, pp. 63–89.

Axelsson, B. and Easton, G. (eds) (1992) *Industrial Network: A New View of Reality*. London: Thomson Learning.

Baker, M. (1999) 'Editorial', *Journal of Marketing Management*, 15(7), October, 583–86.

Beeby, M. and Booth, C. (2000) 'Networks and interorganisational learning: A critical review', *The Learning Organisation*, 7(2), 75–88.

Birley, S. (1985) 'The role of networks in the entrepreneurial process', *Journal of Business Venturing*, 1, 107–17.

Blackburn, R.A., Curran, J. and Jarvis, R. (1990) 'Small firms and local networks: Some theoretical and conceptual explorations', paper presented at the 13th National Small Firms Policy and Research Conference, Harrogate, November.

Blois, K.J. (1990) 'Transaction costs and networks', *Strategic Management Journal*, 11, 493–96.

Boissevain, J. (1974) *Friends of Friends: Networks, Manipulators and Coalitions*. Oxford: Basil Blackwell.

Borch, O.J. and Arthur, M.B. (1995) 'Strategic networks among small firms: Implications for strategy research methodology', *Journal of Management Studies*, 32(4).

Bott, E. (1957) *Family and Social Networks*, London: The Tavistock Institute.

Braddach, J.L. and Eccles, R.G. (1989) 'Price, authority and trust: From ideal types to plural forms', *Annual Review of Sociology*, 15, 97–118.

Carlzon, J. (1987) *Moments of Truth*, Cambridge, MA: Ballinger Books.

Carson, D., Cromie, S., McGowan, P. and Hill, J. (1995) *Marketing and Entrepreneurship in SMEs, An Innovative Approach*. London: Prentice-Hall.

Coase, R.H. (1937) 'The nature of the firm', *Economa*, 4.

Collins, A. and Burt, S. (1999) 'Dependence in manufacturer-retailer relationships: The potential implications of retail internationalisation for indigenous food manufacturers', *Journal of Marketing Management*, 15(7), October, 673–95.

Collinson, E. and Shaw, E. (2001), 'Entrepreneurial marketing – a historical perspective on development and practice', *Management Decision*, 39(9), 761–66.

Conway, S. (1997), 'Informal networks of relationships in successful small firm innovation'. In D. Jones-Evans and M. Klofsten (eds), *Technology, Innovation and Enterprise*.

Cravens, D.W., Ingram, T., LaForge, R.W. and Young, C.E. (1993) 'Behaviour-based and outcome-based sales force control systems', *Journal of Marketing*, 57 (October), 47–59.

Curran, J., Jarvis, R., Blackburn, R.A. and Black, S. (1993) 'Networks and small firms: Constructs, methodological strategies and some findings', *International Small Business Journal*, 11(2), 13–25.

Czepiel, J.A., Soloman, M.R., Suprenant, C.F. (eds) (1985) *The Service Encounter: Managing Employee/Customer Interaction in Service Business*. Lexington, Mass.

DeBresson, C. and Amesse, F. (1991) 'Networks of innovators: A review and introduction to the issue', *Research Policy*, 20, 363–79.

Dion, P., Easterling, D. and Miller, S.J. (1995) 'What is really necessary in successful buyer/ seller relationships', *Industrial Marketing Management*, 24(1).

Doherty, N.F., Ellis-Chadwick, F. and Hart, C. (1999) 'Cyber retailing in the UK: The potential of the Internet as a retailing channel', *International Journal of Retail and Distribution Management*, 27(1), 22–36.

Donckels, R. and Lambrecht, J. (1995) 'Networks and small business growth: An explanatory model', *Small Business Economics*, 7, 237–89.

Easton, G. and Araujo, L. (1994) 'Marketing exchange, social structures and time', *European Journal of Marketing*, 28(3), 72–84.

Ebers, M. (ed.) (1994) *The Formation of Inter-organisational Networks*. Oxford University Press.

Ellis, N. and Mayer, R. (2001) 'Inter-organisational relationships and strategy development in an evolving industrial network: Mapping structure and process', *Journal of Marketing Management*, 17(1–2), February, 183–222.

Eriksson, K. and Hohenthal, J. (2002) 'Learning in international business relationships'. In H. Hakansson and J. Johanson (eds), *Business Network Learning*. Elsevier Science Ltd., Amsterdam, Oxford: Pergamon, pp. 1–16.

Fisk, G. (1997) 'Questioning eschatological questions about marketing apocalypse conditional', *European Journal of Marketing*, Issue 9/10.

Ford, D. (1980) 'The development of buyer-seller relationships in industrial markets', *European Journal of Marketing*, 14, 339–53.

Ford, D. (ed.) (1990) *Understanding Business Markets: Interaction, Relationships and Networks*. The Industrial Marketing and Purchasing Group, Academic Press.

Ford, D., Gadde, L.E., Hakansson, H., Lundgren, A., Snehota, I., Turnbull, P. and Wilson, D. (1998) *Managing Business Relationships*. England: John Wiley and Sons.

Freeman, C. (1991) 'Networks of innovators: A synthesis of research issues', *Research Policy*, 20(5), 499–514.

Gabbott, M. and Hogg, G. (1998) *Consumers and Services*. Chichester: John Wiley and Sons.

Ganesan, S. (1993) 'Negotiation strategies and the nature of channel relationships', *Journal of Marketing Research*, 30 (May), 183–204.

Gardner, J.T., Joseph, W.B. and Thech, S. (1993) 'Modeling the continuum of relationship styles between distributors and suppliers', *Journal of Marketing Channels*, 2, 1–28.

Giddens, A. (1984) *The Constitution of Society*. Cambridge: Polity Press.

Grabher, G. (1993) 'Rediscovering the social in the economics of interfirm relations'. In G. Grabher (ed.), *The Embedded Firm*. London: Routledge.

Grandori, A. and Soda, G. (1995) 'Interfirm networks: Antecedents, mechanisms and forms', *Organisational Studies*, 16(2), 183–214.

Granovetter, M.S. (1973) 'The strength of weak ties', *American Journal of Sociology*, 78(6), 1361–81.

Granovetter, M.S. (1982) 'The strength of weak ties: A network theory revisited'. In P.V. Marsden and V. Lin (eds), *Social Structure and Network Analysis*. London, Sage: pp. 105–30.

Granovetter, M. (1985) 'Economic action and social structure: The problem of embeddedness', *American Journal of Sociology*, November, 55–81.

Granovetter, M.S. (1992) 'Networks and organisations: problems of explanation in economic sociology'. In N. Nohria and R.G. Eccles (eds), *Networks and Organisations: Structure, Form and Action*. Boston, MA: Harvard Business School Press.

Gronroos, C. (1991) 'The marketing strategy continuum', *Management Decision*, 29(1), 7–13.

Gronroos, C. (1994) 'Quo vadis, marketing? Toward a relationship marketing paradigm?', *Journal of Marketing Management*, 10, 347–60.

Gummesson, E. (1994) 'Making relationship marketing operational', *International Journal of Science Management*, 5(5), 5–20.

Gummesson, E. (1995) *Relationship Marketing from 4P to 30 R*. Malmo, Sweden: Liber-Hermods.

Gummesson, E. (1997) 'Relationship marketing as a paradigm shift: Some conclusions from the 30R approach', *Management Decision*, 35(3/4), April–March, 267–73.

Hagedoorn, J. and Schakenraad, J. (1992) 'Leading companies and networks of strategic alliances in information technology', *Research Policy*, 21(2), 163–90.

Hakansson, H. (ed.) (1987) *Industrial Technological Development: A Network Approach*. London: Croom Helm.

Hakansson, H. (1989) *Corporate Technological Behaviour: Cooperation and Network*. London: Thomson Learning.

Hakansson, H. (ed.) (1982) *International Marketing and Purchasing of Industrial Goods: An Interaction Approach*. Chicester: Wiley.

Hakansson, H. and Johanson, J. (1992) 'A model of industrial networks'. In B. Axelsson and G. Easton (eds), *Industrial Network: A New View of Reality*. London: Thomson Learning.

Hakansson, H. and Johanson, J. (2001) 'Business network learning – basic considerations'. In H. Hakansson and J. Johanson (eds), *Business Network Learning*, Elsevier Science Ltd, Amsterdam, Oxford: Pergamon, pp. 1–16.

Hakansson, H. and Snehota, I. (1989) 'No business is an island', *Scandanavian Journal of Management*, 5(3), 187–200.

Hakansson, H. and Snehota, I. (1995) *Developing Relationships in Business Networks*. London: Thomson Learning.

Hamel, G., Doz, Y. and Prahalad, C. (1989) 'Collaborate with your competitors – and win', *Harvard Business Review*, 67 (January–February), 133–39.

Hamfelt, C. and Lindberg, A. (1987) 'Technological development and the individual's contact network'. In H. Hakansson and I. Snehota (1989) 'No business is an island', *Scandanavian Journal of Management*, 5(3), 187–200.

Harland, C.M. (1995) 'Networks and globalisation: A review of research', Warwick University Business School Research Paper, ESRC Grant No: GRK 53178.

Harland, C.M. (1996) 'Supply chain management: Relationships, chains and networks', *British Journal of Management*, , Special Issue, 'Revitalising organisations: The academic contribution', 7 (March), 63–80.

Harris, K., Barron, S. and Ratcliffe, J. (1995) 'Customers as oral participants in the service setting', *Journal of Services Marketing*, 9(4), 64–76.

Harris, S. and Dibben, M. (1999) 'Trust and co-operation in business relationship development: Exploring the influence of national values', *Journal of Marketing Management*, 15(6), July, 463–83.

Henderson, B.D. (1989) 'The origin of strategy', *Harvard Business Review*, November/December, 139–43.

Hill, J. and McGowan, P. (1997) 'Marketing development through networks: A competency based approach for small firm entrepreneurs'. In G.E. Hills, J.J. Giglierano and C.M. Hultman (eds), *Research at the Marketing/Entrepreneurship Interface*. Chicago: University of Illinois at Chicago, pp. 3–15.

Hogg, G., Laing, A.W. and Winkelman, D. (2002) 'The Internet empowered consumer: The professional service encounter in the age of the Internet', *Journal of Services Marketing*, in press.

Hunt, S.D. (1997) 'Competing through relationships: Grounding relationship marketing in resource-advantage theory', *Journal of Marketing Management*, 13, 431–45.

Jarillo, J. (1993) *Strategic Networks: Creating the Borderless Organisation*. Oxford: Butterworth-Heinemann.

Johannison, B. (1986) 'New venture creation: A network approach'. In *Frontiers of Entrepreneurship Research*. Wellesley, MA: Babson College, pp. 236–40.

Johanson, J. and Mattsson, L.G. (1987) 'Interorganisational relations in industrial systems: A network approach compared with the transaction-cost approach', *International Study of Management and Organisation*, XVII(1), 34–48.

Johnson, R. and Lawrence, P. (1988) 'Beyond vertical integration: The rise of the value-adding partnership', *Harvard Business Review*, July–August.

Joseph, W.B., Gardner, J.T., Thach, S.Z. and Vernon, F. (1995) 'How industrial distributors view distributor–supplier partnership arrangements', *Industrial Marketing Management*, 24(1), 27–36.

Kanter, R.M. (1989) 'Becoming PALS; pooling, allying and networking across companies', *Academy of Management Executive*, 111(3), 183–93.

Kanter, R.M. (1994) 'Collaborative advantage', *Harvard Business Review*, 72 (July–August), 96–108.

Kanter, R.M. and Eccles, R.G. (1992) 'Making network research relevant to practice'. In N. Nohria and R.G. Eccles (eds), *Networks and Organisations: Structure, Form and Action*. Boston, MA: Harvard Business School Press.

Kapferer, B. (1969) 'Norms and manipulation of relationships in the work context'. In J.C. Mitchell (ed.), *Social Networks in Urban Situations*. Manchester: University of Manchester Press.

Karunaratna, A., Johnson, L.W. and Rao, C.P. (2001) 'The exporter–import agent contract and the influence of cultural dimensions', *Journal of Marketing Management*, 17(1–2), February, 137–58.

Khanna, T., Gulati, R and Nohria, N. (1998) 'The dynamics of learning alliances: Competition, cooperation and relative scope', *Strategic Management Journal*, 19, 193–210.

Krapfel, R.E., Salmond, D. and Spekman, R. (1991) 'A strategic approach to buyer–seller relationships', *European Journal of Marketing*, 25(9), 22–37.

Li, F. and Nicholls, J.A.F. (2000) 'Transactional or relational marketing: Determinants of strategic choices', *Journal of Marketing Management*, 16(5), June, 449–64.

Littler, D. and Wilson, D. (1991) 'Strategic alliances in computerised business systems', *Technovation*, 11(8), 457–72.

Litvak, I.A. (1990), 'Industry R&D alliances – a key to competitive survival', *Business Quarterly*, 55(1), 61–64.

Lowndes, V., Nanton, P., McCabe, A. and Skelcher, C. (1997) 'Networks, partnerships and urban regeneration', *Local Economy*, February, 333–42.

McDonald, M. (2000) 'Key account management – a domain review', *The Marketing Review*, 1(1), October, 15–34.

Miles, R. and Snow, C. (1986) 'Organisations: new concepts for new firms', *California Management Review*, XXXVIII(5).

Mitchell, J.C. (1969) 'The concept and use of social networks'. In J.C. Mitchell (ed.), *Social Networks in Urban Situations*. Manchester: University of Manchester Press.

References

Moller, K. and Halinen, A. (2000) 'Relationship marketing theory: Its roots and direction', *Journal of Marketing Management*, 16(1–3), Jan/Feb/April, Special Millennium Issue, 29–54.

Morgan, R.M. and Hunt, S.D. (1994) 'The commitment-trust theory of relationship marketing', *Journal of Marketing*, 58 (July), 20–38.

Nohria, N. (1992) 'Is a network perspective a useful way of studying organisations?'. In N. Nohria and R.G. Eccles (eds), *Networks and Organisations: Structure, Form and Action*. Boston, MA: Harvard Business School Press.

Nohria, N. and Eccles, R.G. (eds) (1992) *Networks and Organisations: Structure, Form and Action*. Boston, MA: Harvard Business School Press.

Oakey, R.P. (1993) 'Predatory networking: The role of small firms in the development of the British biotechnology industry', *International Small Business Journal*, 11(4), 9–22.

O'Donnell, A. and Cummins, D. (1999) 'The use of qualitative methods in researching networking in SMEs', *Qualitative Market Research: An International Journal*, 2(2), 82–91.

O'Malley, L. and Tynan, C. (1999) 'The utility of the relationship metaphor in consumer markets: A critical evaluation', *Journal of Marketing Management*, 15(7), October, 587–602.

O'Malley, L. and Tynan, C. (1997) 'A reappraisal of the relationship marketing constructs of commitment and trust', *New and Evolving Paradigms: The Emerging Future of Marketing*, AMA Relationship Marketing Conference, Dublin, Ireland, 13 June, pp. 486–503.

Palmer, A. (2001) 'Co-operation and collusion: Making the distinction in marketing relationships', *Journal of Marketing Management*, 17(7–8), Sept, 761–84.

Patterson, M. and O'Malley, L. (2000) 'The evolution of the direct marketing consumer', *The Marketing Review*, 1(1), October, 89–102.

Pels, J. (1997) 'Actors exchange paradigm and their impact on the choice of marketing models'. In A.W. Falkener (ed.), *Proceedings of the 22nd Macro Marketing Conference*, 2, Bergen.

Perry, M. (1996) 'Network intermediaries and their effectiveness', *International Small Business Journal*, 14(1), July–September, 72–80.

Pfeffer, J. and Salanick, G.R. (1978) *The External Control of Organizations*. New York: Harper and Row.

Powell, W.W. (1990) 'Neither market nor hierarchy: new forms of organisation'. In L.L. Commings and R. Brustaw (eds), *Research in Organisational Behaviour*. Greenwich, CT: JAI Press, pp. 295–36.

Powell, W.W. and Brantley, P. (1992) 'Competitive cooperation in biotechnology: Learning through networks'. In N. Nohria and R.G. Eccles (eds), (1992) *Networks and Organisations: Structure, Form and Action*. Boston, MA: Harvard Business School Press.

Rogers, E. and Kincaid, D.L. (1981) *Communicate Networks*. New York: Free Press.

Rothwell, R. and Dodgson, M. (1991) 'External linkages and innovation in small and medium-sized enterprises', *R&D Management*, 21(2), 258–91.

Salancik, G.R. (1995) 'WANTED: A good networking theory of organisation', *Administrative Science Quarterly*, 40, 345–49.

Saren, M. and Tzokas, N. (1998), 'Some dangerous axioms of relationship marketing', *Journal of Strategic Marketing*, 6, 187–96.

Saxenian, A.L. (1990) ' Regional networks and the resurgence of Silicon Valley', *California Management Review*, 33(1), 89–112.

Shaw, E. (1997) 'The real networks of small firms'. In D. Deakins, P. Jennings and C. Mason (eds), *Small Firms: Entrepreneurship in the 1990s*. London: Paul Chapman Publishing.

Shaw, E. (1998) 'Social networks: Their impact on the innovative behaviour of small service firms', *International Journal of Innovation Management*, 2(2), Special Issue (June), 201–22.

Shaw, E. (1999) 'Networks and their relevance to the entrepreneurial/marketing interface: A review of the evidence', *Journal of Research in Marketing and Entrepreneurship*, 1(1), Fall.

Shaw, E. and Conway, S. (2000) 'Networking and the small firm'. In S. Carter and D Jones-Evans (eds), *Enterprise and Small Business: Principles, Practice and Policies*. Englewood Cliffs, NJ: Prentice-Hall.

Shostack, G.L. (1985) 'Planning the service encounter'. In J.A. Czepiel, M.R. Soloman, C.F. Suprenant (1985) (eds), *The Service Encounter: Managing Employee/Customer Interaction in Service Business*. Lexington, MA.

Smith, W. and Higgins, M. (2000) 'Reconsidering the relationship analogy', *Journal of Marketing Management*, 16(1–3), Jan/Feb/April, Special Millennium Issue, 81–94.

Szarka, J. (1990) 'Networking and small firms', *International Small Business Journal*, 8(2), 10–22.

Tichy, N.N., Tushmann, N.L. and Forbrun, C. (1979) 'Social network analysis for organisations', *Academy of Management Review*, 4(4), 507–19.

Turnbull, P.W., Ford, P. and Cunningham, M. (1996) 'Interactions, relationships and networks in business markets: An evolving perspective', *Journal of Business and Industrial Marketing*, 11(3–4), 44–63.

Turnbull, P.W. and Valla, J.P. (eds) (1986) *Strategies for International, Industrial Marketing*. London: Croom Helm.

Turnbull, P.W. and Wilson, D.T. (1989) 'Developing and protecting profitable customer relationships', *Industrial Marketing Management*, 18, 233–8.

Varadarajan, P. and Cunningham, M. (1995) 'Strategic alliances: a synthesis of conceptual foundations', *Journal of the Academy of Marketing Science*, 23(4), 282–96.

Webster, F.E. (1992) 'The changing role of marketing in the corporation', *Journal of Marketing*, 56 (October), 1–17.

Williamson, O. (1975) *Markets and Hierarchies: Analysis and Antitrust Implications*. New York: The Free Press.

Williamson, O. (1985) *The Economic Institutions of Capitalism*. New York: The Free Press.

Williamson, O. (1991) 'Corporate economic organization; the analysis of discrete structural alternatives', *Administrative Science Quarterly*, 36, 269–96.

Williamson, O. (1996) 'Economic organisation: The case for cander', *Academy of Management Review*, 21(1), 48–57.

Chapter 10

Ames, B.C. (1970) 'Trappings versus substance in industrial marketing', *Harvard Business Review*, 48 (July/August).

Argyris, C. and Schon, D.A. (1978), *Organizational Learning: A Theory of Action Perspective*. Reading, MA: Addison-Wesley.

Baker, K., Harris, P. and O'Brien, J. (1989) 'Data fusion: An appraisal and experimental evaluation', *Journal of the Market Research Society*, 31(3).

Barker, A., Nancarrow, C. and Spakman, N. (2001) 'Informed eclecticism: A research paradigm for the 21st century', *International Journal of Market Research*, 43(1), 1–25.

Blamires, C. (1981) 'Pricing research techniques: A review and new approach', *Journal of the Market Research Society*, 23(3).

Brown, A.D and Ennew, C.T. (1995) 'Market research and the politics of new product development', *Journal of Marketing Management*, 11.

Brown, S. (1995) 'Postmodern marketing research: No representation without taxation', *Journal of the Market Research Society*, 37(3), 287–308.

Bruner II, J.C. and Hensel, P.J. (1996) *Marketing Scales Handbook, vol II: A Compilation of Multi-item Measures*. Chicago: AMA.

Buttery, E.A. and Buttery E.M. (1991) 'Design of the marketing information system: Useful paradigms', *European Journal of Marketing*, 25(1), 26–39.

Carson, D., Gilmore, A., Perry, C. and Gronhaug, K. (2001) *Qualitative Marketing Research*. London: Sage.

Churchill Jr., G.A. (1979) 'A paradigm for developing better measures of marketing constructs', *Journal of Marketing Research*, 16 (Feb), 64–73.

Cobanoglu, C. (2001) 'A comparison of mail, fax and web-based survey methods', *International Journal of Market Research*, 43(4), 441–55.

Curasi, C.F. (2001) 'A critical exploration of face-to-face interviewing vs. computer-mediated interviewing', *International Journal of Market Research*, 43(4), 361–77.

Deshpandé, R. and Zaltman, G. (1982) 'Factors affecting the use of market research information', *Journal of Marketing Research*, 19 (Feb), 14–31.

Deshpandé, R. and Zaltman, G. (1984) 'A comparison of factors affecting researcher and manager perceptions of market research use', *Journal of Marketing Research*, 21 (Feb), 32–38.

Diamantopoulos, A. and Horncastle, S. (1997) 'Use of export marketing research by industrial firms: An application and extension of Deshpandé and Zaltman's model', *International Business Review*, 6(3), 245–70.

Flynn, L.R. (2001) 'Four subtle sins in scale development: Some suggestions for strengthening the current paradigm', *International Journal of Market Research*, 43(4), 409–24.

Garvin, D.A. (1993) 'Building a learning organisation', *Harvard Business Review*, 71(4) (July/ Aug), 78–92.

Gibson, L.D. (1998) 'Defining marketing problems', *Marketing Research*. (Spring 1998). Chicago.

Harvey, M. (2001) 'Decoding competitive propositions: A semiotic alternative to traditional advertising research', *International Journal of Market Research*, 43(2), 171–88.

Higby, M.A. and Farah, B.N. (1991) 'Status of marketing information systems: Decisions support systems and expert systems in the marketing function of USA firms', *Information and Management*, 5, 29–35.

Kohli, A.K. and Jaworski, B.J. (1990) 'Market orientation: The construct, research propositions and managerial implications', *Journal of Marketing*, 54 (April), 1–14.

Kozinets, R.V. (2002) 'The Field behind the screen: Using netnography for marketing research in online communities', *Journal of Marketing Research*, 39(1), 61–72.

Kumar, V., Aaker, D.A. and Day, G.S. (2002) *Essentials of Marketing Research*. New York: Wiley.

Meidan, A. and Moutinho, L. (1999) 'Quantitative methods in marketing', in M. Baker (ed.) *The Marketing Book*, 4th edn. Oxford: Butterworth Heineman.

Menon, A. and Varadarajan, P.R. (1992) 'A model of marketing knowledge used in firms', *Journal of Marketing*, 56 (Oct), 53–71.

Moon, Y. (2000) 'Intimate exchanges: Using computers to elicit self-disclosure from consumers', *Journal of Consumer Research*, 28 (March), 323–39.

Oppermann, M. (1995) 'E-mail surveys: Potentials and pitfalls', *Marketing Research*, 7(3), 29–33.

Piercy, N.F. and Evans, E. (1999) 'Developing marketing information systems', in M.J. Baker (ed.) *The Marketing Book*. Oxford: Butterworth Heineman.

Schnaars, S.P. (1998) *Marketing Strategy: Customer Driven Approach*. New York: Free Press.

Shankar, A. and Patterson, M. (2001) 'Interpreting the past: Writing the future', *Journal of Marketing Management*, 17(5–6), 481–502.

Sinkula, J.M. (1994) 'Market information processing and organisational learning', *Journal of Marketing*, 58 (Jan), 35–45.

Slater, S.S. and Naver, J.C. (2000) 'Intelligence generation and superior customer value', *Journal of the Academy of Marketing Science*, 28(1), 120–27.

Souchon, A.L. and Diamantopoulos, A. (1996) 'A conceptual framework of export marketing information use: Key issues and research propositions', *Journal of International Marketing*, 4(3), 49–71.

Smith, D. and Dexter, A. (2001) 'Whenever I hear the word "paradigm", I reach for my gun: How to stop talking and start walking: Professional development strategy and tactics for the 21st century market researcher', *International Journal of Market Research*, 43(3), 321–40.

Turban, E., Lee, J., King, D. and Chung, H.M. (2000) *Electronic Commerce: A Managerial Perspective*. New Jersey: Prentice Hall.

Valentine, V. and Gordon, W. (2000) 'The 21st century consumer: A new model of thinking', *International Journal of Market Research*, 42(2), 185–209.

Webster, F.E. (1992) 'The changing role of marketing in corporations', *Journal of Marketing* (Oct.), 1–17.

Worcester, R. and Downham, J. (1988) *Consumer Market Research Handbook*, 3rd ed. London: McGraw Hill.

Further reading
Baker, M. and Hart, S. (1989) *Marketing and Competitive Success*. Hemel Hempstead: Philip Allan.

Baker, W.E. and Sinkula, J.M. (1999) 'The synergistic effect of market orientation and learning orientation on organisational performance', *Journal of the Academy of Marketing Science*, 27(4), 411–27.

Freeman, L. (1996) 'The third party suppliers playing greater role', *Advertising Ages Business Marketing*, (June), 12–20.

Huber, G.P. (1991) 'Organizational learning: The contributing processes and the literatures', *Organization Science*, 2 (Feb), 88–115.

Lee, H., Acito, F. and Day, R.L. (1987) 'Evaluation and use of marketing research by decision makers: A behavioural simulation', *Journal of Marketing Research*, 24 (May), 187–97.

Moorman, C., Zaltman, G. and Deshpande, R. (1992) 'Relationship between providers and users of market research: The dynamics of trust within and between organisations', *Journal of Marketing Research*, 29 (Aug), 314–28.

Perkins, W.S. and Rao, R.C. (1990) 'The role of experience in information use and decision making by marketing managers', *Journal of Marketing Research*, 27 (Feb), 1–10.

Slater, S.F. and Narver, J.C. (1995) 'Market orientation and the learning organisation', *Journal of Marketing*, 59 (July), 63–74.

Webb, J. (1999) 'Market research'. In M.J. Baker (ed.) *The Marketing Book*. Oxford: Butterworth Heineman.

Chapter 11

Beane, T.P. and Ennis, D.M. (1987) 'Market segmentation: A review', *European Journal of Marketing*, 21(5), 20–42.

Belk, R.W. (1975) 'Situational variables and consumer behavior', *Journal of Consumer Research*, 2, 157–64.

Bellis-Jones, R. (1989) 'Customer profitability analysis', *Management Accounting* (Feb), 26–28.

Blattberg, R.C. and Deighton, J. (1996) 'Manage marketing by the customer equity test', *Harvard Business Review* (July-Aug), 136–44.

Blattberg, R.C. and Sen, S.K. (1976) 'Market segments and stochastic brand choice models', *Journal of Marketing Research*, 13 (Feb), 34–45.

Bonoma, T.V. and Shapiro, B.P. (1984) 'Evaluating market segmentation approaches', *Industrial Marketing Management*, 13, 257–68.

Brown, H.E., Shivishankar, R. and Brucker, R.W. (1989) 'Requirements-driven market segmentation', *Industrial Marketing Management*, 18, 105–12.

Chandler, G.N. and Hanks, S.H. (1994) 'Market attractiveness, resource-based capabilities, venture strategies and venture performance', *Journal of Business Venturing*, 9(4), 331–49.

Chaffey, D., Mayer, R., Johnston, K. and Ellis-Chadwick, F. (2000) *Internet Marketing*. Harlow: Pearson Education.

Charan, R. and Colvin, G. (1999) 'Why CEOs fail', *Fortune* (Jun 21), 68–80.

Chéron, E.J. and Kleinschmidt, E.J. (1985) 'A review of industrial market segmentation research and a proposal for an integrated segmentation framework', *International Journal of Research in Marketing*, 2, 101–15.

Choffray, J.-M. and Lilien, G.L. (1980) *Marketing Planning for New Industrial Products*. New York: J. Wiley.

Claycamp, H.J. and Massy, W.F. (1968) 'A theory of market segmentation', *Journal of Marketing Research*, 5 (Nov), 388–96.

Coles, G.J. and Culley, J.D. (1986) 'Not all prospects are created equal', *Business Marketing* (May), 52–58.

Dibb, S. (1998) 'Market segmentation: Strategies for success', *Marketing Intelligence and Planning*, 16(7), 394–406.

Dibb, S. (1999) 'Criteria guiding segmentation implementation: Reviewing the evidence', *Journal of Strategic Marketing*, 7, 107–129.

Dibb, S. and Simkin, L. (1996) *The Market Segmentation Workbook: Target Marketing for Marketing Managers*. London: ITBP.

Dibb, S. and Simkin, L. (1997) 'A program for implementing market segmentation', *Journal of Business and Industrial Marketing*, 12(1), 51–65.

Dibb, S. and Simkin, L. (2001) *Marketing Briefs: A Revision and Study Guide*. Oxford: Butterworth-Heinemann.

Dibb, S. and Simkin, L. (2002 forthcoming) 'Market segmentation: Diagnosing and treating the barriers', *Industrial Marketing Management*.

Dibb, S., Simkin, L., Pride, W. and Ferrell, O.C. (2001) *Marketing: Concepts and Strategies*. Boston: Houghton Mifflin.

Dibb, S. and Stern, P. (1995) 'Questioning the reliability of market segmentation techniques', *OMEGA*, 23(6), 625–36.

Dickson, P.R. (1982) 'Person-situation: Segmentation's missing link', *Journal of Marketing*, 46, 56–64.

Dickson, P.R. (1994) *Marketing Management*. Fort Worth: The Dryden Press/Thomson Learning.

Doyle, P., Saunders, J.A. and Wong, V. (1986) 'A comparative study of Japanese marketing strategies in the British market', *Journal of International Business Studies*, 17(1), 27–46.

Doyle, P. (1995) 'Marketing in the new millennium', *European Journal of Marketing*, 29(13), 23–41.

Doyle, P. (1998) *Marketing Management*. London: Pearson.

Engle, J.F., Fiorillo, H.F. and Cayley, M.A. (1972) *Market Segmentation: Concepts and Applications*. New York: Rinehart and Winston Inc.

Frank, R.E., Massy, W.F. and Wind, Y. (1972) *Market Segmentation*. Englewood Cliffs: Prentice Hall.

Gilmore, J.H. and Pine, B.J. II (1997) 'The four faces of mass customization', *Harvard Business Review*, 75 (Jan–Feb), 91–101.

Green, P.E. and Carmone, F.J. (1970) *Multidimensional Scaling and Related Techniques in Marketing Analysis*. Boston: Allyn and Bacon, Inc.

Haley, R.I. (1984) 'Benefit segmentation – 20 years later', *Journal of Consumer Marketing*, 5–13.

Hooley, G.J. (1980) 'The multivariate jungle: The academic's playground but the manager's minefield', *European Journal of Marketing*, 14(7), 379–86.

Hooley, G.J. and Saunders, J.A. (1993) *Competitive Positioning: The Key to Market Success*. New York: Prentice Hall.

Howell, R.A. and Soucy, S.R. (1990) 'Customer profitability – as critical as product profitability', *Management Accounting*, (Oct), 43–47.

Jenkinson, A. (1995) *Valuing Your Customers: From Quality Information to Quality Relationship through Database Marketing*. London: McGraw-Hill.

Kotler, P. (1984, 2000) *Marketing Management*. Englewood Cliffs: Prentice Hall.

Littler, D. (1992) 'Market segmentation', in M.J. Baker (ed.), *Marketing Strategy and Management*. London: Macmillan, 90–103.

McDonald, M. (1995) *Marketing Plans*. Oxford: Butterworth-Heinemann.

McDonald, M. and Dunbar, I. (1995) *Market Segmentation*. Basingstoke: Macmillan Press Ltd.

Meadows, M. and Dibb, S. (1998) 'Assessing the implementation of market segmentation in retail financial services', *The International Journal of Service Industry Management*, 9(3), 266–85.

Mitchell, A. (2000a) 'Databases don't add up to one-to-one marketing', *Marketing Week*, 16 (Mar), 34–35.

Mitchell, A. (2000b) 'Balance of brand power tips to "wired" consumers', *Marketing Week*, 6 (Jan), 28–29.

Müller, K., and Halinen, A. (2000) 'Relationship marketing theory: Its roots and direction', *Journal of Marketing Management*, 16(1), 29–54.

Peppers, D. and Rogers, M. (1993) *The One-to-One Future*. London: Piatkus.

Peppers, D. and Rogers, M. (1999) *The One-to-One Manager*. New York: Currency Doubleday.

Peppers, D., Rogers, M. and Dorf, B. (1999) 'Manager's toolkit: Is your company ready for one-to-one marketing?', *Harvard Business Review*, 77 (Jan-Feb), 151–61.

Piercy, N. (2000) *Market-Led Strategic Change*. Oxford: Butterworth-Heinemann.

Piercy, N.F. and Morgan, N.A. (1993) 'Strategic and operational market segmentation: A managerial analysis', *Journal of Strategic Marketing*, 1, 123–40.

Plank, R.E. (1985) 'A critical review of industrial market segmentation', *Industrial Marketing Management*, 14, 79–91.

Postma, P. (1998) *The New Marketing Era: Marketing to the Imagination in a Technology-Driven World*. New York: McGraw-Hill.

Rapp, S. and Collins, T. (1991) *The Great Marketing Turnaround*. Englewood Cliffs, NJ: Prentice Hall.

Reichheld, F. (1993) 'Loyalty-based management', *Harvard Business Review*, 71 (Mar-Apr), 64–74.

Ries, A. and Trout, J. (1986) *Positioning: The Battle For Your Mind*. New York: McGraw-Hill.

Saunders, J.A. (1987) 'Marketing and competitive success', in M. Baker (ed.) *The Marketing Book*. Oxford: Butterworth-Heinemann.

Shapiro, B.P. and Bonoma, T.B. (1984) 'How to segment industrial markets', *Harvard Business Review* (May–Jun), 104–10.

Shepard, D. (1995) *The New Direct Marketing: How to Implement A Profit-Driven Database Marketing Strategy*. New York: Irwin.

Sheth, J.N., Banwari, M. and Newman, B. (1999) *Customer Behavior: Consumer Behavior and Beyond*. Fort Worth: The Dryden Press/Thomson Learning.

Sheth, J. N., Sisodia, R.S. and Sharma, A. (2000) 'Customer-centric marketing', *Journal of the Academy of Marketing Science*, 28(1), 55–66.

Simkin, L. and Dibb, S. (1998) 'Prioritising target markets', *Marketing Intelligence and Planning*, 16(7), 407–17.

Sleight, P. (1997) *Targeting Customers*. Henley on Thames: NTC Publications.

Smith, W. (1956) 'Product differentiation and market segmentation as alternative marketing strategies', *Journal of Marketing*, 21, 3–8.

Storbacka, K. (1997) 'Segmentation based on customer profitability – retrospective analysis of retail bank customer bases', *Journal of Marketing Management*, 13, 479–92.

Trout, J. and Rivkin, S. (1996) *The New Positioning: The Latest on the World's Number 1 Business Strategy*. New York: McGraw-Hill.

Wedel, M. and Kamakura, W. (2000) *Market Segmentation: Conceptual and Methodological Foundations*. Boston: Kluwer Academic Publishers.

Weinstein, A. (1994) *Market Segmentation*. New York: McGraw-Hill.

Webster, F.E. (1991) *Industrial Marketing Strategy*. New York: John Wiley.

Wensley, R. (1981) 'Strategic marketing: Betas, boxes or basic', *Journal of Marketing*, 45, 173–83.

Wilkinson, A. (2001) 'Retailers are doing it for themselves', *Marketing Week* (Sept 27), 19–20.

Wind, Y. (1978) 'Issue and advances in segmentation research', *Journal of Marketing Research*, 15 (Aug), 317–37.

Young, S., Ott, L. and Feigin, B. (1978) 'Some practical considerations in market segmentation', *Journal of Marketing Research*, 15 (Aug), 405–12.

Zeithaml, V. (2000) 'Service quality, profitability, and the economic worth of customers: What we know and what we need to learn', *Journal of the Academy of Marketing Science*, 28(1), 67–85.

Electronic references

http://www.egg.com
http://www.hsbc.com
http://www.lego.com
http://www.tesco.co.uk

Chapter 12

Allen, T.J. (1985) *Managing the Flow of Technology*. Cambridge: MIT Press.

Anderson, J. (1981) *Cognitive Skills and Their Acquisition*. NJ: Erlbaum.

Ansoff, H.I. (1979) *Strategic Management*. London: Macmillan.

Argyris, C. and Schon, D. (1978) *Organizational Learning*. Reading, MA: Addison-Wesley.

Blackler, F. (1995) 'Knowledge, knowledge work and organization: An overview and interpretation', *Organization Studies*, 16(6), 1021–46.

Bonnet, D. (1986) 'Nature of R&D/marketing co-operation in the design of technologically advanced new industrial products', *R&D Management*, 16(2).

Booz Allen and Hamilton (1982) *Management of New Products for the 1980s*. BAH Inc.

Bourgeois, L. and Eisenhardt, K. (1988) 'Strategic decision processes in high velocity environments', *Management Science*, 14, 816–35.

Brown, A. and Starkey, K. (1994) 'The effect of organisational culture on communication and information', *Journal of Management Studies*, 31(6), 807–28.

Burns, T. and Stalker, G.M. (1961) *The Management of Innovations*. London: Tavistock Publications.

Button, S., Mathieu, J. and Zajac, D. (1996) 'Goal orientation in organisational research: A conceptual and empirical foundation', *Organizational Behavior and Human Decision Processes*, 67(1), 26–48.

Cardozo, R., McLaughlin, K., Harmon, B., Reynolds, P. and Miller, B. (1993) 'Product market choices and growth of new businesses', *Journal of Product Innovation Management*, 10(4), 331–40.

Cohn, S.F. and Turyn, R.M. (1984) 'Organizational structure, decision-making procedures, and the adoption of innovations', *IEEE Transactions on Engineering Management*, EM-31(4), 154–61.

Collins, H. (1993) 'The structure of knowledge', *Social Research*, 60, 95–116.

Cooper, R.G. (1979) 'The dimensions of industrial new product success and failure', *Journal of Marketing*, 43 (Summer), 93–103.

Cooper, R.G. (1993) *Winning at New Product*, 2nd edn. Reading, MA: Addison Wesley.

Cooper, R.G. (1994) 'Third generation new product processes', *Journal of Product Innovation Management*, 11, 3–14.

Cooper, R.G. and Kleinschmidt, E. (1987) 'Success factors in product innovation', *Industrial Marketing Management*, 16, 215–23.

Cooper, R.G. and Kleinschmidt, E.J. (1991) 'The impact of product innovativeness on performance', *Journal of Product Innovation Management*, 8(4), 240–51.

Cooper, R.G. and Kleinschmidt, E.J. (1993) 'New product success in the chemical industry', *Industrial Marketing Management*, 22(2), 85–99.

Cooper, R.G. and Kleinschmidt, E.J. (1994) 'Determinants of timeliness in product development', *Journal of Product Innovation Management*, 11(5), 381–96.

Craig, A. and Hart, S. (1992) 'Where to now in new product development research?', *European Journal of Marketing*, 26(11), 3–49.

Crawford, C.M. (1994) *New Product Management*, 4th edn. IL: Richard D. Irwin.

Daft, R.L. and Weick, K.E. (1984) 'Toward a model of organisations as interpretation systems', *Academy of Management Review*, 9(2), 284–95.

Day, G. and Nedungadi, P. (1994) 'Managerial representations of competitive advantage', *Journal of Marketing*, 58, 31–44.

Day, G.S. (1994) 'The capabilities of market driven organisations', *Journal of Marketing*, 58, 37–52.

De Meyer, A. (1985) 'The flow of technological innovation in an R&D department', *Research Policy*, 14, 315–28.

Dewar, R.D. and Dutton, J.E. (1986) 'The adoption of radical and incremental innovations: An empirical analysis', *Management Science*, 32(11), 1422–33.

Diehl, E. and Sterman, J. (1995) 'Effects of feedback complexity on dynamic decision making', *Organisational Behavior and Human Decision Processes*, 62(2), 198–215.

Dougherty, D. (1992) 'A practice-centered model of organisational renewal through product innovation', *Strategic Management Journal*, 13, 77–92.

Dumaine, B. (1991) 'Earning more by moving faster', *Fortune*, 7 (Oct), 89–90.

Dweck, C. and Leggett E. (1988) 'A social-cognitive approach to motivation and personality', *Psychological Review*, 95, 256–73.

Dweck, C. (1986) 'Motivational processes affecting learning', *American Psychologist*, 41, 1040–48.

Eisenhardt, K., Kahwajy, J. and Bourgeois, L., III (1997) 'Conflict and strategic choice', *California Management Review*, 39(2), 42–62.

Elliott, E. and Dweck, C. (1988) 'Goals: An approach to motivation and achievement', *Journal of Personality and Social Psychology*, 54, 5–12.

Feldman, D. (1976) 'A contingency theory of socialisation', *Administrative Science Quarterly*, 21, 433–50.

Galbraith, J.R. (1986) *Designing Complex Organisations*. Reading, MA: Addison Wesley Publishing Company.

Glazer, R. (1991) 'Marketing in an information intensive environment: Strategic implications of knowledge as an asset', *Journal of Marketing*, 55 (Oct), 1–19.

Goldhar, J.D., Bragaw, L.K. and Schwartz, J.J. (1976) 'Information flows, management styles and technological innovation', *IEEE Transactions on Engineering Management*, EM-23(1), 51–62.

Griffin, A. (1993) 'Metrics for measuring product development cycle time', *Journal of Product Innovation Management*, 10(2), 112–25.

Griffin, A. (1997) 'The effect of project and process characteristics on product development cycle time', *Journal of Marketing Research*, 34 (Feb), 24–35.

Gupta, A.K. and Wilemon, D. (1990) 'Improving R&D/marketing relations: R&D's perspective', *R&D Management*, 20(4), 277–90.

Hall, D. (1987) 'Careers and socialisation', *Journal of Marketing*, 13, 301–21.

Hart, S. (1992) 'An integrative framework for strategy-making processes', *Academy of Management Review*, 17, 327–51.

Hart, S. and Baker, M. (1994) 'Learning from success: Multiple convergent processing in new product development', *International Marketing Review*, 11(1), 77–92.

Hart, S. and Banbury, C. (1994) 'How strategy-making processes can make a difference', *Strategic Management Journal*, 15, 251–69.

Hauptman, O. (1986) 'Influence of task type on the relationship between communication and performance – the case of software-development', *R&D Management*, 16(2), 127–39.

Holbek, J. (1988) 'The innovation design dilemma: Some notes on its relevance and solutions'. In K. Kronhaug and G. Kaufmann (eds), *Innovation: A Cross Disciplinary Perspective*, Norwegian University Press, 253–78.

Huber, G. (1991) 'Organisational learning: The contributing processes and the literatures', *Organisational Science*, 2, 88–115.

Johne, A. (1994) 'Listening to the voice of the market', *International Marketing Review*, 11(1), 47–59.

Kanter, R. (1988) 'When a thousand flowers bloom: Structural, collective and social conditions for innovations in organisations'. In L. Cummings and B. Staw (eds), *Research in Organisational Behavior*, 10, 169–211. Greenwich, CT: JAI Press.

Keeney, R. (1992) *Value-focused Thinking: A Path to Creative Decision Making*. London: Harvard University Press.

Kinnear, T.C. and Taylor, J.R. (1991) *Marketing Research: An Applied Approach*. Singapore: McGraw-Hill.

Kohli, A.K. and Jaworski, B.J. (1990) 'Market orientation – the construct, research propositions and managerial implications', *Journal of Marketing*, 54(2), 1–18.

Lawrence, P.R. and Lorsch, J.W. (1967) 'Differentiation and integration in complex organisations', *Administrative Science Quarterly*, 12(1), 1–47.

Leonard-Barton, D. (1991) 'Inanimate integrators: A block of wood speaks', *Design Management Journal*, 2(3), 60–67.

Levine, J., Rescnick, L. and Higgins, E. (1993) 'Social foundations of cognition', *Annual Review of Psychology*, 41, 585–612.

Levitt, B. and March, J.G. (1988) 'Organisational learning', *Annual Review of Sociology*, 14, 319–40.

Link, P.L. (1987) 'Keys to new product success and failure', *Industrial Marketing Management*, 16, 109–18.

Louis, M. (1980) 'Surprise and sense making: What newcomers experience in entering unfamiliar organisational settings', *Administrative Science Quarterly*, 25, 226–51.

Mahoney, J.S. and Pandian J.R. (1992) 'The resource-based view within the conversations of strategic management', *Strategic Management Journal*, 13, 363–80.

Maidique, M.A. and Zirger, B.J. (1984) 'A study of success and failure in product innovation: The case of the U.S. electronics industry', *IEEE Transactions On Engineering Management*, EM-31(4), 192–203.

Marty, E.O. (1994) 'Process models and the marketing concept'. In *Proceedings of the 24th Conference of the European Academy of Marketing*, 683–702. Paris.

Mayers, S. and Marquis, D.G. (1969) 'Successful industrial innovation', *National Science Foundation*, nsf, 69–117.

McDonough, E.F. III and Leifer, R.P. (1986) 'Effective control of new product projects: The integration of organisation, culture and project leadership', *Journal of Product Innovation Management*, 3(3), 149–57.

McGrath, J. (1984) *Groups: Interaction and Performance*. NJ: Prentice Hall.

Mintzberg, H. (1983) *Structures in Fives: Designing Effective Organisations*. Englewood Cliffs, NJ: Prentice-Hall.

Mintzberg, H., Raisinghani, D. and Thoret, A. (1976) 'The structure of unstructured decisions', *Administrative Science Quarterly*, 21, 246–75.

Moenaert, R.K. and Souder, W.E. (1990) 'An information transfer model for integrating marketing and R&D personnel in NPD projects', *Journal of Product Innovation Management*, 7(2), 91–107.

Montoya-Weiss, M.M. and Colantone, R. (1994) 'Determinants of new product performance: A review and meta-analysis', *Journal of Product Innovation Management*, 11(5), 397–417.

Moorman, C. (1995) 'Organisational market information processes: Cultural antecedents and new product outcomes', *Journal of Marketing Research*, 32 (Aug), 318–35.

More, R.A. (1985) 'Patterns of market research timing for new industrial products', *R&D Management*, 15(4), 271–81.

Nonaka, I. (1988) 'Toward middle-up-down management: Accelerating information creation', *Sloan Management Review*, 29, 9–18.

Olson, E.M., Walker, O.C. Jr. and Ruekert, R.W. (1995) 'Organizing for effective NPD: The moderating role of product innovativeness', *Journal of Marketing*, 59 (Jan), 48–62.

Ortt, R.J. and Schoormans, J.P.L. (1993) 'Consumer research in the development process of a major innovation', *Journal of the Market Research Society*, 35(4), 375–87.

Parks, C. and Cowlin, R. (1996) 'Acceptance of uncommon information into group discussion when that information is or is not demonstrable', *Organisational Behavior and Human Decision Processes*, 66(3), 307–15.

Quinn, R. (1988) *Beyond Rational Management*. CA: Jossey Bass.

Ramanujiam, M. and Mensch, G.O. (1985) 'Improving the strategy-innovation link', *Journal of Product Innovation Management*, 2(4), 213–23.

Reitman, W.R. (1965) *Cognition and Thought: An Information Processing Approach*. NY: John Wiley & Sons.

Roberts, R.W. and Burke, J.E. (1974) 'Six new products–what made them successful?', *Research Management* (May), 21–24.

Robertson, T. (1967) 'The process of innovation and the diffusion of innovation', *Journal of Marketing* (Jan), 14–17.

Rochford, L. and Rudelius, W. (1992) 'How involving more functional areas within a firm affects the new product process', *Journal of Product Innovation Management*, 9(4), 287–99.

Rothwell, R. (1977) 'The characteristics of successful innovators and technically progressive firms', *R&D Management*, 7 (part 3), 191–206.

Rothwell, R., Freeman, C., Horsley, A., Jervis, V., Robertson, A. and Townsend, J. (1974) 'Project SAPPHO Phase II', *Research Policy*, 3, 258–91.

Rothwell, R. and Robertson, A.B. (1973) 'The role of communication in technological innovation', *Research Policy*, 2, 204–25.

Rubenstein, A.H., Chakrabarti, A.K., O'Keefe, R.D., Souder, W.E. and Young, H.C. (1976) 'Factors influencing innovation success at the project level', *Research Management*, 3, 15–20.

Saren, M.S. (1994) 'Reframing the process of new product development: From stages models to a blocks', *Journal of Marketing Management*, 10(7), 633–44.

Schein, E. (1968) 'Organisational socialisation and the profession of management', *Industrial Management Review*, 9, 1–16.

Schroeder, R., Van De Ven, A., Scudder, G. and Polley, D. (1989) 'The development of innovation ideas'. In A. Van De Ven, H. Angle and M. Poole (eds), *Research on the Management of Innovation*, 107–34. NY: Harper & Row.

Senge, P. (1990) *The Fifth Discipline*. NY: Doubleday.

Shanteau, J. (1992) 'Competence in experts: The role of task characteristics', *Organisational Behavior and Human Decision Processes*, 53, 252–66.

Shrivastava, P. (1983) 'A typology of organisational learning systems', *Journal of Management Studies*, 20, 1–28.

Sinkula, J.M. (1994) 'Market information processing and organisational learning', *Journal of Marketing*, 58, 35–45.

Slater, S. and Narver, J. (1995) 'Market orientation and the learning organisation', *Journal of Marketing*, 59, 63–74.

Souder, W.E. and Moenaert, R.K. (1992) 'An information uncertainty model for integrating marketing and R&D personnel in NPD projects', *Journal of Management Studies*, 29(4), 485–512.

Svenson, O. and Malmsten, N. (1996) 'Post-decision consolidation over time as a function of gain or loss of an alternative', *Scandinavian Journal of Psychology*, 85, 39–52.

Svenson, O. (1996) 'Decision making and the search for fundamental psychological regularities', *Organisational Behavior and Human Decision Processes*, 65(3), 252–67.

Takeuchi, H. and Nonaka, I. (1986) 'The new product development game', *Harvard Business Review*, (Jan–Feb), 137–46.

Tull, S.D. and Hawkins, D.I. (1992) *Marketing Research: Measurements and Methods*. NY: Collier Macmillan.

Van Maanen, J. and Schein, E. (1979) 'Toward a theory of organisational socialisation'. In B. Staw (ed.) *Research in Organisational Behavior*. Greenwich, CT: JAI Press.

Victor, B. and Blackburn, R.S. (1987) 'Determinants and consequences of task uncertainty – A laboratory and field investigation', *Journal of Management Studies*, 24(4), 387–404.

Voss, C.A. (1985) 'Determinants of success in the development of application software', *Journal of Product Innovation Management*, 2, 122–29.

Webster, F.E. (1988) 'Developing, disseminating and utilising marketing knowledge', *Journal of Marketing*, 52(4), 48–51.

Wind, J. and Mahajan, V. (1997) 'Issues and opportunities in new product development', *Journal of Marketing Research*, 34, 1–12.

Wind, Y. and Cardozo, R. (1974) 'Industrial Market Segmentation', *Industrial Marketing Management*, 3 (Mar), 153–66.

Chapter 13

Anderson, W.T. (1999) 'Communities in a world of open systems', *Futures*, 31, 457–63.

Anon (1999) 'UK Perspectives Airs Photographic Census', *Precision Marketing*, May 24, 5.

Acland (2001) 'Ruling puts DM industry firmly on back foot', *Marketing Direct*, December, 3.

Arnold, C. (2002) reported by Rubach, E. (2002) 'Up close and too personal', *Precision Marketing*, February, 12.

Borna, S. and Avila, S. (1999) 'Genetic information: Consumers' right to privacy versus insurance companies' right to know: A public opinion survey', *Journal of Business Ethics*, 19, 355–62.

Carson, C.D. (1999) 'What it takes and where to get it', working paper, University of North Carolina.

Channel 4 (1990) 'Direct Marketing', Equinox series.

Chartered Institute of Marketing (2001) 'The impact of E-business on marketing and marketers', October, Cookham. (Website for CIM direct purchase: http://www.connected inmarketin.co.uk, tel. 44 (0)1628 427427)

CIM (2001) 'Marketing trends survey', library@cim.co.uk

Clegg, A. (2001) 'Strong medicine', *Database Marketing*, March, 14–20.

Depres, C. and Chauvel, D. (2000) 'How to map knowledge management'. In D.A. Marchand, T.H. Davenport and T. Dickson (eds), (2000) *Mastering Information Management*. London: Financial Times/Prentice Hall, pp. 170–76.

Dibb, S. (2001) 'New millennium', new segments: Moving towards the segment of one', *Journal of Strategic Marketing*, 9(3), Summer, 193–14.

Evans, M. (1999) 'Direct marketing'. In P. Kitchen, *Marketing Communications: Principles and Practice*. Thomson Business Press, pp. 309–24.

Evans, M. (2000) 'Database marketing: A wider social responsibility', Academy of Marketing Conference, University of Derby, July.

Evans, M. and Fill, C. (2000) 'Extending the communications process: The significance of personal influencers in the UK motor market', *International Journal of Advertising*, 19(2), 43–65.

Evans, M. and Middleton, S. (1998) 'Testing and research in direct mail: the agency perspective', with S Middleton, *Journal of Database Marketing*, 6(2), 127–44.

Evans, M., Nancarrow, C., Tapp, A. and Stone, M. (2002) 'Future marketing, future marketers, future shock', Academy of Marketing Conference, July, University of Nottingham.

Evans, M., O'Malley, L. and Patterson, M. (1997) 'Database marketing: exploring consumer concerns', *Journal of Marketing Communications*, 3(3), 151–74.

Evans, M., O'Malley, L. and Patterson, M. (2001a) 'Bridging the direct marketing-direct consumer gap: Some solutions from qualitative research', *Qualitative Market Research: An International Journal*, 4(1), 17–24.

Evans, M., Wedande, G., Ralston, L. and van t'Hul, S. (2001b) 'Consumer interaction in the virtual era: Some solutions from qualitative research', *Qualitative Market Research: An International Journal*, 4(3), 150–59.

Evans et al. (2001) Web communities, in future marketing series. MA marketing programme for the Open University.

France, E. (1998) as reported by S. Davies (1998) 'New data privacy storm threatens global trade war', *Financial Mail on Sunday*, 29 March, 3.

Gofton, K. (2001) 'Firms fail to relate to customers', *Marketing Direct*, January, 10.

Haeckel (2001) in A. Mitchell (2001) 'Playing cat and mouse games with marketing', *Precision Marketing*, March 16, 14.

Hansard (1999) *House of Commons Debates*, February 3, 22.

Introna, L. and Powlouda, A. (1999) 'Privacy in the information age: Stakeholders, interests and values', *Journal of Business Ethics*, 22, 27–38.

Jephcott, J. and Bock, T. (1998) 'The application and validation of data fusion', *Journal of the Market Research Society*, 40(3), 185–205.

Kennedy, R. and Ehrenberg, A. (2000) 'What's in a Brand?', *Research*, April, 30–32.

Key, A. (2000) 'The taxman: Snooper or helper', *Marketing Direct*, February, 13.

Lavidge, R.J. (1970) 'The growing responsibilities of marketing', *Journal of Marketing*, 34, January, 25–28.

Lazer, W. (1969) 'Marketing's changing social relationships', *Journal of Marketing*, 33, January, 3–9.

Mackintosh, J. (2002) 'Halifax sorry for snub to "cash heavy" businesses', *Financial Times*, February 27.

Marsh, H. (2001) 'Dig deeper into the database goldmine', *Marketing*, January 11, 29–30.

Mitchell, A. (2001) 'The end of the hype', *Marketing Business*, November, 15.

O'Malley, L., Patterson, M. and Evans, M. (1999) *Exploring Direct Marketing*. Thomson Learning.

O'Malley, L. and Tynan, C. (1999) 'A reappraisal of the relationship marketing', *Journal of Marketing Management*.

Packard, V. (1957) *The Hidden Persuaders*. Penguin, p. 195.

Parker, G. (1999) 'Tories accused of GM foods scaremongering', *Financial Times*, February 4, 8.

Precision Marketing (2001–2) November and December 2001, and January 2002, headlines, p. 1 in all cases.

Rheingold, H. (1993) *The Virtual Community: Homesteading on the Electronic Frontier*. Reading, MA: Addison-Wesley Publishing Co.

Rubach, E. (2002) 'Up close and too personal', *Precision Marketing*, February 1, 12.

Shubik, M. (1967) 'Information, rationality and free choice in a future democratic Society', *Daedalus*, 96, 771–78.

Shultz, D., Tannenaum, S. and Lauterborn, R. (1993) *The New Marketing Paradigm*. Lincolnwood, Ill: NTC Business Books.

Smith, G. (1997) 'Letter to IDM Members', September 4, 1.

Specter, M. (1999) 'Cracking the Norse code', *Sunday Times Magazine*, March 21, 45–52.

Wood, J. (1998) 'Mail marketing group to share leads with US firm', *Precision Marketing*, June 15, 6.

Westin, A. (1992) 'Consumer privacy protection: Ten predictions', *Mobus*, February, 5–11.

Chapter 14

Hamill, J. (forthcoming) *Customer Led e-Business.*

Horovitz, J. (2000) 'Using information to bond customers'. In D. Marchand, *Competing With Information.* Wiley.

Newell, F. (2000) *Loyalty.com: Customer Relationship Management in the New Era of Internet Marketing.* New York: McGraw Hill.

Nykamp, M. (2001) *The Customer Differential.* AMACOM.

Peppers, D. and Rogers, M. (1997) *Enterprise One to One: Tools for Competing in the Interactive Age.* London: Piatkus.

Peppers, D., Rogers, M. and Dorf, B. (1999a) 'Is your company ready for one-to-one marketing', *Harvard Business Review*, 77(1), Jan–Feb, 151–60.

Peppers, D., Rogers, M. and Dorf, B. (1999b) *The One to One Fieldbook.* Oxford: Capstone Publishing.

Reinartz, W. and Kumar, V. (2002) 'The mismanagement of customer loyalty', *Harvard Business Review*, July.

Seigel, D. (1999) *Futurize Your Enterprise.* New York: John Wiley & Sons.

Seybold, P. (1998) *Customers.com: How to Create a Profitable Business Strategy for the Internet and Beyond.* London: Century Business.

Further reading

Burnett, K. (2001) *The Handbook of Key Customer Relationship Management.* Prentice-Hall.

Chattel, A. (1998) *Creating Value in the Digital Era.* London: Macmillan Business Press.

Davenport, T.H., Harris, J.G. and Kohli, A.K. (2001) 'How do they know their customers so well?', *MIT Sloan Management Review*, Winter, 63–73.

Ellsworth, J.H. and Ellsworth, M.V. (1995) *Marketing on the Internet.* New York: John Wiley & Sons.

Foss, B. and Stone, M. (2002) *CRM in Financial Services: A Practical Guide to Making Customer Relationship Management Work.* Kogan Page.

Godin, S. (1999) *Permission Marketing: Turning Strangers Into Friends, and Friends into Customers.* New York: Simon & Schuster.

Hamel, G. (2000) *Leading the Revolution.* Boston: Harvard Business School Press.

Hamill, J. (1997) 'The Internet and international marketing', *International Marketing Review*, 14(5), 300–23.

Hamill, J. and Ennis, S. (1999) 'The Internet: The direct route to growth and development'. In M.J. Baker (ed.), *The Marketing Book*, Fourth Edition. Oxford: Butterworth-Heinemann, pp. 693–705.

Hamill, J. and Gregory, K. (1997) 'Internet marketing in the internationalisation of UK SMEs', *Journal of Marketing Management*, 13(1–3), 9–28.

Hoffman, D.L. and Novak, T.P. (1996) 'Marketing in hypermedia computer-mediated environments: Conceptual foundations', *Journal of Marketing*, 60(3), July, 50–68.

Hoffman, D.L. and Novak, T.P. (1997) 'A new marketing paradigm for electronic commerce', *The Information Society*, 13(1), 43–54.

Hoffman, D.L. and Novak, T.P. (2000) 'How to acquire customers on the Web', *Harvard Business Review*, 78(3), May–June, 179–88.

Kaplan, S. and Sawney, M. (2000) 'E-Hubs: The new B2B marketplaces', *Harvard Business Review*, 78(3), May–June, 97–103.

Kenny, D. and Marshall, J.F. (2000) 'Contextual marketing: The real business of the Internet', *Harvard Business Review*, 78(6), Nov–Dec, 119–25.

Kerrigen, R., Roegner, E.V., Swinford, D.D. and Zawada, C.C. (2001) 'B2Basics', *The McKinsey Quarterly*, 1, 45–53.

Molenaar, C. (2002) *The Future of Marketing: Practical Strategies for Marketers in the Post-Internet Age.* Prentice-Hall.

Murphy, J.A. (2001) *The Lifebelt: The Definitive Guide to Managing Customer Retention.* Wiley.

Porter, M.E. (2001) 'Strategy and the Internet', *Harvard Business Review*, 79(3), March, 62–78.

Quelch, J.A. and Klein, L.R. (1996) 'The Internet and international marketing', *Sloan Management Review*, Spring, 60–75.

Raisch, W.D. (2001) *The eMarketplace: Strategies for Success in B2B eCommerce*. New York: McGraw-Hill.

Ramsdell, G. (2000) 'The real business of B2B', *The McKinsey Quarterly*, 3, 174–84.

Rubio, J. and Laughlin, P. (2002) *Planting Flowers, Pulling Weeds: Identifying Your Most Profitable Customers to Ensure a Lifetime of Growth*. Wiley.

Sculley, A.B. and Woods, W.W.A. (1999) *B2B Exchanges: The Killer Application in the Business-to-Business Internet Revolution*. Hamilton, Bermuda: ISI Publications.

Seybold, P.B. (2001) 'Get inside the lives of your customers', *Harvard Business Review*, 79(5), May, 81–89.

Sterne, J. (1996) *Customer Service on the Internet*. New York: John Wiley & Sons.

Tapscott, D., Ticoll, D. and Lowy, A. (2000) *Digital Capital: Harnessing the Power of Business Webs*. London: Nicolas Brealey Publishing.

Varianini, V. and Vaturi, D. (2000) 'Marketing lessons from e-failures', *The McKinsey Quarterly*, 4, 86–97.

Wind, J. and Mahajan, V. (2001) 'The challenge of digital marketing'. In J. Wind and V. Mahajan (eds), *Digital Marketing: Global Strategies from the World's Leading Experts*. New York: John Wiley & Sons, pp. 3–25.

Wise, R. and Morrison, D. (2000) 'Beyond the Exchange: The Future of B2B', *Harvard Business Review*, 78(6), Nov–Dec), 86–96.

Chapter 15

Aaker, D.A. (1991) *Managing Brand Equity*. New York: Free Press.

Aaker, D.A. (1996) *Building Strong Brands*. New York: Free Press.

Agarwal, M.K. and Rao, V.R. (1996) 'An empirical comparison of consumer-based measures of brand equity', *Marketing Letters*, 7(3), 237–47.

Ambler, T. and Barwise, P. (1998) 'The trouble with brand valuation', *Journal of Brand Management*, 5(5 May), 367–77.

Ambler, T. and Kokkinaki, F. (1997) 'Measures of marketing success', *Journal of Marketing Management*, 13, 665–78.

Anderson, E. and Oliver, R.L. (1987) 'Perspectives on behavior-based versus outcome-based salesforce control systems', *Journal of Marketing*, 51 (October), 76–88.

Andersen, A. (1992) *The Valuation of Intangible Assets*, Special Report # P254, London: The Economist Intelligence Unit.

Assmus, G., Farley, J.U. and Lehmann, D. (1984) 'How advertising affects sales: Meta analysis of econometric results', *Journal of Marketing Research*, 21 (February), 65–74.

Aulakh, P.S. and Gencturk, E.F. (2000) 'International principal–agent relationship', *Industrial Marketing Management*, 29, 521–38.

Babakus, E., Cravens, D.W., Grant, K., Ingram, T.N. and LaForge, R.W. (1996) 'Investigating the relationships among sales, management control, sales territory design, salesperson performance, and sales organization effectiveness', *International Journal of Research in Marketing*, 13, 345–63.

Bergen, M., Dutta, S. and Walker Jr, O.C. (1992) 'Agency relationship in marketing: A review of the implications and applications of the agency and related theories', *Journal of Marketing*, 56 (July), 1–24.

Bhargava, M., Dubelaar, C. and Ramaswami, S. (1994) 'Reconciling diverse measures of performance: A conceptual framework and test of a methodology', *Journal of Business Research*, 31, 235–46.

Bonoma, T.V. and Clark, B.C. (1988) *Marketing Performance Assessment*. Boston: Harvard Business School Press.

Brown, C.L. (1999) ' "Do the right thing": diverging effects of accountability in a managerial context', *Marketing Science*, 18(3), 230–46.

Buckley, R., Hall, S., Benson, P.G. and Buckley, M. (1988) 'The impact of rating scale format on rater accuracy: An evaluation', *Journal of Management*, 14(3), 415–23.

Buzzell, R.D. and Gale, B.T. (1987) *The PIMS Principles: Linking Strategy to Performance*. New York: Free Press.

Celly, K.S. and Frazier, G.L. (1996) 'Outcome-based and behavior-based coordination efforts in channel relationships', *Journal of Marketing Research*, 33(May), 200–10.

Chakravarthy, B.S. (1986) 'Measuring strategic performance', *Strategic Management Journal*, 7, 437–58.

Chattopadhyay, P., Glick, W.H., Miller, C.C. and Huber, G.P. (1999) 'Determinants of executive beliefs: Comparing functional conditioning and social influence', *Strategic Management Journal*, 20, 763–89.

Clark, B.H. (1999) 'Marketing performance measures: History and interrelationships', *Journal of Marketing Management*, 15, 711–32.

Collins, J.C. and Porras, J.I. (1995) *Built to Last*. London: Century.

Cravens, D.W., Ingram, T.N., LaForge, R.W. and Young, C.E. (1993) 'Behavior-based and outcome-based salesforce control systems', *Journal of Marketing*, 57 (October), 47–59.

Cutler, M. and Sterne, J. (2000) *E-Metrics: Business Metrics For The New Economy*. Net Genesis and Target Marketing of Santa Barbara.

Davidson, J.H. (1999) 'Transforming the value of company reports through marketing measurement', *Journal of Marketing Management*, 15, 757–77.

Dawes, P.L., Lee, D.Y. and Dowling, G.R. (1998) 'Information control and influence in emergent buying centers', *Journal of Marketing*, 62 (July), 55–68.

Day, G.S. (1994a) 'The capabilities of market driven organizations', *Journal of Marketing*, 58 (October), 37–52.

Day, G.S. (1994b) 'Continuous learning about markets', *California Management Review*, Summer, 9–31.

Day, G.S. and Fahey, L. (1988) 'Valuing market strategies', *Journal of Marketing*, 52 (July), 45–57.

Day, G.S. and Nedungadi, P. (1994) 'Managerial representations of competitive advantage', *Journal of Marketing*, 58 (April), 31–44.

Day, G.S. and Wensley, R. (1988) 'Assessing advantage: A framework for diagnosing competitive superiority', *Journal of Marketing*, 52 (April), 1–20.

Dearborn, D.C. and Herbert, A.S. (1958) 'Selective perception: A note on the departmental identifications of executives', *Sociometry*, 21, 140–44.

Dekimpe, M.G. and Hanssens, D.M. (1995) 'The persistence of marketing effects on sales', *Marketing Science*, 14(1), 1–21.

Dekimpe, M.G. and Hanssens, D.M. (1999) 'Sustained spending and persistent response: A new look at long-term marketing profitability', *Journal of Marketing Research*, 36 (November), 397–412.

Deshpandé, R., Farley, J.U. and Webster Jr, F.E. (1993) 'Corporate culture, customer orientation, and innovativeness in Japanese firms: A quadrad analysis', *Journal of Marketing*, 57 (January), 23–36.

Deshpandé, R. and Webster Jr, F.E. (1989) 'Organizational culture and marketing: Defining the research agenda', *Journal of Marketing*, 53 (January), 3–15.

Dick, A.S. and Basu, K. (1994) 'Customer loyalty: Towards an integrated conceptual framework', *Journal of the Academy of Marketing Science*, 28(5), 5–16.

Dunn, M.G., Norburn, D. and Birley, S. (1994) 'The impact of organizational values, goals, and climate on marketing effectiveness', *Journal of Business Research*, 30, 131–41.

Eccles, R.G. (1991) 'The performance measurement manifesto', *Harvard Business Review*, 69 (Jan–Feb), 131–37.

Eisenhardt, K.M. (1985) 'Control: Organizational and economic approaches', *Management Science*, 31(2), 134–49.

Eisenhardt, K.M. (1988) 'Agency- and institutional-theory explanations: The case of retail sales compensation', *Academy of Management Journal*, 31(3), 488–511.

Eisenhardt, K.M. (1989) 'Agency theory: An assessment and review', *Academy of Management Journal*, 14(1), 57–74.

Fama, E.F. (1980) 'Agency problems and the theory of the firm', *Journal of Political Economy*, 88(2), 288–307.

Fama, E.F. and Jensen, M.C. (1983) 'Separation of ownership and control', *Journal of Law and Economics*, 26 (June), 301–25.

Farquhar, P.H. (1989) 'Managing brand equity', *Marketing Research*, 1 (September), 24–33.

Fattah, H. (2000), 'The metrics system', *Brandweek*, November 13.

Feder, R.A. (1965) 'How to measure marketing performance', *Harvard Business Review*, 43 (May–June), 132–42.

Fisher, R.J., Maltz, E. and Jaworski, B.J. (1997) 'Enhancing communication between marketing and engineering: The moderating role of relative functional identification', *Journal of Marketing*, 61 (July), 54–70.

Fraser, C. and Hite, R.E. (1988) 'An adaptive utility approach for improved use of marketing models', *Journal of Marketing*, 52 (October), 96–103.

Frazier, G.L. and Howell, R.D. (1982) 'Intra-industry marketing strategy effects on the analysis of firm performance', *Journal of Business Research*, 10(4), 431–43.

Glazer, R. (1991) 'Marketing in an information-intensive environment: Strategic implications of knowledge as an asset', *Journal of Marketing*, 55 (October), 1–19.

Grossman, S.J. (1981) 'The role of warranties and private disclosure about product quality', *Journal of Law and Economics*, 24, 461–83.

Guadagni, P.M. and Little, J.D.C. (1983) 'A logit model of brand choice calibrated on scanner data', *Marketing Science*, 2(3), 203–38.

Gupta, A.K. and Govindarajan, V. (1991) 'Knowledge flows and the structure of control within multinational corporations', *Academy of Management Review*, 16(4), 768–92.

Hartline, M.D., Maxham, J.G.I. and McKee, D.O. (2000) 'Corridors of influence in the dissemination of customer-oriented strategy to customer contact service employees', *Journal of Marketing*, 64 (April), 35–50.

Homburg, C. and Pflesser, C. (2000) 'A multiple-layer model of market-oriented organizational culture: Measurement issues and performance outcomes', *Journal of Marketing*, 37 (November), 449–62.

Homburg, C., Workman Jr, J.P. and Krohmer, H. (1999) 'Marketing's influence within the firm', *Journal of Marketing*, 63 (April), 1–17.

IMA (1996) *Cost Management Update*, 64 (June), US Institute of Management Accountants, Cost Management Group.

Ittner, C.D. and Larcker, D.F. (1998) 'Are nonfinancial measures leading indicators of financial performance? an analysis of customer satisfaction', *Journal of Accounting Research*, 36, 1–35.

Jacobson, R. (1990) 'Unobservable effects and business performance', *Marketing Science*, 9(1), 74–85.

Jaworski, B.J. (1988) 'Toward a theory of marketing control: Environmental context, control types, and consequences', *Journal of Marketing*, 52 (July), 23–39.

Jaworski, B.J. and Kohli, A.K. (1993) 'Market orientation: Antecedents and consequences', *Journal of Marketing*, 57 (July), 53–70.

Jaworski, B.J. and MacInnis, D.J. (1989) 'Marketing jobs and management controls: Towards a framework', *Journal of Marketing Research*, 26 (November), 406–19.

Jaworski, B.J., Stathakopoulos, V. and Krishnan, H.S. (1993) 'Control combinations in marketing: conceptual framework and empirical evidence', *Journal of Marketing*, 57 (January), 57–69.

Jensen, M.C. and Meckling, W.H. (1976) 'Theory of the firm: Managerial behavior, agency costs and ownership structure', *Journal of Financial Economics*, 3, 305–60.

Kamakura, W.A. and Russell, G.J. (1993) 'Measuring brand value with scanner data', *International Journal of Research in Marketing*, 10, 9–22.

Keller, K.L. (1993) 'Conceptualizing, measuring, and managing customer-based brand equity', *Journal of Marketing*, 57 (January), 1–22.

Keller, K.L. (1998) *Strategic Brand Management: Building, Measuring and Managing Brand Equity.* Upper Saddle River, NJ: Prentice-Hall.

Kerin, R.A. and Sethuraman, R. (1998) 'Exploring the brand value-shareholder value nexus for consumer goods companies', *Journal of the Academy of Marketing Science*, 26(4), 260–273.

Kohli, A.K. and Jaworski, B.J. (1990) 'Market orientation: The construct, research proposition, and managerial implications', *Journal of Marketing*, 54 (April), 1–18.

Kokkinaki, F. and Ambler, T. (1999) *Marketing Performance Assessment: An Exploratory Investigation into Current Practice and the Role of Firm Orientation.* Cambridge, MA: Marketing Science Institute, Report No. 00–500.

Kotler, P. (2000) *Marketing Management.* Upper Saddle River, NJ: Prentice-Hall.

Krafft, M. (1999) 'An empirical investigation of the antecedents of sales force control systems', *Journal of Marketing*, 63 (July), 120–34.

Lane, V. and Jacobson, R. (1995) 'Stock market reactions to brand extension announcements: The effects of brand attitude and familiarity', *Journal of Marketing*, 59 (January), 63–77.

Lassar, W., Mittal, B. and Sharma, A. (1995) 'Measuring customer-based brand equity', *Journal of Consumer Marketing*, 12(4), 11–19.

Marketing Leadership Council (2001) 'Measuring marketing performance: Results of council survey', (August), Washington, D.C.

Marketing Science Institute (2000) *2000–2002 Research Priorities: A Guide to MSI Research Programs and Procedures*. Cambridge, MA: Marketing Science Institute.

Marketing Week (2001) 'Assessing marketers' worth', February 1, 42–43.

Media Metrix, Press Release, 20 August 2001.

Merchant, K.A. (1988) 'Progressing toward a theory of marketing control: A comment', *Journal of Marketing*, 52 (July), 40–44.

Meyer, J.W. and Rowan, B. (1977) 'Institutionalized organizations: formal structure as mith and ceremony', *American Journal of Sociology*, 83, 340–63.

Meyer, M.W. (1998) 'Finding performance: The new discipline in management', *Performance Measurement – Theory and Practice, Vol. 1*. Cambridge, UK: Centre for Business Performance, xiv–xxi.

Mohammed, R., Fisher, R.J., Jaworski, B.J. and Cahill, A. (2001) *Internet Marketing: Building Advantage in a Networked Economy*. Englewood Cliffs, NJ: McGraw-Hill.

Moorman, C. (1995) 'Organizational market information processes: Cultural antecedents and new product outcomes', *Journal of Marketing Research*, 32 (August), 318–35.

Moorman, C. and Rust, R.T. (1999) 'The role of marketing', *Journal of Marketing*, 63 (Special Issue), 180–97.

Moorman, C. and Zaltman, G. (1985) 'Sharing models of inquiry'. In E. Hirschman and M. Holbrook (eds), *Advances in Consumer Research, Vol 12*. Ann Arbor, MI: Association for Consumer Research, pp. 312–14.

Moorman, C. and Deshpande, R. (1992) 'Relationships between providers and users of market research: the dynamics of trust within and between organizations', *Journal of Marketing Research*, 29 (August), 314–28.

Murphy, G.B., Trailer, J.W. and Hill, R.C. (1996) 'Measuring performance in entrepreneurship research', *Journal of Business Research*, 36, 15–23.

Narver, J.C. and Slater, S.F. (1990) 'The effect of a market orientation on business profitability', *Journal of Marketing*, 54 (October), 20–35.

Nikalant, V. and Rao, H. (1994) 'Agency theory and uncertainty in organizations: An evaluation', *Organization Studies*, 15(5), 649–72.

Noble, C.H. and Mokwa, M.P. (1999) 'Implementing marketing strategies: Developing and testing a managerial theory', *Journal of Marketing*, 63 (October), 57–73.

Novak, T.P. and Hoffman, D.L. (1996) 'New metrics for new media: Towards the development of web measurement standards', *Working Paper Series, Project 2000*, Vanderbilt University.

Oliver, R.L. and Anderson, E. (1994) 'An empirical test of the consequences of behavior- and outcome-based sales control systems', *Journal of Marketing*, 58 (October), 53–67.

Ouchi, W.G. (1979) 'A conceptual framework for the design of organizational control mechanisms', *Management Science*, 25 (September), 833–47.

Park, C.S. and Srinivasan, V. (1994) 'A survey-based method for measuring and understanding brand equity and its extendibility', *Journal of Marketing Research*, 31 (May), 271–88.

Perrier, R. (ed.) (1997) *Brand Valuation* (3rd edition). London: Premier Books.

Riley, D. and Ambler, T. (2000) *Marketing Metrics: A Review of Performance Measures in Use in the UK and Spain*. Cambridge, MA: Marketing Science Institute, Report No. 00–500.

Ross, S.A. (1979) 'Disclosure regulation in financial markets: implications of modern finance theory and signalling theory'. In F. Edwards (ed.), *Issues in Financial Regulation*. New York: McGraw-Hill, pp. 177–202.

Ruekert, R.W. (1992) 'Developing a market orientation: An organizational strategy perspective', *International Journal of Research in Marketing*, 9, 225–45.

Sarin, S. and Mahajan, V. (2001) 'The effect of reward structures on the performance of cross-functional product development teams', *Journal of Marketing*, 65 (April), 35–53.

Sevin, C.H. (1965) *Marketing Productivity Analysis*. New York: McGraw-Hill.

Schultz, D.E. (2000) 'Understanding and measuring brand equity', *Marketing Management*, Spring, 8–9.

Shaw, R. and Mazur, L. (1997) *Marketing Accountability: Improving Business Performance*. London: Financial Times, Retail and Consumer Publishing.

Simon, C.J. and Sullivan, M.W. (1993) 'The measurement and determinants of brand equity: A financial approach', *Marketing Science*, 12(1), 28–51.

Slater, S.F. and Narver, J.C. (1995) 'Market orientation and the learning organization', *Journal of Marketing*, 59 (July), 63–74.

Srivastava, R.K. and Shocker, A.D. (1991) 'Brand equity: A perspective on its meaning and measurement', Working Paper No. 91–124, Cambridge, MA: Marketing Science Institute.

Standard and Poor (1996) *The Outlook*, Special Issue, 68(17), September 30. New York: McGraw-Hill, Section 2.

Swain, J., Erdem, T., Louvriere, J. and Dubelaar, C. (1993) 'The equalization price: A measure of consumer-perceived brand equity', *International Journal of Research in Marketing*, 10, 23–45.

Szymanski, D.M. and Henard, D.H. (2001) 'Customer satisfaction: A meta-analysis of the empirical evidence', *Journal of the Academy of Marketing Science*, 1, 16–35.

Tolbert, P.S. and Zucker, L.G. (1983) 'Institutional sources of change in the formal structure of organizations: The diffusion of civil service reform, 1880–1935', *Administrative Science Quarterly*, 28, 22–39.

Unilever (1998) *Presentation to The Marketing Council Seminar on Measuring Marketing*. London, 2 December.

Webster Jr, F.E. (1992) 'The changing role of marketing in the corporation', *Journal of Marketing*, 56 (October), 1–17.

Workman Jr, J.P. (1993), 'Marketing's limited role in new product development in one computer system firm', *Journal of Marketing Research*, 30 (November), 405–21.

Yoo, B., Donthu, N. and Lee, S. (2000) 'An examination of selected marketing mix elements and brand equity', *Journal of the Academy of Marketing Science*, 28(2), 195–211.

Zucker, L.G. (1987) 'Institutional theories of organizations'. In W.R. Scott (ed.), *Annual Review of Sociology*. Palo Alto: Annual Reviews, pp. 443–64.

Index

Page numbers in *italics* refer to illustrations and tables; page numbers in **bold** refer to main discussion.